STRATEGIC BEHAVIOUR AND INDUSTRIAL COMPETITION

EDITED BY

D. J. MORRIS, P. J. N. SINCLAIR, M. D. E. SLATER
AND J. S. VICKERS

CLARENDON PRESS · OXFORD

1986

Oxford University Press, Walton Street, Oxford OX2 6DP
Oxford New York Toronto
Delhi Bombay Calcutta Madras Karachi
Petaling Jaya Singapore Hong Kong Tokyo
Nairobi Dar es Salaam Cape Town
Melbourne Auckland
and associated companies in
Beirut Berlin Ibadan Nicosia

Oxford is a trade mark of Oxford University Press

Published in the United States
by Oxford University Press, New York

British Library Cataloguing in Publication Data
New industrial economics.
1. Industrial organization (Economic
theory)
I. Morris, Derek J.   II. Oxford economic
papers
338   HD2326
ISBN 0-19-82856-2

Library of Congress Cataloging-in-Publication Data
New industrial economics.
1. Industrial organization (Economic theory)
I. Morris, Derek.
HD2326.N435 1987 338.6 86-28535
ISBN 0-19-828562-0 (pbk.)

Printed in Northern Ireland at
The Universities Press (Belfast) Ltd.

CONTENTS

STRATEGIC BEHAVIOUR AND INDUSTRIAL COMPETITION: AN INTRODUCTION

By D. J. MORRIS, P. J. N. SINCLAIR, M. D. E. SLATER
and J. S. VICKERS

THE economics of industrial organisation is undergoing major change and development. New methods of analysis are forcing substantial rethinking of the causes, nature and effects of competitive behaviour. Traditional views are being reconsidered and replaced by different perspectives, empirical relationships are being reinterpreted, and important implications for anti-trust and industrial policies are being derived from the new approaches. This volume contains twelve original contributions to the economics of industrial organisation which cover a range of topics including contestability theory, predatory pricing, strategic commitment, product differentiation, product compatibility, consumer information, research and innovation. The purpose of this introduction is briefly to identify some prominent themes in recent work on industrial organisation, and to offer a framework for considering the papers in this volume.

These themes are threefold: (a) the ways in which the structure of an industry reacts to, and reflects, the underlying influences of technology and preferences; (b) how one firm can act in order to alter the actions of others, and the timing sequence of such interdependent sets of actions; and (c) the significance of limited information, and in particular of different assumptions about what market participants do not know. Traditionally, problems in the economics of industrial organization were often explored in a static world, where knowledge was perfect and market structure was given. This volume is largely concerned with what can happen these disagreeable and restrictive assumptions are relaxed.

The first theme to highlight is the endogeneity of market structure and the rethinking of causal relationships. The traditional structure-conduct-performance approach to industrial economics emphasised the causal flow *from* industry structure (concentration, conditions of entry, etc.) *via* firms' conduct (price and non-price behaviour) *to* industry performance (profits, innovation, etc.). For example, the number of firms in an industry was regarded as a prime determinant of the degree of cooperation between firms, and hence of their levels of profit. Empirical correlations between structure and performance variables were interpreted causally, with performance seen as being determined by structure. Certain possible barriers to entry were identified as inhibiting potential competitors, notably scale economies, product differentiation, and absolute cost advantages, but the theoretical analysis of entry remained at a relatively simple (and it is now clear unsatisfactory) level.

One of the main objectives of recent work, however, has been to *explain* industrial structure, rather than to regard it primarily as the *explanation* of conduct and performance. Non-cooperative behaviour by firms has typically been assumed, and the approach has been to take nothing as given beyond the fundamental conditions of preferences and technology (or, where demand and technology can be altered, the *opportunities* for influencing them). This is, after all, the basic method of microeconomics. The theory of contestable markets (see Baumol (1982) and the papers by Baumol and Willig and by Schwartz in this volume) is one attempt to explain industrial structure endogenously, albeit under particular assumptions about entry and exit. Another example is the work of Dasgupta and Stiglitz (1980) on the relationships between concentration, innovation, and price-cost margins. They show not only that structure is endogenous, but also that the causal relationships between structure, conduct and performance are different from those emphasised in the traditional approach described above. Rather, all three are determined together by the underlying parameters of demand and technological opportunity. Thus concentration and innovation may go hand in hand because both are fostered by technological opportunity, *not* because one causes the other. Similarly, Shaked and Sutton's (1983) work on vertical product differentiation shows how industry structure can depend in subtle ways upon the interaction between consumer preferences and the technology of product improvement.

Attempts have also been made to explain conditions of entry endogenously. Salop (1979) drew the useful distinction between *innocent* entry barriers, which exist irrespective of the behaviour of incumbent firms, and *strategic* entry barriers, which result from their deliberate actions. Strategic entry barriers are a clear example of how conduct may affect structure, although the scope for this to happen depends once again upon the underlying parameters of demand and technology.

Strategic commitment is the second theme that we wish to highlight. "Strategic" is a word that is perhaps used too much, so it is important to be clear as to its meaning in our context. Schelling in his classic book *The Strategy of Conflict* (1960) defined a strategic move—such as a commitment, threat or promise—as a move designed to influence the behaviour of others. Thus building a high level of capacity to deter entry is a strategic move, which owes its profitability to the influence it has on the decisions of potential entrants. Although much attention has been given to strategic behaviour in the context of entry deterrence, the idea applies equally to competition between existing firms (see for example, the papers by Roberts and by Dixon in this volume).

For a strategic move to be successful, it must influence other firms' expected payoffs from the various courses of action open to them. This can happen essentially in two ways. The first is for the strategic move to have a lasting effect on cost or demand conditions. Investments in capacity (Dixit (1980)), R & D (Gilbert and Newbery (1982); Brander and Spencer (1983)), advertising (Schmalensee (1983)), or brand introduction (Schmalensee

(1978)) are examples of how this might be done. Strategic moves of this kind require *irreversible commitment*—they lose their effect if they can readily be undone. These considerations have led to a greater appreciation of the importance of *sunk costs* (as opposed to fixed costs). In many settings what matters is the degree to which costs are irrecoverable, rather than the relationship between unit cost and output (i.e. scale economies, which were emphasised in the traditional approach). For example, sunk costs play two roles in new theories of entry deterrence. They are important on the one hand to incumbent firms for the making of strategic, irreversible moves to deter entry, and on the other hand the potential entrants will be keenly interested in whether their entry will involve irrecoverable costs on their own part, as contestability theory has detailed.

Another way for a strategic move to work is for it to influence the *beliefs* of those whose behaviour it is designed to affect, even if it does not affect acutal cost and demand conditions. With asymmetric information, a less informed firm will make inferences from the behaviour of a more informed rival. Hence there is an incentive for the latter firm to engage in strategic signalling, which has been examined for example in relation to limit pricing (Milgrom and Roberts (1982a)) and predatory pricing (Kreps and Wilson (1982b); Milgrom and Roberts (1982b); Roberts in this volume).

The analysis of strategic moves is one example of how recent work has explicitly investigated the *dynamics* of competition. Another example is the analysis of collusion in repeated games. These advances beyond traditional static frameworks have been made possible by important developments in theory of dynamic non-cooperative games and its application to oligopoly theory. Many of these developments have stemmed from Selten's (1965, 1975) *perfect equilibrium* solution concept. This requires that firms' strategies be in the equilibrium not only for the game as a whole (as with Nash equilibrium), but also in every subgame of the game—i.e. also when considered from any point (or "node") during the course of the game. A major attraction of this concept is that it captures the intuitive notion of a credible threat—i.e. a threat whose fulfilment is optimal *ex post*. The related solution concept of *sequential equilibrium* (Kreps and Wilson (1982a)) has been most illuminating in contexts of incomplete and imperfect information, for example in the analysis of signalling behaviour (see Roberts' paper in this volume) and of reputation building. The appropriate definition of equilibrium for dynamic games of incomplete and imperfect information is not yet a settled question, and the refinement of existing solution concepts is a very active area of current research.

The discussion above has already moved on to our third and final theme—information and uncertainty—which has recently received extensive treatment in many branches of economics. Akerlof's (1970) classic paper on consumer uncertainty about product quality has stimulated a large literature, and two papers in this volume (those by Eaton and Grossman and by

Perloff and Salop) are concerned with imperfectly informed consumers. The converse problem—firms' uncertainty about consumer demand—is discussed in the paper by Perrakis and Warskett. Asymmetric information about costs as between firms is the subject of Roberts' paper, which has aready been mentioned in relation to signalling. Another major issue, among many in this area, is the acquisition of information, particularly in the process of innovation. The papers by Anderson and Harris and by Bhattacharya, Chatterjee and Samuelson address aspects of this question.

The papers which follow may be loosely divided into two groups. First come those that are principally concerned with entry and/or exit. They are followed by the papers mainly devoted to questions about competition between existing firms. However, this distinction is only really one of emphasis or degree, as the issues involved are so closely related.

The first two papers—by Baumol and Willig and by Schwartz—deal respectively with the pros and cons of the controversial theory of contestable markets. Baumol and Willig review the many contributions to the debate on contestability that have been made since the publication in 1982 of their book *Contestable Markets and the Theory of Industry Structure*, written jointly with John Panzar. It was argued in this book (see Baumol (1982) for a summary statement) that the contestable market—in which the absence of any sunk costs, among other things, renders existing firms completely vulnerable to hit-and-run entry—provides a more useful benchmark for the analysis of industrial structure and conduct than the traditional notion of perfect competition. Thus competition has more to do with ease of entry and exit than with the presence of numerous small firms. Indeed the configuration of firms in a contestable market is determined endogenously, and the existence of only a few firms can be perfectly consistent with strong and desirable competition. The book also made a valuable contribution to the economics of multiproduct firms, and showed the importance of concepts such as economies of scope and transray convexity of costs. However, it is the implications of the theory for antitrust and regulatory policy that have excited the most heated debate. In their paper Baumol and Willig appraise theoretical, econometric and experimental contributions to the debate, as well as policy developments.

Schwartz also reviews recent work on contestability theory, but from a more critical perspective. One issue that he addresses is the robustness of the theory to its admittedly stark assumptions about conditions of entry and exit. This question is central to the applicability of the theory to policy. While all theories have assumptions that can be no more than approximately true, it is undesirable for the implications of a theory to change markedly when its assumptions are altered slightly. Contestability theory has been criticised on these grounds, and it is important to assess the strength of the objection.

Perrakis and Warskett examine strategic entry deterrence by investment in capacity under conditions of demand uncertainty. An incumbent firm and (if it enters) a rival firm decide in turn their respective levels of production capacity before they know the level of industry demand. There are scale economies in the sense that a minimum level of capacity is required for positive output. They show, among other things, that the expected profit from strategic entry deterrence when there is demand uncertainty can substantially exceed the profit in the certainty case. This result illustrates how much difference the presence of uncertainty can make.

Demand uncertainty is also central to Roberts' signalling model of predatory pricing, which examines strategic exit inducement in conditions of asymmetric information about demand. A long-established firm knows the state of demand but a recent entrant does not. The entrant decides whether or not to exit after experiencing market conditions. The established firm seeks to convince the entrant that demand is low by depressing prices, but the entrant realises his incentive to do this. At the equilibrium of this dynamic game of imperfect information, predation occurs and exit is strategically induced if and only if demand is low, which is also what would happen with full information. Demand uncertainty causes predatory signalling, and lower prices, but does not induce more exit than occurs when there is certainty. There are parallels with the work by Milgrom and Roberts (1982a) on limit pricing when there is asymmetric cost information.

The paper by Caves and Ghemawat is an empirical investigation of the relationship between capital commitment and profitability. As was explained above, strategic commitments and sunk costs have featured prominently in recent work on incumbent/entrant interaction and on the nature of competition between existing firms. In a cross-section of concentrated producer goods industries they find that capital intensity and profitability are negatively related, which lends some support to the view that capital commitment is more an instrument of conflict between incumbents than a (profitable) instrument of entry deterrence. They employ a variety of more detailed tests, some of which give unclear results, and it is suggested that empirical work on dynamic interactions in individual markets is called for.

Dixon links strategic commitment with the "consistent conjecture" solution concept for oligopoly games (see, for example, Bresnahan (1981)). The consistent conjective solution concept has aroused much controversy (see Makowski (1986)), and criticisms can be made of the use of conjectural variations more generally. They attempt to capture in a static fashion an idea that is essentially dynamic (how firm A would respond to a change in B's output, and so on). It can be argued, however, that explicitly dynamic models should be used to explore dynamic ideas, and these are now available. Nevertheless, the conjectural variation term continues to be regarded by some as a neat shorthand representation of industry dynamics, and is often interpreted as a measure of the degree of competition between firms. Previous work on strategic commitment has taken as fixed this "degree of competition", and it has been shown that consistent conjectures imply efficient production (no factor bias). But Dixon argues that the conjectural variation term should be treated as endogenous. Thus capital commitment influences the "degree of competition". When this is allowed for, factor bias generally occurs and the capital-labour ratio is too low.

The next two papers are concerned with different aspects of firms' product specification decisions. Caplin and Nalebuff generalise the traditional, one-dimensional Hotelling model of product differentiation to many dimensions. Firms enter sequentially a market in which products have a fixed number of characteristics. Each firm choose irreversibly its product "location" in characteristics space. There is no price competition. It is shown how equilibrium market shares in the two-firm case depend critically upon the number of dimensions of product characteristics. It is suggested that higher dimensionality favours entrants, because they can occupy hitherto unexploited dimensions.

The aspect of product specification examined by Katz and Shapiro is the choice of product compatibility in a technologically progressive industry with network externalities. Telecommunications, computers and video cassettes are examples of such industries. Katz and Shapiro show how firms may use compatibility to reduce competition, and they examine the conflicts that may arise between social and private incentives for compatibility. The paper is a contribution to a new literature on a topic of considerable interest and importance.

The next two papers in the volume are both concerned with consumers' information about the products in a market. The first, by Eaton and Grossman, examines an aspect of marketing—the disclosure by firms of information about their product's quality. The extent of this marketing activity affects equilibrium prices, outputs and profits. Consumers benefit from information insofaras it helps then to buy the product best suited to their tastes, but disclosure tends to raise price because products are effectively more differentiated. The effects of marketing upon competition and welfare are investigated in a variety of contexts.

In the model analysed by Perloff and Salop, consumers have imperfect information about the price charged by each of the firms in an industry. Information is firm-specific: consumers have no additional general market information. As information improves—in the sense that consumers' price estimates become more accurate—equilibrium price falls, because the demand curve facing a firm in effect becomes more elastic. Equilibrium price also falls as the number of firms grows. Results are also presented concerning the existence (and non-existence) of single-price equilibria. The conclusions obtained by Perloff and Salop are contrasted with results in the existing literature on industry equilibrium with imperfectly informed consumers.

The final two papers are both concerned with innovation. Anderson and Harris investigate a dynamic duopoly game in which demand conditions are uncertain until some firm innovates. Each firm decides whether to innovate before knowing demand, to innovate after its rival (when demand is revealed), or not to innovate at all. The model is solved by a continuous-time analogue of Selten's perfect equilibrium concept, which is of independent interest. Because of the informational externality generated by the original innovator, competition can discourage desirable innovation, and the advantages of some regulatory lag are demonstrated Anderson & Harris' model was motivated by, and is applied to, competition between securities exchanges to introduce innovatary financial products.

Bhattacharya, Chatterjee and Samuelson analyse a model of sequential research in which a firm decides, on the basis of its past search, whether to adopt an innovation of uncertain profitability, to continue searching, or to give up. For the single-player problem, the optimal stopping rule is characterised by, and is shown to provide an explanation for, the commonly observed S-shaped diffusion curve. The authors then proceed to a model of interactive search among several firms, in which each firms can obtain additional information from observing the behaviour of others. The paper succeeds in illuminating several facets of a complex problem of competition through innovation.

To conclude, the new theoretical approaches have opened up many new possibilities, and as a result Industrial Organisation is in a state of some turmoil. There is at the moment even some embarrassment of choice among competing theories, and even within theoretical frameworks there is perhaps still too much freedom to choose one's conclusions by selection among many plausible assumptions.

However the broad outlines of a new view of competitive behaviour are beginning to emerge. There is greater agreement now on which are the vital concepts, on general methodological approach, and on which areas of disagreement can only be resolved empirically. This volume seeks to contribute to the process of appraisal and debate, and to stimulate further developments.

University of Oxford

REFERENCES

AKERLOF, G. A. (1970), "The Market for 'Lemons': Quality Uncertainty and the Market Mechanism", *Quarterly Journal of Economics,* Vol. LXXXIV, (August), 488–500.

BAUMOL, W. J. (1982), "Contestable Markets: An Uprising in the Theory of Industrial Structure", *American Economic Review,* Vol. 72, (March), 1–15.

BAUMOL, W. J., PANZAR, J. C. and WILLIG, R. D. (1982), *Contestable Markets and the Theory of Industry Structure,* New York.

BRANDER, J. A., and SPENCER, B. J. (1983), "Strategic Commitment with R & D: the Symmetric Case", *Bell Journal of Economics,* Vol. 14, (Spring), 225–235.

BRESNAHAN, T. (1981), "Duopoly Models with Consistent Conjectures", *American Economic Review, Vol. 71,* (December), 934–945.

DASGUPTA, P. and STIGLITZ, J. (1980), "Industrial Structure and the Nature of Innovative Activity", *Economic Journal,* Vol. 90, (June), 266–293.

DIXIT, A. K. (1980), "The Role of Investment in Entry-Deterrence", *Economic Journal,* Vol. 90, (March), 95–106.

GILBERT, R. J. and NEWBERY, D. M. G. (1982), "Preemptive Patenting and the Persistence of Monopoly", *American Economic Review,* Vol. 72, (June), 514–526.

KREPS, D. M. and WILSON, R. (1982a), "Sequential Equilibria", *Econometrica,* Vol. 50, (July), 863–894.

KREPS, D. M. and WILSON, R. (1982b), "Reputation and Imperfect Information", *Journal of Economic Theory,* Vol. 27, (August), 253–279.

MAKOWSKI, L. (1986), "Are 'Rational Conjectives' Rational?", *Journal of Industrial Economics,* forthcoming.

MILGROM, P. and ROBERTS, J. (1982a), "Limit Pricing and Entry Under Incomplete Information: An Equilibrium Analysis", *Econometrica,* Vol. 50, (March), 443–459.

MILGROM, P. and ROBERTS, J. (1982b), "Predation, Reputation and Entry Deterrence", *Journal of Economic Theory,* Vol. 27, (August), 280–312.

SALOP, S. C. (1979), "Strategic Entry Deterrence", *American Economic Review (Papers & Proceedings),* Vol. 69, (May), 335–338.

SCHELLING, T. C. (1960), *The Strategy of Conflict,* Cambridge, Mass.

SCHMALENSEE, R. (1978), "Entry Deterrence in the Ready-to-Eat Breakfast Cereal Industry", *Bell Journal of Economics,* Vol. 9, (Autumn), 305–327.

SCHMALENSEE, R. (1983), "Advertising and Entry Deterrence: An Exploratory Model", *Journal of Political Economy,* Vol. 91 (4), 636–653.

SELTEN, R. (1965), "Spieltheoretische Behandlung eines Oligopolmodells mit Nachfrage-tragheit", *Zeitschrift fur die gesamte Staatswissenschaft,* Vol. 121, 301–324.

SELTEN, R. (1975), "Re-examination of the Perfectness Concept for Equilibrium Points in Extensive Games", *International Journal of Game Theory,* Vol. 4, 25–55.

SHAKED, A. and SUTTON, J. (1983), "Natural Oligopolies", *Econometrica,* Vol. 51, (September), 1469–1483.

CONTESTABILITY: DEVELOPMENTS SINCE THE BOOK

By WILLIAM J. BAUMOL* and ROBERT D. WILLIG†

THE ideas encompassed in the theory of contestable markets have entered both the academic literature and the discussions of practitioners with surprising speed. At hearings before regulatory agencies in antitrust cases, terms such as "economies of scope," "sustainable prices" and "contestable markets" are interjected casually as though long usage has made their connotations familiar to everyone. This is in part attributable to the steady stream of papers, published and about to be published by authors offering careful theoretical extensions and critiques, empirical and interpretative applications, as well as heated reactions to contestability theory.

The central focus of this paper is a summary of substantive developments relating to contestability since the appearance of our book. We will discuss four subjects: theoretical advances provided by others, econometric studies using the multiproduct cost concepts accompanying contestability analysis, market simulation studies testing various attributes of contestability, and policy developments, covering both policy studies in the economic literature and some remarkable decisions in the regulatory and antitrust arenas, that rely explicitly on the theory of contestability.

However, before reaching these central areas in order to deal with any remaining misunderstandings we shall begin with a brief restatement of some of the things our work does not and was not intended to imply and the things we instead hope it accomplishes. Specifically, we will deny emphatically that it offers carte blanche to mindless deregulation and dismantling of antitrust safeguards. On the contrary, so far as policy is concerned, contestability theory provides guidance in ascertaining where intervention is warranted socially, and it provides a more widely applicable benchmark to guide regulatory agencies and the courts in those arenas where intervention is called for by considerations of economic welfare.

Contestability and "libertarian" ideology

Contestability theory does not, and was not intended to, lend support to those who believe (or almost seem to believe) that the unrestrained market automatically solves all economic problems and that virtually all regulation and antitrust activity constitutes a pointless and costly source of economic inefficiency. In a market that approximates perfect contestability, it is true,

* Princeton and New York Universities.

† Princeton University. The authors want to thank the Information Science and Technology Division and the Regulation and Policy Analysis Program of the National Science Foundation and the C. V. Starr Center for Applied Economics for their generous support of this research. We also wish to acknowledge with gratitude the able assistance of Daniel Schult and the useful comments of Marius Schwartz.

we believe matters can be left to take care of themselves. Small numbers of large firms, vertical and even horizontal mergers and other arrangements which have traditionally been objects of suspicion of monopolistic taint and worse, are rendered harmless and perhaps even beneficent by the presence of contestability. But that observation is no whitewash and establishes no presumption, one way or the other, about the desirability of public sector intervention in any particular market of reality. For before anyone can legitimately use the analysis to infer that virtue reigns in some economic sector and that interference is therefore unwarranted, that person must first provide evidence that the arena in question is, in fact, highly contestable. The economy of reality is composed of sectors which vary widely in the degree to which they approximate the attributes of contestability. Thus, the conclusion that *perfectly* contestable markets require no intervention claims little more than the possibility (which remains to be proven, case by case) that *some* markets in reality may automatically perform in a very acceptable manner despite the small number of firms that inhabit them.

Thus, it is simply incorrect to associate our writings on contestability with an all-pervasive laissez-faire position on the role of regulation and antitrust (for such a characterization of our position see, e.g., Shepherd (1984)). We disagree vehemently with such a view of the world. On the other hand, we reject with equal conviction the position of those who hold that mere large size of a firm means that it *must* serve the economy badly, that high concentration ratios are sufficient to justify governmental restrictions upon the structure or conduct of an industry or that a horizontal merger merits automatic condemnation if it increases concentration ratios substantially. For it is true that a high degree of contestability, where and if it does happen to hold sway, should remove the undesirable consequences which might otherwise stem from these phenomena. Thus, contestability theory supports neither extreme interventionists nor extreme noninterventionists. We believe that antitrust and regulation have valuable roles to play, and that contestability theory can help to identify and sharpen those roles and thereby benefit the public.

Objectives of contestability research

Contestability theory offers an analytic framework within which the fundamental features of demands and production technology determine the shape of industry structure and many of the characteristics of industry prices. The theory accomplishes this via a process of simplification; by stripping away through its assumptions all barriers to entry and exit, and the strategic behavior that goes along with them both in theory and in reality.

The model of perfect competition has also served an analogous simplifying role, and in so doing has provided the foundation for the most elegant and well-articulated portions of economic theory. However, because the model of perfect competition prespecifies industry structure by its very construction, it cannot serve as a useful benchmark for the study of the determinants of industrial structure. Perfect competition is a special case of perfect contestability, and perfect contestability applies with equal force to circumstances where perfect competition is impossible because economies of scale are present. Because of this fact, and because contestability theory encompasses an endogenous determination mechanism from which any industry structure may emerge (depending on circumstances), we feel that it is an extension of the competitive model appropriate for use in the theory of industrial organization.

In addition to this broad purpose in theoretical analysis, we feel that research on contestable markets has two objectives related to policy. The first is the establishment of an improved set of guidelines for appropriate government intervention in the structure and conduct of firms and industries, that is, of the rules to be followed by the regulators and antitrust authorities in those cases in which their intervention is called for. The second objective for policy analysis is the determination of criteria distinguishing between those cases in which intervention by the public sector is warranted and those in which it is not.

With regard to the first policy objective, it is widely understood that the basic guideline for intervention should be replication of the consequences of effective market forces in those cases in which competition, actual or potential, is insufficient to do the job. That is, intervention should aim to induce or compel an industry in which monopoly power is present to perform as it would if effective competitive pressures were available. But, for such cases perfect competition is often unsuitable as a standard, particularly in circumstances common to regulatory and antitrust issues where scale economies and related attributes dictate the presence of only a small number of firms, at least some of them relatively large.

Here, as we will see from recent developments in regulatory practice that will be reviewed presently, contestability theory was, indeed, able to suggest answers where other bodies of theory did not. Moreover, it was able to eliminate curious gaps in the standard theory of policy. Perhaps the most noteworthy of these was the lack of a defensible criterion for regulatory ceilings on prices, though one would have thought that to be the first order of business for social control of firms with monopoly power. Yet, to our knowledge, neither regulators nor courts previously had available to them from the theoretical literature any defensible test to determine just when a particular price set by one of the multiproduct firms of reality was excessive. We will also see later how contestability theory determines how high is enough and will observe that regulatory agencies have begun to adopt the criterion that emerges, with explicit acknowledgement of its source.

In saying this, we do not mean to claim that the theory sheds light on the welfare economics of markets that are highly uncontestable. The theory does not even try to contribute to the analysis of behavior in such cases or to the evaluation of the social cost of any resulting departures from optimality. All the analysis pretends to say about such cases is that if they entail behavior which is deemed socially undesirable and if government undertakes to change this behavior, then it is appropriate to require the individuals to act as they would have if the threat of potential competition had constrained them effectively. If, for example, firms charge prices and earn profits that are deemed excessive, it is appropriate to offer consumers the protection that the threat of barrier free entry would have provided them.

Finally, we feel that contestability theory has helped to show that in *some* cases where regulatory or antitrust intervention was previously common, it was in fact undesirable. Contestability theory, we think, does help to clarify which arenas are the proper candidates for deregulation and cessation of other forms of intervention. But the theory neither calls for anything like universal deregulation nor for its automatic extension without careful study of the pertinent facts, case by case.

Theoretical developments

There has been an outpouring of theoretical work on contestable markets and allied subjects, as there has been recently throughout the field of industrial organization (as this very volume indicates). Our brief overview of the recent developments cannot do justice to the full range of valuable contributions and is, unfortunately, bound to miss important items. This review is organized into four topics: (i) conditions for sustainability of prices set by a monopoly incumbent; (ii) theoretical applications of contestability; (iii) the characteristics of production cost that determine market structure in contestable markets; and (iv) the relationship between strategic firm behavior and contestability.

In our book (1982), we identified one set of conditions sufficient to assure the existence of sustainable prices for a multi-output natural monopolist, and those conditions also were shown to guarantee that the Ramsey optimal prices are sustainable. Among those conditions are the stipulations that the cost function exhibit overall economies of scale and the property of trans-ray convexity. We showed that the sustainability of Ramsey prices could tolerate some deviation from these properties, such as product-specific fixed costs of bounded magnitude. Faulhaber and Levinson (1981) developed the idea of anonymously equitable prices which offered no cross-subsidies to any possible groups of consumers, and connected the properties of such prices to sustainability. Sharkey ((1981) and (1982)) and Spulber (1984) presented new sets of conditions sufficient for the sustainability of monopoly prices, and showed that the Ramsey prices need not be among them. ten Raa ((1983) and (1984)) sharpened the connections among subsidy-free, market-clearing, and sustainable prices. Mirman, Tauman and Zang (1985) further clarified these connections, established novel sets of sufficient conditions for the existence of sustainable prices, and identified conditions under which the Aumann-Shaply prices would be sustainable.

Brown and Heal provided the valuable result that where Ramsey prices are unsustainable, the government can solve the consequent policy conflict between open entry and optimal prices via a system of excise taxes and subsidies to incumbent and any entrants alike. Working in a general equilibrium context with independent demands for the outputs of the natural monopolist, they proved the existence of such a tax system, with zero net effect on government revenues, that permits Ramsey optimal consumers' prices and sustainable producers' prices.

Panzar and Postlewaite (1985) demonstrated the sustainability of Ramsey optimal non-linear prices where costs are linear, and provided counterexamples for other circumstances. In contrast to the usual results for contestable markets, Perry (1982) showed that a natural monopolist can at once earn positive profits and deter entry by commiting itself to the sale of some units of homogeneous output at prices lower than those that apply to marginal purchases.

Our second category of new theoretical work comprises applications of contestability to various issues. Quirmbach (1982) studied vertical integration by an upstream monopolist into a competitive downstream industry. While the welfare effects are, in general, ambiguous, Quirmbach showed that profitable integration would raise social welfare if the upstream market were perfectly contestable.

In their pathbreaking book, Helpman and Krugman (1985) provide a sketch of a new theory of international trade in which industries in the trading nations are perfectly contestable rather than perfectly competitive, as in conventional trade theory. This construction permits them to study the effects of increasing returns to scale in the production processes internal to firms, without the need to specify particular forms of oligopolistic and strategic behavior. Among their conclusions are the result that the sustainable factor-price-equalization equilibrium is a highly useful construct for trade analysis; that even in the presence of economies of scale comparative advantage shapes trade patterns with unequal factor rewards; and that there is a strong presumption that there will be gains from trade when national and international markets are contestable.

Recent work on properties of production costs has been stimulated by the significance they have for the character of industry structure in contestable markets. Weitzman (1983) showed that constant returns to scale must hold when demand can be met by the instantaneous accumulation of inventories created by production that is turned on and off repeatedly without additional costs. He concluded that the hit and run entry opportunities said to be a necessary part of contestability must then be inconsistent with increasing returns to scale. In reply, we pointed out that quantities of services cannot be accumulated in inventories, no matter how short their duration, and that contestability does not require the ability to start and stop production costlessly—only the ability to sell without vulnerability to incumbents' responses for a time long enough to render all production costs economically reversible.

Teece (1982) has contributed illuminating work on the sources of economies of scope, both in theory and in specific applications. Gorman (1985) has recently provided theoretical results on economies of scope where there are complementarities or anticomplementarities in marginal costs and also product specific fixed costs that may be subadditive or superadditive. Bittlingmayer (1985) has provided a theoretical analysis that builds multiservice cost functions for airlines upon the foundation of the costs of operating aircraft. He finds economies of scope among routes arising from the hub and spoke architecture of the cost efficient configuration of routes. He goes on to study the characteristics of rate structures that are sustainable and that are Ramsey optimal.

The final category of theoretical work, the relationships between contestability and strategic firm behavior, is most difficult to review succinctly because it is intertwined with the bulk of new research in industrial organization concerning strategy and oligopoly solution concepts. Perfect contestability is a theoretical benchmark that is by its very construction immune from considerations of strategic behavior by dint of its assumption of the absence of economically sunk costs and irreversible commitments necessary for entry. Nevertheless, as pointed out by our distinguished reviewers, Brock (1983) and Spence (1983), and by our constructive critic Schwartz (1985), it is worthwhile to investigate what forms of game and what models of dynamic strategic oligopoly yield outcomes consistent or inconsistent with contestability. Here, Knieps and Vogelsang (1982) and Brock and Scheinkman (1983) have contributed models of quantity sustainability in which outcomes are quite different from those in contestable markets because potential entrants take incumbents' quantities rather than prices as given. In view of the enlightening work of Kreps and Scheinkman (1983), it is now clear that quantity-taking behavior is a reflection of precommitments to quantity-determining capacity by firms that later simultaneously announce prices.

In contrast, contestable outcomes are yielded by Nash equilibrium in a price setting game without precommitments (Mirman, Tauman, and Zang (1983)), and in a game in which supply schedules comprise the strategy sets (Grossman (1981)). We showed that contestable outcomes are a necessary feature of equilibrium in the limit as sunk costs approach zero, using a model in which incumbents' prices are sticky for at least a short period of time (Baumol, Panzar, and Willig (1983)). Maskin and Tirole (1982) analyze a model of dynamic oligopoly involving firms with fixed costs and show that the solution approaches the contestable outcome as strategic advantages fall to zero. In contrast to these results, Dasgupta and Stiglitz (1985) provide models in which incumbents' strategic advantages over a single potential entrant, no matter how small those advantages may be, permit the incumbents to earn economic profits without danger of entry. And Applebaum and Lim (1985) have contributed a model in which the degree of contestability is endogenous, determined by the incumbent's incentives to commit to quantity-determining capacity in view of demand uncertainty and the pattern of costs over time.

In short, there is a flood of exciting research activity in the area of strategic firm behavior, and one of the ways in which the various models are differentiated is the relationship between the games' solutions and the outcomes that would emerge in perfectly contestable markets. At present, that relationship seems to be highly sensitive to the fine grained structure of the models' game forms, so much so that one suspects that empirical reality embodies relationships more robust and stable than does oligopoly theory in its current tumultuous state.

Experimental market studies of contestability

The fruitful and growing body of research using experimental simulation of market behavior has produced a number of papers investigating contestability issues. This work uses human subjects (usually students), real money payoffs and experimental rules corresponding to preselected cost and other pertinent functions that permit direct calculation of the results predicted by theory and their comparison with those that are observed from the behavior of the experimental subjects.

Taking off from earlier studies on monopoly behavior, Coursey, Isaac and Smith (1984) undertook the first of the experimental studies of contestability. They sought to determine whether complete freedom of entry and exit in a market which could most cheaply be served by one firm but where at least two (potential) participants were available would yield prices closer to the competitive than the monopoly level (they call this the "weak contestable markets hypothesis") or to prices actually equal to the competitive level (the "strong contestable market hypothesis"). Participants were given money which they were required to spend in accord with a strictly decreasing and known marginal cost function, the amount spent depending on how much of the good they decided to "produce". The consumers' demand function was also given but was not known by the sellers (except by experience derived from repeated play) who kept for themselves any excess of sales revenues over costs. A participant made a sale if that person's price offer was not undercut by a rival. Both sellers were required to post their price and quantity offers privately, *and* at the same time. Any seller was permitted (but not required) to sell less than the amount the market demanded at the posted price. The authors concluded that "the . . . experiments strongly support the contestable markets hypothesis, namely, that to observe approximately competitive behavior by a single producing firm with substantially decreasing costs, it is sufficient that (a) sunk costs are zero and (b) there are two contesting firms acting non-cooperatively in the sense that there is no explicit nonprice communication between them that leads to excessive restriction of supply" (Coursey, Isaac, Luke and Smith (1984) p. 69).

Harrison (1985) reaches a rather weaker conclusion from these results and those that emerge from a replication of the experiments (Harrison and McKee (1985) (1987)). Using as test criterion an "index of monopoly effectiveness" $M = (\pi - \pi c)/(\pi m - \pi c)$, where π, πc and πm are, respectively, the total profit that emerges from an experiment, the competitive, and the monopoly profit levels. They note that four of the six experiments did attain the $M = 0$ value expected of perfect contestability after 10 periods (i.e., 10 replications of the experiment by a given set of players). However, over all replications M averaged 29 percent in the original set of experiments and 19 percent in the second set, which while not very far from a competitive result, " . . . is significantly positive." Thus, they conclude, "clearly, we can reject this strong form of the CMH (contestable markets hypothesis)" (p. 13) (the pages refer to the unpublished manuscript).

The Harrison McKee study also concludes from experiments using essentially the same procedure that " . . . the discipline of contestability does serve to mitigate the monopoly (significantly) when we compare it to an unregulated monopoly . . . (but) enlightened monopoly regulation vastly outperforms contestability in terms of reducing monopoly effectiveness" (Harrison, pp. 13–14). (Here the regulator's role is simulated by the offer of a subsidy payment equal to the consumers' surplus from any output exceeding the monopoly level, as calculated from the demand curve.)

In another experiment, Coursey, Isaac, Luke and Smith (1984) evaluate the effects of sunk costs imposed equally on "incumbents" and "entrants". The sunk cost takes the form of a $2 entry permit, valid for five periods. The incumbent is one of two sellers chosen randomly and permitted to operate as a monopolist for five periods. Thereafter, the other seller is permitted to enter and post prices that compete with the incumbent, who is required to purchase an entry permit in period 5 in order to continue operation in periods 6–10. The results, according to Harrison's reanalysis, exhibit no limit pricing behavior and indicate " . . . that the threat of *future* entry in period six imposed virtually no discipline on the incumbent in periods 1–5" (p. 15). He also notes that the sunk costs constitute a differential incremental risk to the entrant (and hence an entry barrier) only in period 6–10. Accordingly, he considers it noteworthy that "For all eighteen periods there is a slight and statistically insignificant effect of sunk costs reducing efficiency. However, there is a significant decline in efficiency in periods 6–10 due to sunk costs" (pp. 19–20).

Finally, Harrison tested the effects of imposition in the Bertrand–Nash (or, perhaps more accurately, the Stackelberg leader–follower) assumption that entrants take the incumbents' prices to be given—a premise widely associated with contestability. This was done by letting all participants post prices simultaneously in the first period, designating the winner as the next periods' incumbent, who is then *required to post a price before anyone else does, and to announce it publicly*, with the following periods handled in the same way. Both two and three participant experiments were run. The author concludes, "... satisfaction of the Bertrand–Nash assumption is associated with a dramatic decline in (*M*) ... Moreover, we find support ... for a *strong form* of the (contestable market hypothesis) that claims that observed prices will converge to *and attain* competitive predictions" p. 37, italics in original).

These results would appear to offer strong support for the conclusions of contestability theory but, unfortunately, they still leave a major gap with which future research will have to deal. As Marius Schwartz, in his latest paper criticizing contestability theory, rightly observes "Harrison's experiments basically do constitute a fair test of behavior under perfect contestability: the incumbent faces a price response lag and the entrant can hit and run costlessly. The real question, however, is not whether competitive results will emerge under perfectly contestable conditions but how often such conditions are likely to exist and what happens when they do not" (Schwartz (1985) p. 20, footnote omitted). Put another way, the critical issue that remains is the determination of the circumstances under which the Bertrand–Nash assumption holds or at least is assumed by the participants to hold approximately. It is noteworthy to have it confirmed that *imposition* of Bertrand–Nash behavior leads to the results predicted by the theory. However, that result still leaves work for future statistical or experimental investigation, which Harrison and his colleagues are pursuing.

Econometric studies: multiproduct cost functions and industry structure

In the past three years there has been an outpouring of empirical studies using the cost concepts derived from the contestable markets literature (see the survey of earlier work by Bailey and Friedlaender (1982)). They provide estimates of the shapes of ray averages cost curves, of economies of scope, of the *M*-locus (the locus of points of minimum ray average costs on each ray in product-quantity space). Many such studies use the functional forms for the multiproduct cost function that were recommended in our book. The empirical studies encompass a wide range of industries, including banking, rail, truck and water transportation, insurance, hospitals and a number of others. Here we can only recapitulate briefly a sample of these studies which, predictably, show that industries differ markedly in their scale and scope attributes and in their degree of approximation to contestability.

I. Cost function estimates

Perhaps the most consistent message of the "new" multiproduct cost studies is that the results of previous work using Cobb–Douglas or CES functional forms cannot be trusted. The more general translog form used by most of the multiproduct literature contains, as special cases, the Cobb–

Douglas and CES forms. The appropriateness of these forms can be tested within the translog framework, and in all such tests reported, those forms are rejected in favor of the general translog form.[1]

A. *Banking and related activities*

Banking institutions seem a natural subject for multiproduct analysis. Gilligan, Smirlock and Marshall (1984) and Gilligan and Smirlock (1984) divide output into deposits and loans, using data on many banks provided by the Federal Reserve System. They find that there are large economies of scope "across the balance sheet." They suggest banking theory explicitly consider that fact, and that bank regulation intended to affect one output also be analyzed in multiproduct terms. They encounter decreasing ray average costs (RAC) for small banks, concluding that some small single-bank markets may indeed be subadditive. Overall scale economies are estimated to dissipate as bank size increases, and banks with deposits of $100 million or more manifest increasing RAC. Product specific dis-economies of scale also appear and the authors conclude that policy that precludes entry and encourages mergers cannot be justified by any cost savings.

Murray and White (1983) examine the investment side of British Columbian credit unions. They find significant economies of scope between mortgages and consumer lending and no economies of scope between all lending and investments. Unlike the U.S. studies, returns to scale are observed in most credit unions in the study. The authors conclude that regulation to "inhibit growth and diversification" hampers market efficiency.

Using the same output categories (mortgages, other lending, and invest-ments) for Californian Savings and Loan data, Mester (1985) finds both overall and product specific constant returns to scale, suggesting that large assets offer no cost advantage. She also finds no advantage to a network of branches, given asset size, and absence of economies of scope between outputs. She rejects cost convexity, although finding pairwise transray convexity, and ray subadditivity along some rays.

Kellner and Mathewson (1983) provide a multiproduct analysis of the life insurance industry. They use a four-output industry model. Scale effects are rejected for the average firm while economies of scope appear in some

---

[1] Note that the translog form is itself unreasonable for cases involving zero output of one product since then the translog form implies that the total cost of the remaining products must be zero, no matter what their output levels. One method used to avoid this problem is recourse to a Box–Cox transformation of the outputs. (See Caves, Christensen, and Tretheway (1980) for a discussion of the translog form.) As an alternative, Friedlaender, Winston, and Kung Wang (1983) use a quadratic approximation to a hedonic function to deal with the problem. The quadratic form also offers a simple measure of economies of scale and scope as well as marginal cost.

product lines. In contrast to previous work, they find no evidence of "natural monopoly tendencies" in the cost structure.

B. *Transportation*

Bailey and Friedlaender (1982) discuss work done on the trucking and railroad industries. Network configurations are reported to offer large economies of scope in both industries. These bias upward the measures of scale effects in single product analyses. In the case of trucking, apparent scale economies disappear for large firms when multiproduct analysis is used. Thus, single product analysis of scale effects may improperly reflect scope effects.

Stimulated by the examination of the regulation of bus transport by the Interstate Commerce Commission (ICC), Tauchen, Fravel, and Gilbert (1983) examine the cost structure, taking regular travel, charter, local service and school busing as the outputs of the industry. Using data on 950 privately owned intercity bus firms in the United States, they find that economies of scale are exhausted at low output levels while economies of scope occur throughout. They point out that price and entry regulation is usually meant to deal with economies of scale which are minor here. Economies of scope can be enhanced by fostering of service cooperation among firms in terms of schedules, interlining of tickets and baggage and use of common terminals.

Friedlaender, Winston, and Kung Wang (1983) examine the American auto industry's cost surface for the individual firm. Output is divided into small cars, large cars and trucks. They find that the size of the firm has little to do with the returns to scope or to scale and that the cost function is not convex; some regions exhibit economies of scale and scope and others exhibit diseconomies. This demonstration of the variability of the industry's cost structures indicates the danger of using the neighborhood of a particular output vector as a basis for the empirical analysis of costs. Generalizations based on studies of aggregate output data are, thus, unreliable.

Caves, Christensen, *et al.* used the multiproduct framework to analyze cost attributes other than economies of scope and scale. In Caves, Christensen and Herriges (1984) they construct models of consumer reactions to peak load electricity rate structures. They also examine productivity growth in U.S. railroads employing multiproduct estimates (Caves, Christensen and Swanson (1981)). And they analyze the effects of deregulation on airline productivity—distinguishing between local service and trunk lines (Caves, Christensen and Tretheway (1983)).

C. *Telecommunications*

Much work has been done on the telecommunications industry. Its output is readily divided at least into local and long distance service, and so constitutes a classic multiproduct case. Evans and Heckman (1984) perform an empirical test of the subadditivity of the industry's costs. To avoid the need for global cost information Evans and Heckman derive a local test for subadditivity by restricting the measurement of subadditivity to a subregion of the observed data. For each year of data they calculate the cost savings offered by a single firm relative to the minimum two-firm cost. Finding all such savings to be positive, they conclude that cost was subadditive during the period 1958–1977.

On the other side, Charnes, Cooper and Sueyoshi (1985) use a goal programing/constrained regression method (derived in operations research studies) and a multiproduct framework, data set and functional form identical with those of Evans and Heckman to obtain opposite results. Basically, they drop the standard economic assumption that the firm always operates on the efficient frontier and seek to derive an envelope from observed costs. While Evans and Heckman found the savings were positive, Charnes, Cooper and Sueyoshi found the maximal savings to be negative. They question the validity of standard econometric procedures, but accept the multiproduct nature of the issue and the test of subadditivity. They stress the importance of use of methods derived from several disciplines, particularly when large issues of policy depend on the outcome.

D. *Other industries*

Cowing and Holtmann (1983) divide hospital care into five care types to analyze the efficiency of general-care hospitals in New York state. They reject the use of a single aggregated measure of output and find the economies of scope "may be at least as important as scale effects in designing more efficient hospital service." They urge policy makers to take scope effects into account when deciding on mergers and encourage future health care research to employ multioutput specifications.

Scott (1982) examines the effects of concentration on manufacturing firms. He investigates the effects of multiproduct competition, or "contact", between firms upon excess profits and resource mobility. He constructs a measure of multimarket contact and then shows that an increase in contact in markets with high sales concentration permits larger profits. However, when sales concentration is low, multiproduct contact can drive profits toward costs.

Vertical integration theory suggests that the presence of economies of scope in an industry need have no categorical implications for the scope of individual firms. Teece (1980) examines this issue and concludes that so long as the economies of scope derive from proprietary information or a specialized indivisible physical asset, a multiproduct enterprise is most efficient. He takes the energy industry as an example of this, where petroleum search and removal techniques can be applied to coal.

Mayo (1984) examines data to pursue Teece's ideas. He uses a cost relationship with coal and petroleum as the outputs. Economies of scope, presumably attributable to similarity of extraction techniques, are found. He also shows that ray average costs decline and, near the axes, declining incremental costs and transray convexity yield evidence of output specific subadditivity. This suggests that divestiture of large laterally integrated petroleum firms may increase costs.

Water supplies are generally run as monopolies in the United States, and Kim and Clark (1983) analyze this industry's cost structure with supplies to residential and nonresidential customers as outputs. Using gallons of water per day as the metric, they find overall constancy in returns to scale. But nonresidential output offers product specific economies while diseconomies appear in residential supply. By analyzing ray average costs for many output mixes, they plot the M-locus for the industry and find it to be concave to the origin. This yields a wide range for the optimal number of firms in a market. In addition, by looking at an "average" ray (79 percent residential), they find that most firms produce near the essentially flat portion of the average cost curve. They conclude that market concentration is generally unnecessary for scale economies and may hinder potential competition in water supply.

II. Tests of the contestability of industries

There have been a number of industry studies seeking to test whether the area of the economy under investigation can legitmately be classed as "contestable". Several, but not all, have yielded results that are somewhat surprising. For example, as we will see below, some studies of the airline industry conclude that the industry is less close to the model of perfect contestability than has sometimes been suggested. On the other hand, one very recent study indicates that the aluminum industry is closer to contestability than might have been expected. Froeb and Geweke (1984) describe the U.S. aluminum industry as an area in which the long term threat of entry drives profits downward. Allowing for short run effects of entry barriers, they test the long run behavior of firms from 1949 to 1972 and find it consistent with that one would expect in an imperfectly contestable market.

On the other hand, the results of some of the studies we are now discussing are less surprising. Extensive work by Davies (1986) for the Canadian Transport Commission on the liner shipping industry concludes that contestability theory may offer the most appropriate model to describe that industry since the transferability and resaleability of capital characterize oceanic shipping. The theory "accounts for the condition of entry to the industry, the cost characteristics and structure of the industry, the existence of loyalty ties (to cartels), the reported absence of supernormal profit and the pricing structure operative in the industry. No other body of theory can explain the existence of all these different phenomena in such a coherent and elegant manner." These conclusions are supported in an independent study of ocean transport by Peter Cassidy (1982).

Contestability and public policy

As has already been said, contestability theory aspires to offer two types of guidance to policy makers: first, it undertakes to provide criteria to distinguish the cases in which government intervention is desirable from those in which it is not and, second, it seeks to offer tools to the regulator that will increase the public welfare benefits of this intervention. There have recently been significant applications of contestability theory on each of these fronts. On both issues we will examine some of the recent discussions in the academic literature and devote the bulk of our attention to pertinent developments in recent regulatory and antitrust decisions.

A. *Contestability as a guide to arenas inappropriate for intervention*

Contestability theory follows the lead of Bain, Sylos-Labini and others in stressing that *potential* competitors, like currently active competitors, can effectively constrain market power, so that when the number of incumbents in a market is few or even where only one firm is present, sufficiently low barriers to entry may make antitrust and regulatory attention unnecessary. Indeed, their costs and the inefficiencies they cause may then offer little or no offsetting benefit.

Since this viewpoint thoroughly antedates contestability theory it is not surprising that it has appeared in a variety of official policies. For example, the 1982 Merger Guidelines of the U.S. Department of Justice defines market power as the ability to profit by raising (and maintaining) price above the competitive level, not referring to market share in that definition. It includes in its market definition firms whose entry would be attracted should an elevation of price be attempted. It asserts, moreover, that mergers will go unchallenged by the Department if they affect only markets subject to potential competition that is sufficiently strong. It proposes to take concentration into account only where potential competition is inadequate.

Similarly, the Federal Communications Commission has shown its awareness of the role of potential competiton. In a recent Notice of Inquiry (FCC (1985)) it adopts a market definition for the analysis of long distance telecommunications similar to that of the Department of Justice. It asserts that " . . . satellite carriers readily can *shift* their capacity from one area to another and terrestrial carriers can readily *expand* their service areas through new facilities, interconnection, or resale." "There may be numerous large *potential* entrants in common carrier or private systems that further check AT & T's market power to some degree." And, "The absence of entry does not show that an existing firm possess market power; existing firms may be charging competitive prices because of competition among themselves or the *threat* of *potential* entry, and thereby make entry unattractive." Thus, the FCC implies that a large market share need not confer any monopoly power.

Contestability theory makes direct appearances in a recent decision of the Federal Trade Commission (FTC (1985)).[2] The case involved the acquisition in 1982 by the Echlin Manufacturing Corporation of the automotive aftermarket divisions of the Borg Warner Corporation, including its carburetor kit activities which overlapped with some activities of Echlin. The FTC staff challenged the acquisition under Section 7 of the Clayton Act and Section 5 of the Federal Trade Commission Act on the grounds that the merger would add significantly to the concentration of this market.

However, testimony before the Administrative Law Judge indicated that the field was not beset by any significant entry barriers and that potential entry was sufficient to deprive the merged firm of any monopoly power over the assembly and sale of carburetor kits. The Commission agreed, and permitted the acquisition. In its decision the Commission asserted (explicitly citing contestability theory and other writings on potential competition):

> "An attempt to exercise market power in an industry without entry barriers would cause new competitors to enter the market. This additional supply would drive prices back to the competitive level. Indeed, the threat of new entry can be as potent a procompetitive force as its realization. As the Supreme Court has recognized, the presence of potential entrants on the fringe of a market can prevent the exercise of market power by the incumbent firms even if the potential entrants never actually enter the market. Thus, in the absence of barriers to entry, incumbent firms cannot exercise market power, regardless of the concentration in the nominal 'market,' and indeed even if that market has been 'monopolized' by a single firm" (pp. 9–10).

The decision goes on to espouse the same definition of entry barriers as that adopted (from Stigler and others) in the contestability literature " . . . as additional long-run costs that must be incurred by an entrant relative to the long-run costs faced by incumbent firms" (p. 12) and, again citing the contestability literature, it concludes that "if sunk costs are considered an entry barrier, it must be because they create a difference in the risk confronting the incumbent firms who have already committed their resources and potential entrants who have yet to make that decision" (p. 17). The decision finds, along with contestability analysis, that " . . . we cannot agree that economies of scale and declining markets necessarily create barriers to entry" (p. 18), and that "the absence of past entry, however, does not prove the existence of entry barriers because it is equally consistent with alternative explanations, such as a declining industry or competitive prices" (p. 19).

---

[2] It should be made clear that the authors of this paper cannot claim to be disinterested reporters, having testified in several of the cases described here.

B. *Deregulatory experience*: *airlines, buses and trucks*

The intellectual foundations of the deregulation of airlines, trucking, and buses included recognition of the power of potential entry. While it was clear that in many transportation markets efficiency is not inconsistent with the operation of enough active carriers to make the replacement of regulation by competition appropriate, it was also clear that on many routes efficient operation is incompatible with the presence of several carriers. Nevertheless, deregulation proceeded in the expectation that potential competition could adequately protect consumers of transportation services in such arenas.

In the initial enthusiasm with which we described contestability analysis we agreed with this assessment, and more than once cited the airline industry as a case in point, using the metaphoric argument that investments in aircraft do not incur any sunk costs because they constitute "capital on wings." Reconsideration has led us to adopt a more qualified position on this score. We now believe that transportation by trucks, barges and even buses may be more highly contestable than passenger air tranportation. Barges and trucks have business firms rather than individual consumers as their primary customers, and that facilitates the provision of service via contracts on which potential entrants can effectively bid against incumbents. Where the contracts apply to long run relationships, as they often do in transportation, even capital costs that are physically irreversible are not economically sunk in the pertinent time period. Moreover, trucks and buses do not face the heavy sunk costs involved in the construction of airports or the shortage of gates and landing slots at busy airports such as that which prevented People Express from acquiring even a single gate of its own at Denver's Stapleton International Airport, so that it was forced instead to lease gates from other carriers, catch as catch can, during a year of flying to that airport.

In fact, post-deregulation experience in the airlines industry has revealed several elements of the structure of supply that conflict significantly with the conditions necessary for the pure theory of contestability to apply without modification. While these structural elements may be transitory, they nevertheless appear to have influenced the performance of the industry in important ways since the advent of deregulation.

First, as the previously noted difficulties of People Express exemplify, there have been constraining shortages of facilities and services of air traffic control at several pivotal airports. These constrain flights in and out of the affected airports and, in addition, they also restrict the prospects of entry and expansion on routes that would otherwise interconnect efficiently with such flights. Second, technological advances, changes in the relative prices of jet fuel and equipment, and changes in the desired configurations of route networks have significantly altered the types and mix of aircraft demanded by the industry. As a result, there have been shortages in the availability of the aircraft demanded, with delivery lags frequently stretching to three years. Third, newly certificated airlines have been able to avoid the costly labor contracts that pervaded the industry before deregulation, so that their labor costs have been substantially lower than those facing the older established carriers. Recently, the older carriers and their unionized work forces have been adapting themselves to this new competitive reality with the aid of more flexible wage contracts, dual wage structures, and less costly contract settlements. Nevertheless, substantial differences in labor costs between older and newer carriers persist.

These conditions make it easy to see why the airline industry does not conform perfectly to the contestability model, even if aircraft are "capital on wings." Thus, it remains to analyze both quantitatively and qualitatively the degree to which the performance of the industry does, or can be expected to, reflect the predictions of contestability theory. This should come as no surprise since most industries can be expected to depart in some important respects from the model of perfect contestability, and it will therefore generally be necessary in applying the theory to assess the economic significance of the deviations.

Several econometric studies have confirmed the imperfection of the contestability of the airline markets (see, e.g., Call and Keeler (1984)). They have shown, for example, that there is a significant positive correlation between profits and concentration in airline markets. Thus the threat of entry does not by itself suffice to keep profits to zero, as perfect contestability would require. Moreover, when new entry does occur, established carriers do reduce their fares in response, something one would expect in a conventional oligopolistic market other than one that is perfectly contestable. Even the study of Morrison and Whinston, which concludes that potential entry does constrain price significantly, finds that the coefficient describing the influence of potential entrants does not become significant until the number of such prospective entrants exceeds three.

The econometric study by Graham, Kaplan, and Sibley (1983) permits comparison among the effects on 1981 route-by-route prices of various influences that lie outside the predictions of contestability theory. They find that prices deviate from costs an additional 10 percent on the average and other things being equal, for routes that utilize one of the major slot-constrained airports in New York, Chicago, or Washington, D.C. In contrast, prices are reduced some 22 percent relative to costs on routes where a newly certificated carrier operates. And, prices are some 18 percent lower relative to costs if four carriers fly the route rather than only one.

These results indicate the significance of the physical constraints on entry and expansion in two ways. First, the direct influence of the slot constraints on prices shows up in the data. Second, the substantial effect of the presence of new carriers, with their low labor costs, demonstrates how much lower fares would generally be if those carriers were able to expand their operations to cover more routes. Finally, the significant effect of the number of carriers on a route shows that active competition plays a role in holding price down toward cost. However, since the size of that effect is so much smaller than would be predicted by most theories of oligopoly that focus on the role of active competitors, it can be concluded that the forces of potential competition still play an important role, despite the structural conditions that impede their workings.

Similar conclusions seem to us to follow from qualitative evaluation of the behavior of the airline markets under deregulation. As we have just seen, the responsive price cuts of incumbents when faced with incursions of low priced entrants is certainly not compatible with the predicted qualitative behavior of contestable markets in the long run. However, there are other qualitative properties that are highly pertinent. In a recent study, Elizabeth Bailey (1986) sets out to examine these. She undertakes to analyze

" . . . the consequences that have emerged under deregulation in terms of the following behavioral properties predicted by contestability theory: a variety of products will emerge, each of which will yield zero economic profit; the revenues from any subset of the products must exceed the incremental costs of those products, so that no cross-subsidy can exist; prices for each product will equal or exceed marginal costs; and an equilibrium market structure will minimize costs of the industry. Thus, if the theory has some degree of validity, more of these properties should be displayed after deregulation than before. Cross-subsidy, which was pervasive in the regulatory era, should be significantly eroded. Prices should move nearer to costs. Products capable of producing zero economic profits, but which were formerly excluded, should now appear." (pp. 2–3, footnote omitted)

Here evidence leads her to conclude that, while the performance in each respect has not been absolutely clear-cut, on balance the patterns predicted by contestability theory have indeed emerged. She writes, in summary of the consequences of deregulation of the airlines, that

"Prices in the cheaper-to-serve long-haul and dense markets were substantially lowered (by about forty percent), whereas prices in the more expensive short-haul and thin markets went up somewhat. A diversity of price-service options arose. Individuals could select between low-service/low-price discount carriers and full-service national carriers. Even among the full-service carriers, prices were lower for customers willing to improve load factors by traveling in off-peak periods or by taking one-stop rather than non-stop flights.

The encouragement to entry under air transport deregulation brought with it a variety of contributions to efficiency. One involved delivery systems. It quickly became clear that hub-and-spoke operations rather than the mostly linear systems imposed by regulation offered savings to the airlines. Hub-and-spoke systems also substantially improved service for consumers. A second efficiency contribution involved input productivity. The post-deregulation period has been characterized by pressures to reduce pay scales toward those in unregulated economic sectors, to increase productivity through changes in work rules, and to choose a more efficient fleet configuration" (p. 22).

In light of these observations and similar evidence drawn from the opening of brokerage commissions to market determination, the deregulation of trucking, and the opening of telecommunications markets to entry, Bailey concludes that performance in these areas has shown no significant inconsistencies with the predictions of contestability analysis.

In short, in terms of the airlines case we can infer that market forces through the pressures of competition, both actual and potential, have done a commendable if imperfect job in protecting consumer interests. This is suggested by a number of developments following deregulation: the decrease in real average prices; the reduction in average time spent in traveling from point to point; the falling real costs of airline operation; the erosion or disappearance of cross subsidies, with the elimination of financing of sparsely traveled routes by those that are heavily traveled, and of peak travelers by off-peak flyers, and the considerable improvements in efficiency through computerized routing and hub-and-spoke operations—approaches that had evaded both executives and the Commission during the era of regulation.

C. *Contestability theory as guide for regulation*

We come, finally, to the arena in which the viewpoint of contestability may make its main contribution—as a guide for regulation, rather than as an argument for its elimination. How does contestability theory help in this domain? After all, perfect competition has long served usefully as the ideal for government intervention to follow; that is, as the model of performance to which it should seek to make the regulated firm adhere. What does contestability analysis have to add to this? The answer is that in some circumstances, notably in the presence of substantial economies of scale and scope, the standard of perfect competition is totally inappropriate. For example, where economies of scale and scope are present society no longer is sure to benefit if firms are required to be small, as they would be under perfect competition. Similarly, a rule that price must be set equal to marginal cost is a prescription for financial disaster. Of course, Ramsey pricing theory is of considerable help here, but in some circumstances its usefulness in practice is limited, particularly where there are no reliable data on elasticities and cross elasticities of demands for the considerable number of products at issue. It is then that contestability theory can come to the rescue (and several times already has). For it can propose, for example, to offer consumers in markets with unavoidable entry barriers just the same sort of protection from excessive pricing that they would have derived from perfect freedom of entry, if such freedom had been possible. This is precisely how the stand-alone cost criterion for price ceilings, which will be described below, emerged from contestability theory and could not have been deduced from the model of perfect competition.

To see just how contestability theory can be used to guide regulation we can do no better than to follow the outlines of a remarkable decision of the Interstate Commerce Commission (1985), a decision that encompasses the foundations of its current policies toward those elements of railroad activities in which competitive pressures are judged to be inadequate (that is, in regulatory terminology, in areas in which a railroad possesses "market dominance," or its shippers are "captive").

Early in the discussion of its economic framework the decision provides a section headed "Contestable Markets." However while, as we will see presently, much is made of the logic of contestability, the decision asserts flatly and quite appropriately that the pertinent arena is *not* contestable: "the railroad industry is recognized to have barriers to entry and exit and thus is not considered contestable for captive traffic" (p. 10).

The question, then, is what is best done to control the pricing terms on which such traffic is served. The Commission adopted a set of rules which it termed "constrained market pricing." Before getting to the details of those rules it is desirable to take note of two fundamental attributes underlying the approach: rate of return-rate base regulation of overall earnings, and acceptance of differential (non uniform) pricing. On the first of these, the Commission undertakes to avoid decisions that preclude a railroad from earning in the long run what it refers to as "adequate revenues." Following long regulatory tradition, these are defined in terms of a permitted rate of return on the railroad's rate base (its total invested capital). What is new here is that the Commission adopts for this purpose most of the criteria called for by economic analysis, for example determining that "'adequate' returns are those that provide a rate of return on net investment equal to the current cost of capital (i.e., the level of return available on alternative investments)" (p. 18).

Second, the Commission recognizes that solvency of the railroads is likely to require differential pricing:

> Most importantly, railroads exhibit significant economies of scope and density. Economy of *scope* refers to the fact that the rail plant is indivisible and can produce numerous services at less cost than those services could be produced by separate rail plants for each service. Economy of *density* refers to the fact that greater use of the fixed plant results in a declining average cost. Thus, the marginal cost of rail service is less than the average cost, because the fixed plant is used in a progressively more efficient manner. The differential between marginal costs and average costs cannot be assigned directly to specific movements by any conventional accounting methodology. Hence, we refer to it as the "unattributable costs." These are the costs which must be covered through differential pricing. (pp. 7–8, footnotes omitted)

The decision goes on to point out that where unattributable costs cannot be covered by marginal cost pricing, then demand considerations as well as cost data must enter into decision making, both in order to permit adequacy of revenues and in order to achieve efficiency.

Any means of allocating these costs among shippers other than actual market demand is arbitrary and may not permit a carrier to cover all of its costs. This is because non-demand-based cost apportionment methods do not necessarily reflect the carrier's ability (or inability) to impose the assigned allocations and cover its costs. Thus, they frequently "over-assign" or "under-assign" the carrier's unattributable costs to particular services. If a carrier sought to apply the formula price to all of its traffic, it would lose that traffic for which the demand could not support the price assigned. In that event, the remaining shippers might be required to pay a larger portion of the carrier's unattributable costs because they would lose the benefit of sharing these costs with the lost traffic.

"Ramsey pricing" is a widely recognized method of differential pricing, that is, pricing in accordance with demand. Under Ramsey pricing, each price or rate contains a mark-up above the long-run marginal cost of the product or service to cover a portion of the unattributable costs. The unattributable costs are allocated among the purchasers or users in inverse relation to their demand elasticity. Thus, in a market where shippers are very sensitive to price changes (a highly elastic market), the mark-up would be smaller than in a market where shippers are less price sensitive. The sum of the mark-ups equals the unattributable costs of an efficient producer. (p. 8, footnote omitted)

Nevertheless, the Commission comments,

Ramsey pricing is based on a mathematical formula which requires both the marginal cost and the elasticity of demand to be quantified for every movement in the carrier's system. Thus, the amount of data and degree of analysis required seemed overwhelming. We concluded that while formula Ramsey pricing is useful as a theoretical guideline, it is too difficult and burdensome for universal application. In setting flat rates, that is, rates which do not vary with the volume shipped, Ramsey pricing, in principle, yields the least inefficient price structure. However, even under pure Ramsey pricing, output levels are less than they would be if rates were set at marginal costs. This results in an economic inefficiency because the value of the lost output to the shipper is greater than the value of the resources saved by reducing output. In such a situation, it may be feasible for the parties to negotiate a contract which will leave both parties better off than at the [flat] Ramsey price. Rail freight differs from financing government services (for which shippers are relatively large and few in number). Thus, the feasibility of contracting is more evident for rail freight than for these other services.

As an alternative to pure Ramsey pricing, we proposed Constrained Market Pricing. (p. 9, footnotes omitted)

The key issue to be faced by constrained market pricing is the formulation of a criterion to be used in setting a ceiling over the price to be charged for traffic over which a railroad possesses market dominance. This is an issue with which the Commission had been struggling only since 1978. Before that, curiously, the Commission had been preoccupied primarily with the setting of floors beneath rail prices, to prevent railroads from undercutting barge and truck competitors (the Commission had once described its role as that of a "a giant handicapper").

In the early 1980's, in its search for a tenable price ceiling rule, it turned initially to the tools it had designed long before in its floor setting endeavors. Here, at least for the bulk of the postwar period, it had been using an accounting concept which it called "fully allocated cost." In essence, this assigned to each part of a railroad's traffic a figure intended to approximate the incremental cost of that traffic, plus a share of the remaining (unattributable) cost proportionate to some criterion of "relative use" such as number of carloads, weight or monetary value of the commodity in question carried by the railroad. The apportionment of the unattributable costs was admittedly arbitrary, bore no necessary relation to the cost data (such as marginal costs) that an economist would consider pertinent, and allowed for no adjustments for variations in demand conditions. Even earlier than the landmark Ingot Molds Case (1967) in which the Supreme Court threw up its hands on the matter, economists had begun to argue before the ICC that the use of a fully distributed cost floor was pernicious and a source of substantial inefficiency, and that marginal or incremental costs were the only defensible cost data for use in the calculation of price floors, a view that gradually acquired acceptance among regulatory agencies, including the ICC.

It seems odd, then, that in 1978, when the Commission began its search for a rate ceiling formula (Interstate Commerce Commission (ICC) (1978)) it turned to fully allocated cost, now discredited as a cost floor, as its candidate for a viable cost ceiling. Initially, it proposed for this purpose to allocate a railroad's unattributable costs in proportion to the variable costs (as a proxy for the incremental costs) of the various portions of its traffic. Because this formula soon proved fatally restrictive, particularly in ignoring demand considerations, the Commission permitted the railroads leeway to charge prices as much as seven percent above fully allocated costs where demand conditions permitted. The courts agreed to the legitimacy of this move toward differential pricing but rejected the use of the arbitrary seven percent range of tolerance (see, e.g., ICC (1979)). The Commission made one more attempt to salvage the fully allocated cost approach to price ceilings, but this time adopted weight and distance traversed (calling it the "ton/ton-mile" method) as its basis of allocation (ICC (1980)). However, in response to careful arguments by the railroads and others, it withdrew from this approach altogether in 1981 (ICC (1981)), and early in 1983 offered constrained market pricing as its alternative.

Here, the ceiling proposed by the Commission was *stand-alone cost,* a concept it acknowledged to have derived from the contestability literature.

" . . . stand-alone cost (SAC) test . . . is used to compute the rate a competitor in the market-place would need to charge in serving a captive shipper or a group of shippers who benefit from sharing joint and common costs. A rate level calculated by the SAC methodology represents the theoretical maximum rate that a railroad could levy on shippers without substantial diversion of traffic to a hypothetical competing service. It is, in other words, a simulated competitive price. (The competing service could be a shipper providing service for itself or a third party competing with the incumbent railroad for traffic. In either case, the SAC represents the minimum cost of an alternative to the service provided by the incumbent railroad.)

The theory behind SAC is best explained by the concept of 'contestable markets.' This recently developed economic theory augments the classical economic model of 'pure competition' with a model which focuses on the entry and exit from an industry as a measure of economic efficiency. The theory of contestable markets is more general than that of 'pure competition' because it does not require a large number of firms. In fact, even a monopoly can be contestable. The underlying premise is that a monopolist or oligopolist will behave efficiently and competitively where there is a threat of losing some or all of its markets to a new entrant. In other words, contestable markets have competitive characteristics which preclude monopoly pricing (p. 10).

Here it is worth reviewing the logic of the stand-alone cost ceiling a bit more closely. The first-best lesson of the perfect competition model, calling for prices to be set equal to marginal costs, has no doubt contributed to the common regulatory ethos which *equates* price to *some* measure of cost. This doctrine has been used frequently where it is completely inappropriate and without logical foundation, that is, in cases where prices should be based on demand as well as cost considerations, because of the presence of economies of scale and scope. Such arbitrary measures as fully distributed costs cannot substitute for marginal cost measures as decision rules for proper pricing, and the search for a substitute is a remnant of inappropriate reliance on the model of perfect competition for guidance in regulation.

In contrast, contestability theory suggests cost measures that are appropriate guideposts for regulated pricing—incremental and stand-alone costs. The incremental cost of a given service is, of course, the increment in the total costs of the supplying firm when that service is added to its product line. In perfectly contestable markets, the price of a product will lie somewhere between its incremental and its stand-alone cost, just where it falls in that range depending on the state of demand. One cannot legitimately infer that monopoly power is exercised from data showing that prices do not exceed stand-alone costs, and stand-alone costs constitute the proper cost-based ceilings upon prices, preventing both cross-subsidization and the exercise of monopoly power (see Faulhaber (1975) for tests of cross-subsidy and their equivalence). A simple example will show why this is so.

First, suppose that a firm supplies two services, A and B, which *share no costs* and that each costs 10 units a year to supply. The availability of effective potential competition would force revenues from each service to equal 10 units a year. For higher earnings would attract (profitable) entry, and lower revenues would drive the supplier out of business. In this case, in which common costs are absent, incremental and stand-alone costs are equal to each other and to revenues, and the competitive and contestability benchmarks yield the same results.

Next, suppose instead that of the 20 unit total costs 4 are fixed and common to A and B, while 16 are variable, 8 of the 16 being attributable to A and 8 to B. If, because of demand conditions, at most only a bit more than 8 can be garnered from consumers of A, then a firm operating and surviving in contestable markets will earn a bit less than 12 from B. These prices lie between incremental costs (8) and stand-alone costs (12), are mutually advantageous to consumers of both services, and will attract no entrants, even in the absence of any entry barriers. In contrast, should the firm attempt to raise the revenues obtained from B above the 12 unit stand-alone cost, it would lose its business to competitors willing to charge less. Similarly, the same fate would befall it in contestable markets if it priced B in a way that earned more than 8 plus the common cost of 4, less the contribution toward that common cost from service A.

Thus, the forces of idealized potential competition in perfectly contestable markets enforce cost constraints on prices, but prices remain sensitive to demands as well. Actual and potential competition are *effective* if they constrain rates in this way, and in such circumstances regulatory intervention is completely unwarranted. But if, in fact, market forces are not sufficiently strong, then there is likely to be a proper role for regulation, and the theoretical guidelines derived from the workings of contestable markets are the appropriate ones to apply. That is, prices must be constrained to lie between incremental and stand-alone costs.[3,4] This is the approach adopted by the ICC to determine maximum rates for railroad services, and the method has already withstood appeals to the Federal courts.

---

[3] Note that, properly applied, the SAC criterion should hold for all subsets of a firm's products and not only for its individual products. Thus, suppose a firm produces three items, A, B and C, and that a widget of limitless capacity must be used in order to produce any A, any B or any combination of the two. The cost of the widget will then not enter either A's or B's incremental cost, but it will clearly consititute part of the incremental cost of supplying them both. Then, the combined total revenue of the two items must suffice to cover the cost of the widget as well as any other incremental cost incurred individually or in common. Note also that efficiency requires that a supplier never set price below either marginal *or* per unit incremental cost, because if it is set so low it may lure away customers from a more efficient supplier, i.e., one who can supply the product at lower marginal or per unit incremental cost, and hence supply either one unit of the product or its entire amount at lower resources cost.

[4] It is easy to prove that if a firm's total earnings are exactly equal to its cost of capital, i.e., if it earns exactly zero economic profits, then if all of its revenues equal or exceed their corresponding incremental costs they are *automatically guaranteed* not to exceed their stand-alone costs and *vice versa*. That is, the passing of either test (the SAC ceiling or the incremental cost floor) automatically demonstrates that the other must also be passed by the prices at issue. To show this simply we deal with the case of two products, though the proof is perfectly general. Let

X_1, X_2 = the quantities of the outputs supplied by a firm

P_1, P_2 = the prices of the products

$C(X_1, X_2)$ = the total cost function

$C(X_1, O)$ = the stand-alone cost of product 1 and

$C(X_1, X_2) - C(X_1, O)$ = the incremental cost of product 2.

Concluding remarks

Whatever one's attitude toward contestability theory or the policy recommendations that have derived from it, it must surely be agreed that it has evoked a flood of imaginative and valuable research and writing in opposition, in extension, and in application. To see how rapidly it and associated concepts have spread one need only recall that as recently as 1970 the concept of Ramsey pricing was unknown to most economists, though the analysis, of course, had appeared in 1927. Indeed, the term "Ramsey pricing" was coined by the present authors less than a decade ago. Terms such as "economies of scope," "stand-alone cost" and "contestable markets" were coined in the 1970's as well. Yet today they are used routinely not only in professional journals, but in hearings before U.S. courts and regulatory agencies. Clearly, propagation of the substance rather than the terminology is what really counts, but this too, is being achieved.

Thus, whatever contribution the future will judge contestability theory to have made, it will surely conclude that the analysis has succeeded in stimulating thought in both the realm of academic research and policy formulation.

Princeton and New York Universities.

REFERENCES

APPLEBAUM, E. and LIM, C., "Contestable Markets Under Uncertainty, *Rand Journal of Economics*, 16, 1, Spring 1985, pp. 28–40.

BAILEY, ELIZABETH, E., "Price and Productivity Change Following Deregulation: The U.S. Experience," *Economic Journal,* March 1986 (forthcoming).

BAILEY, ELIZABETH E. and BAUMOL, WILLIAM J., "Deregulation and the Theory of Contestable Markets," *Yale Journal of Regulation,* 1984, 1, pp. 111–137.

BAILEY, E. E. and FRIEDLAENDER, A. F., "Market Structure and Multiproduct Industries," *Journal of Economic Literature*, Vol. 20, September 1982, pp. 1024–1048.

BAUMOL, W. J., PANZAR, J. C. and WILLIG, R. D., *Contestable Markets and the Theory of Industry Structure*, San Diego: 1982.

BAUMOL, W. J., PANZAR, J. C., and WILLIG, R. D., "Contestable Markets: An Uprising in the Theory of Industry Structure: Reply," *American Economic Review*, 73, June, 1983, pp. 491–496.

BITTLINGMAYER, G., "The Economics of A Simple Airline Network," mimeo, 1985.

Then, zero economic profit requires

(1) $P_1 X_1 + P_2 X_2 = C(X_1, X_2)$

and the incremental cost test for product 2 requires

(2) $P_2 X_2 \geq C(X_1, X_2) - C(X_1, O)$.

Subtraction of (2) from (1) immediately yields the stand-alone cost criterion for product 1,

(3) $P_1 X_1 \leq C(X_1, O)$.

Similarly, subtraction of (3) from (1) immediately yields (2). Q.E.D.

BROCK, W. A., "Contestable Markets and the Theory of Industry Structure: A Review Article," *Journal of Political Economy*, 91, 6, December 1983, pp. 1055–1066.

BROCK, W. A. and SCHEINKMAN, J. A., "Free Entry and the Sustainability of Natural Monopoly: Bertrand Revisited by Cournot," in Evans, D. S. (ed.), *Breaking up Bell*: *Essays on Industrial Organization and Regulation*, 1983.

CALL, GREGORY D. and KEELER, THEODORE E., "Airline Deregulation, Fares, and Market Behavior: Some Empirical Evidence," in *Analytical Studies in Transport Economics*, 1984.

CASSIDY, PETER A., *Australian Overseas Cargo Liner Shipping*, University of Queensland, 1982.

CAVES, D. W., CHRISTENSEN, L. R., and HERRIGES, J. A., "Modelling Alternative Residential Peak-Load Electricity Rate Structures," *Journal of Econometrics*, Vol. 24(3), 1984, pp. 249–268.

CAVES, D. W., CHRISTENSEN, L. R., and SWANSON, J. A., "Productivity Growth, Scale Economies, and Capacity Utilization in U.S. Railroads, 1955–74," *American Economic Review*, December 1981, pp. 994–1002.

CAVES, D. W., CHRISTENSEN, L. R., and TRETHEWAY, M. W., "Flexible Cost Functions for Multiproduct Firms," *Review of Economics and Statistics*, Vol. 62(3), August 1980, pp. 477–481.

CAVES, D. W., CHRISTENSEN, L. R., and TRETHEWAY, M. W., "Productivity Performance of U.S. Trunk and Local Services Airlines in the Era of Deregulation," *Economic Inquiry*, Vol. XXI, July 1983, pp. 312–324.

CHARNES, A., COOPER, W. W., and SUEYOSHI, T., "A Goal Programing/Constrained Regression Review of the Bell System Breakup," Center for Cybernetic Studies Report 513, University of Texas at Austin, May 1985.

COURSEY, D., ISAAC, R. M., and SMITH, V. L., "Natural Monopoly and Contested Markets: Some Experimental Results," *Journal of Law and Economics*, Vol. 27, April, 1984, pp. 91–113.

COURSEY, D., ISAAC, R. M., LUKE, M., and SMITH, V. L., "Market Contestability in the Presence of Sunk (Entry) Costs," *Rand Journal of Economics*, Vol. 15, Spring 1984, pp. 69–84.

COWING, T. G. and HOLTMANN, A. G., "Multiproduct Short-Run Hospital Cost Functions: Evidence and Policy Implications from Cross-Section Data," *Southern Journal of Economics*, January 1983, pp. 637–653.

DASGUPTA, P. and STIGLITZ, J. E., "Sunk Costs, Competition, and Welfare," mineo, 1985.

DAVIES, J. E., "The Theory of Contestable Markets and its Application to the Liner Shipping Industry," Canadian Transport Commission, Ottawa-Hull, 1986.

DENNY, M., FUSS, M., EVERSON, C., and WAVERMAN, L., "Estimating the Effects of Diffusion of Technological Innovations in Telecommunications: The Production Structure of Bell Canada," *Canadian Journal of Economics*, February 1981, pp. 24–43.

EVANS, D. S. and HECKMAN, J. J., "A Test for Subadditivity of the Cost Function with an Application to the Bell System," *American Economic Review*, September, 1984, pp. 615–623.

FAULHABER, G., "Cross-Subsidization: Pricing in Public Enterprise," *American Economic Review*, 65, December 1975, pp. 966–977.

FAULHABER, G. and LEVINSON, S., "Subsidy-Free Prices and Anonymous Equity," *American Economic Review*, 71, 1981, pp. 1083–1091.

FEDERAL COMMUNICATIONS COMMISSION, *Notice of Inquiry, in the Matter of Long-Run Regulation at AT & T's Basic Domestic Interstate Sources*, Washington, D.C., 1985.

FEDERAL TRADE COMMISSION, *Final Order: In the Matter of the Echlin Manufacturing Company, and Borg-Warner Corporation*, Docket Number 9157, Washington, D.C., June 28, 1985.

FRIEDLAENDER, A., WINSTON, C., and KUNG WANG, D., "Costs, Technology and Productivity in the U.S. Automobile Industry," *Bell Journal of Economics*, Spring 1983, pp. 1–20.

FROEB, L. and GEWEKE, J., "Perfect Contestability and the Postwar U.S. Aluminium Industry," Tulane University, December 1984.

GILLIGAN, T. and SMIRLOCK, M., "An Empirical Study of Joint Production and Scale Economies in Commerical Banking," *Journal of Banking and Finance,* vol. 8, 1984, pp. 67–77.

GILLIGAN, T., SMIRLOCK, M., and MARSHALL, W., "Scale and Scope Economies in the Multi-Product Banking Firm," *Journal of Monetary Economics,* Vol. 13, 1984, pp. 393–405.

GORMAN, I. E., "Conditions for Economies of Scope in the Presence of Fixed Costs," *Rand Journal of Economics,* 16, 3, Autumn 1985, pp. 431–436.

GRAHAM, D. R., KAPLAN, D. P., and SIBLEY, D. S., "Efficiency and Competition in the Airline Industry," *Bell Journal of Economics,* Spring 1983, pp. 118–138.

GROSSMAN, S. J., "Nash Equilibrium and the Industrial Organization of Markets with Large Fixed Costs," *Econometrica,* 49, 1981, pp. 1149–1172.

HARRISON, G. W., "Experimental Evaluation of the Contestable Markets Hypothesis," in E. E. Bailey (ed.) *Regulation at the Crossroads,* Cambridge, Mass., 1986.

HARRISON, G. W. and McKEE, M., "Monopoly Behavior, Decentralized Regulation, and Contestable Markets: An Experimental Evaluation," *Rand Journal of Economics,* Spring 1985, 16, pp. 51–69.

HARRISON, G. W., McKEE, M., and RUTSTRÜM, E. E., "Experimental Evaluation of Institutions of Monopoly Restraint," in Green, L. and Kagel, J. H. (eds.), *Advances in Behavioral Economics* (Norwood: Ablex, 1987, forthcoming).

HELPMAN, E. and KRUGMAN, P. R., *Market Structure and Foreign Trade,* 1985.

INTERSTATE COMMERCE COMMISSION, Ex Part No. 347, "Western Coal Investigation—Guidelines for Railroad Rate Structure", 43, *Federal Register,* 22151, May 22, 1978.

INTERSTATE COMMERCE COMMISSION, *Annual Volume Rates on Coal—Wyoming to Flint Creek, Arkansas,* 361, ICC 539, 1979.

INTERSTATE COMMERCE COMMISSION, Ex Parte No. 347 (Sub-No. 1), "Coal Rate Guidelines—Nationwide," 45, *Federal Register,* 80370, December 4, 1980.

INTERSTATE COMMERCE COMMISSION, Ex Parte No. 347 (Sub-No. 1), "Coal Rate Guidelines—Nationwide," December 21, 1981, unpublished.

INTERSTATE COMMERCE COMMISSION, "Coal Rate Guidelines, Nationwide," Ex Parte No. 347 (Sub-No. 1), Washington, D.C., decided August 3, 1985.

KELLNER, S. and MATHEWSON, G. F., "Entry, Size Distribution, Scale, and Scope Economies in the Life Insurance Industry," *Journal of Business,* Vol. 56, No. 1, 1983, pp. 25–44.

KIM, H. Y. and CLARK, R. M., "Estimating Multiproduct Scale Economies: An Application to Water Supplies," U.S. Environmental Protection Agency, Municipal Environment Research Laboratory, Cincinnati, Ohio, July 1983.

KNIEPS, G. and VOGELSANG, I., "The Sustainability Concept under Alternative Behavioral Assumptions," *Bell Journal of Economics,* 13, 1, Spring 1982, pp. 234–241.

KREPS, D. and SCHEINKMAN, J., "Quantity Precommitment and Bertrand Competition Yield Cournot Outcomes," *Bell Journal of Economics,* 14, 2, Auturn 1983, pp. 326–338.

MASKIN, E. and TIROLE, J., "A Theory of Dynamic Oligopoly," mineo, 1982.

MAYO, J. W., "The Technological Determinants of the U.S. Energy Industry Structure," *Review of Economics and Statistics,* January 1984, pp. 51–58.

MESTER, L. J., "A Multiproduct Cost Study of Savings and Loans," essay 1, doctoral dissertation, Princeton University, October 1985.

MIRMAN, L. J., TAUMAN, Y., and ZANG, I., "Monopoly and Sustainable Prices As a Nash Equilibrium in Contestable Markets," Mimeo, 1983.

MIRMAN, L. J., TAUMAN, Y., and ZANG, I., "Supportability, Sustainability and Subsidy-Free Prices," *Rand Journal of Economics,* 16, 1, Spring 1985, pp. 114–126.

MORRISON, S. A. and WINSTON, C., "Empirical Implications and Tests of the Contestability Hypothesis," manuscript, 1985.

MURRAY, J. D. and WHITE, R. W., "Economies of Scale and Economies of Scope in Multiproduct Financial Institutions: A Study of British Columbian Credit Unions," *Journal of Finance,* June 1983, pp. 887–901.

PANZAR, J. C. and POSTLEWAITE, A., "The Sustainability of Ramsey Optimal Non-linear Prices," mimeo, 1985.

PERRY, M., "Sustainable Positive Profit Multiple-Price Strategies in Contestable Markets," mimeo, 1982.

QUIRMBACH, H., "Vertical Integration, Contestable Markets, and the Misfortunes of the Misshaped U," mimeo, 1982.

SCHWARZ, MARIUS, "The Nature and Scope of Contestability Theory," Georgetown University, September 1985, unpublished.

SCHWARTZ, MARIUS and REYNOLDS, ROBERT J., "Contestable Markets: A Uprising in the Theory of Industry Structure: Comment," American Economic Review, June 1983, 73, pp. 488–490.

SCOTT, J. T., "Multimarket Contract and Economic Performance," Review of Economics and Statistics, August 1982, pp. 368–375.

SHARKEY, W. W., "Existence of Sustainable Prices for Natural Monopoly Outputs," Bell Journal of Economics, 12, 1, Spring 1981, pp. 144–154.

SHARKEY, W. W., The Theory of Natural Monopoly, 1982.

SHEPHERD, W. G., "'Contestability' vs. Competition," American Economic Review, 74, September 1984, pp. 572–587.

SPENCE, A. M., "Contestable Markets and the Theory of Industry Structure: A Review Article," Journal of Economic Literature, 21, 1983, pp. 981–990.

SPULBER, D., "Scale Economies and Existence of Sustainable Monopoly Prices," Journal of Economic Theory, 34, 1984, pp. 149–163.

TAUCHEN, H., FRAVEL, F. D., and GILBERT, G., "Cost Structure and the Intercity Bus Industry," Journal of Transport Economics and Policy, January 1983, pp. 25–47.

TEECE, D. J., "Economies of Scope and the Scope of the Enterprise," Journal of Economic Behavior and Organization, Vol. 1, September 1980, pp. 223–247.

TEECE, D. J., "Towards an Economic Theory of the Multiproduct Firm," Journal of Economic Behavior and Organization, March 1982, pp. 39–63.

TEN RAA, T., "Supportability and Anonymous Equity," Journal of Economic Theory, 31, 1983, pp. 176–181.

TEN RAA, T., "Resolution of Conjectures on the Sustainability of Natural Monopoly," Rand Journal of Economics, 15, 1, Spring 1984, pp. 135–141.

U.S. DEPARTMENT OF JUSTICE, Merger Guidelines, Washington, D.C. 1982.

U.S. SUPREME COURT, American Commerical Lines, Inc., et al. vs. Lousiville and Nashville Railroad Co., et al. (Ingot Molds case), October term, 1967, pp. 571–597.

WEITZMAN, M. L., "Contestable Markets: An Uprising in the Theory of Industry Structure: Comment," American Economic Review, 73, June 1983, pp. 486–487.

THE NATURE AND SCOPE OF CONTESTABILITY THEORY

By MARIUS SCHWARTZ

I. Introduction

TRADITIONAL economic thinking holds that some form of policy intervention may be required to check monopolistic behavior when buyers are numerous and sellers are few due to economies of scale. The proposed remedies, however, regulation, public ownership or antitrust, are acknowledged to suffer significant drawbacks. Contestability theory maintains that the dilemma need not arise, because the threat of new entry may be sufficient to discipline incumbent firms. In the extreme, benchmark case of perfect contestability, threat of entry ensures satisfactory performance regardless of the size distribution of incumbent firms and regardless of any oligopolistic interactions among them. More generally, contestability theory shifts attention away from structural measures of market power (such as concentration ratios) and from the nature of oligopoly interactions towards variables that affect the ease of entry and exit. The theory, therefore, has wide-ranging implications both for policy and for economists' research agenda.

The burgeoning literature has sprung off in different directions. Theoretically, it has been questioned whether perfect contestability is logically possible (Weitzman, 1983; Baumol, Panzar and Willig (BPW hereafter), 1983a), whether the theory is robust (Schwartz and Reynolds, 1983; BPW, 1983a; Schwartz and Reynolds, 1984; Farrell, 1984), and what happens when uncertainty is introduced (Brock, 1983; Appelbaum and Lim, 1985). The empirical plausibility of perfect contestability has been questioned in both the single product (Dixit, 1982; Shepherd, 1984) and multiproduct context (Tye, 1984b). And a growing literature is attempting to test the theory both experimentally (Coursey *et al.*, 1983a, 1983b; Harrison, 1984; Harrison and McKee, 1985) and using market data (Call and Keeler, 1985; Froeb and Geweke, 1984; Morrison and Winston, 1985).

The wide diversity of issues addressed, though interesting, threatens to obscure what points are truly fundamental. Perfect contestability, the commonly discussed case, is advanced by the theory's proponents only as a useful theoretical benchmark. As I see it, the key unsettled issues are what is meant by imperfect contestability and whether many actual markets are imperfectly contestable. These issues are addressed in Sections II and III. Section IV considers the different tack recently taken by contestability

The views expressed here do not purport to represent those of the U.S. Department of Justice. Helpful suggestions were received from Henry McFarland, Ted Keeler, Lois Makowski, Tom McCool, Bob McGuckin, Bob Reynolds, Bert Smiley, Jim Tybout, Greg Werden, Cliff Winston, and especially William Baumol, Tim Brennan and Earl Thompson.

authors, that incumbents' pricing may be constrained not by the threat of hit-and-run entry but by the threat of entry through long-term contracts. Before turning to these issues it is useful to clarify what contestability theory says and place the theory in historical context.

In a contestable environment all firms have access to the same technology. The only entry "barrier," therefore, is the fear of price reactions by the incumbent firms. But this fear is removed if exit from the market is costless, as under perfect contestability, because then an entrant can hit-and-run before incumbents can change price. To prevent costless hit-and-run entry incumbents must set price where average cost intersects market demand, which maximizes welfare subject to a breakeven constraint.

The threat of hit-and-run entry is the linchpin of contestability theory. Note that the operative force is threat of entry not actual entry. This distinction is often overlooked, but the radical implications of contestability hinge on threat of entry. To illustrate, suppose contestability is taken to mean that actual entry will occur fairly rapidly if price is set high. In gauging the market's performance at any point in time, the number and size of existing sellers and the interaction among them will be the only relevant variables—potential entry becomes irrelevant. Moreover, if the market cannot profitably accommodate another entrant, due to scale economies and the nature of the oligopoly interaction, entry will be followed by some firm's exit and another period of high prices. Finally, if both firms are active, productive efficiency is sacrificed when the technology is a natural monopoly. In short, the disciplining effect of potential entrants is weaker, less predictable, and less efficient when actual entry—rather than threat of entry—must be invoked. Perfect contestability therefore is a theory of threatened hit-and-run entry and predicts that, barring errors, an incumbent will deter such entry by setting a low price. These observations should be borne in mind as we evaluate the various attempts to test the theory.

A natural objection if that costless hit-and-run entry is impossible in the scale economy markets on which contestability focuses, since scale economies typically derive from fixed costs whose presence is likely to make exit costly. It is here that contestability proponents offer a valuable insight: fixed costs need not be sunk. A fixed cost reflects the indivisibility of some input; it cannot be reduced by reducing output partially but might be avoided by complete shutdown. To illustrate, the cost of railroad tracks is both fixed and sunk, whereas the cost of a locomotive is fixed but avoidable by moving the equipment elsewhere. The feasibility of hit-and-run entry must therefore be acknowledged, at least as a theoretical possibility.

The basic idea that threat of entry may constrain pricing in concentrated industries has long been recognized. The voluminous "limit pricing" literature dating at least to Bain (1949) makes precisely this point. In this literature, potential entrants are assumed to expect that, should they enter, incumbents will maintain constant either their pre-entry price (Gaskins, 1971) or quantity (Bain, 1956; Modigliani, 1958; Sylos-Labini, 1962). The constant price expectation was generally attributed to fringe entrants as in Gaskins.[1] Where entrants must enter on a large-scale, due to scale economies, the constant price expectation was deemed unreasonable—since it would require a completely offsetting output reduction by incumbents. The alternative "Sylos expectation" was invoked—that the incumbent would maintain output constant. Both types of models fell, somewhat misleadingly, under the heading of "limit pricing." The common prediction is that price will be lower and quantity higher that in the absence of threat of entry.

A powerful criticism of this body of thought is that quantity and, especially, price are fairly easy to change. A potential entrant therefore will not learn much about the profitability of entry by observing the pre-entry levels of these variables but should instead look to the oligopoly interaction expected to prevail post entry (Bain, 1949; Needham, 1969; Spence, 1977). Recognizing this, incumbents will ignore the threat of entry and set price as high as the interaction among them permits.[2] This observation led to a change in course of the entry deterrence literature. Pre-entry price was deemphasized and preemptive investments were stressed, since those cannot be undone rapidly should entry occur and thus constitute credible deterrents (Wenders, 1971; Osborne, 1973; Spence, 1977; Friedman, 1979; Dixit, 1979, 1980; Salop, 1979; Eaton and Lipsey, 1980; Schmalensee, 1979; Gilbert and Newberry, 1980). The predictions of this "capital-commitment" literature regarding the effect of threat of entry on price and welfare differ markedly from those of contestability theory. Earlier writers, then, recognized that price might be kept low to deter entry but dismissed this possibility by implicitly assuming that price can be adjusted easily.

Even if capital too can be adjusted easily in some absolute sense, threat of entry need not constrain price. What matters is the relative cost of adjusting capital versus price. Section II shows that no matter how easy it is to exit the market, rapid price responses can always render threat of entry irrelevant to incumbents' pricing. Whether they do is an empirical question addressed in Section III, where I consider how the question should be addressed, evaluate some studies that use market data, and criticize the

---

[1] Implicitly, a fringe firm is viewed as being so small (due to sharply increasing marginal costs) that a large established firm finds it unprofitable to observe and react to its actions. Any one fringe firm therefore is correct in ignoring its own effect on price. However, it should not ignore the collective effect of the entire group of fringe firms. Thus, in Gaskins' model the incumbent selects a price path designed to optimize the rate of fringe entry and along this path price either rises or falls monotonically, yet each entrant takes current price as a proxy for future price. Any fringe firm's price expectation, therefore, is not consistent with the actual price solution.

[2] Recently, models of asymmetric information have been developed where incumbents reduce price in order to portray their costs or market demand as lower and lead entrants to underestimate the profitability of entry (e.g., Milgrom and Roberts, 1982; Saloner, 1982; Matthews and Mirman, 1983). These signalling models have their own shortcomings (Engers and Schwartz, 1984) but, in any event, the bulk of the limit-pricing literature as well as contestability do not feature asymmetric information.

experimental approach. Section IV scrutinizes the effectiveness of threat of entry through long-term contracts (rather than hit-and-run). I conclude in Section V that contestability theory has only limited scope.

II. Ease of entry and exit and the role of rapid price responses

A. *Exit-lag approach*

Consider an incumbent firm and a potential entrant that can produce a homogeneous good with identical cost functions $C = cq + F$ where q is output, c is the constant marginal cost and F is a positive fixed cost incurred at entry (depreciation is ignored for simplicity). Demand is stationary and known. The incumbent sets a price p at time $-E$ and there is an entry lag of length E. If entry occurs at time 0, the incumbent cannot respond by changing price until time T. During this price-response lag the entrant can capture the entire market by matching (or just undercutting) p. After time T the incumbent can change price, hence the entrant faces a duopoly interaction if he stays in the market. We are interested in how threat of entry affects p.

Let $\pi(p)$ denote a firm's operating profit stream, the difference between revenue and variable cost, if it serves the entire market at price p. Assuming an infinite horizon, the "competitive price" p^c is the steady-state price which yields a monopolist zero net profit, $\pi(p^c) = rF$ where r is the competitive interest rate. The monopoly price is denoted p^m.

The incumbent can pursue one of two strategies: exploit the entry lag E and accept entry, or deter entry. If he accepts entry, obviously he sets $p = p^m$ from $-E$ to 0 and loses all sales from 0 to T. If he deters entry, he sets p forever at the entry-deterring level p^*. Which strategy is more profitable depends on the value of p^*, which in turn depends on how easy it is to exit the market.

Schwartz and Reynolds (1983) represented the exit process by assuming that the entrant can leave the market after time $X > 0$ and recover the entire fixed cost F but if he leaves before time X he recovers nothing. The exit lag X is analogous to the Marshallian "short run," the period over which fixed costs cannot be recovered. A shorter exit lag means that exit from the market is easier, making it easier to hit-and-run.

Let π^d denote the entrant's duopoly profit stream if both firms stay in the market beyond time T. Two conditions are necessary (though not sufficient) to make the incumbent choose to deter entry: (1) $\pi^d < rF$ and (2) $T < X$. This is because for any $p > p^c$, hit-and-stay entry is profitable if $\pi^d \geqslant rF$ while hit-and-run entry is profitable if $T \geqslant X$. Thus, if (1) or (2) fails the incumbent must set $p \leqslant p^c$ to deter entry, but instead he would certainly choose p^m and exploit any positive entry lag.

Given $\pi^d < rF$, the entrant's dominant strategy is to exit the market at time X under out assumption that at time X he can fully recoup F. (The model in II.B allows for sunk cost and thus admits the possibility of hit-and-stay being more profitable strategy than hit-and-run.) The entrant's present value as a function of the incumbent's price p, $V(p)$, can be expressed as a weighted sum of net profit streams during the hit period, 0 to T, and the duopoly period, T to X:

$$V(p) = [\pi(p) - rF] \int_0^T e^{-rt}\, dt + [\pi^d - rF] \int_T^X e^{-rt}\, dt$$

Assuming purely for convenience that entry requires strictly positive present value, entry is deterred by setting p to yield $V(p) \leq 0$.

How high can p be set while maintaining $V(p) \leq 0$? This depends on the price-response lag T. To dramatize how swift price responses can negate a short exit lag, Schwartz and Reynolds (1983) considered the case of instantaneous reaction, $T = 0$. Then $V(p) \leq 0$ for any p, hence the incumbent will set $p = p^m$ and deter entry. But this result, that monopoly pricing is consistent with deterring entry, obviously does not hinge on $T = 0$, i.e., on price response being instantaneous. Since $\pi^d < rF$ and $\pi(p^m)$ is bounded, $V(p) \leq 0$ provided the weight on $\pi(p^m) - rF$ is sufficiently small. Thus, for any $X > 0$ there exists a $T < X$ that enables p to be raised all the way to p^m while deterring entry. More generally, for suitable combinations (T, X) in the range $0 < T < X$ the entry deterring price is anywhere in the range $(p^c, p^m]$.

B. Sunk-cost approach

Instead of assuming a positive exit lag, BPW (1983a) propose an alternative representation of imperfect contestability. In their approach exit can take place anytime but a fraction $s \in [0,1]$ of the fixed cost F is lost if exit occurs. Holding c and F constant and letting s approach 0 means that scale economies remain unchanged but the fixed cost that gives rise to them becomes less sunk. This makes exit easier hence the market more contestable. BPW argue that, for any positive price response lag, the entry-deterring price decreases monotonically as s decreases. Neither representation of the exit process, exit lag or sunk cost, is clearly superior; the degree of sunk cost generally increases with exit speed and both variables, sunk cost and exit speed, can influence a potential entrant's profit. It is useful to show, therefore, that nothing substantial hinges on how the ease of exit is modelled.

If the entrant leaves the market at time T, when the incumbent can change price, he recovers $(1 - s)F$. If he stays, there follows a duopoly interaction. Any duopoly interaction is allowed, including temporary shutdown by either firm. This duopoly phase is summarized by an operating profit stream to the entrant whose time-T present value is commonly known

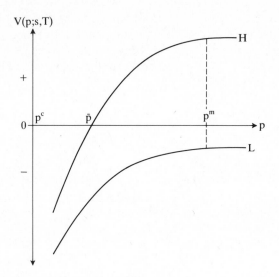

and denoted $V^d \geq 0$. Since the entrant can choose hit-and-run or hit-and-stay, his present value at time 0 is

$$w_1\pi(p) + w_2 \max\left[(1-s)F, V^d\right] - F, \qquad w_1 = \frac{1 - e^{-rT}}{r}, \qquad w_2 = e^{-rT}. \quad (1)$$

Hit-and-run entry (weakly) dominates hit-and-stay if $V^d \leq (1-s)F$. In cases where entry deterrence is chosen, $V^d < F$. Therefore, the above inequality is strict for $s = 0$ and must hold for some $s \in (0,1]$. Assume initially that $V^d = 0$, so hit-and-run entry dominates for all values of s. Later I consider $V^d \in (0, F]$ and allow hit-and-stay to be the more profitable entry strategy.

1. Hit-and-run entry[3]

From equation (1), under hit-and-run the entrant stands to earn

$$V(p, s, T) = w_1\pi(p) + w_2(1-s)F - F, \qquad w_1 = \frac{1 - e^{1rT}}{r}, \qquad w_2 = e^{-rT} \quad (2)$$

where F has been suppressed as an argument because it is constant throughout and T affects V through w_1 and w_2: $T = 0$ implies $w_1 = 0$, $w_2 = 1$ while $T = \infty$ implies $w_1 = 1/r$, $w_2 = 0$, and for $T \in (0, \infty)$ we have $\partial w_1/\partial T > 0$, $\partial w_2/\partial T < 0$. The incumbent wishing to prevent hit-and-run entry chooses the p closest to p^m subject to $V(p) \leq 0$. Let p^* denote this value of p. There are two cases, illustrated by the two curves in Fig. 1. The curves

---

[3] This section draws on Schwartz and Reynolds (1984).

reflect different values of s and T. Both curves reach their maximum at p^m and remain at this level for $p > p^m$, because the entrant will never charge more than p^m. For curve L, $V(p^m) < 0$ so the incumbent ignores threat of hit-and-run entry and $p^* = p^m$. For curve H the entry threat is binding so $p^* = \bar{p}$, the price which yields $V(p) = 0$. Consider this case first.

Substituting $V(p) = 0$ in (2) and rearranging gives

$$\bar{p} = p: \pi(p) = rF\left(1 + \frac{s}{e^{rT} - 1}\right). \tag{3}$$

Under perfect contestability, $T > 0$ and $s = 0$. From (3), $\bar{p}$ is then given by $\pi(p) = rF$, i.e. $\bar{p} = p^c$, the zero-profit price. (In Fig. 1, the profit curve would pass through the origin.) Under imperfect contestability exit is costly, $s > 0$; thus, for $T \in (0, \infty)$ $\bar{p} > p^c$ and

$$\frac{\partial \bar{p}}{\partial s} = \frac{rF}{(e^{rT} - 1)\pi'(p)} > 0 \tag{4}$$

since $\pi'(p) > 0$ for $p < p^m$. In terms of Fig. 1, a reduction in s would shift curve H down, hence shift $\bar{p}$ to the right. The monotonic relationship between $\bar{p}$ and s underlies BPW's (1983a) argument that contestability theory is "robust."

In a technical sense, this robustness claim is correct. Provided price response is not instantaneous, $T > 0$, there is *some* neighborhood of $s = 0$ in which the entry-deterring price rises continuously and monotonically above p^c as s increases. However, this neighbourhood can be *arbitrarily small* and for values of s outside this neighborhood price is unconstrained by threat of entry. To see this, recall that the incumbent's price is

$$p^* = \begin{cases} \bar{p} & \text{if } V(p^m) > 0 & \text{(entry threat binding)} \\ p^m & \text{if } V(p^m) \leq 0 & \text{(entry threat not binding).} \end{cases} \tag{5}$$

$V(p^m)$ depends on s and T. Let $\bar{s}$ be the fraction of sunk cost that, given T, makes hit-and-run entry just unprofitable when the incumbent charges the monopoly price

$$\bar{s} = s: V(s; p^m, T) = 0.$$

Since $\partial V/\partial s > 0$, for $s < \bar{s} V(p^m) > 0$ and for $s \geq \bar{s} V(p^m) \leq 0$. Thus, using (5),

$$p^* = \begin{cases} \bar{p} & \text{if } s < \bar{s} \\ p^m & \text{if } s \geq \bar{s}. \end{cases} \tag{6}$$

Figure 2 shows two $p^*(s)$ curves, OAC and OBC. Each has some range, $s > \bar{s}$, over which equilibrium price declines as s decreases and the market becomes more contestable. But the range for OAC, $s < \bar{s}_1$, is very small, so a small deviation from $s = 0$ is sufficient to make the threat of entry irrelevant and yield the monopoly price. It is in this sense, a low value of $\bar{s}$

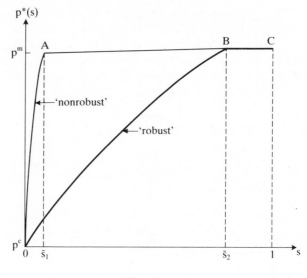

FIG. 2

rather than the shape of the p^* function from 0 to $\bar{s}$ (contrast Shepherd, 1984), that I view contestability theory as nonrobust. After briefly showing that a low $\bar{s}$ also makes hit-and-stay entry unprofitable, I provide some numerical examples showing that in practice $\bar{s}$ is likely to be low.

2. Hit-and-stay entry

From (1), the entrant's present value under hit-and-stay entry is

$$Y(p) = w_1\pi(p) + w_2 V^d - F.$$

So far I assumed $V^d = 0$ so that hit-and-run always dominated hit-and-stay. Assume now $V^d \in [0, F)$ so that $V^d = (1-s)F$ for some $s^* \in (0, 1]$. If $s^* \geq \bar{s}$, hit-and-stay entry can be ignored because it is unprofitable even if the incumbent charges p^m: $Y(p^m) = V(p^m, s^*) \leq V(p^m, \bar{s}) = 0$, the inequality because V decreases in s. Thus, if $s^* \geq \bar{s}$ the preceding hit-and-run analysis continues to apply, with $p^* = \bar{p}(s)$ for $s < \bar{s}$ and $p^* = p^m$ for $s \geq \bar{s}$.

If $s^* < \bar{s}$ the above inequality is reversed and hit-and-stay entry both is profitable at p^m and dominates hit-and-run for values $s > s^*$. For values $s \leq s^*$ hit-and-run dominates. To deter both entry strategies the incumbent therefore sets: $p^* = \bar{p}(s)$, as before, if $s < s^*$; but if $s \geq s^*$ he now sets a lower price, $p^* = \bar{p}(s^*)$.

The possibility of hit-and-stay entry, therefore, modifies the conclusions reached for hit-and-run entry only if $s^* < \bar{s}$. Recall, however, that the value $s^* = 1 - V^d/F$ is independent of the price response lag T, while $\bar{s} \to 0$ as $T \to 0$. Therefore, for sufficiently small T, $s^* \geq \bar{s}$ and hit-and-stay entry, like hit-and-run, is unprofitable even at the monopoly price.

TABLE 1
Values of $\bar{s}$

| | $T = 0.1\ year$ | | | | $T = 0.5\ year$ | | |
| | $r/year$ | | | | $r/year$ | | |
r^m/r	0.1	0.2	0.3	r^m/r	0.1	0.2	0.3
1.5	0.005	0.01	0.15	1.5	0.026	0.053	0.081
2	0.01	0.02	0.03	2	0.051	0.105	0.162
3	0.02	0.04	0.061	3	0.103	0.21	0.324

3. Examples

The question now becomes: is the empirically expected value of $\bar{s}$ "low" or "high"? If for most reasonable parameter values $\bar{s}$ is low, most markets are likely to have values of s exceeding this threshold level and their prices will thus be unaffected by the threat of entry. Substituting p^m in (2), equating to 0 and rearranging gives

$$\bar{s} = \left(\frac{\pi(p^m)}{rF} - 1\right)(e^{rT} - 1). \tag{7}$$

In the scale-economy markets on which contestability focuses, rF is large relative to $\pi(p^m)$, which makes $\bar{s}$ relatively small. More importantly, rapid price responses can make $\bar{s}$ arbitrarily small: $s \to 0$ as $T \to 0$.[4]

To get a crude feel for just how small $\bar{s}$ is likely to be, interpret $\pi(p^m)/F$ as (approximately) the monopoly rate of return, r^m, and r as the competitive rate. Substituting in (7) gives $\bar{s} = (r^m/r - 1)\ (e^{rT} - 1)$. Table 1 shows that $\bar{s}$ is low for most sensible parameter values. For example, if the monopoly rate of return is twice the competitive rate, the latter is twenty percent per annum, and the incumbent must wait over one month before lowering his price ($T = 0.1$), the incumbent can charge the monopoly price if as little as two percent of fixed costs are sunk.[5] As a whole, these examples suggest that contestability theory has very restricted applicability. The experience of the airline industry discussed in Section III reinforces this impression.

C. Synthesis: rapid price responses and noncontestability

The preceding two sections showed that, regardless of how easy exit is, in the class of cases where entry deterrence might be attempted, $V^d < F$, there

[4] In particular $s = 0$ if $T = 0$. From (6) this implies that if $T = 0$ then $p^* = p^m$ for any $s > 0$, which shows that in this model, as in the earlier Exit Lag model, instantaneous price responses enable the incumbent to ignore entry threats and set the monopoly price.

[5] For small rT, $e^{rT} - 1$ approximately equals rT. Therefore, $\bar{s}$ approximately equals $(r^m - r)T$. This approximation provides some indication how large $r^m - r$ must be or how long T must be to make $\bar{s}$ large enough for contestability theory to have significant applicability.

always exists a price response rapid enough to make the entry-deterring price p^* equal the monopoly price p^m. This is true whether the entrant contemplates hit-and-run or hit-and-stay. Intuitively, a rapid price response reduces the hit period and thus its contribution to present value.[6]

If the actual price response is not rapid enough to yield $p^* = p^m$, the incumbent must compare the profitabiltity of two strategies: set $p^* < p^m$ forever and deter entry or accept entry and set p^m during the entry lag phase. Setting p^m obviously becomes more attractive the longer is the entry lag. It also becomes more attractive the swifter is the incumbent's price response, because a swift response shortens the period over which his price is undercut and his sales driven to zero.[7]

To clarify the discussion of empirical evidence I adopt the following terminology: "perfect contestability" exists when threat of entry keeps a monopolist's price at p^c, imperfect contestability when $p \in (p^c, p^m)$, and "noncontestability" when threat of entry has no effect, $p = p^m$. Rapid price responses have been shown to cause noncontestability through the two

---

[6] Anderson (1984) uses a similar quick-response argument in a different context. He emphasizes the role of quick price responses in sustaining cooperative equilibria in repeated games where the payoff matrix has a prisoner's dilemma structure. He notes that as long as there is some cost of changing one's play between periods there always exists a period short enough—a quick enough price response—that makes deviation from the cooperative solution unprofitable.

[7] Ironically, if the entry-deterring price is p^c, because the entrant can costlessly hit-and-run, there always exists a swift price response that leads the incumbent to choose p^m and accept entry rather than choose p^c and deter. Since setting p^c forever yields zero profit, the incumbent would certainly set p^m until entry occurred if he could then exit instantaneously and costlessly. Therefore, a necessary condition for choosing p^c over p^m is that the incumbent cannot exit costlessly—so that if entry occurred he would remain stuck in the market with negative profit (zero revenue and an interest expense on the fixed cost). But this negative profit phase goes to zero as the price response lag goes to zero, making it more profitable to ignore threat of entry and set the monopoly price when the alternative is to set p^c forever.

The preceding discussion raises a paradox. If exit is frictionless to all firms—as under perfect contestability—the threat of hit-and-run entry will never constrain price, because the incumbent will price monopolistically to exploit any entry lag. The familiar perfectly contestable result, $p = p^c$, therefore requires that the incumbent (but not the entrant!) face both an exit lag and a price response lag. But then an equilibrium with positive output may not exist! Consider the exit-lag model and assume that entry cannot be deterred at p^c because duopoly profit $\pi^d > rF$. Assume also that the incumbent's exit lag exceeds his price response lag T. Deterring entry certainly would yield negative profit. The best alternative, setting p^m during the entry lag period and accepting entry, makes present values

incumbent: $w_0[\pi(p^m) - rF] + w_1[0 - rF] + w_2[\pi^d - rF]$

entrant: $w_1[\pi(p^m) - rF] + w_2[\pi^d - rF] > 0.$

where

$$w_0 = \int_{-E}^{0} e^{-rt}\, dt, \qquad w_1 = \int_{0}^{T} e^{-rt}\, dt, \qquad w_2 = \int_{T}^{\infty} e^{-rt}\, dt$$

For E sufficiently short and $\pi^d - rF$ sufficiently small, the incumbent's present value is negative. Anticipating this, no firm would enter the market in the first place for fear of becoming the incumbent. This implausible outcome arises because the entrant can undercut the incumbent's initial price and capture over half the market before the incument can react. The plausibility of such a hit period is discussed further in Section IV.

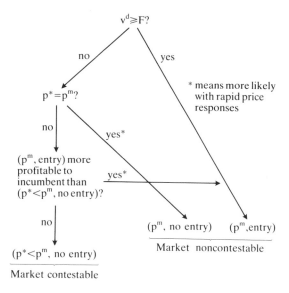

FIG. 3

channels shown in Fig. 3. First, they make the hit period short thereby reducing the potential hit profit, possibly to where entry can be deterred with $p^* = p^m$. Second, they reduce the incumbent's vulnerability if he sets p^m and accepts entry, making this strategy more attractive relative to deterring entry through $p^* < p^m$.

III. Empirical appraisal

A. *Testing for contestability*

To deal with the empirically-prevalent case of an initial oligopoly rather than monopoly, we must examine incumbents' joint profit-maximizing price rather than the actual price charged. For a monopolist the two prices coincide, but in oligopolies competition may keep actual price below the joint-maximizing level. Therefore threat of entry may constrain oligopolists' joint-maximizing price even if it does not constrain their current price. In such a case the market can nevertheless be viewed as imperfectly contestable because the entry threat constraint could become binding in future, if incumbents attempt to raise price.

Let p^m be the joint-maximizing price absent threat of entry, p^j the actual joint-maximizing price and p^c the zero-profit price. Perfect contestability implies $p = p^c = p^j < p^m$. This is empirically refuted for oligopolies by a positive correlation between profitability or price-cost measures and market concentration. The absence of such a correlation, however, does not prove perfect contestability. Interactions among existing producers may be sufficiently competitive across a range of concentration levels to yield competitive performance even if threat of entry were ignored.[8] That is, oligopolies can exhibit $p = p^c$ even if $p^j = p^m$.

Imperfect contestability is much more difficult to refute. If $p^c < p^j < p^m$, actual price p can vary between p^c and p^j according to the number of incumbents and competition among them, yielding a positive correrlation between profitability and concentration. This correlation need not refute imperfect contestability because we could still have $p^j < p^m$ in all the sample markets. Similarly, imperfect contestability is not refuted if oligopoly prices and profits are unaffected by variations in the number and costs of potential entrants (if these were possible to observe). Such variations could affect p^j, and the absence of correlation could mean merely that $p < p^j$ in all markets. If a correlation is present, however, imperfect contestability is supported. Ironically, while perfect contestability seems impossible to prove, imperfect contestability seems impossible to thoroughly disprove.

Nevertheless, suggestive evidence against imperfect contestability and for noncontestability is the occurrence of actual entry and a subsequent reduction in price. Such an observation indicates that entry prevention was either unsuccessful—due to mistakes—or was deemed unprofitable and not attempted. If the mistakes hypothesis can be dismissed, the inference is that threat of entry was ignored in setting price for reasons discussed in Section II.

B. *Market evidence*

Airline city-pair routes are often cited as a prime illustration of a contestable market (e.g., Bailey and Baumol, 1984). Although the fixed costs of planes are substantial relative to market demand (thus limiting the number of airlines on any route), the intrinsic mobility of airplanes between routes strongly suggests that entry and exit is considerably easier than in most industries. These structural conditions are conducive to contestability. But since deregulation airlines can respond quickly to entrants' price cutting.[9] Such rapid price responses can make the threat of entry irrelevant to incumbents' pricing, rendering the market noncontestable.

The available evidence points to noncontestability. Statistical cross-sections studies show a significant, positive correlation between concentration and profits in airline markets, refuting perfect contestability (see Call

---

[8] Another explanation for the absence of a correlation is that both monopoly pricing and superior efficiency are present in a given industry (Demsetz, 1973; Froeb an Geweke, 1984). However, this departs from the structural assumption of contestability that costs are identical.

[9] For example, Delta Airlines assigns 147 employees to track rivals' prices and select quick responses—on a typical day, comparing over 5,000 industry pricing changes against Delta's more than 70,000 fares. New fares filed the prior day with Air Tariff Publishing Co. are tracked by a Delta computer. "Secret" price changes that are deliberately withheld from the Air Traffic Publishing system for several days are tracked through local newspapers or calls to other airlines' reservation offices. Once Delta learns of a competitor's pricing move, it can put matching fare into its reservation system within two hours (Wall Street Journal, August 24, 1983).

and Keeler, 1984, which also provides a good discussion of previous studies). Moreover, new entry does occur and established carriers reduce their fares in response to such entry (Call and Keeler, 1984). In other words, prices are not kept low to deter entry. This evidence points against even imperfect contestability. As Bailey and Baumol (1984) concede, airline behavior has resembled that expected from rival oligoplists in standard analysis not from players in a perfectly contestable world.

Bailey and Baumol attempt to reconcile these results with contestability theory by arguing that the latter pertains to behavior in long run equilibrium, a situation the industry may not yet have reached. In particular, they argue that established carriers found it unprofitable to keep prices low and deter entry because (i) entrants may have enjoyed lower costs and (ii) entrants may have been unable to enter on a large scale. For these reasons, the more profitable strategy may have been to keep prices high initially and reduce them only gradually as entry occurred. Call and Keeler (p. 45) provide a powerful rebuttal: "Given that most *trunk* carriers (my emphasis) have roughly the same costs, and that their capacity is seemingly adequate for rapid entry into new routes, if the contestability hypothesis were correct, the entry of trunk carriers on to new routes would not affect trunk fares. Our statistical evidence goes against that hypothesis."

Morrison and Winston (1985) argue that while airline markets are not perfectly contestable they may be imperfectly contestable. Their testing methodology, conceptually correct, is to include as an explanatory variable of performance[10] not only the number of actual competitors on a route but also the number of potential competitors. They note that testing perfect contestability does not require this regression approach since it predicts no variation in the dependent, performance variable. Imperfect contestability, however, does allow for variation. They find both coefficients to be statistically significant, with that on actual competitors about four times as large. They interpret this as indicating that the airline industry is not perfectly contestable but is imperfectly contestable.

This evidence is interesting but the conclusion that airlines are even imperfectly contestable is premature. First, there is the unanswered question of why entry does occur (Call and Keeler) if prices are set to deter it. Second, Morrison and Winston find the coefficient on the number of potential entrants statistically insignificant until there are *at least* four potential entrants. One would expect precisely the opposite: the marginal effect of large potential entrants should decline rapidly after the first few. This pattern was in fact found in an experimental test of perfect contestability (Harrison, 1984). Morrison and Winston argue, however, that the measured number of potential entrants may overstate the actual number on

---

[10] Their performance measure is consumer surplus relative to the theoretical optimum rather than a profitablity measure, both types of measures are related to price so the distinction is not critical for our purposes.

a given route, since the same firms may be contemplating entry into other routes. A definitive interpretation of their results is probably premature.

Overall, the airline experience since deregulation weights against perfect contestability but is inconclusive regarding imperfect contestability. Airlines, however, are cited as structurally among the most conducive to contestability. If pricing behavior is ultimately found to be largely independent of threat of entry in airlines, contestability is unlikely to be a force in most concentrated industries.

A glimpse of evidence supporting this conjecture is found in Froeb and Geweke's (1984) study of the U.S. primary aluminium industry. Examining time series of profits and concentration, they found no feedback from concentration to profits, but significant negative feedback from profits to concentration. They interpet this as supporting contestability—in the sense that market performance is independent of structure and that profits caused by growing demand or falling costs will be only transient and induce entry. Contestability, however, should be interpreted as saying that threat of entry constrains price, not that actual entry will eventually eliminate profit. In fact, Froeb and Geweke's evidence suggests that price is not affected by threat of entry. First, they find that profits attract entry only after a lag of five years or more. This lag approximately equals the estimated time of construction of a new plant. Given such a long entry lag, it seems implausible that incumbents would find it more profitable to practice limit pricing than to set price high and accept entry. The actual occurrence of entry supports the latter hypothesis. Second, since profit is found to be unaffected by the number of actual competitors, it is difficult to believe that price was being held low to deter potential competitors.

Perhaps the most direct test of whether the threat of entry affects price is to consider situations where potential entrants' costs are reduced by an exogenous structural change such as the removal of a tariff or the expiration of a patent. If incumbents' price is not affected by a change unless actual entry occurs, the inference is of noncontestability. Shaw and Shaw (1977) performed precisely such a test for the West European polyester fiber industry following patent expirations and rejected the hypothesis of limit pricing (or contestability), finding that prices fell only after entry occurred.

C. Experimental evidence

Several authors have recently presented experimental evidence that they claim generally supports contestability theory. I offer the following observations. First, the evidence offered cannot be interpreted as favorable or unfavorable to contestability theory. Second, and more important, it is doubtful whether the entire experimental approach can contribute anything to appraising the empirical importance of contestability theory.

The work of Coursey, Isaac and Smith (1984, hereafter CIS) and Coursey, Isaac, Luke and Smith (1984, hereafter CILS) is representative of the experimental approach. CIS consider two firms with zero fixed costs and identical declining marginal costs. Each period the firms post prices simultaneously and buyers purchase from the lower-price seller. The results showed that in four of six experiments price declined monotonically to competitive levels. (There is a range of such prices since demand is discrete.) In the other two experiments, price was closer to competitive than to monopoly levels but remained above competitive levels. CIS characterize this as evidence for contestability theory.

CILS perform essentially the same experiment except that they introduce a small sunk cost in the form of a permit to serve the market for five periods. One firm, designated the incumbent, is forced to purchase two permits (through period ten) and the other is allowed to contest the market starting in period six after observing the incumbent's price for five periods. CILS find that in five of their twelve experiments both firms entered and price converged monotonically to or close to competitive levels. In two experiments there was tacit collusion—both firms entered and priced at noncompetitive levels. Four experiments revealed price oscillations, with price falling due to entry and then rising—either due to temporarily successful tacit collusion (both firms staying in the market) or one firm's exit from the market. In only one experiment was there a monopolist that kept price at competitive levels—the behavior predicted by perfect contestability.

Harrison (1984) correctly observes, however, that these experiments and others (e.g., Harrison and McKee, 1985) do not implement the key feature of the contestable market hypothesis: the existence of a price response lag for the incumbent which an entrant can exploit. Recall that both CIS and CILS have firms setting prices simultaneously, so that each does not know the other's current period price when choosing its own. Harrison reruns CIS's experiments but allowing the incumbent's price to be known to entrants before they choose their prices. The results, not surprisingly, are more competitive than in CIS, with prices almost always converging to competitive levels.

What do the above papers really show? CIS and CILS are tests not of contestability but of standard duopoly interactions: how two firms behave when prices are chosen simultaneously and marginal costs are decreasing. Noncooperative game theory predicts that there is no pure strategy equilibrium in this environment, with or without fixed costs. The theoretical expectation is for a mixed strategy equilibrium where each firm randomizes its price. The contradictory results of CIS and CILS are therefore interesting in themselves, but not informative about contestability.

Harrison's experiments basically do constitute a fair test of behavior under perfect contestability:[11] the incumbent faces a price response lag and

---

[11] The only caveat is that contestability theory is formulated assuming complete information whereas in Harrison's and other studies demand and rivals' costs are not always commonly known.

the entrant can hit-and-run costlessly. The real question, however, is not whether competitive results will emerge under perfectly contestable conditions but how often such conditions are likely to exist and what happens when they do not. In addressing the latter issue, I have assumed along with BPW that (i) the entrant's present value depends on both a hit phase and a duopoly phase and (ii) that the outcome in the latter can be captured in an expected profit term, V^d, that is common knowledge. Given these assumptions, the outcome is deterministic once parameter values are specified. The key issue is empirical: how rapid are price responses and how low are sunk costs. These questions cannot be answered experimentally.

IV. Contestability and long-term contracts

Rapid price responses eliminate the threat of hit-and-run entry. As an alternative constraint on incumbents' pricing, contestability authors have recently emphasized the threat of entry through long-term contracts (BPW, 1983a). The introduction of long-term price contracts converts contestability into Demsetz's (1968) "competition for the market" argument for a relatively *laissez faire* treatment of natural monopolists.

An obvious objection is that long-term price contracts are simply infeasible in many markets. The severe problems of enforcing quality and making the contracts optimally contingent on different future states, familiar from widespread experience with governmental price controls and price regulation, also plague long-term price contracts employed by private agents and help explain the infrequency of such contracts.[12]

Putting aside the above problems, there is a second objection that is both more subtle and more fundamental. When buyers are numerous and cooperation among them is prohibitively costly, free-rider behavior by individual buyers would foil an entrant's attempt to commit a large fraction of buyers to purchase from him at a given price. Since scale economies force the entrant to capture a large fraction of buyers in order to break even, contracting by an entrant would fail under conditions of scale economies and numerous, noncooperating buyers, And, as argued below, it is largely under such conditions that policy concerns with protecting buyers from monopolistic sellers arise in the first place.

First, suppose the entrant's strategy were to give buyers an unconditional price offer of $p^e \in [p^c, p^m]$, where p^c is the price at which the entrant's decreasing average cost intersects market demand and p^m is the incumbent's monopoly price. Since the offer is unconditional, buyers will inform the

---

[12] The fact that long-term pice contracts suffer from substantially the same problems as price regulation removes much of the bite from Demsetz's proposal (1968) of replacing price regulation of natural monopolies by franchise bidding for the right to serve the market at a fixed price. See, e.g., Williamson (1976).

incumbent of the offer in order to induce a lower counter-offer.[13] The incumbent will respond to the entrant's offer only if it becomes effective, that is, if at least one buyer has signed thereby ensuring entry. At that point the rational response is to undercut p^e to remaining buyers. Since some of his costs are sunk, the incumbent can profitably undercut any $p^e \geq p^c$ if only a few buyers have committed to the entrant. And the entrant will not capture more than a few buyers because each buyer will want to be part of the hold-out group that would obtain the lower price from the incumbent. The prospective losses from serving only a few buyers under the assumed scale economies will deter the entrant from ever making an unconditional price offer.

Now suppose the entrant can offer a price contract that is conditional on a minimum number of buyers accepting. If we grant the entrant the ability to make such conditional offers it is only natural to grant the same ability to the incumbent, in which case the rational incumbent again forestalls entry. Purely for simplicity, suppose that there are N identical buyers so we can speak interchangeably of the number $n \leq N$ that sign exclusively with the entrant and the quantity this implies. The entrant's offer is: p^e only if $n \geq k$ where the critical number specified, k, may be a function of p^e. If n is observable at all times (game theoretically, if buyers act sequentially), the incumbent can easily prevent entry by specifying an integer j, $1 \leq j \leq k - 1$, and committing to undercut p^e if (and only if) $n \geq j$.[14] This ensures holdout once n reaches j.

Matters might seem trickier when n is observable only *ex post*, because then an individual buyer is uncertain whether j others have signed when making his choice (game theoretically, buyers are acting simultaneously). But suppose the incumbent commits to beat p^e if $n \geq j'$, $1 \leq j' \leq k - 2$. Any buyer is better off holding out: if $k - 2$ or less have signed, there will be no entry regardless of his choice; if $k - 1$ or more have signed, the incumbent's superior offer is triggered.

Finally, it might be argued that the precise value of n is not observable even *ex post*. However, whether entry occurs or not reveals if $n \geq k$ or

---

[13] Implausible as it is for the entrant to temporarily capture the entire spot market before the incumbent can react, it is even more implausible to assume that he can do so in the marketing of long-term contracts. For the incumbent now has a much stronger incentive to observe and react to an entrant's pricing overtures. As Brock (1983) points out, it is ridiculous to argue that numerous individual buyers can react to these pricing overtures before the incumbent seller, whose stake is much higher. The argument in the text, however, works even if the incumbent is sluggish because individual buyers have an incentive to inform him of the entrant's offer.

[14] Making an offer that is obviously contingent on the entrant's actions may arouse antitrust suspicion, but the incumbent can give it a less predatory flavor by phrasing it as "I'll beat an entrant's price to my loyal x customers." Choosing $x = N - j$ produces the desired result.

Note that the incumbent may have to be commited to the counter offer, otherwise buyers may fear withdrawal of the counter offer if the entrant's offer fails. Such fears could prevent them from signing with the incumbent. However, we have assumed that the incumbent, like the entrant, can commit to contracts. Moreover, the commitment required is not harsh since by specifying a low j the incumbent can beat the entrant's price while remaining profitable.

$n < k$. (The latter must be observable at least to somebody otherwise it is meaningless to speak of a conditional contract.) The incumbent will offer to beat (or match) p^e only if $n \geq k$. This leaves a small incentive for any buyer to sign with the entrant, namely, the fear that if precisely $k - 1$ others have signed his individual holdout would defeat the entry attempt (and thus also nullify the incumbent's counter offer). The incumbent can overcome this incentive by offering a lump sum, "loyalty bonus" B to his remaining customers if entry does occur.

Suppose the incumbent's offer is: p^m if $n \leq k - 1$, (p^e, B) if $n \geq k$. Consider a buyer's decision. Letting m be the number of other buyers ultimately signing with the entrant, a buyer considers three possible states.

1. If $m \leq k - 2$, entry fails regardless of his choice.
2. If $m = k - 1$, entry succeeds only if he chooses the entrant.
3. If $m \geq k$, entry occurs regardless of his choice.

Let $U(p)$ denote the buyer's consumer surplus from buying the good at price p, and normalize $U(p^m)$ to 0. Let V^M and V^E denote the buyer's expected payoffs from signing with the incumbent and entrant respectively, and L_t the probability the buyer assigns to state t. Then

$$V^M = L_1 \cdot 0 + L_2 \cdot 0 + L_3(B + U(p^e))$$
$$V^E = L_1 \cdot 0 + L_2 \cdot U(p^e) + L_3 U(p^e)$$
$$V^M - V^E = L_3 B - L_2 U(p^e).$$

Since $U(p^e)$ is bounded, for any $L_3 > 0$ there exists a B that will make $V^M - V^E$ positive. Moreover, the requisite B will be "small" since L_2 will be "small": any one of numerous buyers will assign a negligible probability to his being the swing voter.

In short, for any contingent contract the entrant can propose, the incumbent can find a counter that will defeat the entry attempt. Recognizing the sure failure of his offer, a rational entrant would not make it in the first place given any cost of making it. Thus, as pointed out by Thompson (1984), without a mechanism to prevent buyer defection—a mechanism that implies buyer cooperation—there is no equilibrium constrained by competition for the market. Buyers as a group would, of course, prefer an entrant's bid to continue, but individual free riding precludes it. The problem would be absent if there were no economies of scale, because then an entrant's ability to offer a low price would not hinge on numerous buyers going along. Scale economies, however, coupled with noncooperating buyers, create a public good problem with its familiar free-rider incentives.

Scale economies notwithstanding, if buyers' collective purchasing power could be harnessed and offered as a block to the most favorable bidder, concern about seller exploitation of buyers would arise. Indeed, the opposite might be true. Buyers' ability to advance their interests might be excessive—as in monopsony situations. In such cases of "buyer cooperation," signing long-term contracts with entrants would be just one way to protect their interest, a probably inferior way as suggested by its infrequency. Alternatives include bargaining with an incumbent or paying an entrant's sunk cost to ensure the presence of two or more active sellers. But buyer cooperation is infrequently observed, because of the severe informational requirements involved in monitoring and enforcing the behavior of numerous agents. It is in those, rather typical cases of noncooperating buyers and few sellers that concern with monopoly behavior arise.

V. Conclusion

Although proponents of contestability carefully acknowledge the importance of rapid price responses by incumbent firms, this caveat is frequently overlooked. Structural conditions that make entry and exit easy, such as low sunk costs, are incorrectly taken as sufficient to ensure contestability. We have seen that the ability of incumbent firms to change price rapidly in response to entry can offset ease of entry and exit and make markets noncontestable in the sense that pricing behavior becomes unaffected by the threat of entry. Available empirical evidence indicates that this is typically the case.

Nor do long-term contracts salvage contestability. In conclusion, threat of entry is unlikely to be a reliable check on monopolistic behavior in most markets. My own view is that is was a mistake to try and extend contestability beyond the regulatory environment, where regulatory constraints on incumbents' pricing might have provided an explanation for sluggish price responses. The ensuing debate has been of value, forcing a rethinking of conditions implicitly required for competitive outcomes. But given its restricted empirical applicability, contestability theory should not significantly alter either our theoretical thinking about concentrated industries or our policy approach to such industries.

Georgetown University and
U.S. Department of Justice
Washington, D.C., U.S.A.

REFERENCES

ANDERSON, R. "Quick-Response Equilibrium." Manuscript, 1984.

APPELBAUM, E. and LIM,, C. "Contestable Market Under Uncertainty."*Rand Journal of Economics* 16, No. 1 (Spring 1985): 28–40.

BAILEY, E. and BAUMOL, W. "Deregulation and the Theory of Contestable Markets." *Yale Journal on Regulation* 1, No. 2 (1984): 111–37.

BAIN, J. "A Note on Pricing in Monopoly and Oligopoly." *American Economic Review* 39, No. 2 (March 1949): 448–464.

——. *Barriers to New Competition.* Cambridge: Harvard University Press, 1956.

BAUMOL, W. *Microtheory: Applications and Origins.* Brighton: Wheatsheaf Books, 1986.

——, PANZAR, J., and WILLIG, R. *Contestable Markets and the Theory of Industry Structure.* San Diego: Harcourt Brace Jovanovich, 1982.

—— (1983a) "Contestable Markets: An Uprising in the Theory of Industry Structure: Reply." *American Economic Review* 73, No. 3 (June 1983): 491–96.

—— (1983b) "On the Theory of Perfectly Contestable Markets," Bell Laboratories Economic Discussion Paper, 268, forthcoming in *New Developments in the Theory of Industry Structure,* International Economic Association.

BROCK, W. "Contestable Markets and the Theory of Industry Structure: A Review Article." *Journal of Political Economy* 91, No. 6 (December 1983): 1055–56.

CALL, G. and KEELER, T. (1984). "Airline Deregulation, Fares, and Market Behavior: Some Empirical Evidence." in *Analytical Studies in Transport Economics,* Andrew F. Daughety ed., Cambridge University Press (1985), 221–247.

COURSEY, D., ISAAC, R. and SMITH, V. "Natural Monopoly and Contested Markets: Some Experimental Results." *Journal of Law and Economics* 27, No. 1 (April 1984): 91–113.

——, ——, LUKE, M., and SMITH, V. "Market Contestability in the Presence of Sunk (Entry) Costs." *Rand Journal of Economics* 15, No. 1 (Spring 1984): 69–84.

DEMSETZ, H. "Why Regulate Utilities?" *Journal of Law and Economics* 11, (April 1968): 55–65.

——. "Industry Structure, Market Rivalry and Public Policy." *Journal of Law and Economics* 16, (April 1973): 1–9.

DIXIT, A. "The Role of Investment in Entry Deterrence." *Economic Journal* 90, (March 1980): 95–106.

——. "Recent Developments in Oligopoly Theory," *American Economic Review* 72, No. 2 (May 1982): 12–17.

ENGERS, M. and SCHWARTZ, M. "Signalling Equilibria Based on Sensible Beliefs: Limit Pricing Under Incomplete Information." U.S. Department of Justice, Antitrust Division, Economic Policy Office Discussion Paper 84-4 (May 1984). Revised 1986.

FARRELL, J. "The Efficacy of Potential Competition." Manuscript, 1984.

FRIEDMAN, J. "On Entry Preventing Behavior and Limit Pricing Models of Entry." In: *Applied Game Theory,* edited by J. Brams *et al.,* 236–53. Wurzburg: Physica: Verlag, 1979.

FROEB, L. and GEWEKE, J. "Dynamic Contestability and Entry." Manuscript, 1984.

GASKINS, D. "Dynamic Limit Pricing under Threat of Entry." *Journal of Economic Theory* 3, No. 3 (Sept. 1971): 306–22.

GILBERT, R. and NEWBERRY, D. "Preemptive Patenting and the Persistence of Monopoly." *American Economic Review* 72, No. 3 (June 1982): 514–26.

HARRISON, G. "Experimental Evaluation of the Contestable Market Hypothesis." Unpublished Manuscript, Department of Economics, University of Western Ontario, 1984.

—— and McKEE, M. "Monopoly Behavior, Decentralized Regulation, and Contestable Markets: An Experimental Evaluation." *Rand Journal of Economics* 16, No. 1 (Spring 1985): 51–69.

MATTHEWS, S. and MIRMAN, L. "Equilibrium Limit Pricing: The effects of Private Information and Stochastic Demand." *Econometrica* 51, No. 4 (July 1983): 981–995.

MILGROM, P. and ROBERTS, J. "Limit Pricing and Entry Under Incomplete Information: An Equilibrium Analysis." *Econometrica* 50, No. 2 (March 1982): 443–459.

MODIGLIANI, F. "New Developments on the Oligopoly Front." *Journal of Political Economy* 66, No. 3 (June 1958): 215–232.

MORRISON, S. and WINSTON, C. "Empirical Implications and Tests of the Contestability Hypothesis." Manuscript, Brookings Institution, 1985.

NEEDHAM, D. *Economic Analysis and Industrial Structure.* New York: Holt, Reinhart and Winston, Inc., 1969.

OSBORNE, D. "On the Rationality of Limit Pricing." *Journal of Industrial Economics* 22, No. 1 (September 1973): 71–80.

SALONER, G. "Dynamic Limit Pricing in an Uncertain Environment." Ph.D. Dissertation, Stanford University, 1982.

SALOP, S. "Strategic Entry Deterrence." *American Economic Review Proceedings* 69, No. 2 (May 1979): 335–38.

SCHWARTZ, M. and REYNOLDS, R. "Contestable Markets: An Uprising in the Theory of Industry Structure: Comment." *American Economic Review* 73, No. 3 (June 1983): 488–90.

——. "On the Limited Relevance of Contestability Theory." Economic Policy Office Discussion Paper 84–10, U.S. Department of Justice, September 1984.

SCHMALENSEE, R. "Entry Deterrence in the Ready-to-Eat Breakfast Cereal Industry," *Bell Journal of Economics* 9, No. 2 (Autumn 1978): 305–27.

SHAW, R. and SHAW, S. "Patent Expiry and Competition in Polyester Fibres." *Scottish Journal of Political Economy* 24, No. 2 (June 1977): 117–32.

SHEPHERD, W. "Contestability" vs. "Competition," *American Economic Review* 74, No. 4 (September 1984): 572–87.

SPENCE, M. "Entry, Capacity, Investment, and Oligopolistic Pricing." *Bell Journal of Economics* 8, No. 2 (1977): 534–44.

SYLOS-LABINI, P. *Oligopoly and Technical Progress,* Translation Elizabeth Henderson, Cambridge, MA: Harvard University Press, 1962.

THOMPSON, E. "Forms of Competition and Contracting in the Private Marketing of Collective Goods." UCLA Working Paper 346, September 1984.

TYE, W. (1984a) "On the Applicability of the Theory of Contestable Markets to Rail/Water Carrier Mergers," *Logistics and Transportation Review,* Vol. 21, No. 1, March 1985, 57–76.

——, (1984b) "Contestability vs. Competition: Comment." Manuscript.

WALL STREET JOURNAL, August 24, 1984, "In Airline's Rate War, Small Daily Skirmishes Often Decide Winners."

WEITZMAN, M. "Contestable Markets: An Uprising in the Theory of Industry Structure: Comment." *American Economic Review* 73, No. 3 (June 1983): 486–487.

WENDERS, J. "Excess Capacity as a Barrier to Entry." *Journal of Industrial Economics* 20, No. 1 (November 1971): 14–19.

WILLIAMSON, O. "Franchise Bidding for Natural Monopolies in General with Respect to CATV." *Bell Journal of Economics* 7, No. 1 (Spring 1976): 73–104.

UNCERTAINTY, ECONOMIES OF SCALE, AND BARRIER TO ENTRY

By STYLIANOS PERRAKIS *and* GEORGE WARSKETT*

I. Introduction

THIS paper examines the importance of scale economies as a deterrent to market entry under conditions of product demand uncertainty. From the work of Bain [1] it is well-known that barriers to entry are created by the need to enter at a large enough scale to take advantage of lower costs. However, Stigler [16] and others have pointed out that investment in an efficient plant is accessible to the entrant, as well as the incumbent,[1] and once such an investment has been realized there is no post-entry difference between the two firms. Without such a difference, they have argued, there can be no real barrier to entry.

In a recent paper [13], Richard Schmalensee has studied the question of economies of scale within the framework of a post-entry Cournot duopoly model, in which the outcome of the duopoly game is used as an input in the incumbent's capacity choice. If such a choice is irreversible, i.e. if capital costs are sunk, then these costs play no role in the post-entry production decisions. This creates a fundamental asymmetry between incumbent and entrant. The latter's entry decision is dependent on optimal production choices based on total costs, while for the incumbent such choices are based only on variable costs, given its prior irreversible capacity commitment. This asymmetry exists also in the models of [2], [3] and [15], which have also examined entry-deterrence under the assumption of a post-entry Cournot duopoly.[2]

As Schmalensee shows in [13], under certain demand and in the absence of scale economies entry-deterrence is not profitable, since the capacity costs that the incumbent needs to sink in order to credibly deter entry are so large that the monopoly profits become zero. This result, however, is not true when there are scale economies: the monopolist can deter entry with a smaller initial investment, a fact that allows him to enjoy positive profits. These profits, though, are not very "large": the most important result of [13] is that for linear or concave product demand curves the monopoly profits that result from entry-deterrence are at most equal to the flow cost of minimum efficient scale capacity. Schmalensee then argues convincingly that, given that such capacity is "small" relative to total industry demand

---

* We wish to thank Paul Gorecki and two referees of this Journal for helpful advice and comment. Part of the work was done while Perrakis was Visiting Professor at the École Supérieure de Commerce et d'Administration des Entreprises, Reims, France.

[1] Hereafter it will be assumed without loss of generality that the incumbent is a monopolist or a perfectly colluding oligopoly.

[2] Spulber in [15] has also examined a Stackelberg game with the incumbent as the leader.

for most U.S. industries, economies of scale "cannot account for a rate of monopoly profit of even 1 percent" for these industries[3] ([13], p. 1236).

This paper presents a generalization of the Schmalensee model, in which it is recognized that product demand is not known precisely at the time capacity commitments are made. This demand uncertainty arises out of the normal business cycle, and it is a fact of life in most sectors of the economy. It also affects both incumbent and potential entrant symmetrically. In spite of these symmetries, however, it has unexpected consequences with respect to the results of [13].

The following results are derived and presented in this paper. In the next section it is shown that, subject to mild regularity conditions, the Schmalensee upper bound on the profit shield arising from scale economies is also valid under *all* shapes of the demand curve (and not just concave ones), when demand is certain. Section III presents the general model under uncertainty, and examines entry deterrence within this model. In Section IV it is shown that demand uncertainty provides a premium to such deterrence, insofar as the necessary capacity commitment declines *faster* than in the certainty case as the minimum scale rises. The result is that the profit shield bound is no longer necessarily valid, and that it can be violated by a large percentage. These violations are the more important the larger the minimum scale capacity is, as compared to the lowest possible values of product demand.

Thus, this paper supports the Schmalensee results that economies of scale can deter entry, but not his conclusion that such entry deterrence is unimportant. The size of the profitability of entry deterrence under demand uncertainty is a rather complex question, depending (among others) on the size of demand fluctuations around their average value, and the relative size of the cost parameters. Some numerical results are presented in an appendix, in which it is shown that the expected profits from entry deterrence may be more than twice the flow cost of minimum scale capacity, which formed their upper bound in the certainty case.

II. Shielded profits

Let the superscripts $i = 1, 2$ denote the incumbent monopolist, and the potential entrant respectively, with k^i denoting the installed capacity. The incumbent's plant is built at the beginning of the first period, and it produces and sells an unchallenged monopoly at the end of that period. At that point the potential entrant installs capacity, which is used to compete with the incumbent in a Cournot duopoly at the end of period 2, which represents the end of the planning horizon. Only one such entry can take place in the sector. We denote by q the unit cost of capacity k^i and by r the

---

[3] By extension then economies of scale may be a very important source of entry barriers in smaller countries such as Canada, in which the minimum efficient scale is "large" compared to industry demand. See Section V below.

rate of interest, assumed equal to the discount rate for both firms. This last assumption would normally hold under risk-neutrality.[4]

Following [13], we introduce economies of scale by assuming that the marginal cost is constant and equal to c, provided that output[5] x^i is at least equal to the minimum scale k_0 and at most equal to the installed capacity k^i. In other words, the marginal cost function is as in Fig. 1 below. This implies also that capacity may not be increased, once installed, as in [5], [6] and [15]. The relaxation of this assumption will reinforce even more the size of the profit shield. With the exception of this last point (which can be relaxed easily) the cost assumptions are identical to those of Schmalensee in [13].

The post-entry Cournot duopoly game under demand certainty is structured by the usual reaction curves $\gamma^1(x^2)$, $\gamma^2(x^1)$ modified, however, by the presence of a minimal capacity k_0 as illustrated in Fig. 2. the analysis is similar to that of [2], [13] and [15], and will be only briefly summarized here. Since there is no uncertainty, both firms will be operating at full capacity, i.e., $x^i = k^i$, $i = 1, 2$. Hence, the reaction function γ^2 is derived by maximizing $[k^2 p(k^1 + k^2) - [c + q(1 + r)]k^2]$ with respect to k^2, given k^1 and provided $k^2 \geqslant k_0$. As k^1 increases the optimal k^2 declines. For $k^1 \in [\hat{k}^1, K^1]$ the optimal choice of k^2 is equal to k_0, where $\hat{k}^1$ is found from the equation $p(k_0 + \hat{k}^1) + k_0 p'(\hat{k}_0 + k^1) = c + q(1 + r)$, and a prime denotes the derivative. On the other hand, if $k_0 = 0$ then k^2 becomes zero at the entry-deterring capacity $k^1 = K_W^1$. The latter is very simply the competitive output, $p(K_K^1) = c + q(1 + r)$. However, for any $k_0 > 0$ the corresponding entry-deterring value of k^1, denoted by K^1, is easily shown to satisfy $p(k_0 + K^1) =$

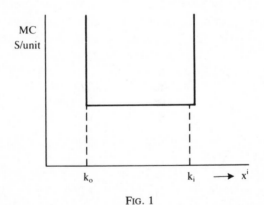

FIG. 1

[4] Since the profit functions are generally different in incumbent and entrant firms, their probability distributions would also differ. Hence, the risk-adjusted discount rates should be different in most cases, if risk-aversion is present.
[5] In other words, we assume that economies of scale affect the operations of the firm (through set-up costs), as well as the capacity installation. The relaxation of this assumption will take place further on in the next section. In the certainty models this point does not arise, since there is no difference between the entrant's capacity and output produced, whereas here the minimum capacity k_0 may exceed production for "low" values of the random demand.

$c + q(1+r)$, or $k_0 + K^1 = K_W^1$ ([13], pp. 1231–1233). Hence, the incumbent can prevent entry by installing capacity equal to or greater than K^1, as suggested by the γ^2 reaction curve in Fig. 2. Schmalensee shows that such a strategy of entry-deterrence can be profitable to the incumbent, but that these profits are at most equal to the flow-cost of minimum scale capacity when product demand is concave. We provide below a simplified and more general proof of this result, and then proceed with an uncertainty model to demonstrate that this bound on shielded profits no longer holds under random demand conditions.

The incumbent's *short-run* profit-maximizing output given entry at k_0 must be at least as large as K^1. In our notation, since the shortrun profit under these consitions is $K^1 p(K^1 + k_0) - cK^1$, we must have

$$K^1 p'(K^1 + k_0) + p(K^1 + k_0) - c \geq 0 \tag{1}$$

Let also $\pi^1(K^1) \equiv K^1 p(K^1) - cK^1$ denote the monopoly's short-run profits given no entry. The Schmalensee upper bound of [13] is given in our notation by the inequality

$$k_0 q(1+r) \geq \pi(K^1) - K^1 q(1+r) \tag{2}$$

Let $f(k_0) \equiv q(1+r)(k_0 + K^1) - \pi^1(K^1) = q(1+r)K_w^1 - \pi^1(K^1)$, since $k_0 + K^1 = K_w^1$ always. This means that $\dfrac{dK^1}{dk_0} = -1$, since K_w^1 is independent of k_0. Hence, $f(0) = [q(1+r) + c - p(K_w^1)] = 0$ as shown earlier, and $f'(k_0) = \pi^{1\prime}(K^1) = K^1 p'(K^1) + p(K^1) - c \geq 0$, since the credibility condition (1)

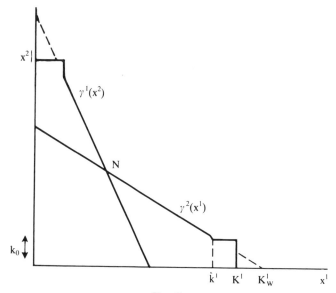

FIG. 2

implies[6] also that the monopolist's marginal revenue given no entry exceeds the short-run marginal cost c for most shapes of the product demand curve. These mean that $f(k_0) \geqslant 0$ always,   Q.E.D.

In contrast to the certainty case discussed above, the bound on shielded profits no longer applies under conditions of uncertainty, permitting profits from entry-deterrence to far exceed the limit given by the flow-cost of minimum scale capacity.

III. The general model

As noted in the previous section, there is intertemporal separation of the capacity and production decisions. Such a separation implies, when uncertainty is present, that the two decisions will take place under different information sets. When capacity is chosen *ex ante*, demand is random. By contrast, production decisions are made *ex post*, after this random demand has been revealed. The already-chosen capacity acts as a constraint on the production decision. This section examines first the *ex post* production decisions, with the chosen capacities already in place.

If x is the total industry output we denote by $p(x, u)$ the corresponding inverse demand function, where u is a random factor. Following the usual specifications we have that $\dfrac{\partial p}{\partial x} < 0$, $\dfrac{\partial p}{\partial u} > 0$ for all x and u. We also assume that the marginal revenue $\dfrac{\partial(xp(x, u))}{\partial x}$ is a decreasing function of x (a necessary, but not sufficient, condition if $p(x, u)$ is concave in x), and that it is a non-decreasing function of u, or that $\dfrac{\partial^2(xp(x, u))}{\partial x \partial u} \geqslant 0$. As pointed out in [9], this assumption is satisfied in most commonly used random demand specifications, including both additive and multiplicative forms.

The random factor u is distributed according to a distribution function $F(u)$, which is assumed continuous without loss of generality. It is also assumed that $F(u)$ is known to both the incumbent and the new entrant, and that the possible range of u is the finite interval $[\underline{u}, \bar{u}]$ of the real line. A consequence of the assumption that $F(u)$ must be common to both incumbent and new entrant is that the random demand distributions in the first and second period must be independent of each other; otherwise, the realization of the demand in period 1 imparts knowledge about the distribution in period 2, which may not be shared by both firms. We further assume, again without loss of generality, that the two periods are of equal length, meaning that $F(u)$ is common to both of them.

---

[6] The proof: let M^1 denote the short-run monopoly profit, i.e. the solution of $\pi^{1\prime}(M^1) = 0$. By the definition of the reaction function $\gamma^1(k_0)$ we have that $\gamma^1(0) \equiv M^1 \gamma^1(k_0)K^1$ (from (1), since the duopolist's marginal revenue is positive at K^1), which implies that $\pi^{1\prime}(K^1) = 0$, Q.E.D. The only requirements are that the monopoly and duopoly revenue functions possess each a unique maximum.

During period 1 the incumbent monopolist, who has invested k^1, produces an amount equal to the short-run profit-maximizing output, or the installed capacity k^1, whichever is less. Let $x^*(u)$ denote the amount produced, which is equal to the smallest of the solution of the equation $\frac{\partial(xp(x, u))}{\partial x} = c$, or of k^1. By the previous assumptions $x^*(u)$ is a non-decreasing function of u, with the result that if $x^*(u) = k^1$ for some u within the set $[\underline{u}, \bar{u}]$ then $x^*(u) = k^1$ for all larger values of u as well.

At the beginning of period 2 the rival firm may enter and install capacity k^2. This will create *ex post*, a Cournot duopoly, with shortrun profits $\pi^1(x^1, x^2, u)$ and $\pi^2(x^2, x^1, u)$, such that $\pi = x^i p(x, u) - cx^i$, $i = 1, 2$ and $x \equiv x^1 + x^2$. The Cournot behavioral assumption implies that x^1 and x^2 are given by the random reaction functions $\gamma^1(x^2, u)$ and $\gamma^2(x^1, u)$, derived from the maximizations of π^1 and π^2 for given x^2 and x^1 respectively. It is easy to see, on the basis of our assumptions that the reaction functions are decreasing in the quantity of the opponent's output and increasing with respect to the random factor u.

We denote by $N^1(u)$ and $N^2(u)$ the coordinates of the Cournot equilibrium point resulting from the intersections of the reaction functions γ^1 and γ^2. Since these reaction functions are symmetric $N^1(u)$ is equal to $N^2(u)$ for all u (hereafter denoted by $N(u)$), meaning that the equilibrium points lie on a 45° line segment passing through the origin, with $N(\underline{u})$ and $N(\bar{u})$ forming the lower and upper limits respectively. In Fig. 3 we show the set of equilibria $N(u)$ with the pair of reaction functions for some value of u.

In Fig. 3 the reaction function $\gamma^2(x^1, u)$ is a smooth curve down to the point where $\gamma^2(x^1, u)$ becomes equal to k_0. If x^1 increases beyond that point

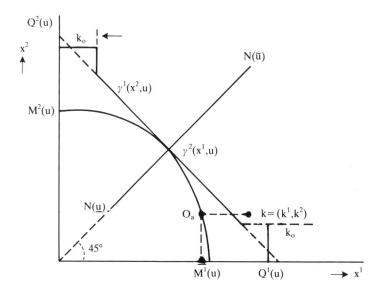

FIG. 3

then the optimal reaction of firm 2 is to produce k_0 as long as $(k_0 p(x, u) - ck_0)$ is positive, where $x = k_0 + x^1$. For $x^1 = Q^1(u)$, the entry-blocking production given u, we have $p(k_0 + Q^1, u) = c$ by definition, and the new entrant ceases production. Conversely, $M^1(u)$ denotes the unconstrained monopoly output, the incumbent firm's preferred output given no competition. If economies of scale didn't exist then the reaction functions would follow the broken lines; this case will be used for comparison purposes.

If entry has occurred, however, it does not necessarily mean that post-entry production will take place at the Cournot point $N(u)$, since the latter may not be feasible. This happens whenever a reaction function γ^i exceeds the corresponding capacity k^i. In Fig. 3 the capacity point k with coordinates k^1 and k^2 is shown, with $k^2 < N(u)$. The corresponding operating equilibrium is at 0_a, where the two firms produce respectively $\gamma^1(k^2, u)$ and k^2.

The exact form of the production equilibrium depends on, among others, the size of the minimum scale k_0 relative to the minimum Cournot equilibrium $N(u)$, and the location of the capacity point k, as in Fig. 3. In Appendix A the entrant's short-run profits are formulated under various assumptions about the relative size of k_0 and $N(u)$. Briefly speaking, the production equilibrium lies on the Cournot locus $[N(\underline{u}), N(\bar{u})]$ of Fig. 3 only if $N(u)$ exceeds both k^1 and k^2. Otherwise, the firm that is being constrained produces at full capacity, while the other operates on its reaction function.

Since the capacity k^1 is observable by the potential entrant, the decision to enter is taken only if the expected profits under the post-entry production equilibrium given k^1 are sufficient to cover the cost of the optimally-chosen capacity k^2. This *ex ante* choice is formulated in Appendix A. The optimal choice of k^1, on the other hand, is carried out by taking into account the anticipated entry. As with the certainty case, we denote by K^1 and K^1_W the entry-deterring levels of k^1 with and without economies of scale.

As shown in Appendix A, the entrant's capacity choice is a non-increasing function $k^2(k^1)$ of the incumbent capacity k^1. Figure 4 below shows the form of this function. As long as $k^2(k^1) > k_0$ the function is strictly decreasing; at some value $\hat{k}^1$ we have $k^2(\hat{k}^1) = k_0$. The value of $\hat{k}^1$ is given by (A.9) or (A.10), with $k^2 = k_0$. For $k^1 > \hat{k}^1$ the entrant's capacity choice will stay equal to k_0 as long as the expected profitability of entering is positive. K^1, the entry-deterring capacity, is the minimum value of k^1 that makes the entrant's expected long-run profit vanish. For $k_0 \leqslant N(u)K^1$ is given by

$$\frac{1}{1+r}\left[\int_{\underline{u}}^{u_2} [p(\gamma^1(k_0, u) + k_0, u) - c]\,\mathrm{d}F(u)\right.$$

$$\left. + \int_{u_2}^{\bar{u}} [p(k_0 + K^1, u) - c]\,\mathrm{d}F(u) = q \quad (3)$$

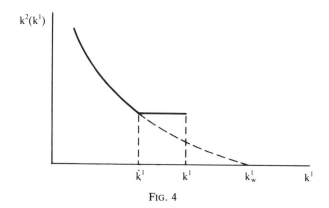

$$\text{FIG. 4}$$

where u_2 is given by $\gamma^1(k_0, u_2) = K^1$. If $k_0 > N(\underline{u})$, on the other hand, then K^1 is given by[7]

$$\frac{1}{1+r}\left[\int_{u_1}^{u_2}[p(2k_0, u) - c]\,dF(u) + \int_{u_2}^{u_4}[p(\gamma^1(k_0, u) + k_0, u) - c]\,dF(u)\right.$$
$$\left. + \int_{u_4}^{\bar{u}}[p(k_0 + K^1, u) - c]\,dF(u)\right] = q, \quad (4)$$

where $p(2k_0, u_1) = c$, $N(u_2) = k_0$ and $\gamma^1(k_0, u_4) = K^1$. Equations (3) and (4) are the counterparts of equation (3b) in [13].

By contrast, the entry-deterring capacity K_W^1 when $k_0 = 0$ is obtained by letting k^2 tend to zero in (A.9) or (A.10). In such a case the value u_4' of the random factor is given by $\gamma^1(0, u_4') = K_W^1$, or $M^1(u_4') = K_W^1$, and instead of (3) or (4) we have

$$\frac{1}{1+r}\left[\int_{\underline{u}}^{u_4'}[p(M^1(u), u) - c]\,dF(u) + \int_{u_4'}^{\bar{u}}[p(K_W^1, u) - c]\,dF(u)\right] = q$$
$$(5)$$

From (5) it can be easily seen that installing K_W^1 is not a profitable action for the incumbent firm, since the discounted expected short-run profit during the second period is less than the cost of capacity.[8] This agrees with

[7] Note that u_1 becomes $\underline{u}$ in (4) if $p(2k_0, \underline{u}) = c$.

[8] The proof: suppressing the arguments of p, we have to show that

$$\int_{\underline{u}}^{u_4'}[M^1p - cM^1]\,dF(u) + K_W^1\int_{u_4}^{\bar{u}}[p - c]\,dF(u) \leqslant q(1+r)K_W^1.$$

Substituting the second integral in the above inequality on the basis of (5) we get, after simplification,

$$\int_{\underline{u}}^{u_4'}[p(M^1(u), u) - c][M^1(u) - K_W^1]\,dF(u) \leqslant 0,$$

which holds since $M^1(u) \leqslant K_W^1$ for all $u \in [\underline{u}, u_4']$.

the certainty conclusion, according to which the monopolist can deter entry only by producing the competitive output.

We close this section by discussing briefly the relaxation of the assumption mentioned in note 5 that economies of scale affect the firm's operations, as well as the capacity installation. Suppose that the marginal cost schedule in Fig. 1 becomes horizontal till the vertical axis to the left of k_0, but that the schedule remains valid only for $k^i \geq k_0$. Then the results for $k_0 \leq N(\underline{u})$ remain unchanged, but (A.6) is now valid for the entire interval $[\underline{u}, u_3]$ when $k_0 > N(\underline{u})$. Consequently, equation (4) now becomes

$$\frac{1}{1+r} \left[\frac{1}{k_0} \int_{\underline{u}}^{u_2} [N(u)p(2N(u), u) - cN(u)] \, dF(u) \right.$$

$$+ \int_{u_2}^{u_4} [p(\gamma^1(k_0, u) + k_0, u) - c] \, dF(u)$$

$$\left. + \int_{u_4}^{\bar{u}} [p(k_0 + K^1, u) - c] \, dF(u) \right] = q \quad (4a)$$

where $k_0 \geq N(u)$ for $u \in [\underline{u}, u_2]$. It is clear that the left-hand-side (LHS) of the above equation exceeds that of (4) for any given K^1. Hence, the entry-deterring capacity derived from (4a) exceeds that yielded by (4). In actual situations (4) and (4a) form two extremes, between which the "true" entry-deterrent capacity lies, since set up costs are not likely to be zero as in (4a), but the breakeven production, at which the marginal cost c becomes valid, may be lower than k_0.

IV. Economies of scale and profit shield

From (5) and (3) or (4) it can be seen easily that K^1 is strictly less[9] than K_W^1 for most shapes of the demand curve. In fact, a stronger result can be proven, namely that $k_0 + K^1 < K_W^1$. This is achieved by equating (3) to (5) for the case where $u_4' < u_4$, and (4) to (5) for the case $u_4' > u_4$, in both instances using the fact that $\gamma^1(k_0, u) + k_0 > M^1(u)$ for all u. The capacity reaction function $k^2(k^1)$ is as shown in Fig. 4, with $k_0 + K^1 < K_W^1$. This last inequality is in sharp contrast to the certainty result, in which the entry-deterring capacity in the absence of scale economies is exactly equal to the minimum scale k_0 plus the entry-deterring capacity with scale economies, as shown in Section II. In other words, under uncertainty the existence of scale economies of size k_0 in output units allows the incumbent to "save" *more than* k_0 in investment (measured in output units) when engaging in entry deterrence. In fact, it can be shown by direct differentiation of (3), (4) or (4a) that the entry-deterring capacity K^1 is a

[9] This is easy to prove formally if we note that $\partial \gamma^1(k^2, u)/\partial k^2 > -1$ for all u and k^2 when the demand function is concave, but also when $p' + \gamma^1 p'' < 0$. This in turn, implies that $M^1(u) < \gamma^1(k_0, u) + k_0$ for all u.

decreasing function of k_0, whose slope is strictly greater (in absolute terms) than 1. Analytically, we get from (3) that

$$\frac{\partial K^1}{\partial k_0} = -1 - \frac{\int_u^{u_2} p'(k_0 + \gamma^1, u)\left[1 + \frac{\partial \gamma^1}{\partial k_0}\right] dF}{\int_{u_2}^{\bar{u}} p'(k_0 + K^1, u)\, dF} \tag{6}$$

For instance, in the case of a linear demand curve, with an additive random factor $p(x, u) = a - bx + u$, we know that $p' = -b$ for all u, and it can be shown that

$$\frac{\partial \gamma^1(k_0, u)}{\partial k_0} = -\frac{1}{2}$$

for all k_0 and u. Hence, from the above expression we get

$$\frac{\partial K^1}{\partial k_0} = -1 - \frac{1}{2}\frac{F(u_2)}{1 - F(u_2)}$$

for all k_0 such that $N(\underline{u}) \geqslant k_0$. For $k_0 > N(\underline{u})$ equation (4) yields in the linear-additive case

$$\frac{\partial K^1}{\partial k_0} = -1 - \frac{[F(u_4) + 3F(u_2)]}{2[1 - F(u_4)]}.$$

In the certainty case, on the other hand, the value of the derivative is always -1.

A geometric demonstration of the effect of an increase in k_0 on the size of K^1 is provided in Fig. 5. Rewriting equation (3) as

$$\int_{\underline{u}}^{u_4} p(\gamma^1(u, k_0) + k_0, u)\, dF(u) + \int_{u_4}^{\bar{u}} p(k_0 + K^1, u) = c + q(1 + r),$$

we note that its LHS is given by the expectation of the ordinates along the

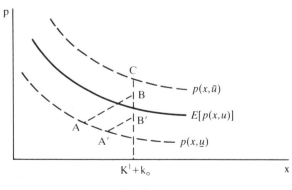

FIG. 5

path ABC as u ranges from $\underline{u}$ to $\bar{u}$. The ordinates along AB are $p(\gamma^1(u, k_0) + k_0, u)$, with point B corresponding to u_4.

Suppose now that k_0 were to increase, the other parameters remaining unchanged. Then, if $K^1 + k_0$ were to remain unchanged as in the certainty case the path AB would shift to A′B′, corresponding to the higher k_0, since $\gamma^1(u, k_0) + k_0$ increases. But it is now clear that the expectation of the ordinates along A′B′C is less than along ABC, thus violating (3). The only way to restore the equation is by shifting $K^1 + k_0$ to the left, i.e. by reducing K^1 more than k_0 has increased.

If the capacity cost $q(1 + r)$ increases sufficiently for any given k_0 then the entry-deterring capacity K^1 solving (3) diminishes. Beyond a certain point the first integral in the LHS of equation (3) disappears and the entry-deterring capacity's equation becomes $E[p(K^1 + k_0, u)] = c + q(1 + r)$. which is similar to the Schmalensee certainty case and, hence, satisfies the profit bound. For entry-deterrence under demand uncertainty to take this form we must have $\gamma^1(k_0, \underline{u}) \geqslant K^1$. Since $M^1(u) > \gamma^1(k_0, u)$ for any u and $k_0 > 0$, it follows that the monopoly who successfully deterred entry is going to be operating at full capacity *for all values of u* under these circumstances, while letting the price fluctuations take care of the randomness in demand. This type of behavior is clearly not very prevalent in most industries, which means that the elegance and simplicity of the certainty case is probably not maintained in practice.

For all these reasons the Schmalensee upper bound on the incumbent firm's monopoly profits arising out of economies of scale when entry is deterred is no longer binding. In our notation, with our formulation and assumptions, this bound if valid would be[10]

$$q(1 + r)k_0 \geqslant \int\limits_{\underline{u}}^{u_4} M^1[p'(M^1, u) - c] \, dF(u)$$

$$+ \int\limits_{u_4}^{\bar{u}} K^1[p(K^1, u) - c] \, dF(u) - q(1 + r)K^1 \quad (7)$$

where $\gamma^1(0, u_4) = K^1$ (or $M^1(u_4) = K^1$), $M^1(u)$ is the optimal monopoly output at u, and $M^1(u) \leqslant K^1$ for $u \in [\underline{u}, u_4]$. To apply the proof developed earlier under certainty we write $g(k_0) = q(1 + r)(k_0 + K^1) - E\pi(K^1)$, where $E\pi(K^1)$ is the expected short-run profits, equal to the sum of the two integrals in the right-hand-side (RHS) of (7); note that M^1 is a function of K^1 via u_4. As argued above, $E\pi(K^1) < q(1 + r)K^1$ for $k_0 = 0$, so that $g(0) > 0$. However, since $dK^1/dk_0 < -1$ the derivative of the first term of

---

[10] Strictly speaking, and according to the formulation of the previous sections, the incumbent stays in business for one period longer than the entrant, which means that (7) underestimates, if anything, the size of his profits. However, we have kept this form of the bound in order to preserve comparability with [13]. If valid, (7) would represent an exact bound on the incumbent's profits if it is assumed that there is an infinite number of post-entry periods, and if r replaces $1 + r$ in the LHS. Such an interpretation preserves completely the Schmalensee assumptions.

$g(k_0)$ is negative and is not necessarily bounded by the derivative of $E\pi(K^1)$, making it possible for $g'(k_0)$ to be negative, and thereby possibly violating (7).

In Appendix B we present the example of a linear demand with additive uncertainty, and binomial or trinomial distribution of the random factor. It is shown that parameter values exist that violate the profit bound (7) under all possible types of equations depending on the relative size of k_0 and $N(\underline{u})$, i.e. (3), (4), or (4a). The violations are more severe, as expected, when (4) is used. In our examples, the bound is exceeded by 8% when (3) is used. The violations increase to more than 20% as k_0 rises to the point of having (4) repalce (3), and they increase even further if an interval of values of u where production of the entrant would be zero is included; in this last case they reach a stunning level of more than 100%. On the other hand, they are "small" (3.5%) when (4a) is the appropriate form. However, there is no simple relationship linking the relative size of k_0 with the violations of the cound, given the highly non-linear nature of the RHS of the alleged bound (7). Thus, all that can be asserted is that the Schmalensee bound is invalid in the presence of uncertainty, and that it may be violated by a "substantial" proportion, depending on the relative value of $N(\underline{u})$ and k_0, even under simple demand and uncertainty forms. It does not seem possible to replace (7) with a valid, yet simple expression, independent of the distribution or the shape of the random demand.

V. Implications and extensions

In this paper we have examined the effect of economies of scale as a barrier to entry in the presence of demand uncertainty. The formulation adopted followed that of [2], [13] and [15], and was a specialization and extension of the model [9].

A particular interest in this study was the validity of Schmalensee's upper bound [13] on the size of the excess profits created by economies of scale. His upper bound equals the flow cost of minimum scale capacity and, under the supposition that plant scale is typically small in relation to U.S. market size, he concludes that economies of scale do not create "sizeable" excess profits. This conclusion was reached by observing that economic profits are the difference of accounting monopoly profits minus accounting "normal" profits, by dividing both sides of the profit inequality by the invested capacity, and by asserting that capacity was approximately equal to market demand.

Several things serve to modify this conclusion when the alleged bound is examined under demand uncertainty. On the one hand, one may argue that observed market demand is always at tor below invested capacity in the presence of demand uncertainty. This would mean that the ratio of minimum scale to market demand (presented as typically less than 0.10 in [13] under the assumption of a national market and homogeneous products) is larger than that of minimum scale to installed industry capacity, which would seem to reinforce the Schmalensee conclusion. However, the source of the estimate ([12], Chapter 4, especially Table 4.10) gives 1967 as the year in which demand was observed. That year was a highly expansionary one for the U.S. economy, implying that for most industries demand was at or near full capacity.

On the other hand, expected profits under entry-deterring policies are simply not bounded by the flow cost of minimum scale capacity when demand is random. The violations of the bound may be quite substantial, as shown in the numerical examples cited above. They become the more substantial the higher the ratio of minimum scale to the "lowest possible" values of market demand. The tendency of firms with high capacity costs (hence with "large" scale) to cut prices deeply in the face of demand downturns is well-known (see, for instance, [12], pp. 205–212). In industries with such firms, therefore, for which the minimum efficient scale is presumably also "large", there is a premium attached to the prevention of entry, since rivalry under depressed demand conditions can have very adverse consequences for firms in the industry. It is this premium that seems to be responsible for the large violations of the bound in our results.

Therefore, if one were to establish conditions under which economies of scale are likely to be important as a source of barriers to entry, how would one summarize the results of [13], as well as this paper? As pointed out in [13] if the minimum scale is less than 10 percent of market demand then under demand certainty scale-economy entry barriers can account for a rate of monopoly profits that exceeds the competitive rate by less than 10 percent. Such a conclusion should be modified if demand fluctuations are "large" in comparison to the minimum scale. The resulting violations must be particularly pronounced in order to create "substantial" monopoly profits, since even a 20 percent violation of the certainty bound would raise such profits to only 12 percent above the normal level if the minimum scale is 10 percent of total industry assets.

A detailed evaluation of all the above effects in those industries in which economies of scale are thought to exist is a major empirical undertaking that transcends the purpose of this paper. Most existing empirical studies in the U.S., U.K. or Canada have not examined demand variability ([4]; [10]; [12], [14]). The list of industries, in which economies of scale are thought to be important is, however, very similar in all three countries:[11] aircraft, refrigerators and freezers, computers, passenger cars and trucks, electric motors, turbo-generators, diesel engines, breweries and cigarettes in the U.S.; the above plus petroleum refining, integrated steel products, cement and detergents in the U.K. and Canada. In some of these industries (such as, for instance, refrigerators) the minimum scale exceeds the market size for the two smaller countries.

[11] The list includes industries with substantial plant or firm-level economies of scale (at least 10 percent of the market), as shown in [4], [14] and [12, pp. 96, 97 and 118].

For the industries in the above list preliminary data from the Canadian market[12] shows that product demand variability is quite pronounced in: aircraft, refrigerators, trucks and trailers, cigarettes, motoe vehicle parts and accessories, and integrated steel products. For these industries one expects on the basis of the model of this paper that successful entry-deterrence would create monopoly profits that are significantly in excess of the upper bound of [13].

The evidence, therefore, for most sectors of U.S. industry, appears to be consistent with Schmalensee's main conclusion about the relative unimportance of scale economies as entry barriers. However, such economies play a role in some sectors (identified above), in which they co-exist with significant uncertainty of product demand. More important, though, is the increased profitability of entry-deterrence in the smaller markets, such as the U.K. and Canada, in which economies of scale as entry barriers may have already been important even under the certain demand model of [13]. In Canada, in particular, in which many product markets are regional because of the large geographical distances, and in which a high tariff policy has served traditionally to isolate many industries from foreign competition, scale economies in combination with demand uncertainty are bound to create powerful incentives to deter new entrants.

As a final remark in this paper we note that the assumption of risk-neutrality for incumbents and entrants understates, if anything, the profitability of entry deterrence. In [9] it is noted that under concave demand risk-aversion decreases the capacity reaction function of the entrant below the risk-neutral level for all values of incumbent capacity, an effect that is consistent with earlier uncertainty results.[13] Such an effect is bound to increase even further the observed *ex post* profits of an incumbent who has successfully deterred entry, although a complete modelling requires also the inclusion of a capital market. The matter is awaiting further study.

University of Ottawa, Ontario
Carleton University, Ontario

APPENDIX

A. *Derivation of the entrant's capacity reaction*

The entrant chooses k^2 by maximizing the discounted expected shortrun profit minus the initial cost of capacity. This discounted shortrun profit is evaluated at the expected equilibria of

[12] The data consisted of unpublished estimates of the variance of industry shipments around the logarithmic trend line, made available to the authors by P. Gorecki. The industry correspondence between these estimates and the economies of scale data of [4], [10], [12] and [14] is only approximate, since the variance estimates were product-based while the economies of scale were estimated on a plant or firm level. The variability of demand was considered substantial if the variance estimate was in excess of 10. It was also implicity assumed that demand uncertainty in an industry in Canada implies similar uncertainty in the other two markets.

[13] See, for instance, [8] and [11]. However, this effect of risk-aversion is not necessarily true in monopolies, whether regulated or not, without the concavity of demand, as in [7].

the Cournot game. We distinguish two cases, when $k_0 \leqslant N(u)$ and $k_0 > N(u)$ respectively. Let $N(u)$ denote, the Cournot equilibrium production, i.e. the solution to the equation $Np(2N, u) + p(2N, u) = c$, and $\gamma^1(k^2, u)$ the reaction function, i.e. the solution of $\gamma^1 p'(\gamma^1 + k^2, u) + p(\gamma^1 + k^2, u) = c$, where a prime denotes the derivative with respect to quantity. Then for $k_0 \leqslant N(u)$ the entrant's short-run profit is given by (A.1)–(A.3).

$$\pi^2 = N(u)p(2N(u), u) - cN(u), \ u \in [\underline{u}, u_1], \ N(u_1) = k^2 \tag{A.1}$$

$$\pi^2 = k^2 p(\gamma^1 + k^2, u) - ck^2, \ u \in (u_1, u_2], \ \gamma^1(k^2, u_2) = k^1 \tag{A.2}$$

$$\pi^2 = k^2 p(k^1 + k^2, u) - ck^2, \ u \in (u_2, \bar{u}]. \tag{A.3}$$

By contrast, for $k_0 > N(u)$ we have (A.4)–(A.8), in which it was assumed that $p(2k_0, u) \leqslant c$ at the first subinterval of values of u, implying that either firm 2 or both will shut down for these low values of demand[14]

$$\pi^2 = 0, \ u \in [\underline{u}, u_1], \ p(2k_0, u_1) = c \tag{A.4}$$

$$\pi^2 = k_0 p(2k_0, u) - ck_0, \ u \in (u_1, u_2), \ N(u_2) = k_0 \tag{A.5}$$

$$\pi^2 = Np(2N, u) - cN, \ u \in (u_2, u_3), \ N(u_3) = k^2 \tag{A.6}$$

$$\pi^2 = k^2 p(\gamma^1 + k^2, u) - ck^2, \ u \in (u_3, u_4), \ \gamma^1(k^2, u_4) = k^1 \tag{A.7}$$

$$\pi^2 = k^2 p(k^1 + k^2, u) - ck^2, \ u \in (u_4, \bar{u}). \tag{A.8}$$

As long as $k^2 > k_0$ the optimal entrant capacity is found by maximizing the discounted expectation of π^2 minus the capacity cost qk^2. This optimal capacity is obviously a non-increasing function[15] of k^1 for all k^1, a *capacity reaction function* $k^2(k^1)$ of a Stackelberg-type game, as in [9] and [15]. As long as $k^2(k^1) > k_0$ the equation for the capacity reaction is (A.9) or (A.10), depending on whether $k_0 \leqslant N(u)$ or $k_0 > N(u)$ respectively.

$$\frac{1}{1+r}\left[\int_{u_1}^{u_2}\left[p + k^2 p'\left(1 + \frac{\partial \gamma^1}{\partial k^2}\right) - c\right]dF(u) + \int_{u_2}^{\bar{u}}[p + k^2 p' - c]\,dF(u)\right] = q \tag{A.9}$$

$$\frac{1}{1+r}\left[\int_{u_3}^{u_4}\left[p + k^2 p'\left(1 + \frac{\partial \gamma^1}{\partial k^2}\right) - c\right]dF(u) + \int_{u_4}^{\bar{u}}[p + k^2 p' - c]\,dF(u)\right] = q \tag{A.10}$$

where $p \equiv p(\gamma^1(k^2, u) + k^2, u)$ and $p \equiv p(k^1 + k^2, u)$ in the first and second integrals respectively in both (A.9) and (A.10).

B. *The profit bound*

Let the demand curve be $p(x, u) = a - bx + u$, where a, b are positive constants with $a > c$, and let u be a stochastic variable distributed on the finite interval $[\underline{u}, \bar{u}]$. The reaction function is given by $\gamma^1(k_0, u) = 1/2b(a - c - bk_0 + u)$, which implies that $M^1(u) = 1/2b(a - c + u)$, and that the coordinates of the Cournot point are $N(u) = (a - c + u)/3b$. We take $\underline{u} = 0$ in each of the cases below. First consider the case of the binominal distribution, $u = 0(= \underline{u})$ with probability $\frac{2}{3}$, and $u = \bar{u}$ with probability $\frac{1}{3}$. The monopoly profits under entry-deterrence become

$$\frac{2}{3}M^1(0)[p(M^1(0), 0) - c] + \frac{1}{3}K^1[p(K^1, \bar{u}) - c] - q(1+r)K^1$$

$$= \frac{2}{3b}\frac{(a-c)^2}{2} + \frac{K^1}{3}(a - c - bK^1 + \bar{u}) - q(1+r)K^1 \tag{B.1}$$

---

[14] If, instead, it is assumed that both will operate at a loss then entry-deterrence becomes, if anything, more profitable, thus reinforcing the subsequent argument.

[15] This is easily seen if we note from (A.1)–(A.3) and (A.5)–(A.8) that π^2 is non-increasing in k^1.

Choose $bk_0 = \dfrac{a-c}{3}$, $3q(1+r) = \tfrac{25}{24}(a-c)$, and $\bar{u} - \dfrac{a-c}{12}$; then we find $K^1 = \dfrac{3(a-c)}{8b} = \gamma^1(k_0, \bar{u})$. Substituting into (B.1) and dividing the result by $q(1+r)k_0$ we find 1.08, i.e. that monopoly profits exceed the Schmalensee upper bound by 8 percent. For $bk_0 = \tfrac{5}{12}(a-c)$, $3q(1+r) = \tfrac{1}{12}[\tfrac{15}{12}(a-c) + \bar{u}]$ and $\bar{u} = a-c$, (B.1) divided by $q(1+r)k_0$ yields 1.207, implying a 20.7 percent violation of the bound. On the other hand, if ecomomies of scale do not affect the firm's operations and the entry-deterring capacity is given by (4a), a similar computation yields a 3.5% violation of the bound for $\bar{u} = 2.1(a-c)$ and $bk_0 = a - c$.

Consider now a trinomial distribution, with $u = 0$, $u = \dfrac{\bar{u}}{2}$ or $u = \bar{u}$, with respective probabilities $\dfrac{1}{3}$, $\dfrac{\mu}{3}$ and $\dfrac{2-\mu}{3}$. Choose

$$bk_0 = \frac{a-c}{2}, \qquad \bar{u} = 1.04(a-c), \qquad 3q(1+r) = (a-c)\left[\frac{1.02}{\mu} + \frac{1.06}{4}\right].$$

Instead of (B.1) the profits are now

$$\tfrac{1}{3}\left[M^1(0)[p(M^1(0), 0) - c] + M^1\frac{(\bar{u})}{2}\left[p\left(M^1\left(\frac{\bar{u}}{2}\right), \frac{\bar{u}}{2}\right) - c\right]\mu\right.$$

$$\left. + K^1[p(K^1, \bar{u}) - c](2 - \mu)\right] - q(1+r)$$

$$= \frac{1}{3}\left[\frac{(a-c)^2}{4b} + \left(\frac{a-c+\dfrac{\bar{u}}{2}}{4b}\right)^2\mu + K^1[a - bK^1 + \bar{u} - c](2-\mu)\right] - q(1+r) \quad \text{(B.2)}$$

Substituting the chosen parameter values into (B.2) and dividing by

$$q(1+r)k_0 = \frac{(a-c)^2}{6b}\left[\frac{1.02}{\mu} + \frac{1.06}{4}\right]$$

we find that the ratio is an increasing function of μ. For $\mu = 1.8$ we get a ratio of 2.046, implying a 104.6 percent violation of the bound.

REFERENCES

1. BAIN, J. S., *Barriers to New Competition,* Cambridge, 1956.
2. DIXIT, A., "The Role of Investment in Entry Deterrence," *Economic Journal* 90, March 1980, 95–106.
3. EATON, B. C. and LIPSEY, R. G., "Capital, Commitment, & Entry Equilibrium," *Bell Journal of Economics* 12, Autumn 1981, 593–604.
4. GORECKI, P., *Economies of Scale in Canadian Manufacturing Industries,* Consumer and Corporate Affairs Canada, Ottawa, 1976.
5. HAHN, F. H., "Excess Capacity and Imperfect Competition," *Oxford Economic Papers* 7, October 1955, 229–240.
6. HICKS, J. R., "The Process of Imperfect Competition," *Oxford Economic Papers* 6, February 1954, 41–54.
7. PERRAKIS, S., "Rate-of-Return Regulation of a Monopoly Firm with Random Demand," *International Economic Review* 17, February 1976, 149–63.
8. PERRAKIS, S., "Factor-Price Uncertainty with Variable Proportions: Note," *American Economic Review* 70, December 1980, 1083–88.
9. PERRAKIS, S. and WARSKETT, G., "Capacity and Entry Under Demand Uncertainty," *Review of Economic Studies* (1983), 495–511.
10. PRATTEN, C. F., *Economies of Scale in Manufacturing Industry,* Cambridge, 1971.

11. SANDMO, A., "On the Theory of the Competitive Firm Under Price Uncertainty," *American Economic Review* 61, March 1971, 65–73.
12. SCHERER, F. M., *Industrial Market Structure and Economic Performance,* 2nd Edition, Chicago, Rand McNally, 1980.
13. SCHMALENSEE, R., "Economies of Scale and Barriers to Entry," *Journal of Political Economy* 89, 6 (December 1981), 1228–1238.
14. SILBERSTON, Z. A., "Economies of Scale in Theory and Practice," *Economic Journal* 82 (March 1972), 369–391.
15. SPULBER, D. F., "Capacity, Output, & Sequential Entry," *American Economic Review* 71(3), June 1981, 503–14.
16. STIGLER, G. J., *The Organization of Industry,* Homewood, Irwin, 1968.

A SIGNALING MODEL OF PREDATORY PRICING

By JOHN ROBERTS

1. Introduction

IN the last five years, recognition of the strategic implications of disparities in the information available to different economic agents has permitted economists to analyze rigorously several important aspects of industrial behavior that have previously defied formal modeling. Nowhere have the results of this work been more striking than in the context of that most controversial issue in industrial economics, predatory pricing.

Apparent instances of firms' temporarily lowering prices to discipline or destroy rivals or to deter future entry date back at least a century to the use of "fighting ships" by the liner conference in the U.K.–China tea trade against nonconference liners. Allegations of predation have been central in U.S. antitrust cases from Standard Oil (New Jersey) through the IBM peripheral computer equipment cases and on up to the current complaints against Hitachi. An active debate in the law journals involves lawyers and economists proposing evidentiary criteria for determining whether predation has occurred. The standard texts in industrial organization present historical evidence and discuss circumstances that seem likely to contribute to the adoption and success of predatory strategies. All this reflects an apparently widely held belief in the existence and efficacy of predatory practices.

Yet, as recently as 1980, the only thoroughgoing, formal analyses of predatory price-cutting that had been developed by economists suggested that it was not a rational, profit maximizing strategy, that instances of actual predation were thus likely to be rare, and that the main effect of legal prohibitions of predation is to permit inefficient firms to use the courts to protect themselves against legitimate competition (see McGee, 1958; 1980). Moreover, despite the difficulty of interpreting a wide variety of historical episodes as anything but predation, in the absence of any competing theory these arguments were gaining important adherents among both economists and legal scholars and seemed to represent the basis for an emerging consensus.

In contrast, we now have several distinct models in which predatory pricing emerges in equilibrium, even though all firms (and even outsiders) are profit-maximizing economic agents who comprehend fully the incentives inherent in the given situation and the implications of making various choices, rationally forecast one another's behavior, and even understand completely the arguments for the irrationality of predation. Among these studies are formalizations of the deep-pocket/long-purse story (Benoit,

The comments of Dick Schmalensee and of two referees and the financial support of the National Science Foundation (grant SES 83-08723) are gratefully acknowledged.

1985; Fudenberg and Tirole, 1985); models where firms accept the losses inherent in preying against a particular rival in order to build a "reputation for toughness" that discourages later challenges (Kreps and Wilson, 1982a; Milgrom and Roberts, 1982b); other models where low prices are an attempt to convince rivals that fundamental market conditions are inherently bad and thereby to induce their exit (Fudenberg and Tirole, 1985) or prevent further entry (Easley, Masson and Reynolds, 1985); and an analysis in which predation is aimed at "softening up" a rival in order to improve the terms for merger (Saloner, 1985).[1]

Two factors are key in obtaining these results. The first is to relax the implicit assumption in earlier arguments that all relevant information is equally available to all concerned parties. The second is to employ explicitly game-theoretic methods to study the resultant behavior.

In this note I offer yet another information-based, game-theoretic model of predation.

The essential idea can be given in terms of a simple example. An incumbent faces a new entrant in a market for a homogeneous good which will be open for two periods. The incumbent knows the demand in the market, which might be either strong or weak, but the entrant does not know the actual level of demand. The firms compete in quantities for a single period, then each observes the price, but not the other's quantity choice. The entrant may then exit. If it does, the incumbent collects its monopoly profit in the second period. If the entrant stays in, the two compete again in quantities.

Assume that if demand were known to be high, continued operation under Cournot equilibrium behavior would be profitable for the entrant, while if demand were known to be low it would want to exit. In these circumstances, it will want to learn the level of demand and it can attempt to infer this information from observing the first-period price.

It is here that informational asymmetries come into play. Note that there are two of these. One is that the entrant cannot observe the incumbent's quantity. If it could, then it could easily infer the level of demand from knowing the price and the total quantity sold. However, with unobservability, the entrant's inference must be based on a conjecture of the incumbent's quantity. The second asymmetry is that the incumbent alone knows the actual demand and can produce different quantities depending on whether demand is high or low.

In particular, the incumbent can increase its quantity when demand is high so that the resultant price is at the level which the entrant expects to see if demand is low. If the entrant took this price as indicating that it will lose money under continued operation and left the market, the incumbent would receive higher second period profits than if the entrant had recognized the true demand conditions and stayed in. Of course, the entrant

---

[1] For a more detailed discussion of these contributions, see Roberts, 1985.

loses by being fooled in this fashion. On the other hand, if demand is weak, both the incumbent and the entrant are better off if the latter exits. In these circumstances, the incumbent would want to convey its information about demand honestly and the entrant would want to receive the information. A simple announcement would not do, however, because the incumbent would gladly make the same announcement if demand were strong. Moreover, producing the simple Cournot quantity will also fail to convey the information credibly so long as the gains to inducing exit when demand is strong are large enough to provide an incentive for mimicry. This means that to signal its information credibly when demand is low the incumbent must depress the price so far that, were demand actually high, it would not be worthwhile to generate this price to induce exit.

Thus, the possibility of inducing exit leads to prices being lower than would obtain absent the possibility for influencing the exit decision. This is the essence of predatory pricing.

Of course, in equilibrium the entrant will recognize the incentives to lower prices and will allow for the resulting behavior. As a consequence, its inferences will not be systematically biased. In fact, in separating equilibrium (in which the prices differ with demand conditions), exit occurs only when demand actually is low, i.e., in exactly the same circumstances as it would if predation were effectively prohibited. Thus, predation aimed at inducing exit occurs and is costly for the incumbent, but no extra exit is induced. Moreover, in the context of this example it turns out that the firm does not deviate from its Cournot best-response when demand is high, although it does deviate when demand is weak to signal this information in a credible fashion. Thus predation occurs (and is followed by exit) only when demand is weak, which is exactly the situation in which exit would occur under full information or the known absence of predation.

If there are more than two possible demand levels, the incumbent may expand output even when there is no possibility of inducing exit. It does so because if the entrant believes demand is weak, it will produce less in the second period. This expansion of output might be interpreted as predation aimed not at inducing exit but rather at "disciplining" a rival.

In equilibrium, however, the entrant still is not fooled. If it stays in, its second-period output is the same as it would have been if it knew there were no predation being practiced.

If we now consider the original entry decision of the entrant, a further twist appears. The entrant, looking forward, will foresee the predatory pricing that will arise if it enters. Even though this pricing does not induce extra exit or lower second-period output, it does reduce the entrant's first-period profits. Thus, entry may be deterred by the credible threat of predation aimed at inducing exit or reducing output, even though this predation will not actually influence the exit or output decisions!

In the next section I specify the model more formally, and in Section 3 I define the equilibrium concept. Section 4 contains the results on equilibrium behavior. In Section 5 I compare this model and its predictions with other recent models of predation and with models of signaling in other contexts. Section 6 contains conclusions.

2. The model

To keep the analysis transparent and facilitate computation, I will work with a very specific, simple model. There are two firms, an incumbent I and a potential entrant E, in a market for a homogeneous, perishable good. Demands in this market in each period are given by $p = a - q_I - q_E$, where p is the price, q_I and q_E are quantities, and a, the choke price, serves to parameterize the strength of demand. The incumbent, by virtue of its experience, knows the market conditions better than does the entrant. Formally, we assume that the value of a is known to I but that the entrant knows only that a lies in some set A of non-negative numbers. The entrant's prior over A is given by a distribution G; G represents E's prior beliefs about demand conditions. As is standard in such problems, these beliefs are assumed to be known by I and, in fact, to be common knowledge.

Each firm has constant marginal costs of production which we will take to be zero for the sake of simplicity.[2] The entrant, however, also incurs fixed costs of f per period. These are assumed to be private information to E, while I knows only that $f \in F \subset R_+$ and holds beliefs about f's value described by a distribution H. Again, the H function is common knowledge, and we assume that a and f are independent.[3]

This asymmetry of having only the entrant face fixed costs is necessitated by the symmetry that will appear elsewhere in the model. In particular, we will assume Cournot, quantity-setting competition, which implies that so long as E's marginal costs are below the monopoly price for I then the entrant can make positive operating profits in full-information Cournot equilibrium.[4] Thus, given marginal costs of zero, exit could never be induced if f were also zero. Since the point is to build a model in which exit might occur, negative profits must be possible. A positive value for f does this, while having the incumbent face zero fixed costs serves to keep matters

---

[2] Thus, non-negativity of prices means that price always (weakly) exceeds marginal and average variable costs. This means that the behavior studied here would not run afoul of the Areeda–Turner test for predation. We will comment further on this below.

[3] If F is a singleton, then the fixed costs are, in effect, commonly known. Much of the sequel will focus on this case.

[4] I will use the term "full information Cournot" to refer to the one-shot game played when the level of a is known and I and E simultaneously and independently select quantities. The unmodified term "Cournot" refers to situations where a is private information to I, the two firms pick quantities simultaneously and independently but with I's choice possibly depending on the value of a, and the payoffs are simply price times quantity for each. With the linearity of demand and cost, Cournot equilibrium best responses are $q(a) = (a - \bar{q}_E)/2$ and $q_E = E(a - \bar{q}(a))/2$, where $\bar{q}_E$ is I's conjecture about E's choice and $\bar{q}(a)$ is E's conjecture about I's strategy. The Cournot equilibrium quantities are $q(a) = [3a - E(a)]/6$ and $q_E = E(a)/3$. Of course, if the distribution of a is degenerate, these reduce to the corresponding full information Cournot quantities.

as simple as possible. It also insures that the incumbent cannot be forced out, so that ignoring the possibility of predation by the entrant is natural.[5] Presumably asymmetries in demand or non-linearities in costs could also be used to this same effect.

The timing of actions is as follows. In period zero, the entrant decides whether or not to enter. If entry does not occur, the game ends with the payoff to E being zero.[6] If entry occurs, we move to period 1. In it, each firm independently picks a quantity q_i^1, $i = E, I$ to place on the market, observes the resultant price, p^1, and receives the corresponding profits. Note that neither observes the other's quantity at this stage. All that is crucial, however, is that E not observe I's output, from which it could, knowing price, infer the value of a. After observing p^1 and knowing f, E decides whether to leave. If it does, its total payoff is $p^1 q_E^1 - f$, and that of I is $p^1 q_I^1 + (a/2)^2$, where the last term is I's monopoly profits in the last period. If E stays in, then the firms again independently and simultaneously pick quantities q_i^2 to sell, the price is $p^2 = a - q_I^2 - q_E^2$, and the resultant total payoffs are $p^1 q_E^1 + p^2 q_E^2 - 2f$ and $p^1 q_I^1 + p^2 q_I^2$. The game then ends.

It is worth noting that the basic results of the paper are robust to the inclusion of discounting, extra periods, nonzero marginal costs, nonlinear demand (with a playing the role of a shift parameter), product differentiation (if the goods are substitutes) and price competition. Also, the private information could be about the incumbent's marginal cost (see Saloner, 1985).

3. The equilibrium concept

By equilibrium I will mean sequential equilibrium, a strengthening of the Nash equilibrium concept due to Kreps and Wilson (1982b). Such an equilibrium consists of strategies for each player as well as beliefs for each about the history of play to date and the values of one another's private information. We describe each of these in turn.

The strategies specify for each player the action it will take at each decision point as a function of the information abailable to it then. For the incumbent, a strategy thus gives its first period quantity, q_E^1, as a function of its information at this point, which is simply the value of a and the fact that E entered, and its second period quantity, q_I^2, as a function of the same data as well as its first-period choice q_I^1 and the first-period price p^1. The entrant's strategies are more complicated. For E a strategy first specifies whether to enter or not as a function of its information, which is the value of f. Further, if it has entered, the strategy specifies q_E^1, again as a function

---

[5] If both faced positive, privately known fixed costs, one could generate price wars such as have been studied by Fudenberg and Tirole (1983) and Mailath (1984).

[6] The payoff here to I is irrelevant, since it takes no action before this point, although it is natural to think of it as receiving its monopoly profits in each future period. If I had to pick its price in period zero, we might well expect limit pricing of the type studied by Milgrom and Roberts (1982a). On this point, see below.

of f. Next, it specifies whether to exit or not. At this point, the entrant knows f, q_E^1 and p^1, so the exit decision can depend on all of these. Finally, if it stays in, the entrant's strategy gives its period 2 quantity as a function of f, q_E^1 and p^1.

The beliefs that are important here are, first, those that the entrant holds initially about the value of a and that the incumbent holds about f. These were specified above in the description of the game. If E enters, the incumbent might update its beliefs about f on this basis, so we must specify beliefs for it when it selects q_I^1. On the other hand, the entrant has learned nothing new at this point, so its beliefs should be given by its prior over a. After observing p^1, however, the entrant might update its beliefs about a, so we must specify beliefs for E at the point where it makes its exit decision. If the entrant stays in, the incumbent might be able to infer something about f from this and so would again update. However, we shall see that these last beliefs are irrelevant. Finally, the entrant's beliefs if and when it selects q_E^2 should be just those it had in deciding to exit, since again it has learned nothing new.

A sequential equilibrium requires that both the beliefs and the strategies have certain properties. In particular, at each decision point, each player must find that continuing to play its equilibrium strategy maximizes its expected profits, given its beliefs and the hypothesis that the other will play its strategy. This best-response condition rules out equilibria supported by threats which would not rationally be carried out. As for the equilibrium beliefs, they should be obtained from the priors G and H by Bayesian updating under the assumption that the equilibrium strategies have been played whenever this is possible, i.e., whenever play of these strategies could (for some values of a and f) have generated the history of play that the player in question has observed. Otherwise, that is, when a history is observed that could not have occurred under play of the given strategies, the beliefs should be consistent with Bayesian updating under the hypothesis that the other player used *some* strategy.[7]

4. Equilibrium behavior

In this section, I first allow for only two levels of demand and explicitly calculate the equilibrium. This example gives insight into the nature of the solution in more general cases, which I also discuss.

Suppose that there are only two possible values, high and low, for the demand intercept and one possible level of the entrant's fixed cost. Assume that if demand were known to be high, the entrant would definitely want to stay in, while if it were known to be low, the entrant would strictly prefer to exit. Let a_H and a_L denote the two possible levels for a, and let ρ be the prior probability assigned to $a = a_L$. Then our assumption is that $(a_L/3)^2 < f < (a_H/3)^2$.

---

[7] This is not quite the Kreps-Wilson condition for consistency of beliefs, but will do here.

Our focus is on separating equilibrium. In standard signaling models, where the action of the signaling player is observable, this term means that this player's strategy is an invertible function of its private information, so that the value of this information can be inferred from the observation of the player's action. Here, the incumbent's first period quantity, q_I, is not observed: instead it is only $a - q_I$ that E can calculate from seeing p and knowing its own choice. However, if $a - q_I(a)$ is monotonic, then E can infer the value of a from observing $(p^1 + q_E^1) = (a - q_I(a))$. It is such a situation, where the observed outcome is an invertible function of I's private information, that I call "separating".

It is by now a commonplace that if any separating equilibrium exists in a signaling game with a discrete set of types of the signaling agent, then there will be a continuum of such equilibria. Interest has centred on the efficient ones of these, where the "weakest" type of signaling player does not deviate from what would otherwise be optimal behavior, while the "stronger" types deviate just enough to deter mimicking by "weaker" ones.[8]

In more standard signaling games, this efficient separating equilibrium has been shown to be the only equilibrium meeting various criteria involving more or less intuitively appealing restrictions on the signal recipient's beliefs after observing messages that ought not to have arisen in equilibrium[9] (Kreps, 1984; Milgrom and Roberts, 1984; Roberts, 1985). Further, Kreps (1984) and Cho and Kreps (1986) have shown that these criteria follow from the property of strategic stability introduced by Kohlberg and Mertens (1984) and thus that the efficient separating equilibrium alone meets this formal, game-theoretic test. However, neither these "intuitive" criteria nor the stability results are directly applicable to the present game, principally because the recipient of the signal (the entrant) takes an action simultaneously with the signaling by the incumbent.

It is beyond the scope of this essay to attempt to generalize all the various intuitive tests to cover the models considered here, let alone to attempt an analysis of strategic stability. However, it is a relatively simple matter to extend the most basic of the intuitive tests, "immunity to elimination of dominated strategies," and to apply it when demand takes on only two values.

In particular, suppose we require that the beliefs of the incumbent after seeing any particular first-period price never put positive probability on demand conditions under which, *given the entrant's first-period output*, producing the quantity necessary to generate this price would represent play of a dominated strategy by the incumbent under these demand conditions.[10]

---

[8] There are many such efficient equilibria, but all have the same equilibrium outcomes. They differ only in the "off the equilibrium path" beliefs and actions.

[9] These beliefs determine the responses to such messages and thus the attractiveness to the signaler of deviating to them.

[10] The extension from the criterion used in standard signaling models involves the italicized clause, which is designed to account for the simultaneity of actions.

Then the only separating equilibria which satisfy this condition are the efficient ones.

All separating sequential equilibria involve the incumbent's producing its Cournot best-response to the entrant's output when demand is high and, when demand is low, its producing at a level that results in a price that would not be profitable to effect if demand actually were high, even though this price would induce exit. The efficient separating equilibria involve the incumbent's generating prices when demand is low such that, if demand were high, the incumbent would be just indifferent between mimicking these prices (which result in exit) and following the equilibrium strategy. In the inefficient equilibria, mimicry that succeeds in inducing exit yields strictly lower profits when demand is high than does the equilibrium play of not mimicking. These inefficient equilibria are supported only by beliefs that more extreme prices than those in the efficient equilibrium signal high demand with enough probability that exit is not optimal. Yet such beliefs mean that the incumbent is believed to play a dominated strategy when demand is strong, and application of the criterion eliminates these equilibria.

Thus, among the separating equilibria, the efficient ones seem particularly central. Note, however, that there will be pooling equilibria that meet our criterion. Nevertheless, we will focus on the efficient separating equilibria in the sequel and will refer only briefly to pooling equilibria.

To solve for equilibrium, begin with the last period and work backward through the game tree.

Suppose (as will be the case in separating equilibrium) that after seeing the first period price, the entrant has point expectations about the value of a. Because the incumbent has access to all the information available to the entrant, it will be able to infer these beliefs. If these beliefs are massed on $a = a_H$ the entrant expects to play the full information Cournot game with $a = a_H$, which yields it profits of $(a_H/3)^2 - f$, while if it believes $a = a_L$ it expects profits of $(a_L/3)^2 - f$ if it stays in. By assumption, in the former case it expects continued operation to be profitable, and so it will stay in, while in the latter case it will exit.

Thus, if the entrant has stayed in because it believed that $a = a_H$, actual play in the last period involves the entrant selecting q_E to maximize $(a_H - \bar{q} - q_E)q_E$, where $\bar{q}$ is its conjecture as to the quantity choice that the incumbent will make. Meanwhile, depending on the true demand conditions, I maximizes either $(a_H - q_H - \bar{q}_E)q_H$ or $(a_L - q_L - \bar{q}_E)q_L$, where $\bar{q}_E$ is its conjecture as to q_E. In separating equilibrium, E will have correctly inferred the value of a, so in equilibrium the profits that accrue in the last period if $a = a_H$ will be $(a_H/3)^2 - f$ for E and $(a_H/3)^2$ for I, while if $a = a_L$ they will be 0 and $(a_L/2)^2$. If, however, the entrant incorrectly inferred that $a = a_L$ when actually $a = a_H$, it will exit and receive 0 while I receives $(a_H/2)^2$. Finally, if the entrant incorrectly believed that $a = a_H$ when actually $a = a_L$, it will stay in. Since the entrant believes that it is playing a game whose unique equilibrium involves it producing $a_H/3$, it will produce this quantity. The incumbent will know that the entrant has these incorrect beliefs and so will expect this output. Its best response is $[a_L - (a_H/3)]/2$ so long as this quantity and the resulting price, $(a_L/2) - (a_H/6)$, are non-negative. Thus, if the entrant mistakenly believes $a = a_H$ and stays in, the incumbent earns $(3a_L - a_H)^2/36$ if $3a_L > a_H$ and zero otherwise.

Knowing the second period payoffs, we can now turn to specifying the efficient separating equilibrium outcome in the first period. This requires three conditions plus some side constraints. First, the choice Q_E of the entrant must maximize its expected profit, given the choices Q_L and Q_H of the two types of incumbent. Second Q_H must be maximizing when $a = a_H$, given Q_E, the exit rule, and the second period profit function. Third, Q_L must be a maximizing response to Q_E when $a = a_L$, given the exit rule, the second period profit function, and the condition that, when $a = a_H$, the incumbent not find that generating the price $a_L - Q_E - Q_L$ that corresponds to low demand and thereby inducing exit is strictly more profitable than selecting Q_H and having the entrant stay in. In addition, we must have all quantities and the resultant prices non-negative, and we must have the incumbent find that selecting Q_L when $a = a_L$ and then receiving $a_L^2/4$ is at least as good as selecting any other output level and receiving either 0 or $(3a_L - a_H)^2/36$ in the second period because E incorrectly believes demand is high and stays in.

The following express the three optimization conditions:

$$Q_E = \frac{\rho(a_L - Q_L) + (1 - \rho)(a_H - Q_H)}{2} \qquad (1)$$

$$Q_H = \frac{a_H - Q_E}{2} \qquad (2)$$

Q_L maximizes $(a_L - Q_E - Q)Q + (a_L/2)^2$ subject to
$$(a_L - Q_E - Q)(Q + a_H - a_L) + (a_H/2)^2$$
$$\leq (a_H - Q_E - Q_H)Q_H + (a_H/3)^2 \qquad (3)$$

Equations (1) and (2) are simply the relevant best responses derived from first order conditions for E's choice given its beliefs and for I's choice when $a = a_H$. The constraint in (3) gives the condition that mimicry be un-profitable. It requires that Q_L not lie in an open interval of quantities. This interval is defined by the condition that if $a = a_H$ but I produces $Q_L + a_H - a_L$, so that the price is $a_L - Q_L - Q_E$, and E then exits, then I does no better than it would by having the true demand be recognized and E stay in. The optimization for I when $a = a_L$ then involves selecting the profit-maximizing output subject to this constraint.

For any given value of Q_E, the constraint and (2) give a quadratic whose solutions are $Q = a_L - (a_H/2) - (Q_E/2) \pm (\sqrt{5}a_H/6)$. Note that the interval defined by these values contains the normal Cournot best response, $(a_L - Q_E)/2$, if $3a_L > (3 - \sqrt{5})a_H$. If this condition does not hold, then

$Q_L = (a - Q_E)/2$ is optimal because mimicking the resultant price would be unprofitable if $a = a_H$: no deviation for signaling purposes is needed. Assume then that $(a_L/a_H) > (3 - \sqrt{5})/3$. Because $(a_L - Q_E - Q)Q$ is symmetric around $Q = (a_L - Q_E)/2$, the root of the quadratic which deviates less from this value actually solves (3). This is

$$Q_L = a_L - (a_H/2) - (Q_E/2) + (\sqrt{5}a_H/6). \qquad (3')$$

Solving (1), (2) and (3') then yields

$$Q_E = \frac{a_H}{3} - \frac{\sqrt{5}}{9}\rho a_H \qquad (4)$$

$$Q_H = \frac{a_H}{3} + \frac{\sqrt{5}}{18}\rho a_H \qquad (5)$$

$$Q_L = a_L + \left(\frac{(3+\rho)\sqrt{5} - 12}{18}\right)a_H \qquad (6)$$

Note that the Cournot solution, which would obtain if E placed probability ρ on $a = a_L$ and the firms were competing for only one period (or predation were otherwise ruled out), is

$$Q_E^* = \frac{\rho a_L + (1 - \rho)a_H}{3},$$

$$Q_H^* = \frac{(2 - \rho)a_H - \rho a_L}{6} = \frac{a_H}{3} + \frac{\rho(a_H - a_L)}{6},$$

$$Q_L^* = \frac{(3 - \rho)a_L - (1 - \rho)a_H}{6} = \frac{a_L}{3} - \frac{(1 - \rho)(a_H - a_L)}{6}$$

where, for non-negativity, we need $\rho > (a_H - 3a_L)/(a_H - a_L)$. Thus, although Q_L exceeds the Cournot best response of $(a_L - Q_E)/2$, it is not automatic that $Q_L > Q_L^*$ or that the price when $a = a_L$ is lower due to predation. However, Q_L does exceed Q_L^* if $a_H(3 - \sqrt{5}) < 3a_L$, which we already saw was necessary for signaling. Further, with this condition both the price when $a = a_L$ and the entrant's output are definitely lower as a result of the expansion of the incumbent's quantity. Finally, it is worth noting that Q_H exceeds Q_H^* and that the price rises when $a = a_H$ relative to the no-predation, Cournot benchmark. This is easily seen by noting that (2) gives I's best response when $a = a_H$ in either circumstance. With $Q_E < Q_E^*$, this means I's output is higher by an amount $(Q_E^* - Q_E)/2$, so the price rises as well. This result is in contrast to standard, sequential-move signaling models, where the signaling player would be (weakly) better off for *all* values of its private information if signaling could be prevented. Here the fear of predation lowers the entrant's quantity to the benefit of the incumbent when demand is strong.

Of course, (4)–(6) can constitute an equilibrium only if the quantities and the resultant prices are all non-negative. However, the quantities will be positive so long as ρ is large enough relative to (a_H/a_L), while prices are positive if $\rho > (3\sqrt{5} - 6)/\sqrt{5} \approx 0.317$.[11]

We must also specify the beliefs to be held by E conditional on the first period price and its own choice. We make these that E assigns probability 1 to a_L if $p + Q \leq a_L - Q_L$, where Q is the quantity E chose, and probability zero to a_L if $p + Q > a_L - Q_L$. Note that these beliefs are consistent Bayesian updating given Q_L and Q_H, that the exit strategy is optimal given these beliefs, and that given them, I has no incentive to deviate from Q_H when $a = a_H$. Obviously, there is no incentive to produce more than Q_L when $a = a_L$. Thus, we have an equilibrium so long as, when $a = a_L$, I does not want to decrease its output, given that E interprets such an output as implying $a = a_H$ and so stays in.[12] This condition is[13]

$$(a_L - Q_E - Q_L)Q_L + (a_L/2)^2$$

$$\geq \max_Q (a_L - Q_E - Q)Q + \left(\frac{3a_L - a_H}{6}\right)\left[\operatorname{Max}\left(0, \frac{3a_L - a_H}{6}\right)\right].$$

This involves an unenlightening condition on (a_H/a_L) versus ρ, but holds if (a_H/a_L) is large enough relative to ρ.

The various requirements that the parameters must meet are not mutually exclusive: separating equilibrium exits for a range of parameter values. Table 1 gives the values of Q_E, Q_L and Q_H for various values of ρ and a_H, given $a_L = 1$. (Note that the linear homogeneity of (4)–(6) means that this suffices in general.) For the sake of comparison, note that for $\rho = 0.6$ and $a_H = 3$, $Q_E^* = 0.6$, $Q_L^* = 0.2$ and $Q_H^* = 1.2$, yielding prices of $P_L = 0.2$ and $P_H = 1.2$, whereas the corresponding equilibrium values are $Q_E = 0.55279$, $Q_L = 0.34164$ and $Q_H = 1.22361$, for prices of 0.10557 and 1.22360.

For extreme values of ρ and a_H/a_L, either no signaling is necessary, non-negativity is violated, or the costs of preventing mimicry are so great that the incumbent is unwilling to signal its information. In the first case Q_E^*, Q_L^* and Q_H^* constitute an equilibrium. In the other cases, if equilibrium exists it involves pooling, because any separating equilibrium involves at least as great deviations from Q_L^*. With the price being the same under both a_H and a_L, E cannot learn the demand conditions from the price and must

[11] If marginal costs were constant, positive, and equal for both firms, then this condition insures that prices exceed marginal costs. If ρ were less than 0.317, prices might still be positive, but they would be less than marginal cost.

[12] It is this that justifies I's output expansion, even though no extra exit is induced relative to Cournot equilibrium. If I reduces its output below Q_L, E sees a high price. It interprets such prices as signaling that demand is high and stays in. Thus, in this sense, I's output expansion does induce exit.

[13] Note that we specify the condition using the equilibrium value for Q_E, which in turn assumes that I will choose Q_L when $a = a_L$. This is appropriate because, if we do have an equilibrium, the entrant will expect that Q_L will be chosen when $a = a_L$, and it must make its quantity choice simultaneously with that of the incumbent, whether or not the incumbent adheres to its equilibrium strategy.

TABLE 1
Values of Q_E, Q_L, and Q_H for $a_L = 1$

a_H	$\rho = 0.4$	$\rho = 0.6$	$\rho = 0.8$
$a_H = 1.5$	0.35093	0.27639	0.20186
	0.63355	0.67082	0.70809
	0.57454	0.61180	0.64907
$a_H = 2$	0.45791	0.36852	0.26914
	0.51140	0.56109	0.61078
	0.76605	0.81574	0.86543
$a_H = 2.5$	0.58488	0.46066	0.33643
	0.38925	0.45137	0.51348
	0.95756	1.01967	1.08179
$a_H = 3.0$	0.70186	0.55279	0.40372
	0.26711	0.34164	0.41618
	1.14907	1.22361	1.29814
$a_H = 3.5$	0.81883	0.64492	0.47100
	0.14496	0.23191	0.31887
	1.34058	1.42754	1.51450

make its exit decision on its priors. Note that in this case, the incumbent must be deviating from its Cournot best-response quantity under at least one of the possible demand conditions.

Finally, we turn to the entry decision at stage zero. If the parameters allow a separating equilibrium, we assume that it will prevail in period 1. Thus, E enters if

$$[\rho(a_L - Q_L - Q_E) + (1 - \rho)(a_H - Q_H - Q_E)]Q_E$$
$$-f + (1 - \rho)[(a_H/3)^2 - f] > 0 \quad (7)$$

and will stay out if the inequality is reversed. Clearly, f may be such that entry is not worthwhile in equilibrium, even though it would be against Cournot pricing. Thus, the lower profits arising from the predation deter entry. For example, in the case $\rho = 0.6$, $a_H = 3$ discussed above, this occurs for $0.41172 < f < 0.43518$.[14]

Let us now extend the analysis to allow for multiple possible levels of the fixed cost and more than two levels of demand. With different values of f possible, the beliefs that I has concerning f during the first period become important. It seems natural to assume that entry will occur in period zero in equilibrium if f is small enough, say, when $f < f^*$. With this assumption, I's beliefs will be given by the distribution $H^*(f)$ defined by $H^*(f) = H(f)/H(f^*)$ for $f \leq f^*$ and by $H^*(f) = 1$ otherwise.

Note that with more than two values for a there are two distinct reasons for the incumbent to increase output in order to attempt to bias the estimate of a. The first is to affect the exit decision, just as above. The second is that even if E does not exit, it will produce less in the second period if it believes

[14] Note that if pooling at a very low price is expected to obtain in period 1, then entry might still be deterred, even though, were entry (mistakenly) to occur, the entrant would stay in to compete in period 2.

that a is low, and this increases the price received by I and I's profit. (For a general treatment of this effect, see Mailath, 1984.) In order to focus on the exit effect, let us first consider an alternate model in which, if the entrant stays in, it becomes informed of the true value of a, although it does not have this information when it makes its exit decision.

Given this, second period payoffs are $(a/3)^2 - f$ and $(a/3)^2$ to E and I respectively whenever E stays in (mistakenly or not) and 0 and $a^2/4$ if E exits. Now suppose that E conjectures that I is using a strategy $\tilde{q}(a)$ in the first period, where $1 - \tilde{q}'(a) > 0$. This latter condition means that E believes it can infer the value of a from observing the price and solving $p + q_E = a - \tilde{q}_I(a)$. For example, if $\tilde{q}_I(a)$ were the Cournot equilibrium quantity $(3a - E(a))/6$, where $E(a) = \int a dG(a)$, then E would estimate a as $2p + 2q_E - (E(a)/3)$, and would exit if this were less than $3\sqrt{f}$. If I's actual output is q, then $p = a - q - q_E$, and E's actual estimate of a would be $\hat{a} = 2a - 2q - E(a)/3$. This estimate is correct only if q actually equals $(3a - E(a))/6$, the conjectured strategy.

More generally, let $\tilde{r}(a) = a - \tilde{q}_I(a)$ and $\tilde{s}(a) = \tilde{r}^{-1}(a)$. Then, if the possible levels of a form a continuum and $\tilde{s}$ is differentiable, we have $\tilde{s}'(a) = 1/(1 - \tilde{q}'(a))$. In any case, E's estimate, given $\tilde{q}_I(\cdot)$, is $\hat{a} = \tilde{r}^{-1}(p + q_E) = \tilde{r}^{-1}(a - q) = \tilde{s}(a - q)$ and E exits if $(\tilde{s}(a - q)/3)^2 < f$. We can now write I's optimization problem: for each a, select $q = q(a)$ to maximize

$$(a - \tilde{q}_E - q)q + \int_0^{(\tilde{s}(a-q)/3)^2} \frac{a^2}{9} dH^*(f) + \int_{\tilde{s}(a-q)/3)^2}^{\infty} \frac{a^2}{4} dH^*(f)$$

where $\tilde{q}_E$ is its conjecture as to $\int q_E(f) dH^*(f)$. The corresponding problem for E is to select $q_E(f)$ for each f to maximize

$$\int [(a - \tilde{q}_I(a) - q)q + \max (0, (\tilde{s}(a)/3)^2 - f)] dG(a).$$

Assuming that H^* has a density h^* and that $\tilde{s}$ is differentiable, the first-order condition for I's maximization gives, for each a,

$$a - \tilde{q}_E - 2q - \left(\frac{5a^2}{162}\right) h^* \left(\left(\frac{\tilde{s}(a - q)}{3}\right)^2\right) \tilde{s}(a - q) \frac{d\tilde{s}(a - q)}{dp} \frac{dp}{dq} = 0,$$

while the first order condition for E is

$$E(a) - E(\tilde{q}(a)) - 2q_E = 0.$$

In equilibrium, the conjectures must be correct. This means that $q_E = \tilde{q}_E$, $q(a) = \tilde{q}(a)$, and (assuming $a - q(a)$ is invertible) that E's estimate of a is correct. Substituting and using $d\tilde{s}/dp = 1/(1 - q'(a))$ then yields

$$a - q_E - 2q(a) + \frac{5a^3 h^*(a^2/9)}{162(1 - q'(a))} = 0 \qquad (8)$$

$$E(a) - E(q(a)) - 2q_E = 0. \qquad (9)$$

Note that, if $h^*(a^2/9)$ and $1 - q'(a)$ are both positive, (8) implies that $q(a)$ exceeds the Cournot best response. This simply reflects the incentive to increase output in order to influence the perception of a and the exit decision. However, by assumption $h^*(f) = 0$ for $f > f^*$, since very high cost firms do not enter. Thus, if $a > 3\sqrt{f^*}$, the first-order condition for I is simply the Cournot best response: at such high levels of a there is no possibility of inducing exit, given $f < f^*$, so there is no deviation from one-period optimizing. For $a < 3\sqrt{f^*}$, $q(a)$ should be defined by (8).

Note that (8) gives a differential equation for $q(a)$, which we can write in terms of the slope of $p + q_E = a - q(a)$ as

$$1 - q'(a) = \frac{-5a^3h^*(a^2/9)}{162(a - q_E - 2q(a))} > 0. \tag{10}$$

Solving this with (9) and using the natural boundary condition that $q(3\sqrt{f^*}) = (a - q_E)/2$ would, assuming no problems with non-negativity, yield the efficient separating equilibrium if it exists. In it, predation is practiced provided demand is low enough. Further, since $E(q(a))$ will be strictly greater than the expectation of the Cournot best response, q_E will be less than the Cournot equilibrium value, $E(a)/3$. This reduction in q_E is not sufficient to offset in expectation the larger value of I's output, so price will be lower too. Thus, first period profits for E will be lower than in Cournot equilibrium.

If we now returned to the original formulation, with a not being publicly revealed after the exit decision, the term in I's objective function reflecting its profits if E stays in becomes

$$\int_0^{(\bar{s}(a-q)/3)^2} \left(\frac{a}{2} - \frac{\bar{s}(a - q)}{6} \right)^2 dH^*(f).$$

Thus, in the first order condition we get an extra term which, in equilibrium, becomes

$$\int_0^{(a/3)^2} \frac{a}{9(1 - q'(a))} dH^*(f) = \frac{aH^*(a^2/9)}{9(1 - q'(a))}.$$

This gives an additional incentive to expand $q(a)$, so that even if $h^*(a^2/9)$ is zero, $1 - q'(a) > 0$ means that $q(a)$ exceeds the Cournot best-response level. As suggested above, this might be interpreted as predation aimed not at inducing exit but rather at disciplining E so that it does not produce too much in the second period.

Now, in stage zero, E must decide whether or not to enter as a function of f. It will enter as long as its expected profits are positive, which implies entry if f is less than some level f^*. With the equilibrium profits for E less than in Cournot equilibrium, f^* will be lower than the value corresponding to Cournot behavior. Thus, the credible threat of predation deters entry.

Although we have treated explicitly only the extreme cases of two levels for a and one for f and of continua for both, the pattern in this latter case will hold with general distributions for each. There will be expansion of output aimed at inducing E's exit and/or at reducing E's second-period output. This will not affect E's choices (relative to the Cournot, known-absence-of-predation benchmark) given that it has entered, but it will tend to reduce entry.

5. Related work

As a game-theoretic analysis of one firm's signaling private information that is relevant to another's decision whether to be an active competitor, the model in this paper derives from and shares many of the features of the Milgrom-Roberts (1982a) analysis of limit pricing.[15] The incentives for I to expand output to try to make E believe that demand (or cost) is low when it actually is high, the resultant incentives to increase output to deter mimicry when demand is low, the failure of this behavior to bias E's inferences in equilibrium, and the consequent failure in separating equilibrium to change E's decision from what it would be if I were known to be following short-run maximizing behavior are all features of the Milgrom-Roberts model. The present analysis does incorporate two important novel features, however.[16]

The first, less significant of these is that E does not directly observe I's choice, but only a function of it and I's private information. Thus, the model combines aspects of both hidden knowledge (the usual factor in signaling models) and hidden actions.[17] The second factor is that the signal recipient, E, chooses its output simultaneously with I in the first round. This means that I's optimal choice as a function of its private information depends on E's action. As a consequence, even when demand is at its highest level, in separating equilibrium I does not produce its simple Cournot output, although (with only two values for a or with a known after the exit decision) it does make its Cournot best response to E's output. However, the latter is reduced in response to I's deviation from Cournot behavior when demand is weak, so that I's best response when demand is high involves a larger output than in Cournot equilibrium. The second effect of the simultaneity is that the separating equilibrium quantities depend on

[15] While that study took I's private information to be the level of its marginal cost, the analysis would not be substantially changed if, instead, the private information were about the level of demand (see Matthews and Mirman, 1983). Also, as noted above, the present analysis would go through if I had positive, privately known marginal costs.

[16] Milgrom-Roberts also assumed that all information became public once the participation decision was made. This eliminated the incentive discussed above to attempt to bias E's estimation in order to affect its output choice if it was active in the second period. See Roberts (1985) for a discussion of the effect of relaxing this assumption in the limit pricing model.

[17] Matthews and Mirman (1983) and Saloner (1982) consider versions of the Milgrom-Roberts model in which the observed price is a stochastic function of the incumbent's unobserved quantity choice. Thus, they have both hidden knowledge and hidden action, but typically it will be impossible in their models to determine I's private information from observing the price.

E's prior beliefs about I's information because these determine its best response function. In contrast, the separating equilibrium choices in standard signaling models are independent of the signal recipient's priors.

The present analysis may also be usefully compared with other information-based models of predation. The first of these to appear were the Kreps-Wilson (1982a) and Milgrom-Roberts (1982b) reputation models, in which the incumbent reacts aggressively to the entry of a particular challenger in order to build a reputation as a predator which will discourage further entry. These models rely on the incumbent facing multiple challenges and can best be interpreted in terms of multi-market situations, whereas predation arises here in the context of a single market. These reputation for toughness models also involve the incumbent's predatory activities being observable to potential entrants. While this does not imply that courts operating under rules of evidence can determine that predation has been practiced, the need to have potential entrants observe an aggressive response would seem risky if predation is illegal.

This point was noted by Easley, Masson and Reynolds (1985), who consider situations where the incumbent's action is unobservable and the profitability of entry is private information to the incumbent. In these aspects, their analysis and the present one coincide, and both lead to predation in which the entrant attempts to make market conditions appear bad. However, as in the reputation for toughness models, the motive for predation in a particular market in Easley-Masson-Reynolds is the desire to protect other markets from entry, and the equilibrium involves firms whose markets are attractive for entry successfully mimicking those whose markets are unprofitable.[18] These features both contrast with the current model.

The signal-jamming model of Fudenberg and Tirole (1985) has several aspects in common with the present model: a single-market setting, unobservable actions, an incentive to lower price to make exit seem the more profitable course, and no impact in equilibrium of the predation on exit but reduction in entry due to the credible threat of predation. The chief difference is that the incumbent in Fudenberg-Tirole has no private information; rather, the two firms are equally informed about the random parameter[19] that determines the relative profitability of exit. This means that the incumbent's predatory output-expansion is independent of the value of profitability parameter, whereas here I's choice is conditioned on this variable. Consequently, price is lower whether demand is high or low in their model, whereas here price may be higher than in Cournot equilibrium when demand is high.

---

[18] An open question is whether such pooling would survive in the Easley-Masson-Reynolds analysis if firms whose markets are unattractive were allowed a choice in their pricing which would permit them then to distinguish themselves.

[19] In Fudenberg-Tirole this is the level of E's fixed cost, and E observes only its profit net of these costs.

The model which is closest to the present one is that presented by Saloner (1985). He considers a three-stage game between I and E. In the first period, I and E select quantities, with I's marginal costs being private information. The second stage models merger or acquisition negotiations between I and E, with I making a take-it-or-leave-it offer to E. If I acquires E, I earns monopoly profits in the third period, while if the offer is rejected, the two again pick quantities simultaneously and independently. Because E's profits in the third stage are positively related to I's costs, the probability that E assigns to low costs influences the price it will accept at the second stage to be acquired. This gives two reasons for I to increase output in the first period so as to signal low costs. First, a perception of low costs means that a merger can be effected on better terms to I. Second, even if the merger fails, perceived low costs benefit I in the third stage competition. The chief technical difference between Saloner's model and the one presented here is that Saloner's involves only hidden information, rather than both hidden information and hidden actions. On the economic side, his treatment focuses on merger as the means of exit. Otherwise, the two analyses have much in common.

Finally, the models of Benoit (1985) and Fudenberg and Tirole (1985) which focus on the effects of financial constraints involve quite different forms of informational asymmetries from those considered here. In the Fudenberg-Tirole formalization of the long-purse story, the key is an informational asymmetry between the prey and outside sources of financing. This prevents the former from obtaining financing for continued operation if the predator has imposed sufficient losses on the prey to lower its capital below some critical level. In this model, predation actually induces extra exit. In Benoit's model, which involves many periods, I is not sure whether E is committed to staying in the market until bankrupted. Absent such uncertainty, a financially constrained E would never enter so long as I is willing to fight one period in order to enjoy monopoly profits ever after. With the asymmetry, E enters, mimicking the behavior of a committed entrant. With positive probability, predation ensues and leads eventually to exit.

6. Conclusion

Recognition of informational asymmetries and the options for strategic behavior that they create has, in the last five years, permitted development of a number of models in which a predatory strategy will be adopted in equilibrium by rational firms. I have developed one such model here. The results of this body of work call into question the McGee arguments that predation is not likely to be consistent with maximizing behavior. At the same time, they also cast doubt upon the validity of many of the legal tests for predation that have been proposed, because the form of predation these models generate need involve no post-entry output expansion and no pricing below marginal costs. Many of these models also suggest that no extra exit is induced by predation, and that incumbents lower prices only because otherwise their prey will interpret the high prices as a sign of weakness and will stay in the market when exit is actually optimal. Yet the predatory behavior is not benign, because the rational anticipation of low prices may deter entry which would be socially desirable and would occur if predation were effectively proscribed.

While these results probably provide a basis for rejecting the presumption that predation will be rarely adopted, it seems premature to draw very definite policy conclusions from them. The results of information-based models are quite sensitive to aspects of the modeling that might, *a priori*, be viewed as elements of the "fine structure." Consequently, unless we are sure we have captured all the relevant strategic options available to firms in the actual situation being examined, we ought not to place as great confidence in intuition derived from such models as we otherwise might. For example, extending our model to require the incumbent to make an output decision before the entry stage would lead to limit pricing as in Milgrom-Roberts (1982a). If there were a separating equilibrium at this stage and if entry still occurred, there would be no predatory expansion of output. On the other hand, both limit pricing and predatory pricing might emerge if there were less-than-perfect separation at the pre-entry stage. Given that incumbents actually do have the option of limit pricing, until we analyze such a model it seems rash to assert to the world that real firms will practice predation for the sort of reasons studied here.

Stanford University, USA

REFERENCES

BENOIT, J.-P. (1984) "Financially Constrained Entry in a Game with Incomplete Information," *RAND Journal of Economics* 15, 490–499.

CHO, IN-KOO and KREPS, D. (1986) "Signaling Games and Stable Equilibria," mimeo, Stanford University Graduate School of Business.

EASLEY, D., MASSON, R. and REYNOLDS, R. (1985) "Preying for Time," *Journal of Industrial Economics* 33, 445–460.

FUDENBERG, D. and TIROLE, J. (1983) "A Theory of Exit in Oligopoly," Technical Report 429, Stanford University Institute for Mathematical Studies in the Social Sciences, Economics Series.

—— (1985) "Predation without Reputation," Working Paper 377, Massachusetts Institute of Technology, Department of Economics.

KOHLBERG, E. and MERTENS, J.-F. (1984) "On the Strategic Stability of Equilibria," Working Paper 1-785-012, Harvard University Graduate School of Business Administration.

KREPS, D. (1984) "Signaling Games and Stable Equilibria," Research Paper 758, Stanford University Graduate School of Business.

KREPS, D. and WILSON, R. (1982a) "Reputation and Imperfect Information," *Journal of Economic Theory* 27, 253–279.

—— (1982b) "Sequential Equilibria," *Econometrica* 50, 863–894.

MAILATH, G. (1984) "The Welfare Implications of Differential Information in a Dynamic Duopoly Model," Princeton University Department of Economics, mimeo.

MATTHEWS, S. and MIRMAN, L. (1983) "Equilibrium Limit Pricing: The Effects of Private Information and Stochastic Demand," *Econometrica* 51, 981–996.

MCGEE, J. (1958) "Predatory Price Cutting: The Standard Oil (N.J.) Case," *Journal of Law and Economics* 1, 137–169.

—— (1980) "Predatory Pricing Revisited," *Journal of Law and Economics* 23, 289–330.

MILGROM, P. and ROBERTS J. (1982a) "Limit Pricing and Entry under Incomplete Information: An Equilibrium Analysis," *Econometrica* 50, 443–459.

—— (1982b) "Predation, Reputation, and Entry Deterrence," *Journal of Economic Theory* 27, 280–312.

—— (1984) "Price and Advertising Signals of Product Quality," Research Paper 742, Stanford University Graduate School of Business. Forthcoming, *Journal of Political Economy*, 1986.

ROBERTS, J. (1985) "Battles for Market Share: Incomplete Information, Aggressive Strategic Pricing, and Competitive Dynamics," Research Paper 827, Stanford University Graduate School of Business.

SALONER, G. (1982) "Dynamic Equilibrium Limit-Pricing," Chapter 2 of *Essays on Information Transmission Under Uncertainty*, Ph.D. dissertation, Stanford University Graduate School of Business.

—— (1985) "Predation, Mergers and Incomplete Information," Working Paper 383, Massachusetts Institute of Technology Department of Economics.

CAPITAL COMMITMENT AND PROFITABILITY: AN EMPIRICAL INVESTIGATION*

By PANKAJ GHEMAWAT and RICHARD E. CAVES

ONE novel element of the 'new industrial economics' is its emphasis on the dynamic aspects of competition. Dynamization has forced a clear distinction between ongoing costs and sunk costs; concurrently, there has been a upsurge of theoretical interest in how the opportunity to sink costs might affect market conduct. Relatively few researchers, however, have attempted to trace the impact of sunk costs all the way through to market performance. We aim to accomplish part of that task here by examining how sunkenness influences profitability.

Two different strands of theoretical work are pertinent to our mission. The first one is the theory of entry (or mobility) deterrence; it has explored how incumbents can render entry unprofitable and generate rents for themselves by investigating in sunk costs. The second strand is the theory of supergames, which has focussed on interactions among incumbents; sunk costs matter within its domain because they reduce incumbents' security levels, potentially shrivelling their rents.

In addition to opposed predictions about how the overall scope for commitment opportunities (measured by the fixed-capital intensity of production processes) will influence profitability, these two distinct lines of theoretical development also predict diverse interactions among commitment opportunities and the elements of market structure that govern their use. We employ this diversity in a cross-sectional statistical research design aimed at assaying the relative weights of the deterrence and supergame (or strategic interaction) theories.

Section I of the paper sets forth the theoretical background for this research. The statistical model is presented in Section II and its results are analyzed in Section III. Section IV summarizes the conclusions from the exercise.

I. Theoretical background

Capital-intensity can affect profitability because, in uncontestable markets, it offers firms the opportunity to make binding commitments of resources. It does so by tilting the cost structure of production from ongoing towards sunk costs: firms that compete in capital-intensive industries typically have to shoulder large, unrecoverable outlays of capital in advance of production decisions. Theory suggests that this will affect both the

* We are indebted to Robert D. Buzzell and the Strategic Planning Institute for access to the data used in this project, to Alejandro Jadresic for research assistance, and to the General Electric Foundation for support.

condition of entry into a market and the interactions among the firms that do choose to enter. These two mechanisms have been addressed, respectively, by work on entry deterrence and on supergames.

Let us start with the entry deterrence story. Its essence can be captured in a simple example (adapted from Salop (1979). Consider two polar production technologies: technology 1 is a capital-extensive one in which all costs are related to *per period* production levels,[1] whereas technology 2 is so capital-intensive that all costs are incurred in advance of the actual production decision. In the assumed absence of other deterrence instruments (such as investments in brand franchise or innovation), an incumbent using technology 1 cannot credibly precommit itself to production levels in advance of a challenger's decision to enter; however, an incumbent using technology 2 can. The ability to make binding commitments can, in turn, affect the challenger's incentive to enter. Given technology 1, the challenger decides to enter as long as the net present value of the profits allotted to it by the rules of the post-entry game, V_1, in greater than zero. But with technology 2, the incumbent has the option of increasing its output beyond the level consistent with a payoff of V_1 to the challenger. Because of the incumbent's ability to precommit to the enhanced level of output, the challenger *must* accept the shrivelling of its payoff to $V_2(< V_1)$; it will not enter if V_2 is less than zero. The only remaining question is whether the incumbent will find it profitable to exclude multiple challengers; given the extreme sunkenness of costs embodied in technology 2, the answer is affirmative so long as industry joint profits are maximized with just one firm.

Two additional points are worth noting. First, the ability to make binding commitments is *necessary* for incumbents to earn positive (economic) profits; in its absence, the logic of contestability decrees that profits will be driven down to zero. (Baumol, Panzar and Willig (1982)). Second, the *magnitude* of sunk costs helps determine the profits that can be generated through preemption; usually, their net present value cannot exceed the irreversible capital cost of a firm of minimal efficient scale (Schmalensee (1981)). In summary, these considerations of entry deterrence lead us to expect a positive correlation between capital-intensity and profitability.

Our example of entry deterrence allotted one firm (the incumbent) a first-mover advantage; what happens if both firms move simultaneously—as might be expected of extant competitors? Define another technology, technology 1.5, that falls between the two extremes considered in the entry-deterrence example. Given technology 1.5, each firms that elects to compete in a particular product market has to incur costs of k in advance of actual production; however, once production begins, all of its remaining costs are incurred on a per-period basis. If the underlying basic conditions in each period remain unchanged over time (i.e., if cost and demand functions are stationary), then the game is repeated in each period and can be analyzed as a supergame (Friedman (1977)).

---

[1] The relation may be a discontinuous one; it allows, for instance, costs that are fixed per period, but not intertemporally.

TABLE 1
Payoffs to a representative competitor

		Technology 1	Technology 1.5
Pre-production Phase		0	$-k$
Production Phase	Minimum	0	0
	Maximum	V_3	V_4
Net Payoffs	Minimax	0	$-k$
	Maximum	V_3	$V_4 - k(>0)$

The analysis of supergames hinges on the Folk Theorem, which asserts that any individual rational outcome (i.e., any outcome which Pareto-dominates an individual firm's minimax point) can be sustained as a subgame—perfect equilibrium in infinitely repeated games with sufficiently little discounting.[2] The multiplicity arises from the fact that actions in repeated games are influenced by anticipated reactions and therefore by fears of retaliation.

What implications does the Folk Theorem hold for capital intensity? Table 1 suggests that for both technology 1 and technology 1.5, a representative firm's minimax payoff in the production phase is zero—it can always shut down, incurring zero losses. Maximal payoffs during the production phase may vary across the two technologies; let us normalize them so that *net* maximum payoffs are the same for technologies 1 and 1.5 ($V_3 = V_4 - k$). Now, because of the constant minimax payoffs of zero during the production phase, the *net security level* for each firms (i.e., its net minimax payoff given that it decides to participate in the industry) is less for technology 1.5 than for technology 1. Increased capital intensity has unfavorably expanded the range of potential payoffs available to a representative firm! In other words, the supergame story predicts a negative correlation between capital-intensity and profitability.[3]

Since the truth of the Folk Theorem, which underpins this prediction, is far from obvious, it is worth recasting in more intuitive terms. Interactions among oligopolists are *a priori* indeterminate in the payoffs that they generate; an upper bound is provided by joint maximization and a lower bound by cut-throat competition that cuts price to the level of on-going average cost.[4] Capital intensity can affect profitability because, despite the up-front incurral of costs, cut-throat competition *might* eliminate all future

[2] For a precise statement of the qualifications and the proof, see Fudenberg and Maskin (1984). They also show that the proof goes through if the infinite horizon is replaced by a small but suitable amount of incomplete information.

[3] Why does the shifting range of outcomes matter? Equivalently, why do firms not secure the Pareto-superior outcome (with a payoff of $V_4 - k$) irrespective of their security levels? The problem is that we are examining noncooperative rather then cooperative equilbria. Even though students of supergames usually select the Pareto-superior equilibrium point, there is no justification for this in the axioms of the noncooperative theory. Selection criteria continue to be researched. In the meantime, if we assume that all subgame-perfect equilibria are equiprobable, supergame considerations lead us to predict that capital-intensity will hurt profitability.

[4] The connection with Chamberlin's (1933, chap. 3) taxonomic approach to imperfect competition is obvious.

profits, depressing each firm's net security level. As a result, the supergame argument suggests that net profits (or profits reported on the basis of an accounting system that "capitalizes" unrecoverable expenditures instead of expensing them immediately) may decline with capital-intensity.

Additional realism can be injected into supergame analysis by grafting monitoring costs and noise onto the demand function; in their presence, firms cannot be certain whether a drop in price is due to chiselling by rivals or simply the handiwork of demand. Green and Porter (1984) derived equilibria in this setting by assuming that firms set a trigger price. If market price ever drops below the trigger level, firms 'punish' each other by increasing production to Cournot levels in the 'reversionary' period that follows. For given interest rates, trigger prices and reversionary period durations, it is possible to calculate the optimal, non-reversionary symmetric outputs. At the margin, these balance the gains from increasing production against the costs of raising the likelihood of (costly) reversionary periods. Roughly speaking, collusion (the ability to sustain payoffs in the neighborhood of V_3 or $V_4 - k$) becomes more difficult as the noise in the demand function increases. For our purposes, it is important to note how sunk costs figure in the calculus of gains and losses from 'cheating'. As capital-intensity increases and costs become increasingly sunk, ongoing costs decline. This increases the incentives to cheat by expanding output and, in consequence, depresses industry profitability.

But the available theory still does not pin down the *net* realized impact of capital-intensity on profitability. The reason is that both the entry-deterrence argument, which predicts a positive correlation, and the super-game argument, which predicts a negative one, are incomplete. Models of entry deterrence typically assume very strong economies of scale, invoke (often without explanation) first-mover advantages and simplify conduct by restricting its dimensions (Fudenberg and Tirole (1983); Gilbert and Harris (1984)). In contrast, supergame models allow competitors a richer array of moves and countermoves but assume the number of competitors and (sometimes) the amount of precommitment to be set exogenously (Brock and Scheinkman (1981); Benoit and Krishna (1985)). In other words, the entry-deterrence models focus on structure and the supergame models on conduct; neither strand of work really integrates these two drivers of performance.[5]

Given the technical difficulty of effecting such an integration, this paper will proceed on an empirical tack. It will interact capital intensity with variables flagged as being important by the entry-deterrence and supergame approaches, and then trace the impact of the interactions on profitability.

---

[5] Kreps and Scheinkman's (1983) model, in which duopolists first build capacity and then engage in Bertrand competition, is only a partial exception because it relies on perfect information and makes specific assumptions about rationing schemes and conjectural variations.

The intent is not to pit the two hypotheses against each other but instead, to compare how well they explain observed patterns.

II. Statistical model

The appropriate statistical model for comparing the entry-deterrence and supergame approaches is the cross-sectional analysis of the determinants of profitability that has seen widespread use in industrial organization. It performs the desired mission of comparing the effcts of commitment opportunities on profitability in different long-run equilibria. By averaging profit rates over a period of time in each market observed and obtaining enough variance among markets in other structural elements, we should be able to assay the relative weights of the effects predicted by the deterrence and supergame models. Our basic model takes the form:

$$\text{ROI} = a_0 + a_1 K + \sum_{i=2}^{n} a_i V_i + u, \tag{1}$$

where ROI is an appropriate measure of the rate of return on investment, K is a measure of fixed-capital intensity, the other additive terms V_i are additional controls for the determinants of profit, and a_1 is an interactive coefficient of the form

$$a_1 = b_0 + \sum_{j=1}^{m} b_j V_j, \tag{2}$$

where the V_j's are interactive variables developed from corollaries of the deterrence and supergame models. This formulation captures the prediction of entry-deterrence models that profits increase with the incumbents' substantive opportunities to precommit (the V_j's) interacted with the technical scope for precommitted outlays (measured by K); the negative effect of strategic interactions on profits depends similarly on opportunities to take part in commitment races interacted with the scope for commitment.

Before developing these hypotheses, we find it helpful to describe the data base used for the test. The PIMS data base of the Strategic Planning Institute contains a large number of observations on individual businesses that operate in narrowly defined industries. Each of these businesses, individual components of (mostly) large enterprises, contributes to the data base a large number of observations on its own activities and on the performance and structure of the market in which it operates. The data are prepared by the business's managers on the basis of detailed instructions from the Strategic Planning Institute. In the research data base, those variables that normally vary substantially from year to year (such as profitability) are expressed as averages for the four most recent years available. The market in which the business competes, defined by the respondent managers, is no wider than a four-digit industry in the United

States Standard Industrial Classification, and apparently is in many cases distinctly narrower.

Any prefabricated data base has both its strengths and weaknesses. For the project at hand, the PIMS data base offers several considerable advantages. Its businesses typically hold rather large shares of their markets and operate in· quite concentrated industries. The mean share of the business in our sample is 26 percent, and the mean value of the four-firm concentration ratio is 92. This is helpful because both the entry deterrence and supergame approaches assume that incumbent firms recognize that they have strategic leverage. A second advantage is that the data base affords a large number of degrees of freedom. Our research sample is confined to manufacturing businesses operating principally in North America; it is also restricted to businesses classified as manufacturing producers' nondurable goods, for which plant capacity decisions should be central strategic variables. Yet the data base still provides 274 observations. A third advantage, as will be seen below, is that PIMS contains variables that are not otherwise readily available or easy to measure, yet which can reasonably be assessed by the respondent managers. The chief disadvantage is that the unit of observation is the business rather than the industry. We do not observe the profit rates of the whole set of interacting market incumbents, only that of the reporting business. We must assume that, after controlling for important specific characteristics of the business (such as its market share), its residual profit rate departs only randomly from the average for all business competing in its market. The same assumption is made for some structural variables that are observed for the business.

The dependent variable is measured as net income before taxes divided by average invested capital. It is adjusted for inflation by applying corrections for price-level changes to depreciation, inventories, working capital, and the net book value of plant and equipment. The adjustment to inventories takes account of the inventory valuation method used by the business.[6] Other variables used in the analysis will be defined below as we develop our substantive hypotheses.

Interactive variables

The measure of capital-intensity used as the fulcrum for this analysis employs as its numerator the net book value of the business's plant and equipment, adjusted to current replacement value and corrected for its current rate of plant utilization. We may normalize this measure of fixed capital by using either value added or net sales in the denominator. We could in fact not discern a clear case for employing the one or the other. The importance of capital relative to other primary factors of production captures

---

[6] This correction seems particularly important for our investigation because the effect of inflation on reported profits is not independent of the business's capital intensity. A corresponding correction will be employed in measuring of capital-intensity itself.

the conventional sense of the importance of capital in the production process. However, the strategic importance of capital as a committed input would seem to depend on capital's importance relative to the market value of output. Rather than try to judge their competing merits, we simply carry through the analysis with two capital-intensity measures, adjusted fixed capital divided by value added (KA) and the same numerator divided by value of net sales (KS).

These measures of capital-intensity were interacted with a number of other variables that seem consistent with the implications of the deterrence and supergame models (the V_j's in equation (2)). The first of these is the lumpiness of additions to capacity in the business's market, indicated by

LUMP = ratio of minimum standard capacity increase in this industry
         to size of the market served by the business.

If capacity can be added only discontinuously and in large units, the effects of capital-intensity as a deterrent to entry should be intensified. This is the classic barrier to entry dependent on the infeasibility of small-scale entry for its effect.[7] The deterrence model thus predicts a positive influence of LUMP, interacted with K, on profitability. In the context of supergames, the lumpiness of an important choice variable reduces the number of 'balanced temptation' equilibria available to sustain tacit collusion— implying a negative influence for LUMP.[8]

The lumpiness of investment has been scaled to the size of the served market, but its influence may also be contingent on other features of the surrounding market. One of these is the unpredictability of the level of demand or, more generally, the realized state of nature. For a risk-averse incumbent, market uncertainty generally reduces the value of the expected payout of capital commitments to deter entry (Spence (1979); Porter and Spence (1982)). The variable that we employ for the interaction with LUMP is:

UNC = variability of demand over a ten-year period, measured by the
        average of absolute values of percentage differences from
        an exponential trend.

Because supergame analysis a la Green and Porter (1984) predicts that uncertainty will depress profitability independently of plant-capacity decisions, we also included UNC interacted with capital-intensity but not with lumpiness.

---

[7] Schmalensee (1981) and Gilbert (1983) have argued that this minimum efficient addition to capacity must be quite substantial for the barrier to generate appreciable monopoly rents for incumbents.

[8] By the "balanced temptation" property, we mean identical incentives for each player to cooperate rather than cheat. In the context of a capacity expansion game, balanced temptation will ensue if equally efficient firms have identical amounts of capacity on stream. Maintaining this state is likely to be less of a problem when new capacity is not lumpy, for it can then be split up more or less equally among the incumbents. For a lengthier discussion and some related evidence, see Scherer et al. (1975, ch. 3).

Another variable with which the lumpiness of capacity additions may interact is the rate of growth of the served market. In the case of entry deterrence, conflicting predictions are obtained. Nakao (1980) showed that under certain conditions the profitability of entry-threatened incumbents will increase with the rate of demand growth. On the other hand, if growth is slow enough, the incumbent is spared the need to make deterring investments with marginal profitability less than the average profitability of the incumbent's plants (Gilbert and Harris (1984)). The effect of growth on the strategic interactions among incumbents should be to raise profits by making it easier, for any given degree of lumpiness, to split capacity additions equally among industry participants—preserving the balanced temptation property and fostering collusion. The variable by which we divide LUMP is:

GROW = exponential growth rate computed for total sales in the served market over a ten-year period.

GROW, uninteracted with lumpiness, should increase profitability on considerations of strategic interaction by raising the payout to cooperative behavior,[9] but its sign is not predictable on considerations of entry deterrence.

Commitment depends not only on the extent to which costs are incurred in advance of production but also on technical factors determining the degree to which costs can be avoided in the short run through reducing the rate of production. These are the factors that determine the shape of the short-run marginal cost curve in the neighborhood of a firm's preferred operating rate. A given capacity commitment binds a firm to produce a larger output subsequently (in any given state of the market) the more inflexible is its plant's output rate. Therefore, inflexibility interacted with capital-intensity should increase profitability if it amplifies incumbents' ability to deter entry, but reduce profitability by pushing incumbents to increase output to noncooperative (reversionary) levels. Our indicator of inflexibility is a simple one:

INFLX = sum of percentages of the reporting business's output produced on assembly lines and by continuous processes.

We assume that these production technologies are less flexible than the remaining categories of customized and batch production.

Market demand elasticity is another influence that should interact with the scope for capital commitment. For purposes of entry deterrence, the less elastic is market demand, the smaller is the capacity that suffices to make entry unprofitable, and the higher should be the profits of the incumbent. With regard to strategic interactions among incumbents, inelasticity lessens

---

[9] Bradburd and Caves (1982) found that the predictable component of the served market's growth wields a positive influence on the profit rates of concentrated industries, a pattern that is consistent with this hypothesis.

the incentive to cheat but also lowers profits in the reversionary state following a breakdown of cooperation. For a class of supergame models studied by Porter (1983), the *net* impact of inelasticity on profitability is negative. The only available proxy is

INLST = an approximately linear function of the share that expenditures on products of the types sold by the reporting business make up of total expenditures by end users.

The inelasticity of demand should increase with this variable, on the familiar rule of derived demand. Therefore, INLST should be positively related to profitability via the effects of entry deterrence, negatively related through the effects of strategic interaction.

Although our model focuses on capital commitment, that is not the only instrument that a business can use to make a strategic commitment. The businesses in our sample are (mostly) components of much larger companies. Commitments can be effected through organizational linkages between the observed business and other parts of the company, in that the curtailment of the business's output would force the enterprise to incur costs of adjustment and reorganization in the balance of its activities, effectively enlarging the sunk costs associated with the business at hand. Such linkages should hence increase the profitability of resources committed to the business insofar as they tend to deter entry, but reduce them by lowering market participants' net security levels. Many forms of linkage may exist between a business and its parent enterprise, but the two that seem to hold the strongest potential for commitment are:

BWDI = fraction of purchased inputs of this business bought from other components of the same company.
FWDI = fraction of sales by this business made to components of the same company.

BWDI and FWDI, interacted with capital-intensity, should be related positively to profitability through the mechanism of entry deterrence, but negatively related through strategic interaction.[10]

Product differentiation should influence the strategic interaction of incumbents and also play a role in entry deterrence. By reducing cross-elasticities of demand between incumbents, structural differentiation of the product reduces the payout to cheating and thus improves the chances for cooperation to prevail. Any effect of product differentiation on profitability through entry deterrence depends on specific mechanisms and opportunities: a conjunction of scale sensitivity and some form of first-mover advantage. Without this conjunction, however, structural heterogeneity may

---

[10] Caves and Porter (1976) found limited evidence to support the hypothesis that these vertical linkages within the enterprise reduce the propensity of the business to exit in the face of unexpectedly low profits.

reduce the profitability of incumbents by multiplying the bases for competitive entry threats (Gilbert and Newbery (1982); also see Yip (1982)). Using the PIMS data base we could not generate a single structural indicator of differentiation, and so were forced to employ several incommensurable variables:

MKTG = total marketing outlays (media advertising, other advertising and promotion, sales force) as a percentage of sales revenue of the reporting business.

AUXL = index of the importance of auxiliary services (such as installation, repair, customer education) to end users.

R & D = expenditures by the reporting business on product research and development as a percentage of its sales revenue.

Interacted with capital-intensity, these three variables should wield a positive effect on profitability by promoting cooperative interactions among incumbents. No clear prediction emerges from the entry deterrence mechanism.

The remaining interactive variables deal with the number of competitors in the market (both sellers and buyers). Seller concentration interacted with the scope for capital commitment should be positively related to opportunities for profits through entry deterrence because entry barriers are in general a collective good, and concentration helps to deter free-riding in their provision. It should also increase profits through strategic interaction because the expected payout to cheating by expanding output decreases with market share—and hence with concentration as an indicator of average share. We use the customary

C4 = share of sales in the served market accounted for by the responding business and its three largest competitors.[11]

A positive influence for C4 interacted with capital-intensity is the outcome predicted by each of our lines of analysis.

Buyer concentration should affect the strategic interaction among incumbents by making it more difficult to maintain a cooperative arrangement. Various mechanisms serve to generate this prediction, a familiar one being Stigler's (1964) model of buyer concentration as a factor that reduces the ability of tacitly colluding sellers to detect cheating by their competitors. No correspondingly clear prediction seems to link buyer concentration to entry deterrence or the structural condition of entry. The PIMS data base contains an inverse measure of buyer concentration:

BNC = the number of the largest immediate customers accounting for 50 percent of the sales of the reporting business.

[11] Because the mean share of the reporting business in our sample is 26 percent, there will be few cases in which the reporting business is in fact not one of the four largest. Because of the focus on strategic interactions, it did not seem appropriate to adjust this concentration ratio for import competition or other such factors that are otherwise employed to adjust the concentration ratio as an indicator of market power.

BNC interacted with capital-intensity should be positively related to profitability through its effect on the strategic interactions of incumbents.[12]

Other exogenous variables

The model is completed by several variables that should affect the profitability of the reporting business independently of its opportunities to make strategic commitments of resources. The first of these is the market share of the reporting business. Although the normative significance of the relationship is subject to controversy, there is widespread agreement that a business's profit increases with its market share as a reflection of underlying elements of luck, still, or strategic pre-emption (mobility barriers). Despite the fact that industry-wide data show no significant increase of profits with share in most industries (Caves and Pugel (1980)), we do expect a positive influence on balance. The variable employed is

SHARE = average percentage share of the served market accounted for by the reporting business.

Although seller and buyer concentration have already been introduced for interaction with capital-intensity, their potential influence is not entirely predicted on the availability of commitment opportunities. With SHARE in the model, care must be exercised in defining seller concentration so as to avoid overlap in the two variables. We define

CON = combined market share of the respondent's three largest rivals (expressed as a percentage) divided by 100— SHARE.

This formulation expresses the three leading rivals' actual combined share as a fraction of its maximum possible value given SHARE. The complexities of coupling SHARE and CON as regressors do not end here. The customary prediction that profitability increases with concentration, and thus with both variables, need not hold when the reporting business is a dominant firm. A dominant firm's profits may well be lower if it has substantial rivals than if it shares the market with a competitive fringe.[13] This consideration suggests that the slope coefficient of CON should be allowed to differ depending on whether SHARE is below (CONLS) or

---

[12] Many of the effects predicted by the supergame hypothesis are underpinned by a previous empirical study. Smith (1981) quizzed corporate planning directors on their level of concern that the industry-wide capacity expansion might break down. Translating the variables that he employed into our own framework, he found that planners' anxieties on this score were significantly fuelled by UNC and INFLX but alleviated by C4. LUMP also increased the level of concern, and GROW and his product differentiation proxy reduced it, but these latter effects did not quite achieve statistical significance.

[13] Kwoka (1979) found that the profit rate of an industry decreases with the shares of firms ranked below the second in size.

above (CONHS) its mean value of 26 percent. We expect a positive coefficient for CONLS but make no sign prediction for CONHS.

A final issue concerning market structure, mentioned above, is whether buyer concentration should influence profitability interactively with seller concentration but independently of commitment opportunities. For a test, we employed the variable RELCON = C4 · BNC, embodying the hypothesis that profitability depends jointly on producer concentration and the absence of substantial buyer concentration.

The last additive variable is capacity utilization. Low utilization implies low profits whether it results from an unexpectedly unfavorable state of demand or from strategic investments in entry deterrence. The PIMS data base contains

> UTIL = average percentage of standard capacity of the reporting business utilized during the four-year observation period.

The variable should wield a positive influence on profitability.

This list of additive regressors completes the cross-sectional model; we should, however, explain the omission of a few candidates suggested by previous studies. Because the sample is confined to markets for producers' nondurable goods, product-differentiation barriers to entry should not arise, and other variables traditionally associated with structural barriers have been specified to interact with capital-intensity. International competition is neglected: potential import competition is covered in the analysis of entry deterrence; actual import competition is neglected on the assumption that mutual dependence among rivals is normally recognized more fully within than between national markets.

III. Statistical results

The results of estimating the model that we have laid out appear in Table 1. Two columns at the left summarize the signs predicted for the variables; in this summary we distinguish between ambiguous predictions (±) and no predictions at all (?). Two regression equations each are presented for capital-intensity measured by sales (KS) and value added (KA).

The model explains about 30 percent of the variance of profitability. The performance of the interactive variables as a group is not particularly strong. Added jointly to a basic specification that consists of only the additive variables and KS (KA), they do not contribute significantly to the variance explained by the model. However, some arresting results do appear.

First, the basic influence of capital-intensity on profitability is clearly negative; the significant negative coefficient persists whether the interactive variables are included or excluded. This result supports the strategic-interactions approach rather convincingly. We should note, however, that certain statistical biases also tend to produce this result. Mismeasurement of fixed capital invested in the business produces an identical error in the

TABLE 2
Determinants of profitability of 274 producer-nondurable businesses

Exogenous variables	Sign predictions		Capital-intensity measure			
	Entry deter- rence	Stra- tegic inter- action	KS		KA	
			(1)	(2)	(3)	(4)
Interactive variables						
KS or KA	+	−	−0.197	−0.200	−9.318	−9.354
			(2.61)	(2.59)	(2.71)	(2.65)
KLUMP	+	−	0.265	0.978	8.543	2.609
			(1.28)	(0.37)	(0.94)	(0.22)
KLUMP*UNC	−	?	−0.212	—	−8.077	—
			(0.52)		(0.45)	
KUNC	?	−	—	−0.537	—	−27.440
				(0.04)		(0.55)
KLUMP/GROW	±	−	−0.868	−0.868	—	−2.320
			(0.31)	(0.31)		(0.18)
KGROW	?	+	0.334	0.285	9.622	8.080
			(2.38)	(1.10)	(1.45)	(0.71)
KINFLX	+	−	−0.067	−0.071	−2.230	−2.253
			(2.61)	(2.75)	(1.77)	(1.74)
KINLST	+	−	0.063	0.011	−0.846	−0.713
			(0.04)	(0.08)	(0.12)	(0.10)
KBWDI	+	−	−0.328	−0.329	2.088	2.272
			(0.59)	(0.59)	(0.95)	(1.01)
KFWDI	+	−	0.192	0.206	4.974	5.458
			(2.57)	(2.64)	(1.47)	(1.55)
KMKT	±	+	0.023	0.010	−3.019	−3.835
			(0.58)	(0.25)	(1.36)	(1.67)
KAUXL	±	+	0.141	0.197	1.785	1.864
			(0.76)	(1.00)	(2.14)	(2.11)
KRND	±	+	−0.142	−0.134	−9.606	−9.391
			(2.09)	(1.94)	(2.45)	(2.31)
KC4	+	+	0.107	0.103	5.522	5.155
			(1.39)	(1.29)	(1.62)	(1.47)
KBNC	?	+	−0.111	0.480	−8.037	5.114
			(1.20)	(1.68)	(1.44)	(1.23)
Additive variables						
SHARE	+		0.145	0.167	0.149	0.172
			(2.51)	(2.80)	(2.70)	(3.03)
CONLS	+		−0.259	−0.221	−0.218	−0.197
			(0.61)	(0.51)	(0.52)	(0.46)
CONHS	±		−0.132	−0.117	−0.150	−0.136
			(2.17)	(1.88)	(2.57)	(2.28)
RELCON	+		0.161	—	0.170	—
			(3.04)		(3.41)	
UTIL	+		0.190	0.176	0.198	0.180
			(3.05)	(2.78)	(3.23)	(2.90)
Constant			9.129	10.050	11.370	12.740
			(1.47)	(1.58)	(1.92)	(2.09)
R^2			0.299	0.275	0.324	0.292

Note. t-statistics appear in parentheses beneath the regression coefficients. The magnitudes of some exogenous variables have been adjusted so as to place their regression coefficients within convenient ranges of values.

numerator of the capital-intensity variable and the denominator of the dependent variable, resulting in a negative bias for the regression coefficient. Furthermore, as Scott and Pascoe (1984) pointed out, the coefficient can also be interpreted as saying that, of two otherwise identical monopolies that obtain the same rents, the one using the more capital-intensive technology will report the lower profit rate.

The significance of the interactive terms is spotty; those that do achieve significance do not uniquely support either the deterrence of the strategic-interaction approach. Forward integration does appear to be a form of commitment that deters entry, and the coefficients of KLUMP point in the same direction. However, the inflexibility of the production process wields a significant negative influence, as predicted from considerations of strategic interaction. Likewise, market growth has the positive influence predicted from strategic interaction, but its significance varies with the specification. The influence of demand uncertainty on profitability is negative, as both approaches predict, but the coefficients are not significant. Our proxy for market demand inelasticity (KINLST, share of customer's purchases) is not remotely significant, nor do commitments through backward integration have any regular influence. The product-differentiation proxies, expected to exert a positive influence on profitability by insulating strategic interactions, provide some puzzles. KAUXL behaves as expected, but the sign of KMKT is erratic, and KRND obtains a significant negative coefficient that conflicts with our expectations. That the conjunction of intensive product R&D and large commitments of capital depresses profits is a plausible consequence of strategic interaction, but the variable is clearly not filling the function that it was originally assigned.

We expected that a more concentrated group of producers would obtain higher profits from a given level of capital commitment; the results tend to support the prediction, but the coefficients are significant only at the 10 percent confidence level. We also expected that the "unconcentration" of buyers (KBNC) would raise the profitability associated with a given level of capital commitment. The results of equations (2) and (4) point in that direction. These equations omit the variable RELCON which, when included among the additive variables, indicates quite strongly that profits increase when buyers are unconcentrated relative to sellers. Thus, buyer concentration and its interaction with seller concentration apparently affect profits independently of the sellers' level of capital commitment.

Of the additive variables, SHARE takes the expected positive and significant coefficient. The concentration of the remaining sellers significantly depresses the profits of dominant firms (CONHS). However, when the reporting business holds a lower share, the concentration of the remaining sellers exerts no net additive effect.[14] Because concentration is

[14] This result holds some importance for the debate over the roles of monopoly and differential (or efficiency) rents in excess profits, as reflected by the dependence of a firm's profits on its own share and its rivals' concentration. Our results suggest that, for high-share firms, the concentration of rivals has a negative influence by impairing their ability to obtain a position of Stackelberg leadership.

also interacted with capital-intensity (KC4), its influence is split between these two variables (and, for the first and third equations, RELCON as well). The influence of capacity utilization is positive, as we expected.

IV. Summary and conclusions

Modern theoretical contributions to industrial organization have emphasized the importance of capital commitment but offered contrary predictions about its consequences for the monopoly rents that market incumbents can accumulate. Models of entry deterrence indicate that incumbents' profits may increase with the scope for capital commitments, while the theory of supergames predicts that they may decline. Overall, our statistical study of firms in concentrated producer-goods markets favors the supergame hypothesis, chiefly because profits decline with capital-intensity. We tested a number of interactive hypotheses in an attempt to discriminate more finely among conditions under which commitment opportunities would repel entrants or promote warfare among incumbents. Some proved insignificant and thus gave no support to either pattern, but the inflexibility of the production process interacted with capital-intensity as predicted by the supergame hypotheses. Other interactions, notably forward integration of the business in question, seem to balance to depict opportunities to deter entry. In accord with the predictions of both approaches, market growth and some aspects of product differentiation, interacted with capital-intensity, increase profitability.

With the negative influence of capital intensity on profits bolstering the supergame hypothesis, what do we make of the unclear results for the variables interacted with capital intensity? A consistent story would be that commitment opportunities can indeed either deter entry or promote rent-eroding races among incumbents.[15] However, which tendency prevails in a market depends on both a vector of market-structure variables and historical accidents of timing in important early moves by incumbent firms. Then a model such as ours might not suffice to detect complex interactions among variables nor to filter out the noise of historical accident. Such an interpretation invites empiricists to study intertemporal interactions in some detail for individual markets. On the other hand, it seems clearly useful to have established that neither model sweeps the other off the field in a broad cross-section of industries.

Harvard University

REFERENCES

BAUMOL, WILLIAM J., PANZAR, JOHN C. and WILLIG, ROBERT D. (1982). *Contestable Markets and the Theory of Industry Structure*. New York: Harcourt Brace Jovanovich.

---

[15] A substantial start at investigating the role of rivalry in investment decisions has been made by Gilbert and Lieberman (1985) and Lieberman (1985).

BENOIT, JEAN-PIERRE and KRISHNA, VIJAY (1985). "Dynamic Duopoly: Prices and Quantities." Working paper, Harvard Business School.

BRADBURD, RALPH M. and CAVES, RICHARD E. (1982). "A Closer Look at the Effect of Market Growth on Industries' Profits." *Review of Economics and Statistics* 64 (November): 635–45.

BROCK, WILLIAM and SCHEINKMAN, JOSE. (1981). "Price Setting Supergames with Capacity Constraints." SSRI Working Series Paper No. 8130, University of Wisconsin.

CAVES, RICHARD E. and PORTER, MICHAEL E. (1976). "Barriers to Exit." In Robert T. Masson and P. David Qualls, eds., *Essays on Industrial Organization in Honor of Joe S. Bain.* Cambridge: Ballinger Publishing Co. Pp. 39–69.

CAVES, RICHARD E. and PUGEL, THOMAS A. (1980). *Intraindustry Differences in Conduct and Performance: Viable Strategies in U.S. Manufacturing Industries.* Monograph No. 1980–2. New York: Graduate School of Business Administration, New York University.

CHAMBERLIN, EDWARD H. (1933). *The Theory of Monopolistic Competition.* Cambridge, Mass: Harvard University Press.

FRIEDMAN, JAMES W. (1977). *Oligopoly and the Theory of Games.* Amsterdam: North-Holland.

FUDENBERG, DREW and MASKIN, ERIC. (1984). "Folk Theorems for Repeated Games with Discounting and with Incomplete Information." Mimeo.

FUDENBERG, DREW and TIROLE, JEAN. (1983). "Dynamic Models of Oligopoly." Institute for Mathematical Studies in the Social Sciences, Technical Report No. 428, Stanford University.

GILBERT, RICHARD J. (1984). "Preemptive Competition." In Frank Mathewson and Joseph E. Stiglitz, eds., *New Developments in the Analysis of Market Structure,* International Economics Association, (forthcoming).

GILBERT, RICHARD J. and HARRIS, RICHARD G. (1984). "Competition with Lumpy Investment." *Rand Journal of Economics* 15 (Summer): 197–212.

GILBERT, RICHARD J. and LIEBERMAN, MARVIN B. (1985). "Investment and Coordination in Oligopolistic Industries," Working paper, Graduate School of Business, Stanford University.

GILBERT, RICHARD J. and NEWBERY, DAVID M. G. (1982). "Preemptive Patenting and the Persistence of Monopoly." *American Economic Review* 72 (June): 514–26.

GREEN, EDWARD J. and PORTER, ROBERT H. (1984). "Noncooperative Collusion under Imperfect Price Information." *Econometrica* 52 (January): 87–100.

KREPS, DAVID M. and SCHEINKMAN, JOSE A. (1983). "Quantity Precommitment and Bertrand Competition Yield Cournot Outcomes." *Bell Journal of Economics* 14 (Autumn): 326–337.

KWOKA, JOHN E., Jr. (1979). "The Effect of Market Share Distribution on Industry Performance." *Review of Economics and Statistics* 61 (February): 101–9.

LIEBERMAN, MARVIN B. (1985). "Excess Capacity, Entry, and Market Structure in the Chemical Processing Industries," Research Paper No. 830, Graduate School of Business, Stanford University.

NAKAO, TAKEO. (1980). "Demand Growth, Profitability, and Entry." *Quarterly Journal of Economics* 94 (March): 397–411.

PORTER, MICHAEL E. and SPENCE, A. MICHAEL (1982). "The Capacity Expansion Process in a Growing Oligopoly." In John J. McCall, ed., *The Economics of Information and Uncertainty.* Chicago: University of Chicago Press.

PORTER, ROBERT H. (1983). "Optimal Cartel Trigger Price Strategies." *Journal of Economic Theory* 29 (April): 313–338.

SALOP, STEVEN C. (1979). "Strategic Entry Deterrence." *American Economic Review* 69 (May): 335–338.

SCHERER, F. M., *et al.* (1975). *The Economics of Multi-Plant Operation: An International Comparisons Study.* Cambridge, Mass.: Harvard University Press.

SCHMALENSEE, RICHARD (1981). "Economies of Scale and Barriers to Entry." *Journal of Political Economy* 89 (December): 1228–38.

SCOTT, JOHN T. and PASCOE, GEORGE (1984). "Capital Costs and Profitability." *International Journal of Industrial Organization* 2 (September): 217–33.

SMITH, RICHARD L., II. (1981). "Efficiency Gains from Strategic Investment." *Journal of Industrial Economics* 30 (September): 1–23.

SPENCE, A. MICHAEL. (1979). "Investment in an Uncertain Environment." Mimeo.

STIGLER, GEORGE J. (1964). "A Theory of Oligopoly." *Journal of Political Economy* 72 (February): 44–61.

YIP, GEORGE S. (1982). *Barriers to Entry: A Corporate-Strategy Perspective*. Lexington, Mass.: Lexington Books.

STRATEGIC INVESTMENT WITH CONSISTENT CONJECTURES

By HUW DIXON

IT IS generally recognised that the flexibility of firms' production will influence the nature of competition in an industry. For example, where production is very inflexible the Cournot outcome seems most appropriate: the Bertrand outcome, however, depends on production being perfectly flexible. The model presented makes both the firms' cost structure (flexibility of production) and the nature of competition endogenous, and thus provides a framework in which both elements of industrial structure and the conduct of firms are explained. We combine two ideas in the recent literature on oligopoly theory: models of strategic investment (Brander and Spencer (1983), Dixon (1985), Eaton and Grossman (1984), Yarrow (1985) inter alia) and notions of the consistency of conjectures (Bresnehan (1981) in particular). The fundamental idea underlying this synthesis is very simple. As we discuss below, there is a precise sense in which Bresnehan's consistency condition relates firm's conjectures about each other's responses—and hence the degree of competition in the product market—to the firms cost functions. Strategic investment models, on the other hand, provide a framework for making the firm's cost functions endogenous: by choosing a level of investment, the firm decides which short-run cost function it will have. By combining the strategic investment framework with Bresnehan's consistency condition, we have a model in which both firm's cost structures and the degree of competition in the product market are endogenously determined. Thus we have a framework in which both a structural characteristic of the market (firms costs), and the conduct of firms are endogenously determined.

For a wide range of industrial processes economists since Marshall have taken the view that it is appropriate to treat the capital stock decision of firms as being taken on a different time scale to output decisions. Insofar as it is appropriate to treat capital as a fixed factor and labour as a variable factor,[1] it follows that when firms compete in the product market they treat their current capital stock as given (output decisions are taken in the long run, output and employment in the short run). The fact that the capital stock is thus committed "before" the firm makes it output decisions implies that the firm can use its investment decision *strategically*: the firm can influence the market outcome through its choice of capital stock.

This paper was awarded the P. W. S. Andrews Memorial Essay Prize for 1985. I would like to thank the Ulph Brothers for useful discussions on this subject, and the referees for their comments. Errors remain inescapably mine.

[1] This can be made a tautology if we treat the capital variable as representing fixed factors in general—including managerial services and skilled labour for example. Alternatively, investment can be interpreted as R&D expenditure as in Brander and Spencer (1983).

Several recent papers have explored the implications of strategic investment. The structure of these models is relatively simple. There are two stages, which capture the distinction between the long[2] and the short-run. In the first "strategic" stage firms choose their capital stock. In the second "market" stage a product market equilibrium occurs given the capital stocks chosen in the strategic stage. The capital stock decisions in the first stage are taken strategically in the sense that firms take into account the effect that investment will have on the outcome in the market stage. In essence, the choice of capital stock determines which short-run cost function the firm will operate on in the market stage. This can also be interpreted as the firm determining the flexibility of production which it will have in the market stage. Following Marshak and Nelson (1972), Production can be characterised as being more "flexible" the less steep the slope of the marginal cost function. For a wide class of cost functions more investment will lead to a decline in the slope of the short run marginal cost function at any given output. An overall equilibrium in the two-stage model is a Nash-equilibrium in capital stocks, since each firm's profits can be given as a function of the capital stocks chosen in the first stage.

What differentiates the models is the assumption made about the market stage, the nature of competition in the product market. Brander and Spencer (1983) explore the model with a Cournot–Nash market stage, Dixon (1985) explores the case with a competitive market stage, whilst Eaton and Grossman (1984) and Yarrow (1985) consider a general conjectural variations model (see also Bulow *et al.* (1985), and Fudenburg and Tirole (1984)). In the case of Cournot–Nash or conjectural variations in the market stage, the firm's investment decision determines the (short run) cost function that the firm will have in the market stage, and hence its reaction function in output space. Thus in essence the firms's choice of capital is ipso facto a choice of reaction function. An equilibrium in this type of strategic investment model is a Nash-equilibrium in a game where firm's strategies are reaction functions. Similarly, in the case of a competitive market stage the firm's investment decision determines its supply function in the market stage and hence we have a Nash-equilibrium in supply functions.[3]

A general (though not universal) property of these models is the phenomena of factor-bias. The strategic use of capital in the first stage means that there is an asymmetry between capital and labour. This asymmetry generally leads to a non-cost minimising capital-labour ratio. In essence, production is inefficient in the sense that firms, whilst on their short-run cost functions, are not on their long-run cost functions. This strategic inefficiency in production gives rise to a welfare loss.

The existing models of strategic investment discussed above have assumed

[2] This is not the Marshallian long run, since there is no entry.
[3] This contrasts with other models with Nash equilibria in supply functions—see Grossman (1981) and Hart (1982). These models allow for a much wider set of supply functions. The main point is that the set of admissable supply functions in Dixon (1985) is defined technologically.

a given degree of competition in the market stage: it is assumed that whilst the investment decision of firms will alter the degree of flexibility of production, this will have no effect on the nature of competition in the product market. It has been argued, however, that the nature of competition will be influenced by the degree of flexibility of production. One particularly interesting way of capturing this is to impose a consisteny condition (as in Bresnehan (1981)) in the market stage with a conjectural variation model. Loosely speaking, a consistency condition can be interpreted as requiring that firms' conjectures about each others responses equal the actual responses firms would make (given their conjectures). In the context or our model, one implication of this is that the more flexible is production, the more competitive will consistent conjectures be (see Section 1). If firms have totally inflexible production ("vertical" marginal cost) then the Cournot conjecture is consistent; if firms have perfectly flexible production ("horizontal" marginal cost) then the Bertrand conjecture is consistent; for intermediate degrees of flexibility, the conjecture will be between the Cournot and Bertrand values (see, Propositions 1–2, and also Bresnehan (1981 pp. 36–7).

In this paper, we combine the strategic investment framework with consistency of conjectures in the market stage. The firm's investment decision will determine its short run cost function, and hence its flexibility of production in the market stage. The flexibility of production then determines the nature of competition in the market stage. This enables us to capture the idea that the firm's investment decision will alter the nature of competition in the market stage, and that the degree of competition in the product market will hance become endogenous in a strategic investment model.

There are three main results in this paper. First, in equilibrium the degree of competition will lie between the Bertrand and Cournot values (Proposition 4(b)). Firms will choose to have an intermediate degree of flexibility of production. This contrasts with Dixon (1986), where with a given degree of competition firms will prefer to have totally inflexible production. Secondly, the wage-rental ratio will influence the degree of competition: a very small wage-rental ratio will lead to Cournot conjectures (see Proposition 4). Thirdly, we are able to evaluate the result that with consistent conjectures there will be no inefficiency in production (Eaton and Grossman (1984 p. 6), Yarrow (1985, Section 6)). This result is shown to hold only when conjectures are exogenous and happen to be consistent in equilibrium. When conjectures are made endogenously consistent, there will generally be factor-bias. In any symmetric equilibrium this factor-bias will lead to undercapitalisation, a capital-labour ratio below the cost minimising level (Proposition 3).

1. Investment, conjectures, and consistency

In this paper we examine a two stage model of strategic investment, where the second market stage is a conjectural variations equilibrium, as in

Eaton and Grossman (1984) and Yarrow (1985). However, unlike these papers, we make the two firms conjecture about each other's output responses endogenous, by imposing a "consistency" condition. There are several related notions of "rationality" or "consistency", which originated out of Hahn's work on conjectural equilibria (1977, 1978)—for example Bresnehan (1981), Hart (1982), Laitner (1980), Ulph (1983). In the framework adopted in this paper these differences are unimportant, although our results draw most on Bresnehan's (1981) work. We restrict our attention to a simple conjectural variations model where reaction functions are linear: consistency here means that firms know the slope of each other's reaction functions. Thus actual and conjectural responses are consistent.

In this section we explore the way in which investment influences the flexibility of production, and how this influences the nature of product market competition through consistency. Firms choose outputs x_i, and have linear conjectures about how the other firm will respond to changes in their own output. Furthermore, this conjecture does not depend on where firms are in the strategy space: that is, from whatever output firms start at, their conjectures about each other's responses are unaffected. Because of these two features—linearity and independence of initial position—firms' conjectures can be expressed as a scalar ϕ_i, which equals firm i's conjecture about j's proportional response to change in x_i, i's belief about $\mathrm{d}x_j/\mathrm{d}x_i$. If $\phi_i = 0$, $i = 1,2$, we have the Cournot model. If $\phi_i > 0$ we obtain a "collusive" model where firms tend to follow each other. If $\phi_i = -1$ and there is a homogeneous product, then we have the competitive or Bertrand model, since firm i believes any change in its own output will be exactly offset by a change in the other firm's output, so that the price is unaffected. The more negative firm i's conjecture, the more accommodating it believes the other firm to be, in the sense that firm j will reduce its output in response to an increase i's output. Given firms' conjectures about each other, we can derive their reaction functions in output space, which give their actual responses. The consistency condition requires that at the equilibrium vector of outputs, the conjectured response equals the slope of the reaction function.

There are several conceptual and technical problems with the concept of consistency. On the technical level, there are no general results about either existence or uniqueness of consistent conjectures. Furthermore, the equilibrium may not be easy to characterise (see Ulph (1983)). On the conceptual level, the conjectural variations model only allows firms to have a very specific type of conjecture: surely we would like to allow for firms to have much more general conjecture (non-linear conjectures, conjectures which allow for initial position). However, if we allow for a more general class of conjectures, the power of the consistency condition is greatly weakened: as Laitner (1980) shows, a continuum of consistent conjectural equilibria will exist (see also Boyer and Moreaux (1983)). Furthermore, it can be very reasonably argued that the conjectural variations model tries to capture in a static model what is really a dynamic problem of firms responses to each other over time. The best way to concieve of a consitent conjectural equilibrium is within a framework of instantaneous responses, where firms can respond immediately to changes in each other's output. This paper does not aim to answer or solve these issues. Rather, we make assumptions about industry demand and firms cost that overcome the technical problems, and partly alleviate the conceptual issues.

There are two firms (the results obviously generalise) $i = 1,2$, which choose outputs $x_i > 0$. They produce a homogeneous product, and there is linear demand.

A1: Industry Demand:

$$p = p^0 - \sum_{i=1}^{2} x_i$$

There are two factors of production, capital and labour. Capital is treated as fixed when output is chosen, but labour is freely varied.

A2: Technology

$$x_i = k_i^{0.5} \cdot L_i^{0.5}$$

Letting wages be the numeraire, r the rental-wage ratio, the firm's short run cost function under A1 is given by:

$$c(x_i, k_i) = r \cdot k_i + x_i^2/k_i \tag{1.1}$$

$$\frac{\partial c}{\partial x_i} = \frac{2}{k_i} \cdot x_i \tag{1.1a}$$

Thus firms have quadratic costs functions, and linear marginal cost, the slope of which is inversely related to investment. In this way the flexibility of the firms production is determined by the level of its investment. We use the term "flexibility" in the technical sense employed in the literature on competitive markets under uncertainty (Stigler (1939), Marshak and Nelson (1972), Mills (1984)). With quadratic costs, the output response of a firm to a change in price will be greater the less steep its marginal cost function is. This sensitivity of output to price is interpreted as flexibility, and defined as $\gamma = (\partial^2 c/\partial x_i^2)^{-1}$. In terms of the Marchak–Nelson definition from (1.1) more capital leads to greater flexibility of production ($\gamma = k_i/2$), since the marginal costs function becomes flatter. In essence, higher investment leads to a shift from variable to fixed costs in the market stage, and low variable costs lead to flexible production.

Given firms investment $\underline{k}$ and conjectures about each other's responses $\phi = (\phi_1, \phi_2)$ we can derive the firm's reaction function in output space. Under A1–2 the firm's profits are:

$$\Pi_i = x_i \cdot (p^0 - x_i - x_j) - rk_i - x_i^2/k_i$$

To derive the firm's reaction function in output space, treating capital as fixed, we set $\partial \Pi_i / \partial x_i = 0$, yielding:

$$x_i = r_i(x_j, k_i, \phi_i) = \frac{p^0 - x_j}{2 + \phi_i + 2/k_i} \qquad (1.2)$$

where $i, j = 1, 2$, $i \neq j$. The reaction function is linear in x_j, with slope:

$$\frac{\mathrm{d}r_i}{\mathrm{d}x_j} = \frac{-1}{2 + \phi_i + 2/k_i} \qquad (1.3)$$

The consistency condition requires that the actual responses equal the conjectural responses, $\phi_i = \mathrm{d}r_j/\mathrm{d}x_i$, which under A1–2 yields the two equations:

$$\phi_i(2 + \phi_j + 2/k_j) + 1 = 0 \qquad i,j = 1,2, \, i \neq j \qquad (1.4)$$

Under A1–2, firms have linear reaction functions, and the consistency condition seems particularly appropriate. Although consistency only requires the conjecture to equal the slope of the reaction function at a point, with linear reaction functions this is equivalent to each firm knowing the whole of the other firm's reaction function. Also, since the reaction functions are linear, we don't need to solve for the equilibrium outputs to solve for consistent conjectures, as is clear from (1.4). By convention, we let $\phi_i = 0$ whenever $k_j = 0$.

What is the relationship between consistent conjectures and the capital stocks $\underline{k}$? From (1.4) it is clear that consistency implies that $\phi_i < 0$ whenever $\underline{k} \gg 0$. In addition to (1.4) we have the second order conditions for the reaction function:

$$\phi_i > -(1 + 1/k_i) \qquad i = 1, 2 \qquad (1.5)$$

Equations (1.4) and (1.5) define uniquely the consistent conjectures:

Proposition 1: Let $\underline{k} \gg 0$. There exist unique consistent conjectures

$$\phi_i \in (-1, 0) \qquad i = 1, 2$$

(all proofs are in the appendix.)

Thus, for $\underline{k} \gg 0$, the consistent conjectures are between the Bertrand value -1 and the Cournot value 0.[4] Let the implicit function defined by (1.4) be $\phi : [0, \infty)^2 \rightarrow (-1, 0]^2$ where:

$$\phi_i = \phi_i(\underline{k}) \qquad (1.6)$$

Total differentiation of (1.4) yields the response of conjectures to changes in

---

[4] Consistency implies non-positive conjectures within the context of perfect information. Hviid and Ireland (1986) show that allowing for imperfect information may yield positive consistent conjectures.

$\underline{k}$. Differentiating with respect to k_i, using (1.3):

$$
\begin{bmatrix}
\phi_2 & \dfrac{-1}{\phi_2} \\[2ex]
\dfrac{-1}{\phi_1} & \phi_1
\end{bmatrix}
\begin{bmatrix}
d\phi_1/dk_1 \\[1ex]
d\phi_2/dk_2
\end{bmatrix}
=
\begin{bmatrix}
\dfrac{2}{k_1^2} & \phi_2 \\[2ex]
0 &
\end{bmatrix}
\tag{1.7}
$$

The determinant is $\Delta_\phi = \phi_1\phi_2 - (\phi_1\phi_2)^{-1} < 0$, since $\phi_i \in (-1, 0)$. Hence:

$$
\frac{d\phi_1}{dk_1} = \frac{1}{\Delta_\phi} \cdot \phi_1\phi_2 \frac{2}{k_1^2} < 0
\tag{1.8a}
$$

$$
\frac{d\phi_2}{dk_1} = \frac{1}{\Delta_\phi} \cdot \frac{\phi_2}{\phi_1} \frac{2}{k_1^2} < 0
\tag{1.8b}
$$

and similarly for $d\phi_i/dk_2$.

Hence, an increase in k_1 leads to both firms' consistent conjectures becoming more negative, more accommodating. Under consistency $\phi_1 = dr_2/dx_1$: so that (1.8a) implies that the increase in k_1 leads to the slope of firm 2's reaction function becoming more negative, and (1.8b) implies that its *own* reaction function becomes more negatively sloped. This will subsequently prove very important: with consistent conjectures, *each* firm's reaction function is determined by *both* firms capital stocks. As either firm invests more, the market will become more competitive since firms will be encouraged to expand their own output as the other firm's reaction function become more accommodating. Consider sequences $\{\underline{k}_n\}$ where $\underline{k}_n \gg 0$ and the corresponding sequences $\{\underline{\phi}_n\}$ where $\phi_n =_{\text{def}} \phi(\underline{k}_n)$:

Proposition 2: (a) If $\underline{k}_n \to \infty$, then $\phi_{in} \to -1$

(b) If $\underline{k}_n \to \underline{0}$, then $\phi_{in} \to 0$ $\quad i = 1, 2$.

Proposition 2 tells us that as *both* firms' production become perfectly flexible ($\underline{k}_n \to \infty$), then consistent conjectures tend to the Bertrand value: as both firms' production become perfectly inflexible, the consistent conjectures become Cournot.

In this section we have examined the relationship between investment and the flexibility of production, and the relationship between the flexibility of production and consistent conjectures. The more each firm invests in capital, the greater is its flexibility of production, and the more competitive the consistent conjecture of *both* firms become. This relationship implies that firms can manipulate the degree of competition in the product market through their investment decisions.

2. Strategic investment with consistent conjectures

In this section we explore the full two-stage strategic investment model when firms take into account the effect of their investment decisions on the degree of competition in the market stage. As a first step, we will consider the firm's output decision in the market stage *given* conjectures $\phi \in (-1, 0]^2$ and $\underline{k} \geq 0$, *without* imposing consistency $\phi = \phi(\underline{k})$. Firms choose outputs to maximise profits given ϕ and $\underline{k}$. This yields the firms' reaction functions in output space, 1.2). Given the two firms' reaction functions, we can solve for the equilibrium outputs. Whilst 1.2) can be solved explicitly, we shall write the solution outputs as general functions of ϕ and $\underline{k}$:

$$x_i = R_i(\phi, \underline{k}) \qquad i = 1, 2 \tag{2.1}$$

We can totally differentiate 2.1) to discover the response of the equilibrium outputs in the market stage to changes in $\underline{k}$ and ϕ. Defining the determinant $\Delta = (2 + \phi_1 + 2/k_1)(2 + \phi_2 + 2/k_2) - 1 > 0$, this yields:

$$\frac{\partial R_1}{\partial k_1} = \frac{1}{\Delta} \frac{2x_1}{k_1^2} \left(2 + \phi_2 + \frac{2}{k_2}\right) > 0 \tag{2.2}$$

$$\frac{\partial R_2}{\partial k_1} = \frac{-1}{\Delta} \frac{2x_1}{k_1^2} < 0 \tag{2.3}$$

and similarly $\partial R_2 / \partial k_2 > 0 > \partial R_1 / \partial k_2$. Note that:

$$\frac{\partial R_2 / \partial k_1}{\partial R_1 / \partial k_1} = \frac{-1}{2 + \phi_2 + 2w/k_2} \tag{2.4}$$

The RHS of (2.4) is the slope of firm 2's reaction function: the LHS the ratio of the change in x_1 to the change in x_2 caused by the shift in firm 1's reaction function resulting from the increase in k^1. Intuitively equality 2.4 must hold since varying k_1 merely shifts firm 1's) reaction function, whilst firm 2's reaction function is unaffected. Hence the change in both firms' output in the market stage is simply a move along firm 2's reaction function as in Fig. 1. Note also that the increase in firm 1's output as it increases investment exceeds the reduction in firm 2's output, so that total industry output increases.

How does the equilibrium output vary with ϕ given $\underline{k}$? Again, total differentiation of equations (1.2) with respect to ϕ yields:

$$\frac{\partial R_1}{\partial \phi_1} = \frac{-1}{\Delta} x_1 \cdot \left(2 + \phi_2 + \frac{2}{k_2}\right) < 0 \tag{2.5}$$

$$\frac{\partial R_2}{\partial \phi_1} = \frac{x_1}{\Delta} > 0 \tag{2.6}$$

and similarly $\partial R_1 / \partial \phi_2 > 0 > \partial R_2 / \partial \phi_2$.

Thus as firm 1 conjectures that firm 2's output response becomes less accommodating (ϕ_1 increases), its own reaction function shifts to the left, again as in Fig. 1, so that:

$$\frac{\partial R_2 / \partial \phi_1}{\partial R_1 / \partial \phi_1} = \frac{-1}{2 + \phi_2 + 2/k_2} \tag{2.8}$$

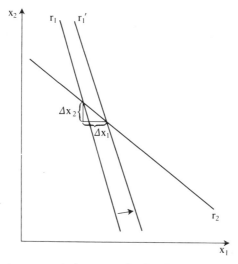

FIG. 1. Output responses to investment by firm 1 with exogenous conjectures

since firm 2's reaction function is unaffected by changes in ϕ_1. Note that as ϕ_1 increases, and firm 2 is believed to be less competitive, total industry output *falls*.

We have up to now examined what happens to the equilibrium outputs in the market stage as ϕ and $\underline{k}$ vary. We have *not* imposed consistency $\phi = \phi(\underline{k})$ as in 1.6). Eaton and Grossman (1984) and Yarrow (1985) consider a strategic investment model where firms choose $\underline{k}$, but treat the nature of competition in the product market as exogenous. To briefly outline this type of model, firms' payoffs can be written as a function π_i of capital stocks chosen; given ϕ:

$$\pi_i(\underline{k}) = R_i(\phi, \underline{k}) \left[P^0 - \sum_{j=1}^{2} R_j(\phi, \underline{k}) \right] - rk_i - \frac{R_i(\phi, \underline{k})^2}{k_i} \tag{2.8}$$

Firms then choose their capital stocks k_i, and we assume a Nash-equilibrium occurs, which seems reasonable given that capital expenditures are irreversible. In essence, this is a model where firms choose their output reaction-functions through teir choice of k_i. The resultant equilibrium can thus be seen as a Nash-equilibrium in reaction functions. A necessary condition for equilibrium is that firms are in their reaction functions. Setting $\partial \pi_i / \partial k_i = 0$ we have:

$$\frac{\partial c}{\partial k_i} = x_1 \cdot \frac{\partial R_1}{\partial k_1} \left[\phi_1 - \frac{\partial R_2 / \partial k_1}{\partial R_1 / \partial k_1} \right] \tag{2.9}$$

where $\partial c / \partial k_1$ is the partial derivative of the cost function $c(x_1, k_1)$ with respect to k_1, from A2. Turning first to the LHS of (2.9), if $\partial c / \partial k_1 = 0$ then the capital stock minimises the cost of producing x_1. If $\partial c/\partial k_1 < 0$, then there is *undercapitalisation*, too little capital then that which minimises cost, the technology being too labour-intensive. If $\partial c/\partial k_1 > 0$, then we have *overcapitalisation*, with more capital than mimimises the cost of producing x_1. Turning to the RHS of (2.9), if we consider the term in brackets, we have the difference between the firm 1's conjecture about the firm 2's output response ϕ_1, and the actual response of firm 2 (recall that $(\partial R_2/\partial k_1)/(\partial R_1/\partial k_1)$ is the *slope* of firm 2's reaction function, (2.7)). Thus we obtain Eaton and Grossman's result that if the conjecture is greater (less) than the actual response, there will be a factor bias of overcapitalisation (undercapitalisation) (Eaton and Grossman, (1984) Proposition 2.1). If the actual and conjectured responses are equal, however, then there will be no factor bias, and the technology will be efficient.

For example, if firms have Cournot conjectures ($\phi_i = 0$) as in Brander and Spencer (1983), then there will be over-capitalisation under A1–2. To take the other extreme, where firms have Bertrand conjectures as in Dixon (1985), then there will be under-capitalisation. If there is a factor bias of under- or over-capitalisation, then this will lead to a welfare loss relative to the social optimum. If we adopt the consumer surplus approach, then there will be two sources of welfare loss. The first will be the standard "welfare triangle" due to output being restricted below the perfectly competitive level. The second will be due to average costs being above their minimum level, which follows from the factor bias. In Dixon (1985), it is shown that in the case where the market stage is competitive, the lost surplus due to factor bias can exceed the surplus lost due to the restriction of output.

Eaton and Grossman's conclusion (1984 p. 6–7) is that if the product market is a consistent conjectural equilibrium, then there will be no factor bias. This result, however, is derived only for an exogenously given conjecture which happens to be consistent for the values of k the firms choose in equilibrium. If ϕ *happen* to be consistent for a particular (equilibrium) k, then they will certainly be inconsistent for all other k, since the slopes of the firm's reaction functions will be different. If we believe that consistency of conjectures is a desirable property, then surely we ought to impose consistency on the firm's conjectures over the whole strategy space, for all k. Unless we impose $\phi = \phi(k)$, then it is very unlikely that exogenously given conjectures will happen to be consistent at any particular (equilibrium) k.

Indeed, strategic investment models with inconsistent conjectures are rather unsatisfactory. If $\phi_1 \neq dr_j/dx_i$, then it is difficult to give a convincing account of the firm's decision making in the two stages of the model. In the strategic stage, when the firm chooses its capital stock, it knows the true structure of the market—its own reaction function and the reaction function of the other firm. Thus when the investment decision is made, the firm is assumed to know the actual slope of the other firms's reaction function. However, when it enters the market stage, the firm chooses its own output according to its exogenously given (and almost certainly incorrect) conjecture about the slope of the other firm's reaction function. Thus in passing from the strategic to the market stage, a veil of ignorance seems to descend on the firm, since it loses its former knowledge of the other firm's reaction function. In essence, there is a conflict between the assumption of perfect foresight which the firm possess in the strategic stage, and inconsistency of conjectures in the market stage. If firms are going to have "rational" expectations in the strategic stage, then surely the conjectures should also be consistent in the market stage.

When we impose the consistency condition on conjectures, so that $\phi = \phi(k)$, then the outputs given $\underline{k}$ are:

$$x_i(\underline{k}) =_{\text{def}} R_i(\phi(\underline{k}), \underline{k}) \tag{2.11}$$

When firm i varies its capital stock k_i, it shifts the reaction functions of *both* firms. Since the conjectures of both firms become more competitive as k_i increases (1.8), both firms reaction functions will move out as in Fig. 2. This makes the overall effect of an increase in k_1 on x_1 ambiguous:

$$\overset{(-)(-)}{\underset{}{}}\quad\overset{(+)(-)}{\underset{}{}}\quad\overset{(+)}{\underset{}{}}$$
$$\frac{\mathrm{d}x_1}{\mathrm{d}k_1} = \frac{\partial R_1}{\partial \phi_1}\frac{\mathrm{d}\phi_1}{\mathrm{d}k_1} + \frac{\partial R_1}{\partial \phi_2}\frac{\mathrm{d}\phi_2}{\mathrm{d}k_1} + \frac{\partial R_1}{\partial k_1} \tag{2.12}$$

Since the analysis is rather complex, it is useful if we break the overall effect

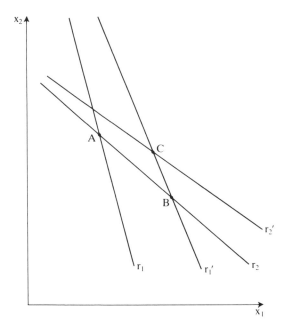

FIG. 2. Output responses to investment by firm 1 with consistent conjectures

into two parts, the first being the effect of k_1 on x_1 holding ϕ_2 constant:

$$\left.\frac{dx_1}{dk_1}\right|_{\phi_2} = \frac{\partial R_1}{\partial \phi_1}\frac{d\phi_1}{dk_1} + \frac{\partial R_1}{\partial k_1} = \frac{1}{\Delta\Delta_\phi}\cdot\frac{2x_1}{k_1^2}\left[\frac{\phi_2\phi_1-\Delta_\phi}{\phi_1}\right] > 0 \qquad (2.12)$$

Similarly,

$$\begin{array}{c}(+)(-)(-)\\[4pt]\left.\frac{dx_2}{dk_1}\right|_{\phi_2} = \frac{\partial R_2}{\partial \phi_1}\frac{d\phi_1}{dk_1} + \frac{\partial R_2}{\partial k_1} = \frac{1}{\Delta\Delta_\phi}\cdot\frac{2x_1}{k_1^2}[\phi_1\phi_2-\Delta_\phi] < 0\end{array} \qquad (2.13)$$

In calculating $dx_i/dk_1|_{\phi_2}$ we are only taking into account the effects of dk_1 in shifting firm 1's reaction function: by holding ϕ_2 constant, we are in effect holding firm 2's reaction function constant. Thus, in terms of Fig. 2, we are considering the move along firm 2's reaction function from point A to B. The crucial point is that since we are moving along firm 2's reaction function:

$$\left.\frac{dx_2/dk_1}{dx_1/dk_1}\right|_{\phi_2} = \phi_1 \qquad (2.15)$$

If we hold ϕ_2 constant, then, the change in ϕ_1 caused by k_1 shifts firm 1's reaction function further out, enhancing the effect with exogenous conjectures (see 2.12).

However, the effect of increasing k_1 is to make firm 2's conjecture ϕ_2 more competitive, shifting out firm 2's reaction function. This mitigates the expansionary effect, and the overall effect on x_i seems to be ambiguous (although a negative sign seems unlikely, we haven't been able to rule it out).

$$\frac{dx_1}{dk_1} = \left.\frac{dx_1}{dk_1}\right|_{\phi_2} + \frac{\partial R_1}{\partial \phi_2}\frac{d\phi_1}{dk_1} \lesssim 0? \qquad (2.15)$$
$$\begin{array}{cc}(+)&(+)(-)\end{array}$$

$$= \frac{1}{\Delta\cdot\Delta_\phi}\cdot\frac{2\cdot x_1}{k_1^2}\left[\phi_2 - \frac{\Delta_\phi}{\phi_1} + \frac{\phi_2\cdot x_1}{\phi_1\cdot x_2}\right] \qquad (2.16)$$

In the symmetric case where $k_1 = k_2$, $x_1 = x_2 = x$, $\phi_1 = \phi_2 = \phi$ clearly $dx_1/dk_1 > 0$.

Turning to the overall effect of k_1 on x_2 when we take into account the change in ϕ_2 we have:

$$\begin{array}{cc}(-)&(-)\ (-)\end{array}$$
$$\frac{dx_2}{dk_1} = \left.\frac{dx_2}{dk_1}\right|_{\phi_2} + \frac{\partial R_2}{\partial \phi_2}\cdot\frac{d\phi_2}{dk_1} \qquad (2.17)$$

Again, the conjectural effect via ϕ_2 works in the opposite direction to the other effects, and may reverse them. However, in the symmetric case we have $dx_j/dk_i < 0$.

Having related firms' output to investment under consistent conjectures (2.11), we now turn to the firm's strategic investment decision. The payoff function is:

$$U_i(\underline{k}) = x_i(\underline{k})\left(P^0 - \sum_{j=1}^{2} x_j(\underline{k})\right) - \frac{x_i(\underline{k})^2}{k_i} - rk_i \qquad (2.18)$$

Setting $\partial U_i/\partial k_i = 0$, we obtain:

$$\frac{\partial_c}{\partial k_1} = x_1 \cdot \frac{dx_1}{dk_1}\left[\phi_1 - \frac{dx_1/dk_1}{dx_2/dk_2}\right] \qquad (2.19)$$

If we consider the RHS bracket, this is the difference between the actual output response in market stage (since ϕ_i are consistent), and the tradeoff between x_1 and x_2 which the firm in effect faces in the strategic stage. As is clear from Fig. 2, since an increase in k_1 makes both conjecture more competitive and shifts both reaction functions out, the trade off the firm faces in the market stage must be less negative than the slope of the other firm's reaction function (the slope $A-B$ is more negative than the slope $A-C$). Combining 2.14), 2.15) and 2.16) we have:

$$\frac{dx_2/dk_1}{dx_1/dk_1} > \frac{dx_2/dk_1}{dx_1/dk_1}\bigg|_{\phi_2} = \phi_1 \qquad (2.20)$$
$$(A-C) \qquad (A-B)$$

Hence the RHs bracket of (2.19) must always be negative with *endogenously* consistent conjectures, in contrast to the zero value with *exogenously* consistent conjectures as in Eaton and Grossman (1984). Whether this will give rise to under or overcapitalisation will depend on the sign of dx_1/dk_1:

$$\frac{\partial c}{\partial k_i} > 0 \quad \text{if} \quad \frac{dx_1}{dk_1} < 0 \quad \text{(overcapitalisation)}$$

$$\frac{\partial c}{\partial k_i} < 0 \quad \text{if} \quad \frac{dx_1}{dk_1} > 0 \quad \text{(undercapitalisation)}$$

Efficiency will only occur iff $dx_1/dk_1 = 0$. In the symmetric case, $dx_1/dk_1 > 0$, so that we obtain undercapitalisation. To summarise this:

Proposition 3: Suppose an equilibrium $\underline{k}^*$ exists in the strategic investment model. There will be undercapitalisation if output responds positively to investment. In a symmetric equilibrium there will be undercapitalisation.

Although we have not been able to rule it out, the case of overcapitalisation seems a rather unlikely curiosity.

We have not established whether or not an equilibrium exists: equation (2.19) is merely a necessary condition for firms to be on their reaction functions in the strategic stage. Even under such simple assumptions as A1–2, making conjectures consistent leads to a very complex relation between capitals $\underline{k}$ and outputs $\underline{x}$. U_i may well not be concave in k_i. However, Proposition 3 at least provides a counter example to Eaton and Grossman's result, and shows how it depends crucially on conjectures being exogenous.

Because it is not possible to formulate useful conditions for the existence and uniqueness of equilibria in this model, we cannot perform meaningful comparative statics on the model using the equilibrium conditions (2.19). However, we can use more general analysis to characterise the properties of any equilibria that exist. We close this section with an analysis of the impact of the rental-wage ratio r on equilibrium conjectures. As r increases, the cost of capital becomes expensive relative to labour. Intuitively, as r becomes very expensive, this will lead eventually to small levels of investment, which implies conjectures close to the cournot value.

Proposition 4: Consider the strategic investment model $[R_+, U_i : i = 1 . . n]$.
(a) If $r \geq (p^0/2)^2$, there exists a unique equilibrium where $\phi^* = \underline{k}^* = \underline{0}$.
(b) if $r < (p^0/2)^2$, then for any equilibrium that exists where $\underline{k}^* \gg \underline{0}$, conjectures are between the Cournot and Bertrand values $\phi^* \in (-1, 0)$.

Thus relative prices in the factor market eventualy have an influence on the degree of competition in the product market. The basic point to remember is that changes in r have no direct influence on the consistent conjectures, which are determined only by the level of investment by the two firms (this stems from the fact that marginal cost in the market stage is unaffected by r, since capital is a fixed cost). The level of r will, however, influence the degree of investment in the industry in equilibrium.

An immediate implication of this analysis is that in the strategic investment framework, with a technology that has a strictly increasing smooth relationship between the labour input and output given capital, the assumption of either Cournot or Bertrand competition are too extreme. Of course, if the technology were Leontief in the market stage, then the choice of capital would tie down the capacity (i.e. maximum output) of the firm in the market stage, and hence lead to inflexible production (a "vertical" marginal cost at capacity). In this case the *equilibrium* consistent conjectures would be Cournot (out of equilibrium the analysis is more complex, depending on whether the capacity constraint binds). In order to have a Leontief technology in the market stage, we need not assume that the underlying technology is Leontief: it would suffice to have a putty-clay technology, where the capital-labour ratio is freely chosen with the investment decision in the strategic stage, but becomes fixed in the market stage. At the other extreme, if capital and labour are perfect substitutes in production, and cost the same $(r = 1)$, then marginal cost is "horizontal" and output is perfectly flexible whatever the level of investment. In this case the equilibrium conjectures are Bertrand.

In the framework presented, firms are only able to influence the flexibility of production through their investment decision. It is possible to widen the firm's choice, for example, by allowing the firm to choose whether to precommit one or both inputs in the strategic stage (as in Dixon (1986)). Alternatively, the firm could choose the type of technology to influence the flexibility of production in the market stage. We leave these possibilities for future research.

Conclusion

This paper explores a model of strategic investment with consistent conjectures. This is a model in which the firm's cost structure and the nature of competition in the product market are endogenous. Thus aspects of both the industry structure (in this case costs) and conduct are determined. Two basic insights are explored. Firstly, that the nature of product market competition depends on the flexibility of firms' production. This is captured by imposing a consistency condition on conjectures. Secondly, the idea that firms can influence the flexibility of production, as in strategic investment models where firms choose their short run cost function through their investment decision. The model combines these two ideas, so that firms take into account the impact of their investment decisions on competition in the product market.

There are three main results in this paper. First, in equilibrium, the degree of competition will lie between the Bertrand and Cournot values. Secondly, there will generally be a factor bias, with undercapitalisation in any symmetric equilibrium. Thirdly, the degree of competition is ultimately sensitive to the wage-rental ratio. As capital becomes very expensive, equilibrium conjectures converge to the Cournot value.

The relationships explored in this paper are ultimately very complex. In order to understand complex phenomenon it is often necessary to construct simple models. This paper is no exception to this tendency. Even a slight relaxation of the A1–2 would make the model intractable and ambiguous. Thus the model should certainly be interpreted as an example rather than a general theory. However, it is hoped that the example is stimulating, and provides a useful first step.

Birkbeck College, London

APPENDIX: PROOFS

The proofs are briefly sketched.

Proposition 1: For an explicit solution to the quadratic system, see Bresnehan (1981, pp. 994–5). We give an alternative and more intuitive proof. We demonstrate that: (a) there is a unique solution to 1.4) and 1.5) such that $\phi_i \in (-1, 0)$ $i = 1, 2$; (b) there are no solutions with $\phi_i < -1$.

(a) There exists a unique solution $\underline{\phi} \in (-1, 0)^2$. If $\phi_2 \in (-1, 0)$ then from 1.4)

$$\phi_1 \in [-(1 + 2/k_2)^{-1}, \ -(2 + 2/k_2)^{-1}] =_{\text{def}} C_1$$

Similarly if $\phi_1 \in (-1, 0)$ then:

$$\phi_2 \in [-(1 + 2/k_1)^{-1}, \ -(2 + 2/k_1)^{-1}] =_{\text{def}} C_2$$

Any consistent conjectures in $(-1, 0)^2$ most lie in the subset $C = C_1 \times C_2$. Expressing both consistency conditions 1.4) so that ϕ_1 is a function of ϕ_2, we have:

$$\phi_1 = Z_1(\phi_2) = -(2 + \phi_2 + 2/k_2)^{-1}$$
$$\phi_1 = Z_2(\phi_2) = -1/\phi_2 - 2(1 + 1/k_1)$$

If conjectures are consitent, then $\phi_1 = Z_i(\phi_2)$ $i = 1, 2$. Restricting ourselves to $\phi_2 \in C_2$, consider $Z: C_2 \to [-1, 0]$, where $Z(\phi_2) =_{\text{def}} Z_1 - Z_2$.

$$Z(\phi_2) = -(2 + \phi_2 + 2/k_2)^{-1} + 1/\phi_2 + 2(1 + 1/k_1)$$

$$Z(-(2 + 2/k_1)) < 0 < Z(-(1 + 2/k_1))$$

Since Z is continuous and strictly decreasing, there exists a unique ϕ' in the interior of C_2 such that $Z = 0$, so that $\phi_1' = Z_i(\phi')$. Hence (ϕ_1', ϕ') are unique consistent conjectures in C. (b) To see that no other consistent conjectures exist, note that Z is strictly decreasing whenever the second order condition is satisfied.

Proposition 2: $-1 < \phi_i(\underline{k}) < 0$ for all $\underline{k} \gg 0$, and from (1.4):

$$\phi_i > -1/(1 + 2/k_{jn})$$

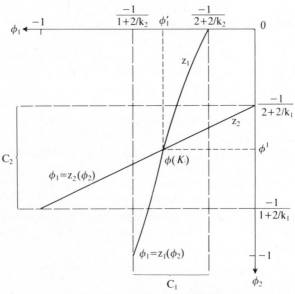

FIG. 3. Illustration of Proposition 1

Hence

$$\underset{k_{jn}\to+\infty}{\text{Liminf}}\ \phi_{in} > \text{Lim}\ \frac{-1}{1+2/k_{jn}} = -1$$

Since Limsup $\phi_{jn} < -1$, it follows that $\underset{k_n\to+\infty}{\text{Lim}}\ \phi_{jn} = -1$ QED

Proposition 4:
(a) Minimum average cost is $2 \cdot \sqrt{r}$. If $\sqrt{r} \geqslant p^0/2$ then firms earn negative profits whenever $k_i > 0$.
(b) If $\sqrt{r} < p^0/2$, then $\underline{0}$ cannot be an equilibrium, since either firm can produce a small output efficiently and earn strictly positive profits, hence in any symmetric equilibrium $\phi_i < 0$. To obtain a lower bound on ϕ_i, we define an upper bound on k_i. A necessary condition for $U_i(\underline{k}) \geqslant 0$ is that $p^0 - x_i \geqslant 2 \cdot \sqrt{r}$. Since with symmetry production is undercapitalised, $x_i \geqslant k_i \cdot \sqrt{r}$. Hence $k_i \leqslant (p^0/\sqrt{r}) - 2$, ensuring $\phi_i < -1$.

BIBLIOGRAPHY

BRANDER, J. and SPENCER, B. (1983). "Strategic Commitment with R&D: the Symmetric Case", *Bell Journal of Economics,* Vol. 14, pp. 225–35.

BRESNAHAN, T. (1982). "Duopoly Models with Consistent Conjectures", *American Economic Review,* vol. 71, pp. 934–45.

BOYER, M. and MOREAU, M. (1983): "Conjectures, Rationality, and Duopoly Theory", *International Journal of Industrial Organisation,* vol. 1, pp. 23–41.

BULOW, J., GEANAKOPLOS, J. and KLEMPERER, P. (1985). "Multimarket oligopoly: Strategic Substitutes and Complements", *Journal of Political Economy,* June.

DIXON, H. (1985). "Strategic Investment with Competitive Product Markets", *Journal of Industrial Economics,* vol. 33, pp. 483–500.

DIXON, H. (1986). "Cournot and Bertrand Outcomes as equilibria in a Strategic Metagame", *Economic Journal,* Conference Supplement. pp. 59–70.

EATON, J. and GROSSMAN, G. (1984). "Strategic Capacity Investment and Product Market Competition", Woodrow Wilson School, Discussion Paper No. 80.

FUDENBERG, D. and TIROLE, J. (1984). "The Fat-Cat Effect, The Puppy-Dog Ploy, and the Lean and Hungry Look", *American Economic Review,* vol. 74, pp. 361–366.

GROSSMAN, S. (1981). "Nash-Equilibrium and the Industrial Organisation of Markets with Large Fixed Costs", *Econometrica* Vol 49, 1149–77.

HAHN, F. (1977). "Exercises in Conjectural Equilibria", *Scandinavian Journal of Economics,* vol. 79(2).

HAHN, F. (1978). "On Non-Walrasian Equilibria", *Review of Economic Studies,* vol. 45, pp. 1–17.

HART, O. (1982). "Reasonable Conjectures", ICERD Discussion Paper 82/61.

HVIID, M. and IRELAND, N. (1986). "Consistent Conjectures with Information Transmission", (Mimeo) Warwick University.

MARSHAK, T. and NELSON, R. (1962). "Flexibility, Uncertainty and Economic Theory", *Metroeconomica,* vol. 14, pp. 42–64.

MILLS, E. (1984). "Demand Fluctuations and Endogenous Firm Flexibility", *Journal of Industrial Economics,* vol. 33, pp. 55–72.

LAITNER, J. (1980). "Rational Duopoly Equilibria", *Quarterly Journal of Economics,* pp. 641–662.

MARSHAK, T. and NELSON, R. (1962). "Flexibility, Uncertainty, and Economic Theory", *Metroeconomica,* vol. 14, pp. 42–60.

MILLS, D. (1984). "Demand Fluctuations and Endogenous Firm Flexibility", *Journal of Industrial Economics,* vol. 33, pp. 55–72.

STIGLER, G. (1939). "Production and Distribution in the short Run", *Journal of Political Economy,* vol. 47, pp. 305–27.

ULPH, D. (1983). "Rational Conjectures and the Theory of Oligopoly", *International Journal of Industrial Organisation,* vol. 1, pp. 131–54.

VENABLES, T. (1984). *Does Protection Reduce Productivity?,* Mimeo, Sussex University (September).

VIVAS, X. (1985). "Capacity Precommitment, Technology Flexibility, and Oligopoly Outcomes", Mimeo, University of Pennsylvania.

YARROW, G. (1985). "Measures of Monopoly Welfare Loss in Markets With Differentiated Products", *Journal of Industrial Economics* vol. 33, pp. 515–530.

MULTI-DIMENSIONAL PRODUCT DIFFERENTIATION AND PRICE COMPETITION

By ANDREW S. CAPLIN and BARRY J. NALEBUFF

1. Introduction

BEGINNING with Hotelling's (1929) study of spatial competition, location theory has provided important insights into imperfect competition. However, the applicability of the classical approach is limited; it leaves two major issues unresolved. First, what impact does price competition have on the process of product selection? Second, what results are available when products differ across more than one dimension? We develop a simple framework to study competition through product differentiation and prices in a multi-dimensional setting.

Efforts to model price competition, even in a one dimensional setting, have proved discouraging. Equilibrium may not exist if firms locate too close together (d'Aspremont *et al.*, 1979). When equilibrium exists, its nature depends heavily on an exogenously specified transport cost function, be it fixed, linear, or quadratic (Gabszewicz and Thisse, 1985; Economides, 1985). In general, it is hard to provide an economic interpretation and justification for these types of transportation costs in a model of product differentiation.

Most location models follow Hotelling in focussing on competition along a single dimension. In one dimension, a firm has at most two neighbors; this places an artificial limit on the extent of competition. Only in higher dimensions is this problem eliminated (Archibald and Rosenbluth, 1975; Stiglitz, 1984). Realistically, product differentiation is almost always multi-dimensional. Computer printers vary in terms of speed, noise, and clarity of output. Cars vary in size, comfort, sportiness, fuel economy, reliability, and in many other dimensions.

The multi-dimensional nature of product design is particularly evident in marketing new products. Products are frequently launched to fill a perceived market niche; low alcohol beer and caffeine free soft drinks are two recent examples. These products take advantage of a characteristic under-exploited by existing competitors. This suggests that a multi-dimensional setting is important both to the theory of product design and to the theory of advertising. However, to understand product design first requires an understanding of price competition.

Product selection and pricing strategy is typically a two-stage process. Initially, product characteristics are chosen. Then given a set of commodities with fixed characteristics, competition takes place through prices.

Multi-dimensional product differentiation and price competition are brought together in our study of imperfect competition. We use Grandmont's

(1978) theory of intermediate preferences to build a tractable multi-dimensional location model. This provides a framework to address important issues in industrial organization: when are there first-mover advantages in product design (Guasch and Weiss, 1980); how is location chosen to deter entry (Schmalansee, 1978); what are the signs of collusive behaviour in product design; how do cost differences affect product differentiation, prices, and market shares?

If location choice is followed by price competition Proposition 4.1 provides conditions for existence of a price equilibrium given any location pair. The significance of this result stems from the historic difficulty in attaining existence of price equilibria in location models. In addition, it allows us to examine the effects of *cost asymmetries* on product differentiation. Proposition 4.2 shows that a low cost entrant seeking to capture the entire market from a higher cost incumbent does best to imitate his product. We also show that a high cost firm, by locating well away from the center of the market, may be able to avoid destructive competition with its low cost rival, and guarantee itself a market niche.

We present more precise results for product differentiation in a price-regulated duopoly. The first firm to fix a location is at a disadvantage. The second mover advantage increases with the dimension of the product space. For arbitrary distributions of consumer preferences over n-dimensional goods ($n \geq 2$), the second firm can capture up to $(n-1)/n$ of the market. However, when there is a measure of agreement (defined in Section 5) about which mix of characteristics is most desirable, the incumbent firm can always locate so as to guarantee a 36.8% ($1/e$) market share.

Section 2 presents a brief survey of location theory. Section 3 outlines our general model. Section 4 integrates product design with endogenous price competition in a two-dimensional setting. Section 5 analyzes product differentiation in arbitrary dimensions for price regulated duopolists. Section 6 offers our conclusions.

2. Location theory

Location theory begins with the work of Hotelling (1929). In his analysis, the set of possible locations for a given product is represented by the unit interval, [0,1]. Each firm produces at a single location. Market demand is generated by consumers who differ in their location along a line. Each consumer prefers products closer to their own location. Prices are taken as fixed and identical and hence consumers always buy the closest product. This basic model has been applied by political scientists to study the choice of party platforms (Black, 1948; Kramer, 1977), and by economists to examine product differentiation (Chamberlin, 1933; Eaton and Lipsey, 1975; Prescott and Visscher, 1977; Lane, 1980).

Attempts to incorporate prices have encountered a major difficulty in even proving the existence of equilibrium strategies. It is largely this difficulty which has prevented the more widespread adoption of the model. To compute the equilibria for a two-stage model requires the existence of Nash equilibria in prices for *arbitrarily* close product specifications. The disturbing result of d'Aspremont *et al.* (1979) is that no pure strategy pricing equilibrium may exist when firms are located too close to one another. But, if no price equilibrium exists for certain locational choices then there is no way for firms to estimate the profitability of those locations.

Resolutions of the existence problem have concentrated on three areas: changing the transport cost function, allowing for mixed strategies, and focussing on vertical as opposed to horizontal location problems.

Gabszewicz and Thisse (1986) have demonstrated the existence of a pure strategy price equilibrium for the Hotelling model when there are quadratic as opposed to linear transportation costs. The equilibrium locations are at the two ends of the unit interval. Similar are the results of Economides (1983) who shows that when consumers have a maximal or reservation distance that a pricing equilibrium exists and firms locate far apart. The equilibrium depends heavily on the form of the transportation cost function (Gabszewicz and Thisse, 1986). As a consequence, few applications have been developed.

Even when there is no equilibrium in pure strategies, there may be mixed strategy solutions (Dasgupta and Maskin, 1986). It is of interest that Hotelling's model with linear transportation costs and bounded reservation prices possesses no equilibrium even in mixed strategies. In games where mixed strategy equilibria do exist (see examples by Osborne and Pitchik (1982) and Stiglitz (1984)), their complexity effectively rules out comparative static analysis.

Shaked and Sutton (1982) attain important positive results in price/location theory by examining vertical rather than horizontal product differentiation. In their model, firms compete over quality and price. Quality choice is a "vertical" location problem because all consumers prefer higher quality to lower quality. By contrast, in "horizontal" location problems, changing the product specification is a move towards some consumers and away from others. Their results are encouraging, but so far limited to problems of one dimension (quality). It has proved difficult to develop generalizations that include horizontal product differentiation.

An entirely different approach to multi-dimensional product differentiation and pricing is taken by Spence (1976), Dixit-Stiglitz (1977). They address Chamberlin's question of whether the competitive market will provide the optimal amount of product diversity. To focus on this question, they use a completely symmetric model. This bypasses issues of product design and questions where asymmetries play a prominent role.

To achieve greater applicability of the location model to multi-dimensional horizontal product differentiation with price competition, we begin by reformulating the basic framework.

3. The general model

The formal model provides a precise specification of the consumer and producer sides of the economy and the definition of equilibrium. After presenting the general framework, we specialize to the case of duopolistic competition.

Consumers

Products are identified by an n-dimensional vector of salient characteristics (Lancaster, 1966; Gorman, 1980). Consumers face a variety of commodities each offering a different bundle of characteristics. There is exclusivity in consumption; each consumer chooses only one of the products. The characteristics of the commodities cannot be combined to yield intermediate mixes.

Our approach to the price/location model separates the space of consumer preferences from the space of product characteristics. The population is represented by a distribution on the space of utility functions. Specifically, we assume that consumers have Cobb–Douglas utility functions. Heterogeneity of tastes is then specified by a distribution function over the Cobb–Douglas parameters, as in Lane (1980).

In the traditional location model, a single space is traditionally used to represent both the diversity of products and the diversity of consumer preferences. A product is represented as a point in characteristic space. A consumer is represented by a most preferred characteristic mix and by a "transport cost" function. This function specifies the price difference needed for the consumer to be indifferent between a unit of any given good and a unit of their most preferred good. The model of consumer preferences underlying the transport cost function is left unspecified. A conceptual advantage of our approach is that "transport costs" are defined endogenously from the utility function rather than being exogenously set as either fixed, linear or quadratic.

An additional motivation for assuming Cobb–Douglas utility functions is tractability. There should be a simple calculation determining which consumers prefer good X to Y and which prefer Y to X. In one dimensional problems, this is straightforward. But, even in the two-dimensional location model with linear transportation costs, market areas are defined by hyperbolas when the two firms charge different prices. In contrast, when consumer preferences are derived from Cobb–Douglas utility functions, for all prices (P_x, P_y) the set of consumers who prefer X to Y is divided from those who prefer Y to X by a hyperplane in the space of Cobb–Douglas parameters [Grandmont (1978)].

Producers

On the supply side, there is a fixed list of potential competitors, $i = (1, \ldots, j)$. We assume that the order of entry into the market is sequential, with a fixed known order of entry. Based on the expected competition, the ith firm is either deterred from entering or pays market entry costs of A^i and produces one product. If it enters, competitor i has cost function $C_i(W)$ giving its unit cost of production for any list of product characteristics, W. Once chosen, product characteristics are fixed. Behind this assumption is the belief that changing product design is both time consuming and costly relative to changing price.

Each potential entrant decides on its location rationally, taking account of the existing products, future product selection, and the anticipated price competition. After all product locations are chosen, the prices are determined in a Bertrand–Nash equilibrium for the given products.

Equilibrium

An equilibrium of the game is an ordered list of j firms $\{f_1, f_2, \ldots, f_j\}$, j products $\{W_1, W_2, \ldots, W_j\}$, and j prices $\{p_1, p_2, \ldots, p_j\}$ where

(i) $\{p_1, p_2, \ldots, p_j\}$ is a Nash equilibrium in prices given products $\{W_1, W_2, \ldots, W_j\}$.

(ii) Each firm in the list $\{f_1, f_2, \ldots, f_j\}$ picks its location optimally in relation to other firms' prior locations, predicted future locations, and the ensuing price competition. Each firm that locates correctly anticipates making sufficient profits to justify entry.

(iii) Each non-entering firm rationally predicts a loss should it choose to enter.

Duopoly

In a duopoly, the incumbent firm first chooses its product, $X \in \mathbb{R}^n$. The rival firm responds with its product $Y \in \mathbb{R}^n$. Firm X has cost function $C_x(X)$, firm Y has cost function $C_y(Y)$. Entry into the market is free.

In this n-dimensional setting, a consumer of type $\alpha = (\alpha_1, \ldots, \alpha_n)$ has Cobb–Douglas utility function,

$$U(\alpha, Q, w_1, \ldots, w_n) = Q^b w_1^{\alpha_1} \ldots w_n^{\alpha_n}, \tag{1}$$

where w_i represents the ith characteristic of commodity W and Q represents the total consumption of other products. Consumption of any given commodity is treated as a continuous variable.

For simplicity, all consumers are assumed to have identical values of $b \geqslant 0$, and equal incomes $I > 0$. We normalize so that $\alpha \in S^n$, the n-dimensional unit simplex, i.e. $\alpha_i \geqslant 0$ and $\sum_{i=1}^{n} \alpha_i = 1$. Thus all individuals spend the same amount, $I/(1+b)$, on commodity X or Y, whichever they purchase.[1] Units are chosen so that $I/(1+b)=1$.

Given commodities X and Y, the duopolists simultaneously choose prices P_x and P_y. A consumer with Cobb–Douglas parameter $\alpha \in S^n$ will purchase X over Y if and only if,

$$\frac{x_1^{\alpha_1} \ldots x_n^{\alpha_n}}{P_x} > \frac{y_1^{\alpha_1} \ldots y_n^{\alpha_n}}{P_y} \tag{2}$$

Taking logarithms and rearranging yields

$$\sum_{i=1}^{n-1} \alpha_i \ln \left(\frac{x_i y_n}{y_i x_n}\right) > \log \left(\frac{y_n}{x_n}\right) + \log \left(\frac{P_x}{P_y}\right) \tag{3}$$

Equation (3) asserts that the set of consumers preferring X to Y can be separated from those preferring Y to X by a hyperplane in the space of Cobb–Douglas parameters. This observation follows closely from Grandmont's (1978) demonstration that Cobb–Douglas utility functions lie in the class of intermediate preferences. The dividing hyperplane has normal vector

$$\left(\log \left(\frac{x_1 y_n}{y_1 x_n}\right), \ldots, \log \left(\frac{x_{n-1} y_n}{y_{n-1} x_n}\right)\right),$$

which depends only on the products' specifications, not on their prices. Hence price changes cause parallel shifts in the hyperplane dividing the population between the two products. The central role of hyperplanes greatly simplifies our analysis. This is most evident in Section 5, which presents a multi-dimensional extension of the fix-price models of Hotelling (1929) and Prescott and Visscher (1977).

4. Existence of a price equilibrium

We focus on a two-dimensional version of the general duopoly model. We assume that both firms have constant returns to scale and that production of either characteristic is equally costly. This allows us to consider the effect of cost differences between the two firms. Since the goods are infinitely divisible, no generality is lost in choosing a scale so that $x_1 + x_2 = y_1 + y_2 = 1$. Unit costs for Firm X are C_x and for Firm Y are C_y.

In two dimensions the determination of market shares is considerably simplified. Consumers buy (X, P_x) over (Y, P_y) if $\alpha_1 \geq \alpha_1^*$, where

$$\alpha_1^* = [\log (y_2/x_2) + \log (P_x/P_y)]/K, \tag{3'}$$

and $K \equiv \ln [(x_1 y_2)/(y_1 x_2)]$.[2]

---

[1] If expenditure differed across the population, an additional integration would be required holding $\sum_{i=1}^{n} \alpha_i$ constant.

[2] When locations are fixed, we assume that X is more intensive in the first characteristic so that $k>0$. If $k<0$, then market areas are reversed.

Without loss of generality, total population is 1. Firm X's revenue is then $F(\alpha_1^*)$, where $F(\alpha_1^*)$ is the proportion of the population with $\alpha_1 \leq \alpha_1^*$.[3] Consumers with Cobb–Douglas preferences who purchase X spend a fixed amount on X regardless of its price. Higher prices lead to lower production costs as each consumer's demand is inversely proportional to price. Thus profits obey

$$\begin{aligned} \Pi_x &= [1 - F(\alpha_1^*)][1 - C_x/P_x], \\ \Pi_y &= F(\alpha_1^*)[1 - C_y/P_y]. \end{aligned} \tag{4}$$

The major result of this section is an existence result for a pure strategy Nash equilibrium in prices given any two distinct commodities (X, Y). Existence depends on an assumption about the distribution of consumer preferences.

Assumption A1: The distribution function $F(\alpha_1)$ is concave and twice differentiable over its support (a, b); $F'(\alpha_1) = f(\alpha_1)$, $F''(\alpha_1) = f'(\alpha_1) \leq 0$.

One special case of A1 is a uniform density over a connected subset of the unit interval.

The point of this assumption is to prevent extreme distributions of consumer preferences. Profit is guaranteed to be well behaved if a sufficient fraction of the population is "centrally" located in relation to the consumers with "extreme" tastes. An equivalent assumption plays a central role in providing stability to a broad class of voting problems (see Caplin and Nalebuff, 1986).

To review, the order of events is that Firm X first chooses its characteristic mix (x_1, x_2) and then Firm Y selects (y_1, y_2). The prices (P_x, P_y) are subsequently determined as a Bertrand–Nash equilibrium for the given pair of products. To solve the game, it is necessary to work backwards and calculate the expected price equilibrium for any pair of locations.

Given locations and Firm Y's price, the derivative of Firm X's profit function must be zero in equilibrium:

$$d\Pi_x/dP_x = \frac{[1 - F(\alpha_1^*)]C_x}{P_x^2} - \frac{f(\alpha_1^*)(1 - C_x/P_x)}{KP_x} = 0, \tag{5}$$

where we have substituted in the value of $d\alpha_1^*/dP_x$,

$$d\alpha_1^*/dP_x = 1/[KP_x]. \tag{6}$$

Parallel calculations determine the derivative conditions for Firm Y,

$$d\,\Pi_y/dP_y = \frac{F(\alpha_1^*)C_y}{P_y^2} - \frac{f(\alpha_1^*)(1 - C_y/P_y)}{KP_y} = 0. \tag{7}$$

---

[3] We assume that the density of F is non-atomic so that consumers indifferent between distinct goods X and Y are negligible.

Proposition 4.1 demonstrates that the first-order conditions, (5) and (7) are also *sufficient* to identify Bertrand–Nash equilibria. This is the key step in our proof of existence of an equilibrium.

Proposition 4.1: For consumer preferences satisfying A1, any joint solution to the first-order conditions is a Bertrand–Nash equilibrium.

Proof
   In Appendix.   □

Proposition 4.2 shows that there exists a joint solution to the first-order conditions and that it is unique. In equilibrium, $d\Pi_x/dP_x = 0$ and $d\Pi_y/dP_y = 0$ simultaneously. This implies:

$$P_x/C_x = 1 + K[1 - F(\alpha_1^*)]/f(\alpha_1^*),$$
$$P_y/C_y = 1 + KF(\alpha_1^*)/f(\alpha_1^*). \tag{8}$$

Taking ratios and substituting in the value of α_1^* in terms of P_x/P_y from equation (3′) yields the following implicit equation for any equilibrium value of α_1^* interior to the support of F,

$$\psi(\alpha_1^*) \equiv K\alpha_1^* - \log\left[\left(\frac{C_y}{C_x}\right)\left(\frac{f(\alpha_1^*) + K[1 - F(\alpha_1^*)]}{f(\alpha_1^*) + KF(\alpha_1^*)}\right)\left(\frac{y_2}{x_2}\right)\right] = 0. \tag{9}$$

Proposition 4.2: Under Assumption A1, there exists a unique equilibrium price pair (P_x, P_y) given locations (X, Y).

Proof
   If X and Y are identical, then $P_x = P_y = \text{Max}[C_x, C_y]$ and the lower cost firm monopolizes the market. For X and Y distinct, Lemma A1 in the appendix, demonstrates that ψ is a strictly monotonic function for α_1 in the support of F. Hence, any solution to $\psi(\alpha_1^*) = 0$ is unique. If $\psi(\alpha_1)$ is everywhere negative then $F(\alpha_1^*) = 1$, $P_x = C_x$, and $P_y = C_x[1 + K \mid f(\alpha_1^*)]$. If $\psi(\alpha_1)$ is everywhere positive, then $F(\alpha_1^*) = 0$, $P_y = C_y$, and $P_x = C_y[1 + K \mid f(\alpha_1^*)]$. If a solution to $\psi(\alpha_1) = 0$ exists, then equilibrium prices are determined by substitution back into equation (8)   □

Consider Firm Y's location decision in light of Proposition 4.2. It faces an incumbent of known location. If Firm Y has lower costs, it faces a dichotomous choice: it must decide between choosing a location in order to monopolize the market and choosing a location which results in a shared market.[4] Proposition 4.3 characterizes the optimal exclusionary tactic. There is an interesting analogy here with Hotelling's principle of minimum differentiation—the optimal exclusionary tactic is to locate in the identical

---

[4] On this point, Lane (1980) makes an a priori assumption that exclusion will never occur. Yet, to calculate equilibrium locations, one must allow for exclusion out of equilibrium.

spot as the incumbent. However, the motivation for imitation is entirely different than in Hotelling. Rather than agreeably splitting the market, the new entrant steals the entire market.

Proposition 4.3: When a low cost entrant (Firm Y) faces a high cost incumbent (Firm X) located in $[a, b]$, its optimal exclusionary strategy is to produce an identical product.

Proof

Consider all equilibria to the pricing game where Firm Y captures the entire market, $F(\alpha_1^*) = 1$. Since Firm X's profits in all of these equilibria are zero, it follows that $P_y \leqslant C_x$. If not, Firm X could earn positive profits by charging P_y and selling to consumers who prefer its product. Hence, over all positions (X, Y) such that $F(\alpha_1^*) = 1$, the highest value of P_y is C_x. Thus

$$\Pi_y \leqslant 1 - C_y/C_x. \tag{10}$$

But by locating in the same place as X and charging C_x, Firm Y manages to achieve a monopoly position with a profit of

$$\Pi_y = 1 - C_y/C_x, \tag{11}$$

proving the proposition $\square$

Note that if the high cost incumbent is located outside the support of F then the optimal exclusionary tactic is to locate at the nearest boundary, a or b.

The alternative to exclusion is accommodation. Whether Firm Y chooses to exclude or accommodate depends on the density function and Firm X's initial location. If the density is continuous at both boundaries of the support, $f(a) = f(b) = 0$, then Firm X is guaranteed a positive equilibrium market share and hence positive profits for any initial location. This follows from the first-order conditions. If Firm Y has the entire market, it will wish to raise its price since the density of marginal consumers is zero. This allows Firm X to gain a positive market share.

With $f(a)$, $f(b)$ strictly postive, a high cost firm may be excluded from the market. For example, if the low cost firm locates first, then there is no guarantee that the high cost firm can fit into the market. Alternatively there may be uncertainty about the competitor's costs. In this case, even if the high cost firm locates first, it is not sure how much of an extreme position to take. There will then be a tradeoff between lower profits at more extreme positions and a higher probability of being excluded.

5. Multi-dimensional product differentiation without price competition

Consider competition in product design in an industry with regulated pricing. To focus on product differentiation, we assume that the cost functions, in addition to being linear and additive in characteristics, are identical for the two firms X and Y. With an appropriate choice of units, cost are

$$C_x(w_1, \ldots, w_n) = C_y(w_1, \ldots, w_n) = \sum_{i=1}^{n} w_i.$$

Prices are a fixed mark-up over input costs $P_x/C_x = P_y/C_y = 1 + m$, for $m \geq 0$. With these assumptions, any two goods X and Y both in S^n will have an equal price.

With mark-ups fixed, total industry profits obey,

$$\Pi_x + \Pi_y = \left[1 - F(\alpha_1^*)\right]\left(1 - \frac{C_x}{P_x}\right) + F(\alpha_1^*)\left(1 - \frac{C_y}{P_y}\right)$$

$$= \frac{m}{1 + m}.$$

Hence total profits are independent of product choice, and the two firms are playing a zero-sum game. They choose product design to maximize their own market share, or equivalently to minimize the competitors market share.

There is a simple correspondence between product choice and points in the space of Cobb–Douglas parameters. For a consumer of type $\alpha \in S^n$, the product $X = \alpha$ is most preferred among the possible equally priced products. This allows us to speak of product selection in the space of utility parameters. A product of type $\alpha \in S^n$ represents the most preferred point for the α type.

According to equation (3) of Section 3, the population is divided between products of type α_1 and α_2 by a hyperplane containing α_1, on one side, and α_2 on the other. The goal of Firm X is to produce for a type α_x in order to maximize its market share. It must anticipate that Firm Y's product α_y will depend on α_x: α_y will be chosen to minimize Firm X's market share. In equilibrium, Firm X chooses that type α^* which minimizes Firm Y's maximal market share.

Facing a given product α_x, Firm Y's maximization problem is straightforward. It picks α_y so that the hyperplane in the space of Cobb–Douglas parameters dividing the population between the two products contains maximal area on the side of α_y. The central observation is Lemma 5.1. Firm Y can, by an appropriate choice of product, secure for itself the population on *either* side of *any* hyperplane through α_x.

Lemma 5.1: Consider any given hyperplane in $\mathbb{R}^n$ which passes through the origin, and has a non-empty intersection with the unit simplex, S^n. For any product $X \in S^n$ which does not lie on this hyperplane, there exists a distinct product $Y \in S^n$ so that the given hyperplane separates those who prefer X from those who prefer Y.

Proof

A hyperplane is uniquely defined by a point on its surface and its normal. Given any normal vector $\pi = (\pi_1, \ldots, \pi_n)$ and a commodity $X \in S^n$, we construct a good $Y \in S^n$ so that the separating hyperplane has normal π and passes through the origin.

Let the ith characteristic of Y be $y_i = x_i e^{-\lambda \pi_i}$. Consumers indifferent between X and Y satisfy $\alpha \cdot \pi = 0$. Thus, for any non-zero λ, the separating hyperplane passes through the origin and has normal vector π. The scale λ is chosen so that $Y \in S^n$. □

With Lemma 5.1, the problem is formally identical to existing models in the social choice literature (see for example Grandmont (1978), Greenberg (1979) and Kramer (1977)). The optimal policy for Firm X is to produce for the type α^* that minimizes the maximal proportion of the population on one side of any hyperplane passing through α^*.[5]

We exploit the analogy with social choice to present some examples and some general results on equilibrium market shares.[6] The results explore the relationship between dimensionality, population preferences, and the order of entry into the market.

The case with $n = 2$ is straightforward with a non-atomic distribution of parameters. Two firms locating sequentially will share the market evenly. To secure a fifty percent market share, Firm X produces the product α^* which is most preferred by the median type, $F(\alpha^*) = \frac{1}{2}$. The political analogue is the well-known median voter result for a population with single-peaked preferences along a line (Black [1948]).

The simplicity of the two-dimensional case is misleading. Equal division does not generalize to higher dimensions, except in the special case where the distribution of Cobb–Douglas parameters is radially symmetric (Plott, 1967).

A more interesting example involves Cobb–Douglas parameters distributed uniformly in the three-dimensional unit simplex. Whenever the first firm locates, the second can receive more than one-half of the market. In fact it is optimal for the Firm X to produce the good $(\frac{1}{3}, \frac{1}{3}, \frac{1}{3})$ designed for the individual at the center of mass of the simplex.[7] At the center of mass, Firm X serves four-ninths of the population when the second firm locates optimally [Fig. 1(a)]. If Firm X locates elsewhere, Firm Y gets a greater than five-ninths share of the market [Fig. 1(b)].

In three dimensions, the worst possibility for Firm X involves an atomic

---

[5] In fact Lemma 5.1 shows only that Firm Y can achieve market areas arbitrarily close to those defined by hyperplanes through α_x. The epsilon-equilibrium is the relevant solution concept.

[6] Caplin and Nalebuff (1986) present a thorough treatment of the equivalent problem in the context of social choice.

[7] It is tempting to conjecture that the first firm always locates at the center of mass of population preferences even with more complex densities. This is false (Caplin and Nalebuff, 1986).

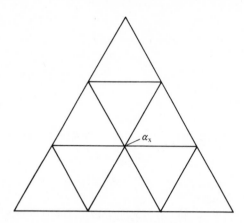

FIG. 1(a). The lines inside the triangle divide it into nine identical triangles. With Firm X locating at α_x, Firm Y can secure five of the nine triangles. To do this it produces products α_Y for which the dividing lines approach α_x at an angle perpendicular to any side of the outer triangle. There are no other lines in the triangle which secure as much as five-ninths of the population for Firm Y.

distribution of parameters. Assume that one third of the population is of type α_A, one third is of type α_B, and one third of type α_C, with α_A, α_B and α_C non-colinear. In this case, Firm Y can secure a two-thirds market share regardless of Firm X's location (Figure 2).

Insights from these planar examples are central to understanding higher-dimensional problems. There are two main results, both drawn from the social choice literature.

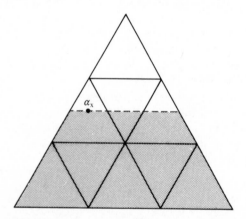

FIG. 1(b). Here, Firm X locates at α_x away from the centroid of the simples. Firm Y can now get more than five-ninths of the triangle. For example, it can pick α_Y so that the dividing lines approach α_X at an angle perpendicular to the farthest side.

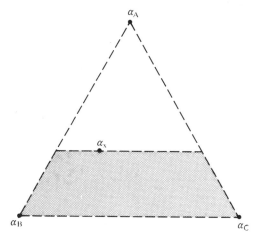

FIG. 2. The market consists of equal numbers of the three types α_A, α_B, α_C. Firm X locates at α_x. To secure the two types α_B and α_C, Firm Y produces a product giving rise to the dividing line drawn in the figure.

Proposition 5.1: With Cobb–Douglas parameters distributed arbitrarily over $S^n, n \geqslant 2$, Firm X locating optimally will receive between $\frac{1}{2}$ and $1/n$ of the total market. No tighter bound is possible.

Proof

This follows from the result of Greenberg (1979) in light of Lemma 5.1 □

Proposition 5.2: Consider Cobb–Douglas parameters distributed according to a non-atomic density $f(\alpha)$ on $\alpha \in S^n, n \geqslant 2$. Assume that the density $f(\alpha)$ is concave on its support $B \subset S^n$. Then Firm X locating optimally will receive a market share of between $\frac{1}{2}$ and $((n-1)/n)^{n-1}$. No tighter bound is possible.

Proof

This follows from the result of Caplin and Nalebuff (1986) in light of Lemma 5.1 □

These results highlight the importance of the dimensionality of the commodity space. In both propositions, the first firm's market share falls as the dimensionality rises. This suggests that entrants can improve their market share by differentiating their product along a previously unexploited dimension. Advertising is one tool used to expand the number of a product's salient characteristics. Burger King's advertising campaign introduce the distinction between flame-broiled and fried hamburgers. The recently introduced low-alcohol beer, LA, added a new dimension to beer marketing.

6. Concluding remarks

Our concluding remarks offer three directions for further research on multi-dimensional product differentiation and price competition.

Further development of the basic duopoly model

The solution to the simple duopoly model can be applied to examine a wide variety of other questions. Two important issues are the introduction of uncertainty into the locational model, and a comparison with the collusive solution.

The introduction of uncertainty will greatly enhance the model's realism. Typically, firms are not fully informed about competitors' costs. This informational asymmetry introduces entirely new issues. For example, the choice of a particular product may act as a signal of the firm's costs. This has implications both for an incumbent's choice of an initial location and the nature of the subsequent price competition. Here it is of interest that a central location by the first firm appears to be a high risk strategy once one takes account of uncertainty. Taking a central location is good for a low cost producer, but is bad should the rival turn out to have lower costs. Hence increased uncertainty about the other firm's cost may push both away from the center of the market. In equilibrium, locating centrally would send a strong entry-deterring signal that costs are very low.

The duopoly model can also be applied to study anti-trust questions. Collusion can take place in pricing decisions and/or location choices. Traditionally, anti-trust focus has been on recognizing price collusion rather than collusion in product design. Less obvious are instances where firms collude in product design, anticipating non-cooperative pricing strategies. For example, in the case of airlines, given that they pursue competitive pricing policies, are they colluding or competing in scheduling their flights?

Extensions

While the two firm, two-dimensional version of the model is revealing it is important to extend the framework to more realistic environments. Existence of a price equilibrium for an arbitrary pair of locations can be generalized beyond the two-dimensional existence result in Section 4. Our assumption of concavity (A1) plays a central role in extending the existence results to higher dimensions.

It is also important to specify in a more satisfactory manner the determinants of the order of entry into a particular market (e.g. see Hay, 1976). Frequently, the decision on whether or not to enter is being made by a number of firms at the same time. This raises entirely new issues. Will firms agree on an order of entry? If not, will there be a sudden rush to enter, with several firms entering simultaneously? Conversely, may the prospective actions of future competitors deter entry altogether, and so prevent the development of potentially profitable markets? The issues are suggestive of a possible asymmetric war of attrition (Nalebuff and Riley, 1985).

Applications

For policy design, we must compare the socially optimal pattern of product location with the non-cooperative oligopoly solution. It may then be possible to separately understand market departures from optimality in (a) the design of products, (b) pricing strategies, and (c) the number of competing products.

Finally, a potentially important application of our model is to the theory of the product cycle in international trade theory. It is frequently contended that the U.S. acts as a leader in innovation but ultimately has its markets taken away by lower cost foreign producers. There is then the question of which kinds of products and innovations will be least susceptible to this kind of potentially destructive low cost competition. The answer has implications for R&D strategies both at the corporate and national levels as well as for the design of tariffs as part of an overall industrial policy. Our model appears well suited to studying product cycle dynamics since the central elements are the known order of entry into the market and the underlying asymmetry of costs.

APPENDIX

Proposition 4.1: For consumer preferences satisfying A1, any joint solution to the first-order conditions is a Bertrand–Nash equilibrium.

Proof

Consider first a joint solution, (P_x^*, P_y^*), with $F(\alpha_1^*) \in (0, 1)$. If Firm X (symmetrically, Firm Y) has a price better than P_x^* against P_y^*, this implies that there is some other price, P_x, with $F(\alpha_1^*) \in (0, 1)$, which is a local minimum of the profit function. But (1a)–(5a) prove this is impossible as any solution to the first-order condition with $F(\alpha_1^*) \in (0, 1)$ is always a local maximum.

$$\left. \frac{d^2\Pi_x}{dP_x^2} \right|_{(d\Pi_x/dP_x)=0} \sim -f(\alpha_1^*)C_x/P_x - f(\alpha_1^*) - f'(\alpha_1^*)(1 - C_x/P_x)/K \tag{1a}$$

$$\sim -2f(\alpha_1^*)^2 - f(\alpha_1^*)[1 - F(\alpha_1^*)]K - f'(\alpha_1^*)[1 - F(\alpha_1^*)] \tag{2a}$$

$$\leqslant -2f(\alpha_1^*)^2 - f'(\alpha_1^*)[1 - F(\alpha_1^*)] \tag{3a}$$

$$\leqslant -(\tfrac{3}{2})f(\alpha_1^*)^2 \tag{4a}$$

$$< 0. \tag{5a}$$

Equation (2a) follows by substitution of the first-order condition solution for C_x/P_x into (1a). Equation (3a) follows as $K > 0$. Equation (4a) follows as $-f'(\alpha_1^*)[1 - F(\alpha_1^*)] \leqslant (\tfrac{1}{2})f(\alpha_1^*)^2$ for any concave function F. To confirm this, note that the worst case occurs when f' is a negative constant. Then for any α_1, $1 - F(\alpha_1) \leqslant -\tfrac{1}{2}f(\alpha_1)^2/f'(\alpha_1)$. Equation (5a) follows by A1 as $f(\alpha_1^*) > 0$ for $F(\alpha_1^*) \in (0, 1)$.

The only other possibility is that at the joint solution, (P_x^*, P_y^*), one firm, say Firm X, receives a zero market share. In this case, by equation (7), $F(\alpha_1^*) = 1$ implies $f(\alpha_1^*) > 0$. From equation (5), this then requires that $P_x = C_x$. This is a best response for Firm X. Any lower price leads to losses, while higher prices maintain a zero market share. Since Firm Y has a positive market share (and $f(\alpha_1^*) > 0$) the previous argument proves the optimality of P_y^*.[8] □

Lemma A1 to *Proposition* 4.2: Under A1, $\psi'(\alpha_1^*) > 0$ for $\alpha_1^* \in (a, b)$.

Proof
Taking the derivative of equation (9) shows

$$\psi'(\alpha_1^*) = K\left[1 + \frac{2f^2 + f + f'[1 - 2F]}{(f + K[1 - F])(f + KF)}\right] \tag{6a}$$

$$\geq K\left[1 + \frac{(3/2)f^2 + f}{(f + K[1 - F])(f + KF)}\right] \tag{7a}$$

$$> 0 \quad \text{for} \quad \alpha_1^* \in (a, b). \tag{8a}$$

In this derivation, we have shortened $f(\alpha_1^*)$ to f and similarly for F and f'. Equation (7a) follows from (6a) by the concavity assumption A1. Again a triangular distribution is the worst case; with f' a constant, either positive or negative, $f'[1 - 2F] \geq -(\frac{1}{2})f^2$. Substituting this inequality in (6a) yields the desired result. □

Princeton University, USA.

REFERENCES

ARCHIBALD, G. C. and ROSENBLUTH, G. (1975), "The "New" Theory of Consumer Demand and Monopolistic Competition," *Quarterly Journal of Economics* 89, 569–90.

BLACK, D. (1948), "On the Rationale of Group Decision-Making," *Journal of Political Economy* 56, 23–34.

CAPLIN, A. and NALEBUFF, B. (1986), "On 64% Majority Rule," *Econometrica* forthcoming.

CHAMBERLIN, E. H. (1933), The Theory of Monopolistic Competition, Harvard University Press, Cambridge, MA.

DASGUPTA, P. and MASKIN, E. (1986) "The Existence of Equilibrium in Discontinuous Economic Games, II: Applications," *Review of Economic Studies* 53, 27–42.

D'ASPREMONT, C., GABSZEWICZ, J., and THISSE, J. F. (1979), "On Hotelling's "Stability in Competition"," *Econometrica* 47, 1145–1150.

DIXIT, A. K. and STIGLITZ, J. E. (1977), "Monopolistic Competition and Optimum Product Diversity," *American Economic Review* 67, 297–308.

EATON, B. C. and LIPSEY, R. G. (1975), "The Principle of Minimum Differentiation Reconsidered: Some New Developments in the Theory of Spatial Competition," *Review of Economic Studies* 42, 27–49.

ECONOMIDES, N. (1984), "The Principle of Minimum Differentiation Revisited," *European Economic Review* 24, 345–368.

GABSZEWICZ, J. J. and THISSE, J. F. (1986), "Spatial Competition and the Location of Firms," *Fundamentals of Pure and Applied Economics*, J. Lesourne and H. Sonnenschein (eds.), Harwood, London.

GORMAN, W. M. (1980), "A Possible Procedure for Analysing Quality Differentials in the Egg Market," *Review of Economic Studies* 47, 843–856.

GRANDMONT, J. M. (1978), "Intermediate Preferences and the Majority Rule," *Econometrica* 46, 317-330.

[8] For his model, Lane (1980) constructs a unique joint solution to the first-order conditions. However, he does not consider whether the resulting prices form mutually best responses.

GREENBERG, J. (1979), "Consistent Majority Rules Over Compact Sets of Alternatives," *Econometrica* 47, 627–636.

GUASCH, J. L. and WEISS, A. (1980), "Adverse Selection by Markets and the Advantage of Being Late," *Quarterly Journal of Economics* 96, 453–466.

HAY, D. A. (1976), "Sequential Entry and Entry Deterring Strategies," *Oxford Economic Papers* 28, 240–257.

HOTELLING, H. (1929), "Stability in Competition," *Economic Journal* 39, 41–57.

KRAMER, G. H. (1977) "A Dynamic Model of Political Equilibrium," *Journal of Economic Theory* 16, 310–334.

LANCASTER, K. J. (1966), "A New Approach to Consumer Theory," *Journal of Political Economy* 74, 132–157.

LANE, W. (1980), "Product Differentiation in a Market with Endogenous Sequential Entry," *Bell Journal of Economics* 11, 237–260.

NALEBUFF, B. and RILEY, J. (1985), "Asymmetric Equilibria in the War of Attrition," *Journal of Theoretical Biology* 115, 81–97.

OSBORNE, M. J. and PITCHIK, C. (1983), "Equilibrium for a Three-Person Location Problem," Discussion Paper No. 123, Department of Economics, Columbia University.

PLOTT, C. (1967), "A Notion of Equilibrium and its Possibility under Majority Rule," *American Economic Review* 57, 787–806.

PRESCOTT, E. C. and VISSCHER, M. (1977), "Sequential Location among Firms with Foresight," *Bell Journal of Economics* 8, 378–393.

SCHMALENSEE, R. (1978), "Entry Deterence in the Ready-to-Eat Breakfast Cereal Industry," *Bell Journal of Economics* 9, 305–327.

SHAKED, A. and SUTTON, J. (1982), "Relaxing Price Competition Through Product Differentiation," *Review of Economic Studies* 49, 3–14.

SPENCE, A. M. (1976), "Product Selection, Fixed Costs and Monopolistic Competition," *Review of Economic Studies* 43, 217–235.

STIGLITZ, J. E. (1984) "Towards a General Theory of Monopolistic Competition," Working Paper, Department of Economics, Princeton University.

PRODUCT COMPATIBILITY CHOICE IN A MARKET WITH TECHNOLOGICAL PROGRESS*

By MICHAEL L. KATZ *and* CARL SHAPIRO

I. Introduction

THE benefit that a consumer derives from the use of a good often is an increasing function of the number of other consumers purchasing compatible items. This effect has long been recognized in the context of communications networks such as the telephone and Telex. In these cases, there is a direct externality; the more subscribers there are on a given communications network, the greater are the services provided by that network. Because they were first recognized in these industries, we call these positive external consumption benefits *network externalities.*

Network externalities are significant in many important industries where there are no physical networks. In fact, most examples of network effects entail indirect externalities associated with the provision of a durable good (hardware) and a complementary good or service (software). In these cases the externality arises when the amount and variety of software available increase with the number of hardware units sold. For instance, computers and programs must be used together to produce computing services, and the greater the sales of hardware, the more surplus the consumer is likely to enjoy in the software market due to increased entry. With video cassette players, the playback machine and a cassette jointly produce video services. Any technology that requires specific training also is subject to network externalities; the training is more valuable if the associated technology is more widely adopted. The arrangement of typewriter keyboards is an often noted example. Similarly, durable goods, such as automobiles, that require specialized servicing often are subject to network externalities.

When network externalities are significant, so too are the benefits to having all consumers purchase units of the durable that can utilize identical units of the complementary good.[1] If two units of hardware can utilize identical units of software, they are said to be *compatible.* All television sets, for example, are compatible in that they can receive and process the same broadcasts. Understanding the extent to which products will be compatible with one another is central to the analysis of markets in which network externalities arise.

* This material is based on work supported by the National Science Foundation under Grant No. SES-8510746 (Katz) and Grant No. SES-8408622 (Shapiro). We thank seminar participants at the FTC, Hebrew University, Michigan, Pittsburgh, Princeton, State University of New York at Albany, and Yale for comments and suggestions.

[1] With communications networks the question of compatibility has a somewhat different structure. The question is one of whether consumers using one firm's facilities can contact consumers who subscribe to the services of other firms.

There are two ways in which such industrywide compatibility or standardization may be achieved. For some products (e.g., video cassette recorders), the competing technologies may be inherently incompatible. In such cases, the only way to enjoy the full benefits of network externalities is to achieve *de facto* standardization by having all consumers purchase the same technology. The adoption of the QWERTY keyboard arrangement in the typewriter industry followed this pattern of standardization.[2] Arthur (1985) and Farrell and Saloner (1985 and 1986) study consumer choice among incompatible technologies in a market where the firms do not behave strategically. In Katz and Shapiro (1986), we examine the dynamics of competition between incompatible technologies in a market where firms do engage in strategic pricing.

The second way of exploiting network benefits to their fullest is to design products utilizing different technologies to work with one another. This type of technical compatibility might be thought of as creating a "standardized interface." By this we mean that each firm continues to produce according to its own technology, but the products of the two firms use the same software or may communicate directly with one another. Typically, achieving technical compatibility will be costly. These costs may include the costs of redesigning the products to work with the same complementary products, or the costs that one firm incurs in producing an adapter that allows its hardware to utilize software designed for the product of another firm. In many markets, this may be done at reasonable cost. For example, the use of standardized interfaces allows a variety of components in a personal computer system to operate together; several different brands of personal computer (the hardware) may utilize a given brand of printer (here, the "software").

In this paper, we use a modified version of our (1986) model to study the private and social incentives to achieve technical compatibility in the context of dynamic rivalry and industry evolution. The competitive environment is dynamic for two reasons. First, over time each product or network establishes an *installed base* of physical capital, in the form of previously sold equipment, and human capital, in the form of users who are trained to operate that network's products. The installed bases at any point in time influence competition at that time, due to the positive network externalities that such bases confer on current adopters. The second source of change in the environment comes from technological progress, which we take as exogenous. The relative costs of competing technologies may shift over time. In the presence of network externalities, it is important for current adopters to form expectations about the future costs of the rival technologies, since these cost will influence the future sizes of the networks among which current consumers must choose. Both the case of known

---

[2] David (1985) provides an interesting history of the adoption of the QWERTY keyboard as the standard arrangement.

technological progress and the case of uncertain progress are examined below.

We find that the dynamics of competition have a powerful effect on private compatibility decisions. In an earlier paper, Katz and Shapiro (1985), we showed that in a static environment (i.e., a single-period model) the industry's collective incentives to achieve full compatibility always are less than the social incentives. In our dynamic framework, however, we find that private firms often have excessive collective compatibility incentives. The reason is the following one. When firms produce incompatible products, consumer valuation of a unit of the good depends on the network size of the specific manufacturer of the unit. Thus, in the early stages of industry evolution, there may be extremely intense competition among producers as each seeks to get ahead of its rivals by building up an installed base. With compatible products, however, all brands are part of a single network. Hence, there is no mechanism by which a firm may establish a lead in terms of installed base. Thus, compatibility may serve to diminish competition in a new or rapidly growing industry. The resulting increase in profits is a private, but not social, benefit which gives rise to excessive compatibility incentives.

The paper is organized as follows. In Section II, we formulate a model of dynamic network competition. We describe market equilibria in this model for the case of nonstochastic technological progress, and examine the effect of compatibility on consumers, firms, and aggregate welfare. Section III treats the case of uncertain technological advance. A conclusion follows.

II. Network competition with certain technological progress

We examine the sub-game perfect equilibrium of a three stage game in which there are two competing technologies. We assume that each technology is patented and hence proprietary. At time zero, the firms choose whether to design their products to be compatible. At date $t = 1$ each firm selects a price for its product or technology. In response to these prices, each of the N_1 consumers in the market at $t = 1$ chooses which technology to adopt. Again at time $t = 2$, each firm sets a price and each of the N_2 consumers in the market at that time responds. N_1 and N_2 are given exogenously. Figure 1 presents a schematic diagram of our three stage game.

The technologies may have different production costs over the two periods. Denote by c_t the per-unit production cost for technology A during period t; let d_t denote firm B's unit costs at time t. As we shall see, the crucial variable is the difference between the two technology's costs, which we denote by $\alpha_t \equiv d_t - c_t$. α_t measures *firm A's cost advantage* during period t.

Apart from the firms' costs, the problem is symmetric across the two firms. Therefore we can, without loss of generality, adopt the labeling

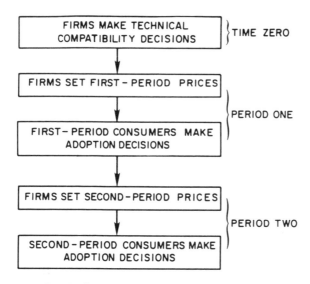

FIG. 1. Compatibility choice in a three-stage game

convention that technology B is cheaper during the second period: $\alpha_2 \leq 0$. If α_1 also is negative, then technology B is superior in both periods. The more interesting case will turn out to be the one in which $\alpha_1 > 0$. In that case, technology A holds the initial cost advantage, but is overtaken technologically by B in the second period. When $\alpha_1 > 0$ and $\alpha_2 < 0$, it is useful to think of technology B as the new or emerging technology.

A consumer shopping in period t has a completely inelastic demand for one unit of the good. The gross benefit that a consumer derives from consumption of one unit of the good, $v(z)$, depends on how many other consumers, z, ultimately purchase compatible units. In other words, the extent of consumption externalities depends only on the final network sizes.[3] Consumers in our model are homogeneous in that all of them have the same surplus function $v(z) - p$, where p is the price paid. The prices of technologies A and B in period t are denoted by p_t and q_t, respectively.

If the products are compatible, each consumer enjoys gross benefits of $v(N_1 + N_2)$ from either technology, since (under our assumption of inelastic demand) all other consumers ultimately purchase compatible units. When the technologies are incompatible, gross consumption benefits depend upon the number of consumers purchasing the *same* technology. Let x_t and y_t denote the quantities of technologies A and B, respectively, that are sold in period t. A consumer who purchases technology A in period t derives net

---

[3] As we discuss more fully in Katz and Shapiro (1986), it is straightforward to allow first-period consumers to derive intermediate benefits from the good that depend solely on the first-period network size. Such benefits would only strengthen the incentives for first-period consumers to form a bandwagon.

benefits of $v(x_1 + x_2) - p_t$. The corresponding value for a consumer who purchases technology B in period t is $v(y_1 + y_2) - q_t$.

A. *Equilibrium with compatible products*

If the products of the two firms are compatible, consumers in each period purchase units from the firm offering the lower price. This choice generates net benefits of $v(N_1 + N_2) - \min(p_t, q_t)$ for a consumer in period t. The allocation of first-period sales across firms has no effect on the second-period outcome. In the second period, the firms play a standard Nash-Bertrand pricing game. The equilibrium entails the firm with the lower costs winning all of the second-period sales at a price "just under" the costs of its rival. With our labeling convention that $\alpha_2 \leqslant 0$, firm B wins all of the second-period sales at a price of c_2 and earns second-period profits of $\pi_2^B = -N_2\alpha_2$.

The first-period pricing game has the same structure as the second-period one. When $\alpha_1 > 0$, firm A captures first-period sales at a price of d_1, earning profits of $\pi_1^A = N_1\alpha_1$. For $\alpha_1 \leqslant 0$, firm B wins the first-period sales and earns $\pi_1^B = -N_1\alpha_1$ from those sales.

Total industry profits over the two periods are equal to $N_1 |\alpha_1| + N_2 |\alpha_2|$. Consumers in period t enjoy net benefits of $N_t\{v(N_1 + N_2) - \max[c_t, d_t]\}$. Aggregate welfare, which we take to be the sum of consumer surplus and profits, is simply the excess of gross consumption benefits over production costs. It is given by $W = (N_1 + N_2)v(N_1 + N_2) - N_1 \min[c_1, d_1] - N_2 d_2$.

B. *Equilibrium with incompatible products*

When the technologies are incompatible, each consumer cares about the adoption decisions of all other consumers. Not surprisingly, bandwagons arise. In fact, in response to any pair of prices (p_t, q_t) in period t, there is no equilibrium in which consumers in that period choose different technologies from one another. To see this fact, consider period two. Given homogeneous tastes, a second-period equilibrium among consumers could involve positive sales of both technologies only if all consumers were indifferent between the two networks. But then a single consumer who was adopting product A could increase her payoff by shifting to network B. Such a shift would, given the positive consumption externalities, raise the payoff from adopting B above its previous level, which in turn equalled the consumer's previous payoff.[4] Therefore, only corner equilibria are possible in the second period. The argument for bandwagon equilibria is even stronger in the initial period. At that time, an individual's switch from A to B might also cause more second-period consumers to adopt B, and cannot cause more of them to choose A. Of course, our strong within-period bandwagon result relies on consumer homogeneity.

[4] If consumers ignored their influence on network size (i.e., if there were a continuum of consumers), then an unstable interior equilibrium might exist.

There may exist more than one perfect equilibrium involving within-period bandwagons.[5] For example, if everyone else chooses technology A at time t, it may well be optimal for any given period-t consumer also to choose A in order to stay with the crowd. But the same may hold true for technology B. It is our view that the Pareto-preferred equilibrium serves as a focal point when there are multiple equilibria. In particular, we assume that consumers in the market at a given date all select the technology yielding them each the greater surplus when two corner equilibria (for consumer choices at a given date) exist. Note this "coordination" does not require any side payments, since the consumers purchasing at a given date have coincident interests.

Solving the game backwards, we begin with second-period competition. Using the argument above, the only possible histories all entail a single firm having "won," i.e., having made all of the sales, during the first period. As we shall see, a key feature of a given market is whether the second-period consumers will match the first-period consumers' technology choice.

The firms play Nash in second-period prices, and thus either firm is willing to go down as far as its marginal cost in order to undercut the other firm. With our Pareto-selection criterion, the technology that can offer second-period consumers the greater level of surplus (were it to price as low as its marginal cost) captures all second-period sales. The winning technology is priced so that it marginally beats the losing one.

Competition in the second period hinges on the two differences between the firms that exist at that time. The first difference is the *cost advantage* that firm B enjoys, $-\alpha_2$. The second difference is the *installed base advantage* that accrues to whichever firm won the sales during the initial period. The firm with the installed base can offer gross benefits of $v(N_1 + N_2)$ if second-period consumers adopt it. In contrast, the firm with no base can only offer benefits of $v(N_2)$; effectively, its product is inferior. Formally, the installed base advantage is given by $\beta_2 \equiv v(N_1 + N_2) - v(N_2)$, the additional benefits that a technology offers due to its already having N_1 users.

Technology B's second-period cost advantage may be so large that it will be chosen even if technology A is priced at cost in the second period and all first-period consumers purchased A. This will occur if $v(N_2) - d_2$, the maximum surplus that B can offer without an installed base, exceeds $v(N_1 + N_2) - c_2$, A's best surplus offer when it does have a base of users. $v(N_2) - d_2 > v(N_1 + N_2) - c_2$ is equivalent to $-\alpha_2 > \beta_2$, i.e., B's cost advantage exceeds A's installed base advantage.

Consider first-period competition when $-\alpha_2 > \beta_2$, recalling that in a perfect equilibrium first-period consumers rationally anticipate second-period pricing and adoption decisions as a function of their own (collective) choice. If first-period consumers opt for technology A, then in the second

---

[5] We explore the structure of multiple equilibria in our (1985) paper.

period the maximal price that B can charge satisfies $v(N_1 + N_2) - c_2 = v(N_2) - q_2$, or $q_2 = c_2 - \beta_2$. Firm B earns total profits of $N_2(-\alpha_2 - \beta_2)$. Alternatively, firm B can undercut firm A in the first period. First-period consumers recognize that second-period consumers will purchase technology B. Thus, first-period consumers compare $v(N_1) - p_1$ and $v(N_1 + N_2) - q_1$. Firm B enjoys an *anticipated base advantage* of $\beta_1 \equiv v(N_1 + N_2) - v(N_1)$. Using the fact that firm A is willing to price as low as c_1 to win first-period sales, firm B must set its price at $q_1 = c_1 + \beta_1$ in order to win first-period sales. In this event, firm B earns profits of $N_1(-\alpha_1 + \beta_1)$ in the first period. Given that technology B prevails during the first period, firm B can set a higher second-period price than it could had it lost in the first period. Its maximal second-period price is $q_2 = c_2 + \beta_2$, generating second-period profits of $N_2(-\alpha_2 + \beta_2)$. Comparing total profits under each of the two first-period strategies, we see that it is profitable for firm B to win first-period sales if and only if

$$\beta_1 + (2N_2/N_1)\beta_2 > \alpha_1. \tag{1}$$

Next, suppose that B does *not* have a sufficient cost advantage in the second period to guarantee that it will win the second-period competition (i.e., $-\alpha_2 \leqslant \beta_2$). In this case, network effects dominate cost differences. Whichever firm captures the first-period sales will make the second-period sales as well. First-period consumers realize that, as a group, they play a leadership role and their choice will be matched by second-period consumers. Firms also are aware that winning in the initial period is essential to making any sales, or profits, at all.

Conditional on winning the first-period sales, second-period profits are $N_2(\beta_2 + \alpha_2)$ for firm A and $N_2(\beta_2 - \alpha_2)$ for firm B. Turning to the first period, we investigate the lowest first-period price that would be profitable for each technology. If firm A loses the first-period competition, then it earns no profits in either period. If it wins the first-period sales at a price of p_1, firm A's profits are

$$(p_1 - c_1)N_1 + (\beta_2 + \alpha_2)N_2. \tag{2}$$

Solving (2) for the price that yields zero profits, we obtain

$$\hat{p}_1 = c_1 - (N_2/N_1)(\beta_2 + \alpha_2). \tag{3}$$

Similar calculations show that the minimal price at which firm B would seek first-period sales is

$$\hat{q}_1 = d_1 - (N_2/N_1)(\beta_2 - \alpha_2). \tag{4}$$

The firm that has the lower minimal price is the one that will serve all consumers in both periods. Comparing equations (3) and (4), we find that firm B wins if and only if

$$N_1\alpha_1 + 2N_2\alpha_2 \leqslant 0. \tag{5}$$

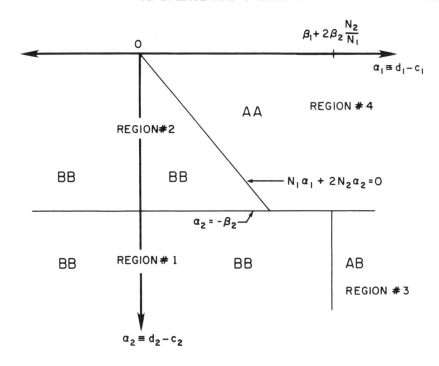

FIG. 2. Equilibrium technology adoption under incompatibility

The equilibrium market outcome under incompatibility is illustrated in Fig. 2. As the asymmetry of the figure illustrates, there is a *second-mover advantage* among firms in the dynamic competition. Suppose that $N_1 = N_2$, and that firm A's initial cost advantage just equals firm B's later advantage, i.e., $0 < \alpha_1 = -\alpha_2$. As long as the cost differences are not too large, the market equilibrium entails all consumers purchasing technology B. The reason is that firm A cannot promise to price below cost in the second period, but firm B *can* price below cost in the first period.[6]

It is straightforward to compute the firms' profits and total welfare for each of the types of equilibria shown in Fig. 2. In Region #1, firm B wins in both periods, $\pi^B = N_1(\beta_1 - \alpha_1) + N_2(\beta_2 - \alpha_2)$, $\pi^A = 0$, and $W = (N_1 + N_2)v(N_1 + N_2) - d_1N_1 - d_2N_2$. The same outcome and welfare arises in Region #2, but there firm A competes more strongly in the first period, and $\pi^B = -\alpha_1N_1 - 2\alpha_2N_2$. In Region #3, the pattern of technology choice is A followed by B, $\pi^A = N_1(\alpha_1 - \beta_1) - 2N_2\beta_2$, $\pi^B = N_2(-\beta_2 - \alpha_2)$, and $W = N_1(v(N_1) - c_1) + N_2(v(N_2) - d_2)$. Finally, in Region #4, firm A wins in both periods, $\pi^A = \alpha_1N_1 - 2\alpha_2N_2$, $\pi^B = 0$, and $W = (N_1 + N_2)v(N_1 + N_2) - c_1N_1 - c_2N_2$.

---

[6] We have more fully explored this and other biases in the market choice between incompatible technologies in Katz and Shapiro (1986).

C. *Compatibility choice*

When network externalities are large, the choice of whether to make the products or technologies compatible is one of the most important dimensions of industry performance. We assume that the decision to design a standardized interface linking the networks of the two firms' products is made prior to production of the goods, i.e., before the period-one competition. By studying perfect equilibria, we are making the assumption that the firms accurately forecast industry competition with and without compatibility when making their compatibility decisions.

We denote by $\Delta\pi$ the change in the firms' joint profits in going from the incompatibility regime to the compatibility regime, gross of any costs of achieving compatibility. $\Delta\pi$ measures the firms' joint private incentives to achieve compatibility. A particular firm's incentives are denoted by $\Delta\pi^i$, $i = A,B$. With obvious notation, the social incentive to achieve compatibility is given by ΔW. The difference between social and private incentives is given by the change in consumer surplus, $\Delta S \equiv \Delta W - \Delta\pi$. We say that a firm or a consumer cohort prefers compatibility if its payoff (weakly) rises on account of compatibility (before any costs associated with achieving compatibility are considered). Recall our labeling convention, $\alpha_2 \leqslant 0$. Comparing the profits and consumer surplus in the two regimes, as calculated in Sections IIA and IIB above, one obtains:

Proposition 1: Firm A always prefers compatibility, as do second-period consumers. First-period consumers prefer compatibility if and only if technology B is sufficiently superior during period 2 that first-period consumers would be stranded if they chose technology A. Firm B may or may not prefer compatibility, but it's interests always are opposed to those of consumers as a whole.

When α_1, as well as α_2, is nonpositive, firm A has higher production costs in both periods and earns zero profits under either compatibility regime. In the case where $\alpha_1 > 0$, firm A, the owner of the currently superior technology, prefers compatibility because this dampens its rival's competitive zeal during the initial period. Compatibility removes the strategic linkages between the two periods of competition; since each firm's competitive position in the second period is independent of who won the sales during the first period, neither firm is willing to set first-period price below cost. With compatibility, firm A can exploit its early cost advantage, independently of any future disadvantages it will face. Consumers are content to purchase A's products without fear of being stranded with an obsolete model.

Figure 3 indicates the qualitative effects of compatibility on firm B, and on the firms jointly. The diagonally striped area in the Figure indicates those cost pairs (α_1, α_2) for which firm B prefers compatibility. Firm B tends to prefer compatibility if its cost disadvantage during the first period,

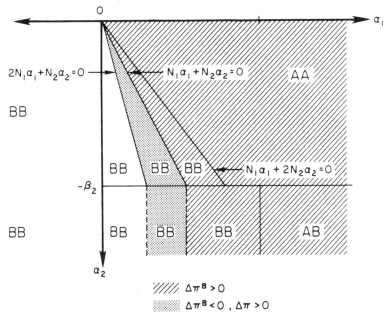

FIG. 3. The effect of compatibility on profits

α_1, is large, or if its cost advantage during the second period, $-\alpha_2$, is small. The shaded region corresponds to those cost pairs for which $\Delta\pi^B < 0$, but $\Delta\pi > 0$; the firms jointly gain from compatibility, although firm B alone does not.

Firm B always likes compatibility if it would lose the initial period competition without compatibility (Regions #3 and #4 from Figure 2). In these cases, compatibility makes the B technology more attractive in period 2. But firm B may prefer incompatibility if a lack of compatibility drives A from the market or weakens A as a competitor. In the case where technology B has a cost advantage in both periods, firm B always prefers incompatibility.[7] More generally, a firm developing a new technology that will enjoy a sufficiently large cost advantage tomorrow (relative to its cost disadvantage today), has an incentive to design its products to be *in*compatible with the technology having lower costs today. Doing so cripples its rival's ability to compete today, since first-period consumers know that they will be stranded tomorrow if they purchase the older technology with the early cost advantage.

Shifting attention to the demand side of the market, the effect of compatibility on consumers can be best understood by recognizing the following fact. Since the firms engage in pricing competition, consumers in a given period enjoy the surplus that the *less* well-placed firm can offer. That

---

[7] This is analogous to our [1985] finding that a firm that is expected to have a large network prefers incompatibility.

surplus level determines how low a price is offered by the other firm, which actually makes the sales.

Because of this principle, second-period consumers always prefer compatibility. Compatibility increases the competitive position of the technology that did *not* prevail during the initial period; that technology is no longer handicapped by a smaller in-place base of units. Under compatibility, second-period consumers obtain the greatest surplus that they can hope to earn, $v(N_1 + N_2) - c_2$.

Turning to first-period consumers, if $-\alpha_2 > \beta_2$, so that firm B will surely prevail in the second period, then these consumers prefer compatibility. Compatibility increases the size of A's network and enhances the surplus that firm A can offer at price c_1, which is the lowest price that firm A will offer under either regime. If, however, $-\alpha_2 \leqslant \beta_2$, then first-period sales determine second-period sales, and first-period consumers need not worry about being stranded. Therefore, they benefit from the intensified first-period competition to which incompatibility leads.

Given these incentives, we can now examine whether the firms will in fact achieve compatibility and how the social and private decisions compare. As we have seen, there are cases in which the move to compatibility increases the profits of firm A, yet reduces those of firm B. Thus, we must be careful to specify the process by which compatibility is achieved and whether side payments between the firms are feasible. We denote by $F^i \geqslant 0$ the costs that must be incurred by firm i if the two technologies are made compatible. F denotes total standardization costs for the industry; $F^A + F^B = F$. We assume that compatibility does not alter the marginal costs of production.

When the firms are able to make side payments between each other, the private compatibility decision hinges on the sign of $\Delta\pi - F$. The social decision rule is to achieve compatibility if and only if $\Delta W \geqslant F$. Proposition 1 indicates that whenever firm B prefers incompatibility, the firms' *joint* compatibility incentives are too low; $\Delta\pi^B < 0$ implies that $\Delta S > 0$ and, hence, that $\Delta\pi < \Delta\pi + \Delta S = \Delta W$. The firms fail to achieve socially efficient compatibility when $\Delta\pi < F < \Delta W$.

It is also possible that the firms have *excessive* incentives to achieve compatibility. Again by Proposition 1, they have excessive incentives whenever firm B prefers compatibility. When $\Delta\pi > F > \Delta W$, the firms choose compatibility although its costs exceed the social benefits. The reason for these excessive incentives is the same as the reason why firm A prefers compatibility: compatibility leads to reduced competition during the first period (i.e., there is no below-cost pricing during the first period).

The result that the firms jointly have excess private compatibility incentives contrasts markedly with the usual results that firms would like to differentiate their products to relax competition.[8] With compatibility the

---

[8] Neven (1985) and Shaked and Sutton (1982) study the diminution of competition through product differentiation in a market without network externalities.

firms are selling perfect substitutes, while incompatible products are differentiated on the basis of network size. In the presence of network externalities, the firms diminish their rivalry in the initial period by producing perfect substitutes.

This result is analogous to the fact that firms may jointly prefer not to be able to make sunk capital investments in the context of dynamic rivalry. When capital investments (such as physical capital investments or advertising) are possible, each firm may have an incentive to overcapitalize in order to bolster its competitive position in the future. But the ability of all firms to make such investments may reduce the profits of each firm. In this analogy, increased compatibility corresponds to a reduced degree of sunkness of any such investments. If the investments are not sunk, they cannot constitute a form of commitment, and collective over-investment does not occur in equilibrium. Likewise, with compatibility each of the firms is unwilling to sustain loses during the early stages of competition.

When side payments are not feasible, and the firms disagree on the desirability of making their products compatible, it is important to specify whether unilateral standardization is feasible, or if decisions must be made jointly. Both cases may arise in practice. Often, a single firm can act unilaterally to make its product compatible with those of another firm by constructing an adapter. For example, some video game manufacturers have developed physical adapters that allow their machines to run games initially written for their competitors' hardware. Similarly, one firm may be able unilaterally to adopt another network's specifications for its product design. An example of this pattern is the manufacture by several companies of personal computers that are sufficiently similar to the IBM PC that they can run software written for the IBM PC.

In other cases, compatibility is attainable only through the joint adoption of a product standard; the firms must act together to make their products compatible. These cases arise when the interface or product design is proprietary or when an adapter is prohibitively expensive (e.g., equal to the cost of the product itself). The CPM operating system for personal computers and the broadcast television standards are both examples of jointly adopted standards.[9]

When a single firm is able unilaterally to construct an adapter, the adapting firm bears all of the compatibility costs, F. An adapter will be built if and only if $\Delta \pi^i \geq F$ for at least one of the two firms. Proposition 1 establishes that firm A will find it profitable to construct an adapter if F is sufficiently small. In other words, we find that the owner of an older

---

[9] In a variety of manufacturing industries, standards are promulgated to encourage compatibility. The American National Standards Institute establishes domestic standards and represents the U.S. in the International Organization for Standardization. Carlton and Klamer (1983) discuss compatibility in telephony, as well as in the electronic funds transfer and rail transportation industries.

technology will make an effort to become compatible with future technologies. Yet the newer technology may resist designing its product to be
compatible with the older technology. If the firm controlling the emerging
technology does construct an adapter, then we know that consumers, in
particular first-period consumers, are made worse off as a result. This result
may appear to be an odd one, but is is not hard to understand. Firm B
constructs the adapter in those cases where the dominant effect of
compatibility is to dampen first-period competition.

For an industry standard to be established, the firms must act together.
Compatibility will be achieved if and only if $\Delta \pi^i \geq F^i$ for both firms. Hence,
compatibility can arise only if firm B, the emerging technology, consents, in
which case (by Proposition 1) consumers as a whole must be made worse
off. If $\Delta \pi < \Delta W$, then $\Delta \pi^B < 0$ and firm B will block what may be efficient
compatibility. This result is not surprising given our earlier analysis of side
payments; the private compatibility rule when the compatibility mechanism
is an industry standard is more stringent absent side payments than it is
when side payments are feasible. Of course, when firm B likes standardization, the firms' *joint* incentives are excessive, and side payments may
allow firm B to bribe firm A (perhaps by covering the bulk of the
standardization costs) in order to bring about standards that are socially
inefficient.[10]

III. Network competition with uncertain technological progress

Often, consumers and firms are uncertain about the future costs of the
competing technologies. In this section, we consider a market in which the
second-period costs of the two technologies are unknown in the first period.
As we have seen, given our assumption that demand is inelastic in each
period, the market equilibrium depends only on the difference in second-
period costs, α_2. Let $f(\cdot)$ denote the density function of α_2. We assume that
all agents know this distribution of the cost difference. For simplicity, we
assume that the two firms have identical first-period costs, i.e., $\alpha_1 = 0$.

A. Equilibrium with compatible products

Suppose that the two products are compatible. For any given realization
of α_2, the second-period outcome is determined as in our earlier case where
the second-period costs were known with certainty in the first period.
Taking expectations over the possible realizations of α_2, the expected
second-period profits of firm A are

$$N_2 \int_0^\infty \alpha_2 f(\alpha_2) \, d\alpha_2. \tag{6}$$

---

[10] An example would be: $\Delta W < F < \Delta \pi$, $\Delta \pi^A < F^A$, and $\Delta \pi^B > F^B$.

Similarly, the expected second-period profits of firm B are

$$N_2 \int_{-\infty}^{0} -\alpha_2 f(\alpha_2) \, d\alpha_2. \tag{7}$$

The outcome in the first period has no effect on second-period profits, and as before competition in the first period is essentially a single-period Nash-Bertrand pricing game. Thus, the equilibrium price in the first period is $p_1 = c_1 = d_1 = q_1$, and the firms earn zero profits in that period. Thus, the firms' total profits over the two periods are given by equations (6) and (7).

B. Equilibrium with incompatible products

As we have shown in Section II, for any given realization of α_2, first-period sales enter into the calculation of the second-period outcome when the products are incompatible. Let R^i denote firm i's expected second-period profits conditional on its having won all of the first-period sales, and let L^i denote expected second-period profits conditional on having made no first-period sales. Integrating over the relevant regions, we obtain

$$R^A = N_2 \int_{-\beta_2}^{\infty} \{\alpha_2 + \beta_2\} f(\alpha_2) \, d\alpha_2 \tag{8}$$

and

$$L^A = N_2 \int_{\beta_2}^{\infty} \{\alpha_2 - \beta_2\} f(\alpha_2) \, d\alpha_2. \tag{9}$$

The difference between the expected profits conditional on winning and losing first-period sales tells us the maximal amount that firm A would be willing to pay to obtain the first-period sales (i.e., how much the firm would be willing to subsidize first-period consumers). Letting M^A denote this difference, $R^A - L^A$, we have

$$M^A = N_2 \beta_2 \left\{ \int_{\beta_2}^{\infty} f(\alpha_2) \, d\alpha_2 + \int_{-\beta_2}^{\infty} f(\alpha_2) \, d\alpha_2 \right\} + N_2 \int_{-\beta_2}^{\beta_2} \alpha_2 f(\alpha_2) \, d\alpha_2. \tag{10}$$

Similar calculations show that firm B's maximal willingness to subsidize first-period consumers is

$$M^B = N_2 \beta_2 \left\{ \int_{-\infty}^{-\beta_2} f(\alpha_2) \, d\alpha_2 + \int_{-\infty}^{\beta_2} f(\alpha_2) \, d\alpha_2 \right\} - N_2 \int_{-\beta_2}^{\beta_2} \alpha_2 f(\alpha_2) \, d\alpha_2. \tag{11}$$

In setting its first-period price, firm A is willing to go as low as $c_1 - M^A/N_1$. Firm B is willing to go as low as $d_1 - M^B/N_1$. Consumers choose the firm from whom expected surplus is greater.

C. Compatibility choice

The general case of uncertain technological progress is difficult to analyze. There are, however, two important special cases where we can characterize the compatibility incentives fully. First, suppose that $f(\cdot)$ is symmetric around 0, i.e., that the firms are ex ante symmetrically placed. In this case, the expressions for M^A and M^B simplify greatly. Since

$$\int_{\beta_2}^{\infty} f(\alpha_2)\, d\alpha_2 = \int_{-\infty}^{-\beta_2} f(\alpha_2)\, d\alpha_2 \quad \text{and} \quad \int_{-\infty}^{\infty} f(\alpha_2)\, d\alpha_2 = 1,$$

we have $M^A = N_2\beta_2 = M^B$. Hence, the first-period equilibrium price is $c_1 - \beta_2(N_2/N_1)$, because each firm is willing to pay up to $N_2\beta_2$ to win the first-period sales. Total expected profits for firm i thus are equal to

$$L^A = N_2 \int_{\beta_2}^{\infty} \{\alpha_2 - \beta_2\} f(\alpha_2)\, d\alpha_2. \tag{12}$$

Comparing equations (6) and (12), and using the fact that the two firms earn equal expected profits, we find that compatibility raises expected profits.[11]

The reason why symmetrically placed firms always prefer compatibility is similar to the incentives noted in the certainty model of Section II. In the second period, the firms are asymmetric (with or without compatibility) and competition does not fully dissipate profits. With incompatible products, however, competition in the first period strongly tends to dissipate second-period profits; they earn combined losses in the first period absent compatibility. With incompatibility, the firms each earn the "loser's" level of expected second-period profits, i.e., the profits earned by a firm with an installed base *dis*advantage. Under compatibility, there is no scope for installed base investment, and second-period profits are not dissipated in the first period. Thus, in our uncertainty model, the firms want to reduce ex ante competition, which occurs while they are in a symmetric position.

Summarizing the effects of compatibility on consumers as well as firms:

Proposition 2: Suppose that the firms are ex ante symmetric. Then compatibility raises expected profits. For any realization of α_2, compability raises or leaves unchanged second-period consumer surplus and total welfare. If $N_1\beta_1 \leqslant N_2\beta_2$, then for any realization of α_2, compatibility lowers first-period consumer surplus and total consumer surplus.

Proof The result for profits is established above. Total welfare reaches its maximum under compatibility, since each consumer enjoys gross benefits of $v(N_1 + N_2)$ and the cheaper technology is produced in each period. Second-period consumers must benefit from compatibility by Proposition 1. The final part of the proposition is established by direct computation.   Q.E.D.

---

[11] For particular realizations of α_2, however, ex post industry profits would have been higher had the products not been compatible. One such case arises when the firm that wins first-period sales is the one with higher second-period costs and $\beta_2 - |\alpha_2| < |\alpha_2|$.

Given ex ante symmetry, first-period consumers and consumers as a whole will prefer incompatibility if the realized cost advantage of the firm that lost in the first period is less then β_2. In such cases, *de facto* standardization arises even absent compatibility, and first-period consumers benefit from the increased competition to serve them under incompatibility. If, however, the firm that wins the first-period sales has much higher costs in the second period, then first-period consumers will be stranded. In this case, they must compare the network benefits that arise from compatibility, $N_1\beta_1$, with the loss of their subsidy from below-cost pricing, $N_2\beta_2$. When $N_1\beta_1 \leqslant N_2\beta_2$, the subsidy is worth more than is the larger network, and these consumers prefer incompatibility, despite stranding.

Now consider a second special case in which α_2 always lies within the interval $[-\beta_2, \beta_2]$, although the firms need not be ex ante symmetric. In this case, whichever firm wins the first-period sales also wins the second. Hence, $L^i = 0$, and

$$M^A = N_2 \int_{-\beta_2}^{\beta_2} \{\alpha_2 + \beta_2\} f(\alpha_2) \, d\alpha_2.$$
$$= N_2\{\bar{\alpha}_2 + \beta_2\}, \tag{13}$$

where $\bar{\alpha}_2$ is the mean of α_2. Similarly, $M^B = N_2\{-\bar{\alpha}_2 + \beta_2\}$. Given the labeling convention that $\bar{\alpha}_2 \leqslant 0$, $M^B \geqslant M^A$, and firm B "outbids" firm A for first-period sales. Firm B earns total profits of

$$M^B - M^A = -2N_2\bar{\alpha}_2. \tag{14}$$

Comparing the sum of equations (6) and (7) with equation (14), making straightforward algebraic manipulations, and applying Proposition 1 to the effects of compatibility on consumers, we obtain

Proposition 3: Suppose that the support of α_2 lies within the interval $[-\beta_2, \beta_2]$ and that the mean of α_2 is nonpositive. Then first-period consumers prefer incompatibility, and second-period consumers prefer compatibility for any realization of α_2. The firms' expected profits under compatibility exceed expected profits under incompatibility if

$$0 \leqslant E[\Delta \pi] = N_2 \left\{ 3 \int_0^{\beta_2} \alpha_2 f(\alpha_2) \, d\alpha_2 + \int_{-\beta_2}^0 \alpha_2 f(\alpha_2) \, d\alpha_2 \right\}. \tag{15}$$

Welfare attains its first-best level under compatibility, and thus compatibility cannot lower total surplus. In fact, it may strictly raise welfare. Since consumers match across periods, the full network benefits are realized in either case, and any welfare gains must come on the production side of the market. Under compatibility, production costs are minimized. But under incompatibility, firm B will have positive second period sales (given that it has won the first-period sales) even when it is the higher-cost producer. Hence, compatibility raises expected welfare by

$$E[\Delta W] = N_2 \int_0^{\beta_2} \alpha_2 f(\alpha_2)\, d\alpha_2 > 0. \tag{16}$$

Using the definition of total surplus, equations (15) and (16) imply that the expected change in total consumer surplus from the move to compatibility is

$$E[\Delta S] = -N_2 \left\{ \int_0^{\beta_2} 2\alpha_2 f(\alpha_2)\, d\alpha_2 + \int_{-\beta_2}^0 \alpha_2 f(\alpha_2)\, d\alpha_2 \right\}. \tag{17}$$

The right-hand side of equation (17) may be either positive or negative. Note that $E[\Delta W] > 0$ implies that whenever $E[\Delta \pi] < 0$, $E[\Delta S] > 0$; when the firms jointly oppose compatibility, consumer always collectively favor it.

Equation (15) suggests that the firms collectively prefer compatibility as long as they have similar expected second-period costs. When $\bar{\alpha}_2 = 0$, for example,

$$\int_{-\beta_2}^0 -\alpha_2 f(\alpha_2)\, d\alpha_2 = \int_0^{\beta_2} \alpha_2 f(\alpha_2)\, d\alpha_2,$$

and the right-hand side of equation (15) is positive; the firms prefer compatibility. The competition to obtain installed base is strongest when the firms are evenly matched ex ante. At the other extreme, if α_2 is always negative, then the right-hand side of equation (15) is negative, and the firms, in particular firm B, prefer incompatibility. This result generalizes our earlier finding in the certainty case that a firm prefers incompatibility if it enjoys a cost advantage at each date.

Proposition 3 compares total profits under the two compatibility regimes. Given that $\pi^A = 0$ under incompatibility, clearly $\Delta \pi^A \geq 0$. Since

$$\Delta \pi^B = 2N_2 \int_0^{\beta_2} \alpha_2 f(\alpha_2)\, d\alpha_2 + N_2 \int_{-\beta_2}^0 \alpha_2 f(\alpha_2)\, d\alpha_2, \tag{18}$$

which may be positive or negative, firm B's attitude towards compatibility is more sensitive to the distribution of α_2. For $\bar{\alpha}_2 = 0$, $\Delta \pi^B > 0$, and the firms both prefer compatibility.

In addition to examining the effects of changes in $\bar{\alpha}_2$, we can examine the incentive effects of a mean-preserving spread in the distribution of α_2.

Corollary: Suppose that α_2 lies within the interval $[-\beta_2, \beta_2]$ and the mean of α_2 is nonpositive. Then a mean preserving spread in the distribution of α_2 increases the firms' collective incentives to achieve compatibility.[12]

Proof Rewriting equation (15),

$$E[\Delta \pi] = N_2 \int_0^{\beta_2} \alpha_2 f(\alpha_2)\, d\alpha_2 + N_2 \int_{-\beta_2}^0 -\alpha_2 f(\alpha_2)\, d\alpha_2 + 2N_2 \bar{a}_2. \tag{19}$$

---

[12] We assume the spread does not expand the support of α_2 beyond $[-\beta_2, \beta_2]$.

Of course, $\bar{\alpha}_2$ is unaffected by a mean preserving spread. The mean preserving spread must, however, raise (or leave unchanged) the first integral on the right-hand side of the equation since this integral is taken over a tail (the mean of α_2 is nonpositive). Since the first integral rises,

$$\int_{-\beta_2}^{0} \alpha_2 f(\alpha_2)\, d\alpha_2 = \bar{\alpha}_2 - \int_{0}^{\beta_2} \alpha_2 f(\alpha_2)\, d\alpha_2$$

must fall. Thus, the second right-hand side integral must rise. This fact implies that the mean-preserving spread raises the right-hand side of equation (19).   Q.E.D.

A mean-preserving spread in α_2 may be interpreted as a change in the correlation between the two firms' second-period costs. See, for example, the two panels of Fig. 4, in each of which (c_2, d_2) is distributed over the

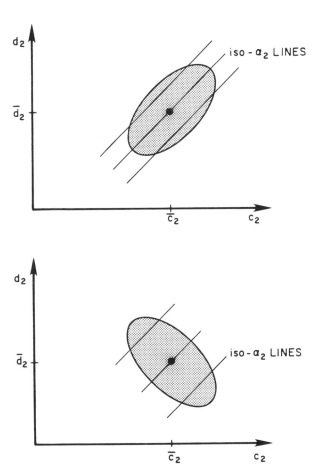

FIG. 4. Positively and negatively correlated c_2 and d_2

shaded region. The shaded regions in Figs 4a and 4b are assumed to have the same center of mass. In Fig. 4a, c_2 and d_2 are highly correlated, and their difference, α_2, exhibits little spread. In Fig. 4b, the two firms' costs are less correlated; the corresponding distribution of α_2 is a mean-preserving spread of the distribution from Fig. 4a. Therefore, the Corollary suggests that the firms are more likely to prefer compatibility when their second-period costs are uncorrelated or negatively correlated. It is exactly in such circumstances that compatibility generates the greatest social benefits.

In closing this section, we should note that one could use Propositions 2 and 3 to analyze the compatibility decision, as in Section II. The same basic forces that may lead to insufficient or excessive private compatibility incentives remain present in the uncertainty case.

IV. Conclusion

Our analysis demonstrates that the social and private incentives to achieve compatibility may diverge. The most striking result is that firms may use product compatibility as a means of reducing competition among themselves. By choosing compatible technologies, the firms prevent themselves from going through an early phase of extremely intense competition where each firm tries to build up its network to get ahead of its rival. As a result, product compatibility tends to lower the surplus of first-period consumers, and the firms' compatibility incentives may be socially excessive. The private incentives are not always excessive, however. Product compatibility tends to strengthen second-period competition since no firm falls behind in terms of its first-period installed base. Thus, second-period consumers derive greater surplus under compatibility than under incompatibility, and the firms' compatibility incentives may be too low.

There are several directions in which it would be useful to extend our analysis. One would be to endogenize the rate of technological progress. Obviously, such an extension would raise a host of interesting and difficult issues. For example, how might firms commit themselves to vigorous R&D activities in the future as a way of building a base today?

A second extension would be to consider elastic demands. By assuming that demand is perfectly inelastic over the relevant range, we have assumed away one motivation for below-cost pricing during the first period. If the firms produce compatible products and demands are inelastic, neither firm is willing to set its first-period price below cost. With elastic demand, however, low first-period prices can help second-period profits even under compatibility. The reason is that the quantity purchased at a given price will be an increasing function of the network size, and second-period profits for the winning firm are equal to $|\alpha_2|$ times the number of units demanded at max $[c_2, d_2]$.[13] Of course, in the first period each firm is uncertain as to

---

[13] Here, we are assuming that the monopoly price given costs of min $[c_2, d_2]$ is more than max $[c_2, d_2]$.

whether it will make second-period sales; expanding the network base may merely be helping its rival. Thus, there is a free-rider problem. But as long as a firm's chance of having the lower second-period cost is positive, it will have incentives to set price in the first period below costs to win the sales.[14] Although elastic demand introduces a number of additional effects, the fundamental forces that we have identified in the simple model above clearly remain.

Princeton University, USA.

REFERENCES

ARTHUR, B. (1985), "Competing Technologies and Lock-in by Historical Small Events: The Dynamics of Allocation Under Increasing Returns," Policy Paper, Center for Economic Policy Research, Stanford University, January.

CARLTON, D. and KLAMER, J. (1983), "The Need for Coordination Among Firms, with Special Reference to Network Industries," *The University of Chicago Law Review,* Spring.

DAVID, P. (1985), "Understanding the Economics of QWERTY or Is History Necessary?" *American Economic Review,* May.

FARRELL, J. and SALONER, G. (1985), "Standardization, Compatibility, and Innovation," *Rand Journal of Economics,* Spring.

FARRELL, J. and SALONER, G. (1986), "Installed Base and Compatibility: Innovation, Product Preannouncements, and Predation," GTE Labs Economics Working Paper 86-2, February.

KATZ, M. and SHAPIRO, C. (1985), "Network Externalities, Competition, and Compatibility," *American Economic Review,* June.

KATZ, M. and SHAPIRO, C. (1986), "Technology Adoption in the Presence of Network Externalities," *Journal of Political Economy,* August.

NEVEN, D. (1985), "Two-Stage (Perfect) Equilibrium in Hotelling's Model," *Journal of Industrial Economics,* March.

SHAKED, A. and SUTTON, J. (1982), "Relaxing Price Competition Through Product Differentiation," *Review of Economic Studies,* January.

[14] Another consequence of elastic demand is that compatibility, by strengthening second-period competition, represents a commitment to lower second-period prices, and thus shifts *first-period* demand outwards.

THE PROVISION OF INFORMATION AS MARKETING STRATEGY*

By JONATHAN EATON and GENE M. GROSSMAN

1. Introduction

DECISIONS about marketing strategy are an important component of competition among firms. Marketing can take many forms: advertising, developing ongoing relationships with retailers, and packaging are examples. With some types of products, marketing serves the purpose simply of delivering the product to the consumer. Implicit in the marketing of many other types of products, however, is the provision of information about relevant characteristics of the product. Many processed food items, for example, include on their packaging pertinent information concerning vitamin, caloric, protein and carbohydrate content; soft drinks include information about caffeine. Advertising for books and films provides information to attract the audience to which these products are most likely to appeal. Firms do not necessarily provide information about *all* product characteristics that are likely to be of interest to consumers: many food items do not report their contents, and many aspects of a book or movie are not revealed in advertising.

Disclosure of product characteristics is of course an issue of considerable interest to regulatory policy. Governments frequently require firms to disclose information about their products, the case of pharmaceuticals being a most obvious example. At the same time, many countries place restrictions on advertising in certain media, thereby inhibiting firms in their efforts to convey information.

This paper treats the disclosure of information about product characteristics as part of a firm's overall competitive strategy.[1] We consider two firms which sell differentiated products to consumers with heterogeneous tastes. A component of each firm's marketing strategy is its decision to reveal information about its product.[2] The outcome of the decisions of the two

* Financial support for this research was provided by the National Science Foundation under grant no. SES 8207643 and by the Alfred P. Sloan Foundation. We thank Jim Brander, Alan Deardorff and Carl Shapiro for helpful comments, and Arthur Murton for excellent research assistance.

[1] In a somewhat related paper, Grossman (1981) considers the incentives that a monopolist has to disclose information about the quality of its product. The emphasis there is on what consumers will infer about true quality from a firm's failure to reveal information.

[2] The role of advertising in providing information to consumers has been analyzed by Butters (1977) and Grossman and Shapiro (1984). Each of these papers addresses rather different aspects of the marketing decision from what we consider here, however. Butters looks at advertising that discloses information about price rather than about product characteristics. Grossman and Shapiro do consider a marketing activity that informs consumers about product characteristics, but assume that if this information is not revealed, no sales can be made. Hence the possibility of consumers buying a product about which their information is imperfect is precluded.

firms to disclose this information has important implications for the nature of the rivalry between the firms, and hence for each firm's profit and for consumer welfare.

Section 2 of the paper sets forth the basic assumptions of the model. Here we discuss the implications of discolsing information about product characteristics for equilibrium prices, sales and profits. One finding is that firms do not necessarily benefit from having information about their product revealed. If the two products available in the market are actually very similar, both firms benefit if only one firm's product is known to consumers, since the intensity of the price competition between the firms is then diminished.

In Section 3 we consider disclosure of information on product characteristics as a component of firms' profit maximizing behavior. First we study the marketing behavior of an initially unknown firm competing in the market with a firm whose product is already known to consumers. This analysis is relevant to instances of market penetration, when a new entrant challenges an established incumbent. Next we study a symmetric two-stage game in which two initially unknown firms with given product types simultaneously choose marketing strategies in a first stage and then engage in price competition in the product market. Finally, we investigate a three-stage game in which firms can select their product characteristics in a stage of competition prior to the marketing phase.

Implications of the model for consumer welfare are discussed in Section 4. We find that a movement from a situation in which neither firm's product characteristic is known to one in which both are known can never benefit, and almost always lowers the welfare of the average consumer. Even though product information allows consumers to buy the brand that is more compatible with their tastes, it also acts to differentiate the products, reducing the intensity of the price competition between firms. The loss to consumers from having to pay higher prices exceeds the gain from their ability to buy a more suitable product. Furthermore, if one product's characteristic is known, revelation of the other can benefit consumers only if the two products are actually quite similar, or if the known product is of a type very near to the preferred product of the median consumer and the unknown product appeals to consumers in the tail of the taste distribution.

In Section 5 we summarize our findings, and note some of the limitations of the present analysis.

2. Marketing and firm profits

We assume that each firm's product embodies a characteristic θ that takes on values in the real line. A typical consumer i, purchasing at price p a unit of the commodity embodying characteristic θ, derives utility

$$-p - a(\theta^i - \theta)^2 \tag{2.1}$$

Here θ^i represents the specification of consumer i's ideal product. Utility falls as the distance between the ideal product type of the characteristic of the product actually consumed rises. Each consumer demands exactly one unit of the brand that generates the greatest surplus.

We assume that utility declines with the *square* of the distance between the ideal and the product actually consumed. The linear specification used by Hotelling (1929) and many others since implies non-existence of an equilibrium price solution if firms' products are too close in characteristics space, as D'Aspremont, Gabszewicz and Thisse (1979) have shown. As they also show, this problem does not arise with a quadratic specification.

We consider a market with consumers whose ideal characteristic θ^i is distributed uniformly on the interval [0, 1]. Consumers may know exactly the characteristic of a product available for sale, or else may have a uniform prior about the specification of a firm's product on the interval [0, 1]. We consider two alternative marketing strategies. We term a marketing campaign *revealing* if advertising serves to disclose to all consumers the characteristic embodied in the firm's product. A *non-revealing* marketing campaign is one that only generates brand-name recognition. We implicitly assume that participation in the market requires that one of these types of marketing activities be undertaken.

In this section we consider the equilibrium in the market when two firms with exogenous product types compete under a given state of consumer information. We distinguish three cases depending upon whether consumers are informed about the characteristics of both, one or neither of the products. This analysis serves as an input into the next section, where we consider the endogenous choice of marketing strategy. Furthermore, the analysis of the asymmetric case is interesting in its own right, since it describes oligopolistic competition in markets where one firm is at an informational disadvantage. Such situations often arise, for example, in international trade, where products of home firms are for historical reasons generally better known than those of foreign firms, as well as in cases where a new firm enters into an already established market.[3]

2.1. *Both firms known*

We denote by θ_j the characteristic embodied in the good produced by firm j, for $j = A, B$, and choose labels such that $\theta_A \leq \theta_B$. As a function of the prices charged by the two firms, p_A and p_B respectively, we can determine which consumer will be indifferent between the two products. Let this consumer's ideal product be denoted by θ^*. Consumers for whom $\theta^i < \theta^*$ will strictly prefer firms A's product, while those for whom $\theta^i > \theta^*$ will prefer product B.

---

[3] Schmalansee (1982) has studied the informational disadvantage of a new entrant into a market in which quality is valued but difficult to verify. In his work, information is conveyed only by experience with the goods.

For the indifferent consumer, the utility of purchasing from firm A and firm B is the same. Therefore,

$$-p_A - a(\theta^* - \theta_A)^2 = -p_B - a(\theta^* - \theta_B)^2 \tag{2.2}$$

Solving (2.2) for θ^* gives

$$\theta^* = \frac{p_B - p_A}{2a\delta} + \bar{\theta} \tag{2.3}$$

where

$$\delta \equiv \theta_B - \theta_A,$$

the distance between the two firms' product characteristics, and

$$\bar{\theta} \equiv (\theta_A + \theta_B)/2,$$

the average of the two product specifications.

Firm A sales equal θ^* while firm B sells to the remaining $1 - \theta^*$ consumers. Assuming constant marginal production costs of c_A and c_B, respectively, the firms' profit levels gross of fixed costs (including marketing costs) are given by

$$\pi_A = (p_A - c_A)\theta^* = (p_A - c_A)\frac{p_B - p_A}{2a\delta} + \bar{\theta} \tag{2.4a}$$

and

$$\pi_B = (p_B - c_B)(1 - \theta^*) = (p_B - c_B)\frac{p_A - p_B}{2a\delta} + (1 - \bar{\theta}) \tag{2.4b}$$

We assume that each firm sets a price for its product taking the price of the other firm's product as given, i.e., competition is Bertrand–Nash or Nash in prices. Firm A's profit maximizing price, given p_B, is

$$p_A = \frac{c_A + p_B}{2} + a\delta\bar{\theta} \tag{2.5a}$$

and similarly firm B's reaction function is given by

$$p_B = \frac{c_B + p_A}{2} + a\delta(1 - \bar{\theta}) \tag{2.5b}$$

Solving (2.5a) and (2.5b) for p_A and p_B yields the Bertrand–Nash prices:

$$p_A = [2c_A + c_B + 2a\delta(1 + \bar{\theta})]/3 \tag{2.6a}$$

$$p_B = [2c_B + c_A + 2a\delta(2 - \bar{\theta})]/3 \tag{2.6b}$$

The indifferent consumer is at location

$$\theta^* = \frac{c_B - c_A}{6a\delta} + \frac{1 + \bar{\theta}}{3} \tag{2.7}$$

and profits of firm A and firm B as a function of the exogenous parameters are, respectively,

$$\pi_A = \frac{1}{2a\delta} \frac{(c_B - c_A) + 2a\delta(1 + \bar{\theta})^2}{3} \tag{2.8a}$$

$$\pi_B = \frac{1}{2a\delta} \frac{(c_A - c_B) + 2a\delta(2 - \bar{\theta})^2}{3} \tag{2.8b}$$

Not surprisingly, firm A benefits and firm B loses as $\bar{\theta}$, the *average* product characteristic, rises, making firm A's product relatively more desirable to a wider spectrum of the market. Firm A also benefits from having a cost advantage relative to firm B. The effect of an increase in the *distance* between the products (δ) or in consumers' sensitivity to product characteristics relative to price (as reflected in the parameter a), is ambiguous, however. The direction of the effect of an increase in a or δ on firm A's profit is given by the sign of the expression:

$$c_A - c_B + 2a\delta(1 + \bar{\theta})$$

which can be negative if firm A has a strong cost *advantage*. The corresponding condition for firm b is

$$c_B - c_A + 2a\delta(2 - \bar{\theta})$$

Thus, greater distance between the firms or greater sensitivity to the product characteristic *may* act to the disadvantage of the firm with a relative cost advantage. The reason is that greater distance or sensitivity to distance inhibits that firm in its attempt to exploit its cost advantage by competing for customers at the other firm's end of the spectrum. The firm with the cost *dis*advantage necessarily benefits from an increase in a or δ. Also, when $c_A = c_B$, so relative costs are same, *both* firms necessarily benefit from increases in a and δ.

2.2. One firm known, one firm unknown

We now consider the case in which consumers know the characteristic embodied in firm A's product, but not the one embodied in firm B's good. Consumers are assumed to have a prior distribution for θ_B that is uniform on $[0, 1]$. Without loss of generality (by symmetry) we suppose $\theta_A \leqslant 1/2$.

The utility consumer i derives from purchasing product B is subjectively uncertain. Expected utility is given by

$$U_B^i = -p_B - \int_0^1 a(\theta^i - z)^2 \, \mathrm{d}z$$
$$= -p_B - a(\theta^{i2} - \theta^i + \tfrac{1}{3})$$

Note that the consumer for whom $\theta^i = 1/2$ derives the highest expected utility from purchasing firm B's product, while consumers at either extreme experience lowest expected utility from this good.

To determine each firm's market share, price and profits, we distinguish two cases.

Case 1: $\theta_A = 1/2$. In this case the product of firm A is preferred by the *entire* market if $p_A - p_B < a/12$, while firm B captures the whole market if $p_A - p_B > a/12$. It follows from the assumption of Betrand competition that if $c_B > c_A - a/12$, firm A sets $p_A = c_B + a/12$ and earns a profit (gross of fixed costs) of $c_B - c_A + a/12$. Otherwise, firm B captures the entire market by setting a price $p_B = c_A - a/12$, and has a profit of $c_A - c_B - a/12$.

Case 2: $\theta_A < 1/2$. Let us assume, provisionally, that both firms make positive sales in the equilibrium for this case. Then firm A will sell to all consumers with tastes on the interval $[0, \theta^*]$, where θ^* is given by

$$\theta^* = \frac{p_B - p_A}{a(1 - 2\theta_A)} + \tfrac{1}{3} - \theta_A^2 \tag{2.10}$$

The remaining $1 - \theta^*$ consumers will purchase the product of firm B. The Bertrand prices that emerge from maximization of the respective expressions for profits are

$$p_A = \frac{2c_A - c_B}{3} + \frac{a(4 - 6\theta_A - 3\theta_A^2)}{9} \tag{2.11a}$$

and

$$p_B = \frac{c_A + 2c_B}{3} + \frac{a(5 - 12\theta_A + 3\theta_A^2)}{9} \tag{2.11b}$$

Solving for θ^* gives

$$\theta^* = \frac{c_B - c_A}{3a(1 - 2\theta_A)} + \frac{4 - 6\theta_A - 3\theta_A^2}{(1 - 2\theta_A)} \tag{2.12}$$

Now, for the firms to sell in positive amounts requires that $\theta^* \in (0, 1)$. This condition places certain restrictions on the parameter values, as is evident from (2.12). For example, if $c_A = c_B$, then the condition is met if and only if

$$0 \leqslant \theta_A \leqslant 2 - \sqrt{21}/3 \cong 0.4725$$

Thus, there is a range of specifications for the product of firm A in the vicinity of $\theta_A = 1/2$ such that firm B, if its product characteristic is unknown, cannot profitably enter the market, unless is has cost advantage. Evidently, there is significant advantage to being *known* when a firm offers a product near the center of the market's taste spectrum.

Assuming that θ^* from (2.12) does indeed fall between zero and one, so that both firms make positive sales, the firms' profits are

$$\pi_A = \frac{1}{a(1-2\theta_A)} + \frac{c_B - c_A}{3} + \frac{a(4 - 6\theta_A - 3\theta_A^2)^2}{9} \qquad (2.13a)$$

$$\pi_B = \frac{1}{a(1-2\theta_A)} + \frac{c_A - c_B}{3} + \frac{a(5 - 12\theta_A + 3\theta_A^2)^2}{9} \qquad (2.13b)$$

If marginal costs are equal across firms, the known firm (A) earns higher profits provided that $\theta_A > 1/2 - \sqrt{3}/6 \cong 0.211$. However, being known becomes a disadvantage when a firm produces a product near to or at an extreme end of the taste distribution; for example, if $\theta_A = 0$ and $c_A = c_B$, then $\pi_A = 16a/81$ while $\pi_B = 25a/81$.

Intuitively it might seem that the profit of the known firm would rise as its product approaches the center of the taste distribution. Somewhat surprisingly, this is not the case. The derivative of π_A with respect to θ_A is negative in the range $[0, \sqrt{2/3}]$. The reason is that, as θ_A approaches $1/2$, price competition between the known firm and the unknown firm becomes more intense. From equation (2.11a) and (2.11b) we note that both prices fall as θ_A tends to $1/2$. Thus, even though firm A's share of the market rises as its product approaches the center, its price falls. There is an advantage to a known firm, in competing with a unknown firm, of having a product that appeals to an extreme of the market rather than to the center of the market.

Finally, consider the effect on the firms' profits of an increased consumer sensitivity to product characteristics. If marginal production costs are equal, we see from differentiating equations (2.14) with respect to ϱ that firm A, the known firm, benefits from increased sensitivity, whereas firm B necessarily loses. This result is in contrast to the case in which both firms are known, where we found that $c_A = c_B$ is sufficient for both firms to gain whenever ϱ increases.

2.3. Both firms unknown

If consumers in the market are ignorant of both θ_A and θ_B, then the two products are undifferentiated from their perspective. Consumers will choose the goods which has the lowest price. Price competition between the two firms will establish $p_A = c_B$ if $c_B > c_A$, with firm A making all sales and earning a profit $c_B - c_A$. Conversely, if $c_A > c_B$, then $p_B = c_A$, firm B captures the entire market, and $\pi_B = c_A - c_B$. Finally, if $c_A = c_B = c$, then $p_A = p_B = c$, each firm's sales are indeterminant and profits for both firms are zero.

3. Marketing strategy: to reveal or not to reveal?

Having characterized equilibrium profits under regimes in which (i) the attributes of both firms' products are known by consumers, (ii) one firm's product is known and the other's is not, and (iii) consumers are informed about neither product, we can now investigate firms' incentives to provide information about their products, and the consequent equilibrium choice of marketing strategies. In performing this analysis, we assume that an informative advertising campaign involves the same cost as a non-revealing one, and that advertising costs are fixed under either strategy (i.e. they are independent of the sales level). The principles that we shall expound remain valid if revelation is a mosre costly strategy, although, of course, the range of parameter values over which it will be chosen is contracted accordingly.

We begin our analysis of the marketing-strategy decision by considering the incentives facing a firm whose product is initially unknown, in competition with a firm producing a good that is familiar to consumers. This analysis applies, for example, to a firm that is attempting to penetrate a foreign market. We then investigate the case of competition between two firms both of which are initially unknown. Finally we consider the case when firms can choose their products' types, as when characteristics are the outgrowth of a deterministic R & D project. In each case we assume that marketing decisions are made prior to pricing decisions, and in the case of endogenous characteristics, we further assume that firms choose their products before they choose their marketing strategies. In considering their choices at any of the earlier stages of competition, we assume that firms correctly anticipate the effect of those decisions on the outcome of competition in subsequent stages.[4] In other words, we treat firm rivalry as a multi-stage game, and apply the equilibrium concept of subgame perfection, as defined by Selten (1975).

3.1. Marketing strategy of an initially unknown firm competing with a known firm

Consider the case of an unknown firm, firm B, contemplating entry into a new market where it will compete with firm A, whose product is already known by consumers to embody a characteristic θ_A. We restrict our attention to the situation in which marginal production costs are equal.

If firm B chooses a strategy of non-revelation, its profit is given by expression (2.13b), assuming that $\theta^* \in [0, 1]$. Disclosing its product characteristic to the market will lead to a level of profit given by expression (2.8b).[5] The profitability to firm B of revelation rises as δ rises: i.e., the more firm B's product differs from that of firm A the more it will be in firm B's interest to advertise that fact. Figure 1 indicates those values of θ_B for

---

[4] We also assume throughout the analysis that consumers do not draw inferences about product characteristics when they observe that a firm has chosen a marketing strategy of non-revelation. Implicity we are assuming that consumer have limited information about the structure of the market under consideration.

[5] Corresponding formulae for the case when $0.5 < \theta_A \leqslant 1$ are easily derived.

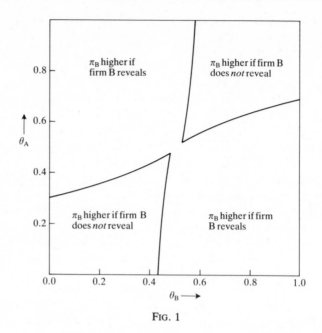

FIG. 1

which it is in firm *B*'s interest to have consumers informed about its product.

Disclosure is advantageous to firm *B* when its product is very different from that of its competitor, or when firm *A* provides a good close to the center of the market's taste distribution. (In the latter case, a revealing marketing campaign may be a pre-requisite for market entry.) Conversely, when the two firms offer similar products, revelation by firm *B* will result in intense price competition in the production stage, to the detriment of both firms.

3.2. *Marketing by two initially unknown firms*

When two firms enter a new market simultaneously, neither product is initially familiar to consumers. Then each firm must choose a marketing strategy, taking into account its beliefs about the other's choice. In addition, each must consider how its decision will affect the subsequent pricing competition.

We consider only the case when the two firms have equal production costs (i.e. $c_A = c_B = c$). Note first that equilibrium cannot involve each firm choosing a pure strategy of non-revelation. Each would then earn zero profits in the resulting Bertrand competition, and either could increase its profits by altering its decision (taking that of its rival as given), thereby becoming the only firm to reveal.

The payoff matrix at the marketing stage has the following general form:

Firm B

	Reveal	Don't Reveal
Reveal	π_A^2, π_B^2	π_A^A, π_B^A
Don't Reveal	π_A^B, π_B^B	$0, 0$

Firm A { Reveal / Don't Reveal }

Here we have introduced the notation $\pi_j^z(\theta_A, \theta_B)$ for $j = A$, B, and $z = A$, B or 2, which is the profit that firm j earns in the product market competition if consumer's are informed about the characteristics of product z only (where $z = 2$ indicates that consumers are informed about *both* goods).

The product characteristic space now can be divided into four regions (see Fig. 2). If, given θ_A and θ_B, $\pi_A^2 > \pi_A^B$ and $\pi_B^2 > \pi_B^A$, then the unique equilibrium in the two-stage game involves both firms revealing their product characteristic in their marketing campaigns. The part of the characteristic space in which this configuration of profits results is labelled "R" in the figure. If $\pi_A^2 > \pi_A^B$ and $\pi_B^2 < \pi_B^A$, then the unique equilibrium has A revealing and B not revealing. Similarly, B will choose to reveal and A not to reveal if $\pi_B^2 > \pi_B^A$ and $\pi_A^2 < \pi_A^B$. These regions are labelled "A" and "B", respectively. Finally, if $\pi_B^2 < \pi_B^A$ and $\pi_A^2 < \pi_A^B$, then there exist two

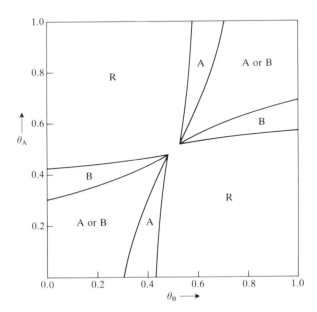

FIG. 2

equilibria in pure strategies; these involve either of the firms selecting a revealing marketing strategy, while the other opts for non-revelation.[6] This final possibility is indicated in the figure by the designation "*A* or *B*."

The figure shows that revelation by both firms will be the outcome in a market where the competitors have very dissimilar products, or in one where at least one of the firms has a product close to the center of the taste distribution. In the former case, revelation occurs because the price competition that results when both products are known to consumers is not too intense, and each firm can exploit its market power on consumers who, if informed, would prefer its product by a wide margin. In the latter case, when one firm has a good near the center, the other will need to reveal either as a prequisite for market entry or to avoid being relegated a very small market share at the tail of the distribution of consumer tastes. Given that this firm reveals, the other will choose to reveal as well, so as to capture the larger portion of the market associated with its central positioning.

When the two products are actually quite similar the resulting game has two equilibria in pure strategies, each with one of the firms revealing and the other not. This result obtains because price competition would be intense if both firms were to reveal, or if neither were to do so. Thus, in any situation where one is revealing and the other not, neither would wish to change and thereby cause a highly competitive outcome in the (second-stage) product market. It is interesting to note that where the two products are similar and near the center of the taste distribution, the firm that reveals generally earns higher profits than that which does not. However, the opposite is true when the two products are actually closer to one of the tails of the taste distribution.[7]

A unique equilibrium involving one firm selecting an informative advertising campaign and the other doing the opposite arises when one of the firms has a product located toward an extreme end of the taste distribution, while its rival's product is located on the same side of the median, but somewhat closer to the center. Then, the firm at the extreme position will be the one to reveal, this being its dominant marketing strategy. If its rival were to choose "not reveal", then by revealing it averts a zero-profit equilibrium. If its rival chooses "reveal", then it must reveal to avoid being relegated a small market share at the tail of the market, and then facing relatively severe competition even for this segment. Given the choice of this firm to reveal, the rival prefers to avoid the competition that would result were consumers to be aware that the two offer somewhat similar products. By not revealing, the rival also can take advantage of the fact that its

---

[6] In this case there will also exist a mixed strategy equilibrium defined by (λ_A, λ_B), where λ_j is the probability that firm j chooses to reveal. Each firm would pursue a mixed strategy only if the expected profit from revealing were equal to that for not revealing. It is easy to verify that this condition implies $\lambda_A = \pi_B^B/(\pi_B^B + \pi_B^A - \pi_B^2)$ and $\lambda_B = \pi_A^A/(\pi_A^A + \pi_A^B - \pi_A^2)$.

[7] In a situation of this latter sort, firms may actually attempt to provide consumers with information about the attributes of their competitor's product.

competitor has staked out a position that appeals only to those with exotic tastes.

3.3. *The three-stage game with endogenous product types*

To this point, we have been assuming that product characteristics are exogenously given to the firms engaged in marketing and pricing competition. This analysis is relevant to situations where product development is subject to a large random component, or in the context of international trade, when firms with pre-existing products designed for the home market decide to enter into new markets abroad. However, in some emerging industries, firms will have the opportunity to select the characteristics of their goods during a product-design phase of competition. In such circumstances it is interesting to ask which product types they will choose to develop in light of the bearing that these decisions will have on subsequent stages of rivalry.

The apparatus that we have developed allows us to analyze a duopoly game in which firms first choose their product type, then undertake an advertising campaign (informative or otherwise), and finally set prices and make sales in a third stage of competition. In our model, *the unique equilibrium in this three-stage game has firms developing products at opposite extreme ends of the spectrum of characteristics, and then opting for marketing campaigns that fully inform consumers.*[8]

It is easy to show that these are indeed an equilibrium set of strategies. Suppose that firm A has chosen $\theta_A = 0$ (which firm B takes as given) and consider the optimal response by firm B. Referring to Fig. 2, we note that for a range of choices of θ_B greater than approximately 0.44, the outcome of the marketing game would be for both firms to reveal. Within such a regime, firm B's profits increase with the distance between the two products. Thus, $\theta_B = 1$, yielding profits to firm B of $0.5a$, is the best among these. Next consider values for θ_B such that only firm A will reveal in the resulting marketing competition. For all of these values, firm B earns profits of $0.309a$, less than those associated with a choice of $\theta_B = 1$. Finally, for a range of values of θ_B less than approximately 0.31, there exists an equilibrium in the marketing subgame where only firms B reveals. Among these, profits are maximized when firm B's product is located as far from the center as possible, i.e. when $\theta_B = 0$. (Recall this result from Section 2.2.) Then firm B has profits of $0.198a$, again less than those it could earn by setting $\theta_B = 1$. Thus, $\theta_B = 1$ is the profit maximizing response by firm B to $\theta_A = 0$. Obviously, the reverse must be true as well, so this pair of choices of product types is an equilibrium in the three-stage game.

The uniqueness of this equilibrium is somewhat more difficult to establish.

---

[8] Strictly speaking, there are two such equilibria, the second found by reversing the names by the firms. D'Aspremont *et al.* (1979) also establish this "principle of maximum differentiation" as the equilibrium location of two firms whose locations are known.

The result follows from the fact that, for *any* $\theta_A \leq 0.5$, a dominant strategy for firm B is to choose $\theta_B = 1$ and then to undertake an informative advertising campaign.[9] To see this, note that for any value of $\theta_A \leq 0.5$, if firm B chooses $\theta_B = 1$ the resulting marketing subgame has both firms revealing. Furthermore, $\theta_B = 1$ yields higher profits for firm B than any other location yielding a marketing equilibrium of this type.

For most values of θ_A, firm B will be able to choose among a range of values for θ_B such that an equilibrium to the marketing subgame exists involving only firm A revealing. Within this range, π_B is invariant to the choice of θ_B. We have verified that for all values of $\theta_A \in [0, 0.5]$, $\pi_B^A(\theta_A, \theta_B)$ is less than $\pi_B^2(\theta_A, 1)$.

Finally, firm B might choose a location that is consistent with the existence of an equilibrium in the marketing subgame in which only firm B reveals. As we have noted above, among the equilibria of this type, firm B has highest profits when its position is as far to an extreme of the taste distribution as is possible. For all θ_A less than approximately 0.43 firm B can choose $\theta_B = 0$, and an equilibrium will exist with only B revealing. Then $\pi_B^B(\theta_A, 0) = 0.198a$, but this is less than $\pi_B^2(\theta_A, 1)$ for all $\theta_A < 0.43$. When $\theta_A > 0.43$, firm B will need to set θ_B greater than some strictly positive minimum value to ensure the existence of an equilibrium in the marketing subgame in which only firm B reveals. Again, we have verified that for each value of $\theta_A \in [0.43, 0.5]$, π_B is greater when, rather than choosing this minimum value, firm B sets $\theta_B = 1$.

Having established that $\theta_B = 1$ is a dominant strategy for firm B whenever $\theta_A \leq 0.5$, it should be clear that the equilibrium with the two firms locating at opposite extremes is unique. If either firm were to take an interior position, it would find that profits could be increased by moving to the end opposite from its rival. It follows, therefore, that equilibrium marketing campaigns are always informative in situations where it is appropriate to extend the model to allow endogenous product choices by firms.

4. Consumer welfare and product information

So far we have considered the effect of two alternative marketing strategies on firm profits, and the consequent incentive to undertake a marketing campaign that discloses information on product characteristics. We now look at the marketing issue from the point of view of consumers, investigating whether or not consumers benefit from the provision of information by firms. Since the market we consider consists of a continuum of consumers with different tastes, changes in exogenous parameters and in the marketing strategy of firms may not affect the welfare of *all* consumers in the same direction. Rather than undertaking a taxonomic discussion of how consumers in different segments of the taste distribution are affected, we focus instead on the average welfare of consumers as a group.

---

[9] By symmetry, firm B should choose $\theta_B = 0$ and reveal if $\theta_A > 1/2$.

4.1. *Both products known*

When both products are known, the utility of an individual purchasing product A is given by $-p_A - a(\theta - \theta_A)^2$ while an individual buying product B obtains $-p_B - a(\theta - \theta_B)$.[2] Assuming $\theta_B > \theta_A$, individuals with θ in the interval $[0, \theta^*)$ purchase A and those on $(\theta^*, 1]$ purchase B. Here the relevant values of p_A, p_B and θ^* are given in equation (2.6) and (2.7). In general, the expression for average utility is

$$\bar{U} = \int_0^{\theta^*} [-p_A - a(\theta - \theta_A)^2] \, d\theta + \int_{\theta^*}^1 [-p_B - a(\theta - \theta_B)^2] \, d\theta \qquad (4.1)$$

which, after substitution of the parameters for the full-information case, yields

$$\bar{U}^k = -c - \frac{a}{3} + a\left(1 - \frac{\delta}{9}\right)\bar{\theta}(1 - \bar{\theta}) - \frac{a\delta^2}{4} - \left(\frac{13}{18}\right)a\delta \qquad (4.2)$$

when $c_A = c_B = c$.

Differentiating $\bar{U}^k$ with respect to δ yields a negative expression: an increase in the difference between the two commodities *lowers* averages consumer welfare. Even though (when $\delta < 1/2$) an increase in δ benefits the average consumer by providing him with a product that more closely approximates his ideal, the increase in price due to the reduction in the competitiveness of the market more than offsets this first effect on consumer welfare. Differentiating $\bar{U}^k$ with respect to $\bar{\theta}$ yields an expression that has the same sign as $1 - 2\bar{\theta}$; a movement of the mean product characteristic toward the center of the taste distribution raises welfare.

4.2. *One product known*

When consumers are informed only about the characteristic of the good produced by firm A, the *ex post* or realized utility of an individual who purchases firm B's product will in general differ from his *ex ante* expected utility. It is possible, therefore, to look at average utility either from an *ex ante* perspective (i.e. based on consumers' prior belief about the distribution of θ_B) or from an *ex post* perspective (based on the actual value of θ_B). The first comparison would be relevant, for example, to a case in which government policy regarding disclosure must be set in the absence of government information about the true characteristics of the various brands; the second is relevant when the government can undertake tests on the products to learn the actual value of θ_B. In what follows, we shall take both of these perspectives to compare average consumer welfare when information about firm B's product is not revealed with the welfare that obtains under full information.

Consider the *ex ante* comparison first, and assume that $\theta_A < 1/2$ and that both products are purchased in positive amounts in equilibrium. Then consumers in the range $[0, \theta^*)$ purchase from firm A, and achieve utility $-p_A - (\theta - \theta_A)^2$, whereas those in the range $(\theta^*, 1]$ purchase product B with expected utility

$$-p_B - a \int_0^1 (\theta - \theta_B)^2 \, d\theta_B \tag{4.3}$$

The relevant equilibrium values of p_A, p_B and θ^* are given in expressions (2.11) and (2.12).

Integrating over the expected utilities of both types of consumers, we obtain the expected utility of the average individual, conditional on θ_A but not θ_B, for the equal cost case ($c_A = c_B = c$):

$$E[\bar{U}^A \mid \theta_A] = -c - \frac{a(13 - 24\theta_A + 6\theta_A^2)}{18} + \frac{a(4 - 6\theta_A - 3\theta_A^2)^2}{162(1 - 2\theta_A)} \tag{4.4}$$

This should be compared with the *ex ante* expectation of the average level of utility which would obtain if θ_B were revealed through marketing. This latter expression is found by integrating the expression for $\bar{U}^k$ as a function of θ_B (equation 4.2) with respect to the prior distribution for θ_B, i.e.

$$E[\bar{U}^k \mid \theta_A] = \int_0^1 \bar{U}^k \, d\theta_B$$

$$= -c - \frac{269}{432}a - \frac{a}{216}(\theta_A^3 + 198\theta_A^2 - 262\theta_A) \tag{4.5}$$

Comparing (4.4) and (4.5), we find that for all $\theta_A \in [0.02, 0.5]$, $E(\bar{U}^A) > E(\bar{U}^k)$ when $c_A = c_B = c$. That is, except when the known product is located at the extreme end of the market's taste distribution, average consumer welfare is higher when the characteristics of the product of firm B is *not* revealed. A law requiring product disclosure may well affect consumers adversely by lessening the extent of price competition between firms.

We turn now to the *ex post* comparison, focusing again on the equal cost case. The average utility when consumers are fully informed, $\bar{U}^k$, is given in (4.2). Alternatively, when consumers know only the characteristics of brand A, their average expected utility is found by substituting in equation (4.1) the equilibrium values for θ^*, p_A and p_B given in expressions (2.10) and (2.11).

Unlike the case for the *ex ante* comparison, here the relative benefit to consumers of product disclosure depends on the actual value of θ_B. In Figure 3 we illustrate the regions in characteristic space in which the provision of information by firm B leads to higher average consumer welfare than otherwise. We find that when the two products are in fact very different, revelation of θ_B is detrimental to consumers, because it reduces the intensity of price competition. The closer is θ_A to the middle of the

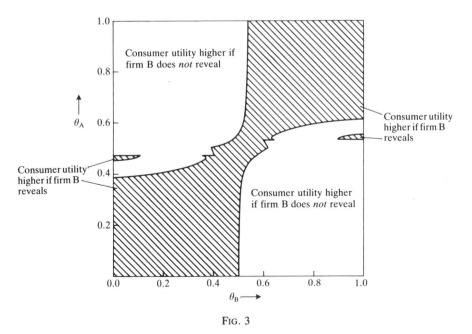

FIG. 3

spectrum of potential products types, the larger is the range of values of θ_B for which consumers achieve on average greater utility when θ_B is not revealed. However, when θ_A is very near the center and θ_B is on the same side of the median but at the extreme end of the distribution, consumers do again benefit, on average, from revelation by firm B. Here, a strategy of non-revelation by firm B ensures that only consumers at the far and of the taste distribution opposite from θ_A will choose to purchase the product of firm B; but these are exactly the individuals who are least suited to consuming firm B's good.

Compare these findings with the discussion of firm B's incentive to disclose its product characteristics in Section 3.1. Over much of the parameter space the interests of firm B and those of consumers are in conflict. When the offerings of the two firms are similar, consumers would benefit from information about firm B's product, but firm B would not wish to provide this information. The converse is true when the products are in fact highly differentiated. In our model, a social welfare criterion always resolves this conflict of interest in favor of disclosure. This is so because when more information is provided, there is improved matching of consumers and products, a social benefit, whereas the effect of disclosure on price competition only implies transfers between firms and consumers under the maintained assumption of unit-inelastic demand. Of course, such would not necessarily be the case in a model with a more general demand structure.

4.3. *Neither product known*

If neither product is known and costs are the same, consumers pay a price c for either commodity. Since a typical consumer has identical prior expectations about each commodity, he is, *ex ante*, indifferent between them. *Ex ante* the expected utility of a consumer with taste parameter θ purchasing from firm A is

$$-c - a \int_0^1 (\theta - \theta_A)^2 \, \mathrm{d}\theta_A = -c - \frac{a}{3}[3\theta^2 - 3\theta + 1] \qquad (4.9)$$

The expected utility to this individual of purchasing product B is the same. The average value of this expression is given by

$$-c - \frac{a}{3} \int_0^1 [3\theta^2 - 3\theta + 1] \, \mathrm{d}\theta = -c - \frac{a}{6} \qquad (4.10)$$

The *ex ante* expected utility of knowing both firms' product characteristics can be obtained by taking the expectation of expression (4.6) not conditional on θ_A. The consequent expression equals $-c - \dfrac{279}{864} a$, which is less than expression (4.10): *ex ante*, consumers are better off *not* knowing the characteristics of either product being sold than knowing both; the benefit to the average consumer of the more intense price competition that arises when the products are *ex ante* undifferentiated exceeds the cost of the inability to buy the more appropriate product.

If the government has information about product characteristics, one might expect that for some values of θ_A and θ_B total disclosure would raise average consumer welfare. This is in fact not the case. The expected utility, *ex post*, of the average consumer, when product information is not revealed, is given by

$$\bar{U}^I = -c - \frac{a}{3} + a\bar{\theta}(1 - \bar{\theta}) - \frac{a\delta^2}{4}$$

(We have assumed that a typical consumer purchases each product with probability 1/2.) This expression exceeds expression (4.2), average consumer welfare when both products are known, by an amount

$$\frac{a\delta}{9}\left[\bar{\theta}(1 - \bar{\theta}) + \frac{13}{2}\right],$$

which is always non-negative. When the two products are identical ($\delta = 0$) consumer welfare is the same regardless of whether or not consumers know the characteristics of the two products. Otherwise, the public disclosure of information about product characteristics harms consumers via its effect on equilibrium prices by more than it benefits them via its improvement in the matching of consumers and brands. Information is more harmful to consumers the greater is the actual difference between the two models produced.

5. Conclusion

The decision to reveal information about a product's characteristics is an important component of a firm's marketing strategy. This paper has developed a model of marketing behavior to analyse the implications of this decision for profits and consumer welfare.

The model is limited in a number of respects. Only horizontal differentiation of the product is introduced; consumers are identical except with respect to their tastes for this product; demand is unit inelastic; a very simple cost structure is assumed; and there are only two firms. Even within this restrictive context, a number of results emerge with implications for more general situations. First, firms may benefit from not having information about their products revealed. This strategy may allow them to disguise the similarity of their goods to other brands available on the market. Second, the strategic interaction among firms in their marketing activity can give rise to many possible outcomes, with all, some, or no firms pursuing a policy of revelation (although in our model the last of those only can result if firms pursue mixed strategies). Third, if firms can choose their product types, they will do so to minimize competition at later stages, by locating at opposite ends of the product spectrum and then engaging in informative advertising campaigns. Finally, revelation of information about products can harm consumers by increasing the perceived differentiation of products in the market, thereby reducing the extent of price competition among firms.

University of Virginia,
Princeton University

REFERENCES

BUTTERS, G. (1977) "Equilibrium Distributions of Sales and Advertising Prices," *Review of Economic Studies* 44 (3), 465–491.

D'ASPREMONT, C., GABSZEWICZ, J. J., and THISSE, J.-F. (1979) "On Hotelling's 'Stability in Competition.'" *Econometrica* 47 (5), 1145–1150.

GROSSMAN, G. M. and SHAPIRO, C. (1984) "Informative Advertising and Differentiated Products," *Review of Economic Studies* 51 (1), 63–81.

GROSSMAN, S. (1981) "The Informational Role of Warranties and Private Disclosure about Product Quality," *Journal of Law and Economics* 24 (3), 461–484.

HOTELLING, H. (1929) "Stability in Competition," *Economic Journal* 39 (1), 41–57.

SCHMALANSEE, R. (1982) "Product Differentiation Advantages of Pioneering Brands," *American Economic Review* 72 (3), 349–365.

SELTEN, R. (1975) "Re-examination of the Perfectness Concept for Equilibrium Points in Extensive Games," *International Journal of Game Theory* 4 (1), 25–55.

FIRM-SPECIFIC INFORMATION, PRODUCT DIFFERENTIATION, AND INDUSTRY EQUILIBRIUM*

By JEFFREY M. PERLOFF and STEVEN C. SALOP

I. Introduction

RESEARCH over the last three decades has shown that imperfect consumer information may enable even small firms to set their prices above marginal cost.[1] Much of the recent literature has assumed that consumers possess information about the general market but lack information about specific firms. This paper presents a new model in which consumers have imperfect information about specific firms and lack information about the market. The resulting equilibrium has very different properties than in previous models.[2]

Consumers gather information in a number of diverse ways. One method is a personal inspection or search before purchase. This prepurchase inspection may be aided by the use of screening devices and signals. Prepurchase information may also be purchased from diagnostic and testing agencies, certifiers, newspapers, and brokers. Recommendations from friends may also be used. Finally, advertising by sellers and personal experience yield information that is more or less reliable.

Most attention has been paid to the information-gathering role of search or inspection, perhaps because it contains both the result of *informational market power* and the possibility of nonexistence of equilibrium as emphasized by Stiglitz (1979). Search or inspection has been studied by Wilde and Schwartz (1979) and a number of others since Diamond (1971).

At the same time, however, the other information-gathering institutions have been analyzed in detail. For example, Phelps (1972) analyzes screening devices. Nelson (1974) examines the role of product market signals, particularly advertising and market share. The educational signaling literature of Spence (1973, 1974), Stiglitz (1975), Gausch and Weiss (1980), and others may be reinterpreted as product testing and certification. Leland

* This work was partially funded by the Federal Trade Commission. The opinions expressed here are those of the authors and may not reflect the views of the Federal Trade Commission or any individual commissioners or other staff members.

The authors wish to thank B. Allen, H. Beales, P. Berck, D. Cass, D. Crawford, J. Galambos, S. Grossman, O. Hart, M. Katz, T. Romer, M. Rothschild, D. Sant, D. Scheffman, an anonymous referee, and especially R. Willig for useful discussions and advice.

Giannini Foundation Paper No. 787 (for identification purposes only).

[1] The concept that imperfect consumer information endows even small firms with *informational market power* was developed by Scitovsky (1950), Arrow (1958), and Stigler (1961) among others. The elegant modeling of this phenomenon by Diamond (1971) and the discovery of the lemons principle by Akerlof (1970) has stimulated research by economists and policy analysts on both the scope of and potential remedies for imperfect information. The policy implications are emphasized by Pitofsky (1977), Schwartz and Wilde (1979), and the Federal Trade Commission (1978, 1979).

[2] Stiglitz (1979) surveys most of the major models and discusses their properties.

(1979) analyzes the effect of licensing to ensure minimum quality standards. Plott and Wilde (1979) have studied diagnosticians both theoretically and experimentally. Newspaper information has been analyzed by Salop and Stiglitz (1977) and Varian (1980).

Recommendations from friends have been paid less attention, except to the extent that such information may be similar to that gained from using market share as a positive signal. The role of advertising in directly providing firm-specific information has been analyzed by Butters (1977). The behavior of brokers has been implicitly modeled in the agency literature. Moreover, the direct mailing advertising in Butters (1977) may be reinterpreted as an independent broker or salesman. The matchmaking role of brokers has been examined by Salop (1980). Personal experience has been analyzed by Phelps and Winter (1970); Grossman, Kihlstrom, and Mirman (1977); Smallwood and Conlisk (1979); and Shapiro (1980).

The model presented here might be best described as a newspaper model in that consumers are endowed with some imperfect information about each firm in the market, though the equilibrium in the market for information is not explicitly analyzed. Alternatively, it might be better described as an amalgam of all information gathering, past and present, about *specific* firms and brands where the number of consumers perfectly informed about every firm is initially taken to be insignificant.

On the other hand, unlike the other search, newspaper, and signaling models, the consumers here are restricted to *firm-specific information.* Additional *general market information,* such as the range or density of actual prices in the market, is not known to the consumer. His general market information is limited to only that which may be inferred from firm-specific data and, therefore, is redundant. This model has strikingly different properties from those of earlier models which were driven by their assumptions of perfect general market information. Indeed, in many ways, this firm-specific information model represents a retrenchment for it has none of the strange and wondrous properties of search and other models. In a market restricted to firm-specific information gathering, if only an insignificant proportion of consumers are perfectly informed about all firms, market breakdown is far less likely; instead, equilibrium generally exists for the model presented here.[3]

Given that firms' profit-maximizing conditions hold, a unique single-price equilibrium does obtain; however, we have not ruled out the existence of additional multiple-price equilibria from pure or mixed strategies. Moreover, we show that price dispersion may occur if a significant number of consumers are perfectly informed. As the degree of information about all firms improves from perfect ignorance to perfect information, the equilibrium price falls continuously to the competitive price. In contrast, as

---

[3] This assertion is true for those cases in which the usual second-order conditions for profit maximization hold for each firm (see Section II).

Stiglitz (1979) discusses, most models have a discontinuity in that any imperfection of information causes price to be above marginal cost.

Finally, perhaps the most striking contrast with previous models occurs with respect to entry competition. In the search models, entry does not reduce price; if anything, it increases the equilibrium price by making discovery of the lowest price firm more costly on average. On the other hand, the firm-specific information model has the property that, as the number of firms becomes sufficiently large, the equilibrium price falls to the perfectly competitive price.

These results are discussed below. Section II sets out the basic specific-firm information framework, derives the equilibrium, and analyzes improvements in consumer information. Entry competition is examined in Section III and multiple-price equilibria in Section IV.

In Section V we show how the basic model may be reinterpreted and applied to industry equilibrium when products are differentiated. This product differentiation may be spurious, arising out of consumers' misperceptions; or it may be due to actual differences in product formulations and consumer preferences. As a model of product differentiation, the formal structure is a synthesis of the spatial approach of Hotelling (1929), Lancaster (1979), and others with the representative consumer approach of Spence (1976), Dixit and Stiglitz (1977), and Hart (1979). An analogous model of product differentiation is analyzed in detail in Perloff and Salop (1985). The welfare implications of a similar model are discussed in Sattinger (1984). Possible improvements and extensions are discussed in the conclusions.

II. Equilibrium with imperfect information

In this section we analyze a model of industry equilibrium when consumers are perfectly informed. As discussed in the introduction, this model differs somewhat from other work in its conceptualization of information imperfections and consumer decision making.

Two classes of price and quality data may be distinguished-firm-specific and general market information. By firm-specific information, we mean consumers' direct estimates of the prices and qualities of various commodities available from different firms. By general market information, we mean consumers' estimates of these parameters for the market generally. For example, in the case of price uncertainty, a consumer's firm-specific information may be a prior probability distribution $F_i(p_i)$ over the possible prices, p_i, of each firm, $i = 1, 2,..., n$; or it may simply be a point estimate, s_i, of each price. With respect to the market in general, the consumer may have a probability distribution $F(\underline{p})$ of the set of all prices charged for the commodity in question or simply the range of prices charged.

Of course, these two classes of information are related. The general market distribution $F(\underline{p})$ may be derived from the appropriate aggregation of the firm-specific distributions, $F_i(p_i)$. Similarly, in the absence of any additional firm-specific information, a consumer treats $F(\underline{p})$ as the firm-specific distribution as well.

Models of search equilibrium, such as Diamond (1971), generally assume that consumers' general market information is rational; that is, the prior price distribution, $F(\underline{p})$, is self-fulfilled by the actual equilibrium distribution of prices in the market. Additional firm-specific information is gathered from search; in particular, a consumer obtains perfect firm-specific information by sampling a store or product. For example, Butters' (1977) advertising model has a diffuse prior $F(\underline{p})$ and perfect firm-specific information if an advertisement is received. The newspaper model of Salop and Stiglitz (1977) has a rational $F(\underline{p})$ and, additionally, perfect firm-specific information for all firms if the newspaper is purchased.

We take a different approach here. We assume that consumers have only imperfect firm-specific information and no additional general market information about prices beyond that implied by the firm-specific distributions. This formalization is more in the spirit of estimation models rather than the search literature.

Specifically, we assume each consumer $j(j = 1, 2,..., L)$ enters the market armed with a point estimate s_i^j for each of the $i = 1, 2,..., n$ firms in the market and purchases from the firm estimated to have the lowest price or $\min_i s_i^j$. For now, we focus on the case in which products in the industry are homogeneous and known to be homogeneous (i.e., this general market information does exist).[4]

Consumers may form their estimates, s_i^j, by gathering information in a variety of ways according to the costs and benefits of each. As discussed previously, inspection, reliable and unreliable experience, truthful and deceptive advertising, and friends and neutral third parties are among the information-gathering methods analyzed in the literature.[5] According to the exact structure of information gathering assumed, particular restrictions on the estimates are implied. For example, if a price is sampled, it will yield a perfect price estimate. For other information-gathering methods, it is difficult to determine exactly what sort of rationality restrictions to place on consumers' estimates.

In this model, we do not derive the structure of the estimates from an explicit information-gathering technology. Instead, we begin with an exogenously generated set of estimates, satisfying certain plausible conditions. In particular, we assume that consumer j's estimates $(s_1^j, s_2^j,..., s_n^j)$ are generated as follows:

$$s_i^j = p_i + \beta \theta_i^j \qquad (1)$$

[4] We might note here that the estimates, s_i^j, could easily be re-interpreted as estimates of expected consumer surplus so that real or spurious product differentiation may be incorporated into this model. This extension is made below in Section V.

[5] For a nontechnical discussion of these different methods, see Federal Trade Commission (1979).

where $\theta_i^j \sim F_i^j(\theta)$, $\theta \in [a, b]$, $E(\theta_i^j) = 0$, $\mathrm{Var}\,(\theta_i^j) > 0$, and $F_i^j(\theta)$ is a continuously differentiable distribution function with density $f_i^j(\theta)$.[6]

Thus, estimates are taken to be unbiased and, if $\beta > 0$, as imperfect.[7] The scale parameter β permits a range of information states from perfect information ($\beta = 0$) to perfect ignorance ($\beta \to \infty$). Those consumers who draw $\theta = 0$ have accurate estimates, those who draw $\theta < 0$ have an underestimate, and those with $\theta > 0$ have an overestimate of price. Estimates are related to the actual price, p_i, charged by the firm.[8] Finally, the support of θ, $\theta \in [a, b]$ may be finite or infinite. One natural restriction would be to assume price estimates must be nonnegative although, as will be demonstrated below, weaker restrictions will suffice.

Given his estimates $(s_1^j, s_2^j, \ldots, s_n^j)$, each consumer j selects the firm with the lowest estimated price, $\min_i s_i^j$, and shops there. Further comparison shopping is not permitted although the model could accommodate it; thus, we implicitly assume the cost of further search is prohibitive.[9] Instead, once at the selected store, the consumer observes the actual price, p_i, and purchases $D(p_i)$ units.

As a result of this information, a disproportionate share of each firm's sales is made to customers who underestimated its price. Comparison shopping would affect this proportion. Finally, in the static model analyzed here, no additional learning is permitted; every period is independent of the past. In contrast, a richer intertemporal model would include an analysis of the evolution of estimates over time as experienced consumers learn and eventually die, and new ignorant buyers enter the market.[10]

Given this formal structure, we may derive the form of the demand curves facing each firm in the market. It is apparent that, for $\beta > 0$, these demand curves are downward sloping even though all products are homogeneous. Since consumers are not perfectly informed of the lowest price store, higher priced stores do obtain some unlucky customers.[11] Under

[6] Mass points to $F_i^j(\theta)$ are discussed in Section IV. The other assumed properties of these functions are presented in Appendix B. We assume that $E(s_i^j) = p_i$; that is, the coefficient of p_i in equation (1) is one. Were S_i^j a more complicated function of p_i, consumers' estimates would be biased; however, the results reported below would still hold (see footnote 7).

[7] In fact, this restriction of unbiased estimates is not necessary for many of the results derived below. A weaker restriction of identical bias for all estimates would suffice.

[8] There exists some evidence on the nature of $F_i^j(\theta)$. For example, the *Progressive Grocer* (November, 1974, p. 39) conducted a survey of 560 shoppers in four Providence and Boston area supermarkets in July, 1974. The consumers were asked to cite the selling price of 44 popular brand-name and nationally advertised items. Only 24 percent of the shoppers tested knew the "correct" price (within 5 percent) for a specific product compared to 32 percent in a similar study in 1963. Other evidence is provided by Gabor and Granger (1961), Uhl and Brown (1972), and Devine and Marion (1979).

[9] Further search would be induced if the actual price, p_i, exceeded the second lowest estimate, $\min_k s_k^j$, in excess of the consumer's search cost. This topic is discussed in more detail below.

[10] *Cf.* Phelps and Winter (1970) and Smallwood and Conlisk (1979).

[11] For example, if store 1 charges $10 and estimates are $(8, 10, 12)$ and if store 2 charges $11 with estimates $(9, 11, 13)$, then store 2 will obtain customers who draw the estimate pairs $\{(10, 9); (12, 9); (12, 11)\}$.

these circumstances, demand is elastic for two reasons: A price reduction brings forth additional customers, and each customer purchases additional units.

In the case of perfect information ($\beta = 0$), however, the lowest price store does obtain all the customers; thus, shading one's price below a common level $\bar{p}$ does yield a discontinuous demand increase (i.e., demand is perfectly elastic). In contrast, in the perfect ignorance case ($\beta \to \infty$), the flow of customers is unrelated to actual price; demand elasticity comes only from additional purchases from each customer obtained.

We now derive the exact form of the firms' demand curves from the theory of order statistics. For a representative firm i, the probability that it is selected by consumer j is the probability that s_i^j is the lowest estimate. Dropping the superscript j for convenience and substituting from equation (1), we have[12]

$$\Pr_i \equiv \Pr(s_i \leqslant s_1, s_i \leqslant s_2, \ldots, s_i \leqslant s_n)$$
$$= \int \prod_{k=i} \left\{ 1 - F_k\left(\frac{p_i - p_k}{\beta} + \theta\right) \right\} f_i(\theta) \, d\theta. \tag{2}$$

After selecting a firm, each consumer observes the actual price, p_i, and purchases $D(p_i)$ units there. If there are L consumers with identical demand curves, then the expected demand of firm i is given by

$$Q_i(p_1, p_2, \ldots, p_n) = LD(p_i)\Pr_i. \tag{3}$$

Given these demand curves for each firm, the industry equilibrium for an exogenous number of firms n may be derived using conventional methods. If firm i has a constant marginal cost c_i and fixed cost K_i, then its expected operating profits are given by

$$\pi_i(p_1, p_2, \ldots, p_n) = (p_i - c_i)Q_i(p_1, p_2, \ldots, p_n) - K_i. \tag{4}$$

Each firm maximizes expected operating profits, taking the prices at other firms as given; that is, we derive a Nash-in-price equilibrium. Note that this approach assumes firms have perfect information regarding their competitors' prices in contrast to consumers.[13] Differentiating equation (4) with

---

[12] If $s_i \leqslant s_k$, then

$$\theta_k > \frac{p_i - p_k}{\beta} + \theta_i.$$

Thus, given θ_i, the probability that $s_i \leqslant s_k$ is

$$1 - F\left(\frac{p_i - p_k}{\beta} + \theta_i\right).$$

Since θ_i is drawn independently, equation (2) follows.

[13] This assumption may be justified on the grounds that the gains to gathering this information are higher for firms than for individual consumers.

respect to p_i under the Nash conjectural variation and rewriting, we have[14]

$$p_i = c_i - \frac{Q_i}{\partial Q_i / \partial p_i}. \tag{5}$$

We now derive a *symmetric, single price, Nash equilibrium*, given the structure of demand given by equation (3). By symmetry, we mean that the degree of imperfect information for all consumers and costs are identical for all firms, or

$$F_i^j(\theta) = F(\theta), \tag{6}$$
$$c_i = c.$$

Moreover, we *assume* that equilibrium entails identical prices for all firms,[15]

$$p_i = p. \tag{7}$$

We derive the equilibrium as follows: Assuming that all firms except firm i charge an identical price p, then after substituting into equation (3), we have

$$Q_i(p, \ldots, p_i, \ldots, p) = LD(p_i) \int \left\{ 1 - F\left(\frac{p_i - p}{\beta} + \theta\right) \right\}^{n-1} f(\theta)\, d\theta. \tag{8}$$

Differentiating (8) with respect to p_i under the Nash conjecture, the demand slope is given by

$$\frac{\partial Q_i}{\partial p_i} = \frac{D'(p_i)}{D(p_i)} Q_i - \left(\frac{n-1}{\beta}\right) LD(p_i)$$
$$\int \left\{ 1 - F\left(\frac{p_i - p}{\beta} + \theta\right) \right\}^{n-2} f\left(\frac{p_i - p}{\beta} + \theta\right) f(\theta)\, d\theta. \tag{9}$$

Substituting the equilibrium value $p_i = p$ into (8) and (9), we have

$$Q_i = LD(p) \int \{1 - F(\theta)\}^{n-1} f(\theta)\, D\theta = \frac{L}{n} D(p),^{16} \tag{10}$$

$$\frac{\partial Q_i}{\partial p_i} = \frac{L}{n} D'(p) - \left(\frac{n-1}{\beta}\right) LD(p) \int \{1 - F(\theta)\}^{n-2} \{f(\theta)\}^2\, d\theta. \tag{11}$$

[14] We assume that the second-order conditions are fulfilled, an assumption that is not true in general for all $F(\theta)$ and $D(p)$. For a discussion of sufficient conditions for the second-order condition to hold, see Perloff and Salop (1985); see also footnote 21.

[15] It should be emphasized that we assume a single-price equilibrium. Although this assumption may be easily proved for the case of $n = 2$, we have not ruled out multiprice equilibria for larger n. This issue is discussed in more detail in Section IV.

[16] Since

$$\int \{1 - F(\theta)\}^{n-1} F(\theta)\, d\theta = \frac{1}{n}.$$

The individual consumer's demand elasticity is

$$\eta \equiv -\frac{\partial Q_i}{\partial p_i}\frac{p_i}{Q_i} = -\frac{p_i D'(p_i)}{D(p_i)}.$$ (12)

Substituting equations (10)–(12) into (5), the symmetric, single-price equilibrium price, $p(n)$, is characterized as follows when there are n firms in the market:

$$p(n) = c + \frac{1}{M(n)},$$ (13)

where

$$M(n) = \frac{\eta}{p(n)} + \frac{n(n-1)}{\beta} \int \{1 - F(\theta)\}^{n-2}\{f(\theta)\}^2 \, d\theta.$$ (14)

Equations (13) and (14) define a single-price equilibrium between the competitive and monopoly prices. For example, if $\beta = 0$ (perfect information), then $M(n) \to \infty$ and $p = c$, that is, perfect competition obtains.[17] This result, of course, is analogous to the usual "Bertrand" equilibrium. At the other extreme, if $\beta \to \infty$ (perfect ignorance), then $M(n) = \eta/p$ and the monopoly price p^m obtains, where p^m satisfies the usual Lerner markup condition

$$\frac{p^m - c}{p^m} = \frac{1}{\eta}.$$

Improved information is captured by decreases in the scale parameter β. If the elasticity η is nondecreasing in price, then it is easily shown that a firm's aggregate demand becomes more elastic; thus, the equilibrium price falls. Differentiating equations (13) and (14) with respect to β, we have $\partial p/\partial \beta > 0$. That is,

Theorem 1: A reduction in consumer information (in the sense of an increase in β) raises the equilibrium price.

Moreover, as information becomes perfect, the equilibrium price approaches the perfectly competitive price continuously. This result is in contrast to Diamond's result that small but strictly positive search costs yield an equilibrium at the monopoly price. That is, in this model a small degree of imperfect information gives only a small degree of informational market power.

This difference from Diamond's result is not difficult to explain. A small search cost does not, in fact, imply a low cost to becoming perfectly informed. In fact, Diamond's result obtains because, at his monopoly price equilibrium, becoming perfectly informed entails sampling an infinite

[17] Of course, if $\eta \to \infty$, then $p(n) = c$ as well.

number of stores, and thus an infinite cost, if search costs are strictly positive.

It should be added that, if decreased information is formalized as a general mean-preserving spread of the density $f(\theta)$, the effect on the equilibrium price is indeterminate. This ambiguity arises because the firm's demand elasticity depends on the entire noise distribution as discussed in Appendix A. This result takes on greater importance in the analysis of product differentiation in Section V.

III. Entry competition

In this section we examine the effect of entry competition (increases in the exogenous number of firms n) on the single price equilibrium. It is a property of even traditional Cournot models of imperfect competition that entry may not lower the equilibrium price (Seade, 1980). We have not yet obtained a general entry result for small changes in the number of firms, but we have derived some asymptotic properties.

Although entry shifts each firm's demand curve inward, the elasticity of demand may not rise and, thus, equilibrium price may not fall. This ambiguity may be confirmed by differentiating the expression for $M(n)$ in equation (14) with respect to n.

On the other hand, for the limiting case of $n \to \infty$ $(k \to 0)$, a complete characterization does obtain. Of course, if each firm has strictly positive fixed costs $(k_i > 0)$, the market is unable to support an infinite number of firms. Instead, ignoring the integer problem, a zero profit equilibrium is characterized by the usual tangency of demand with average cost. Only if the level of fixed costs approaches zero (*perfectly free entry*) may the number of competitors become infinite.

The following theorem presents a condition under which the perfectly free entry price equals the perfectly competitive price under full information. The proof is contained in Appendix B.[18]

Theorem 2: If the support $[a, b]$ of the noise density $f(\theta)$ is bounded from below (i.e., if a is finite), then

$$\lim_{n \to \infty} p(n) = c.$$

The support $[a, b]$ must be bounded from below since all price estimates, s_i, must be positive.

Intuitively, the Nash equilibrium price approaches the competitive price if firm's Nash demand curves become perfectly elastic. If so, then even the smallest price increase causes the loss of all customers. Recall that a

---

[18] Robert Willig and Janos Galambos provided us with more general proofs.

representative firm obtains only those customers who most underestimate its price. Indeed, for $n \to \infty$ and finite lower bound a, a firm obtains only those customers who draw the maximum underestimate $\theta = a$ since each customer chooses a firm from an infinite sized sample from $f(\theta)$, that is, the first (lowest) order statistic equals the lower bound a. Similarly, since the sample is infinitely large, the second-order statistic also approaches the lower bound a. In other words, all of the firm's customers represent close wins, and each of these close wins is converted into a close loss if the firm raises its price even slightly. Thus, its demand is perfectly elastic and Theorem 2 holds.

Thus, perfectly free entry implies perfect competition. Setting profits equal to zero (allowing free entry) in equation (4) and substituting for p from equation (5)—the marginal revenue equals marginal cost condition— we obtain the equal number of firms.

$$n = \frac{L}{KM(n)}. \tag{15}$$

Above, we assumed $K \to 0$ so the equilibrium number of firms, n, grew without bound. Similarly, increases in the size of the market (as measured by L) increase the number of firms n which, in turn, increases $M(n)$. In the limit, as $L \to \infty$, then $n \to \infty$, $M(n) \to \infty$, and the equilibrium price approaches the perfectly competitive level. In these cases, the firm-consumer ratio (n/L) does become zero as in Hart (1979).

Although biased estimates have not been formally analyzed here, the reader may confirm that the theorems generalize to the case of a common biased distribution $F(\theta)$. In this sense, deceptive (biased) advertising does not destroy perfect competition in the perfectly free entry case as long as the degree of bias is identical for all firms.[19]

IV. Uniqueness, mass points, and multiprice equilibria

Thus far, we have restricted our attention to single price equilibria. In this section we discuss the possible existence of multiprice equilibria as well as the uniqueness of the single-price equilibrium derived above. We turn first to the uniqueness issue.

In principle, there could be multiple single-price equilibria; however, for the conventional case where the individual consumer's demand elasticity, $\eta(p)$, is nondecreasing in price, multiple single-price equilibria cannot occur:

Theorem 3: If $\eta(p)$ is nondecreasing in price and if a single-price equilibrium exists, then it is unique.

This result may be shown by rewriting (13) as follows:

$$\frac{p - c}{p} = \frac{1}{pM(n)}.$$

---

[19] Of course, if advertising is treated as a fixed cost, the perfectly free entry condition is not satisfied by a zero profit equilibrium.

The left-hand side is monotonically increasing in p, while the right-hand side is monotonically decreasing. Since the left-hand side equals zero when $p = c$ and the right-side approaches zero as p becomes infinitely large, the two sides must intersect exactly once at a positive price markup

$$\frac{p - c}{p} > 0.$$

This result does not rule out the additional possibility of multiple-price equilibria, even under the symmetric information and cost conditions set out in Section II. We do not have a general theorem on the nonexistence of multiprice equilibria; however, such equilibria can be rejected in a duopoly ($n = 2$) model to which we now turn.

For simplicity, suppose that consumers have perfectly inelastic demands ($\eta = 0$). Normalizing $\beta = 1$, the probability that firm 1 obtains a representative customer is

$$\Pr(s_1 \leqslant s_2) = \Pr(\theta_1 - \theta_2 \leqslant p_2 - p_1). \tag{16}$$

The distribution of $\mu \equiv \theta_1 - \theta_2$, $H(\mu)$, is symmetric with mean equal to zero so that $H(0) = \frac{1}{2}$.[20] Substituting the definition of μ into equation (16) and normalizing $L = 1$ so that expected sales equal the representative probability, we have

$$Q_1(p_1, p_2) = H(p_2 - p_1), \tag{17a}$$
$$Q_2(p_1, p_2) = 1 - H(p_2 - p_1). \tag{17b}$$

Calculating expected profits and substituting into the profit-maximizing condition analogous to equation (5), we obtain

$$p_1 = c + \frac{H(p_2 - p_1)}{h(p_2 - p_1)}, \tag{18a}$$

$$p_2 = c + \frac{1 - H(p_2 - p_1)}{h(p_2 - p_1)}, \tag{18b}$$

where $h(\mu)$ is the density of $H(\mu)$. Subtracting (18a) from (18b), we have

$$p_2 - p_1 = \frac{1}{h(p_2 - p_1)} \{1 - 2H(p_2 - p_1)\}. \tag{19}$$

Since $H(0) = \frac{1}{2}$, equation (19) is only satisfied for $p = p_1 = p_2$; and the unique single-price equilibrium is given by[21]

$$p = c + \frac{H(0)}{h(0)}. \tag{20}$$

---

[20] Symmetry may be shown by deriving $h(\mu)$, the density of $H(\mu)$, using a convolution with substitutions $\mu = \theta_1 - \theta_2$ and $\zeta = \theta_1 + \theta_2$. With a little manipulation, it can be shown that $h(\mu) = h(-\mu)$.

[21] When $n = 2$, in the symmetric equilibrium $(p_i = p)$, if $D(p_i) = $ a constant, $\partial^2 \pi_i / \partial p_i^2 = 2\partial Q_i / \partial p_i < 0$. Where $D'(p_i) < 0$, $\partial^2 \pi_i / \partial p_i^2 = 2\partial Q_i / \partial p_i + $ other negative terms < 0. This result does not necessarily hold for $n > 2$.

Two price equilibria may be ruled out by examining (19). If $p_2 - p_1 > 0$, then $H(p_2 - p_1) > \frac{1}{2}$ and, since $h(p_2 - p_1) > 0$, the right-hand side of (19) is negative while the left-hand side is positive. A similar contradiction obtains for $p_2 - p_1 < 0$.[22]

Thus, if $n = 2$ and $\eta = 0$, only a single-price equilibrium obtains. For $\eta > 0$, the result obtains if η is nondecreasing in price. However, this method of proof cannot be easily extended to the case of more than two firms. Beginning from a single price satisfying the equilibrium conditions, suppose a deviant firm, say, firm 1, sets its price at a level other than the common price p. In this case, letting $\mu_i = \theta_1 - \theta_i$, $i = 2, \ldots, n$, the n-firm equation analogous to (19) might be derived. Unfortunately, the marginal distributions of the μ_i's are not independent, complicating the calculations.

Until now, we have ruled out mass points. Mass points are important because they lead to the possibility of ties between the lowest estimates. These ties, in turn, lead to discontinuities in demand. Mass points may occur at $\theta = 0$ if some consumers are perfectly informed.[23] The introduction of mass points greatly changes the analysis.

Theorem 4: If the distribution function $F(\theta)$ has a mass point at $\theta = 0$, no single-price equilibrium exists.

We show this result by first ruling out a single-price equilibrium at $p > c$ and then by ruling out a single-price equilibrium at $p = c$. For any $p > c$, one deviant firm could break all previous "ties" by shading its price slightly. Sales would jump discontinuously if there were a strict proportion of ties raising its profits.

For $p = c$, unless absolutely all consumers were perfectly informed about all firms, a deviant could earn positive profits by charging $p_i > c$ and relying on the occasional unlucky buyer. In contrast, nondeviants set $p = c$ and earn zero profits.

The presence of mass points also has implications for the nature of multiprice equilibria:

Theorem 5: If the distribution function $F(\theta)$ has a mass point at $\theta = 0$, an equilibrium price vector cannot contain two or more prices which are equal.

If two prices were equal, the previous argument would apply. One of the firms could increase its sales and profits discontinuously by shading its price slightly.

As yet, we have not been able to take the analysis much further. It appears possible for a multiprice equilibrium to exist with (given appropriate reordering of firms) $p_1 < p_2 < \ldots < p_n$. It is clear that $p_1 > c$ and

---

[22] A similar analysis can be used to analyze the case of differential costs. If $c_1 < c_2$, then it can be shown that $p_1 < p_2$, that $p_1 - c_1 > p_2 - c_2$, and that the low-cost firm has a higher gross margin $(p_1 - c_1)/p_1$.

[23] By perfect information, we mean that the vectors $\underline{s}^j = \underline{p}^j$ (e.g., $\underline{Q}^j \equiv 0$ or $\beta \equiv 0$).

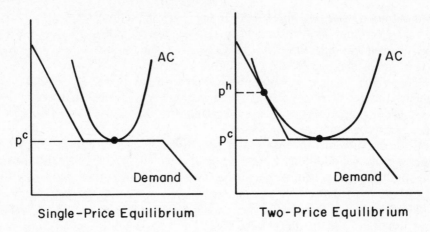

Single-Price Equilibrium   Two-Price Equilibrium

FIG. 1

$p_n \leqslant p^m$, the monopoly price. We have obtained no further restrictions beyond equal profitability.

Given mass points, if average costs are U-shaped, however, either single price or two or more price equilibria may obtain. Figure 1 illustrates possible single-price and two-price equilibria for this structure. This result is similar to Salop and Stiglitz's (1977) newspaper model. The difference is that the uninformed consumers here purchase according to their different estimates while, in the newspaper model, they purchase randomly.

These results are possible because of the demand discontinuities. Thus, common prices may only occur at the competitive price. There may still be a two-price equilibrium if there is only one high price (say, at p^h in Fig. 1) deviant. Three-price equilibria require only two deviants and so forth.

Although the existence of multiprice equilibria might cause an embarrassing nonuniqueness, they would enrich the model considerably. In particular, they would permit general market information to be more easily incorporated into the formal model, allowing the conventional search model to be more easily compared to this one. The existence of multiprice equilibria would remove the necessity of the restriction of only firm-specific information as follows: In the current model, where equilibrium entails only a single price, a consumer with that general market information would purchase randomly, regardless of the actual estimates drawn. Further analysis along these lines must await a sequel.

V. Spurious and actual product differentiation

As discussed earlier, the model may be reinterpreted to include both spurious and actual product differentiation. By spurious product differentiation, we mean that consumers mistakenly perceive brands to differ by more then they do actually, including the purely spurious differentiation case in which brands are actually homogeneous but are perceived to differ.[24] By actual product differentiation, we mean the case in which consumers differ in their actual valuation of different brands.

The model may easily handle spurious product differentiation by interpreting θ_i^j as quality misperceptions rather than price misperceptions. Similarly, actual product differentiation may be treated by reinterpreting θ_i^j as actual (cardinal) brand preferences. In both cases, s_i^j is redefined as the negative of consumer surplus.

All of the previous theorems hold for these variants of the basic model. Interestingly, the addition of quality misperceptions to price misperceptions may not raise the equilibrium price. As is shown in Appendix A, a mean-preserving spread in the noise density may raise or lower the equilibrium price. The actual product differentiation model is examined in more detail in Perloff and Salop (1985).

As this discussion indicates, the current price or quality uncertainty (spurious differentiation) model is very similar to the actual product differentiation model in Perloff and Salop (1985). That is, there is a near equivalence between spurious and actual price dispersion. Mathematically, there are only two important differences between the two models. First, in the current model, individual demand curves may slope downward; whereas, in the actual differentiation model, the individual demand curves were inelastic. Second, in this model, price is inherently bounded (Theorem 2); while, in the other model, quality is not so obviously bounded. The focus of the two papers, however, is quite different; and we believe both models are independently interesting.

VI. Extensions and conclusions

To recapitulate the main results of the firm-specific information model, if second-order conditions are satisfied, then at least one single-price equilibrium obtains. There is a unique single-price equilibrium if individual demand elasticities are nondecreasing in price. Multiprice equilibria appear

---

[24] The classic story of spurious product differentiation concerns the consumer who forms a false belief that one aspirin brand is superior to another after it relieves a mild headache and the "inferior" brand does not relieve a more serious one. This story may not be too farfetched: Even a placebo achieves a relief rate of around 45 percent compared to a relief rate of around 80 percent for actual aspirin (Food and Drug Administration, 1977). Such spurious product differentiation has been suggested by a number of writers including Chamberlin and Galbraith with respect to a wide variety of consumer products such as beer, detergents, lemon juice, and even soft drinks. The experimental evidence is interesting on this point. Blind tests of consumers' preferences after use do not replicate market shares. In addition, they vary according to whether products are labeled with brand names. For evidence, see Tucker (1964), McConnell (1968), Morris and Bronson (1969), and Monroe (1976); for a related model, see Schmalensee (1979); and for a good discussion of some of the policy implications of this phenomenon, see Craswell (1979).

to be possible as well although more work needs to be done to rigorously establish existence and additional properties of such equilibria.

If a mass of consumers are well informed, a single-price equilibrium cannot exist if marginal costs are constant. If average costs are U-shaped, however, then single-price equilibria at the competitive price or multiprice-equilibria may obtain.

If there are an insignificant number of well-informed consumers, then the single-price equilibrium has the following properties. Improved information, in the sense of the scaling parameter defined above, lowers the equilibrium price. Devine and Marion (1979) indicate this effect may be empirically important. Entry competition lowers price for sufficiently vigorous entry; and in the case of perfectly free entry, equilibrium price falls to the competitive price.

Beyond these results, few other properties have been established. More work needs to be done here with respect to both symmetric multiprice equilibria and multiprice equilibria arising from differential costs and information endowments. The degree of information must be made endogenous. Particular distributions should be examined. The dynamics of the model must be analyzed.

Finally, and probably most important, search must be explicitly introduced into the model. This modification may be done in either of two ways. First, having arrived at a store, a consumer will often find he has underestimated the price charged so he may have a sufficient incentive to sample the firm with the second lowest estimate. Such search will probably have little or no effect on the general qualitative properties of the model.

Of course, a more sophisticated or experienced consumer may infer that his lowest estimate tends to be an underestimate. This information will not alter his behavior significantly unless he also infers that all prices are identical if, in fact, they are.[25] In that case, if consumers ignore their firm-specific estimates and choose firms randomly, price rises to the monopoly level. Of course, in this case, if a deviant lowers his price and, hence, the firm-specific estimates of his price, will consumers rely on the information? This is the usual logical difficulty arising in search and newspaper models.[26] The problem can be avoided in the case of multiprice equilibria. At such an equilibrium, general market information corresponding to the full rational expectations hypothesis of the search and newspaper models can be well accommodated.

University of California, Berkeley
Georgetown University Law Center

[25] The level of the expected benefits of search, of course, will be altered.
[26] *Cf.* the solutions of Salop and Stiglitz (1977) and Diamond and Rothschild (1978).

APPENDIX A

We rewrite the density as $f(\theta; \alpha)$ where α is a parameter representing the level of uncertainty: As α increases, uncertainty increases due to a mean-preserving spread. Differentiating (13), it may be shown that the sign of $\partial p/\partial \alpha$ is the same as the sign of

$$\frac{\partial}{\partial \alpha} \int_a^b \{f(\theta; \alpha)\}^2 \, d\theta.$$

Appendix Fig. 2 shows a symmetric density to which a mean-preserving spread has been applied. Various size regions are shown and identified by capital letters: All regions with the same letter are of the same size.

If $F(\theta)$ is the original density and $h(\theta)$ is the density after two sections (labeled A, which are e by x as shown in Appendix Fig. 2) are removed from the center and added to the tails, then the change in the integral of the squared density is given as follows:

$$\int_a^b \{h^2(\theta) - f^2(\theta)\} \, d\theta = 2 \left\{ \int_0^x [f(\theta) - e]^2 \, d\theta - \int_0^x f^2(\theta) \, d\theta \right.$$

$$+ \int_y^{y+x} [f(\theta) + e]^2 \, d\theta - \int_y^{y+x} f^2(\theta) \, d\theta \bigg\}$$

$$= 4e(ex + \{[F(y+x) - F(y)] - [F(x) - F(0)]\}).$$

This value may be either positive or negative. Graphically, it is positive if the areas A and B are greater than C and negative if A plus B is less than C.

Heuristically, if the density is nearly uniform, this value is positive, so price rises as uncertainty increases. If the density is single peaked with a large mode, then the price will fall as uncertainty increases. Thus, the price effect depends on the density and the type of mean-preserving spread used.

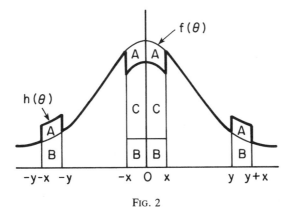

FIG. 2

APPENDIX B

The proof of Theorem 2 is given here. This proof assumes that the density function $f(\theta)$ has the following properties (which could be relaxed at the cost of greater complexity in the proofs):

1. $f(\theta) > 0$, $\theta \in (a, b)$.
2. $f(\theta)$ is analytic.

We wish to prove that, under the conditions given in Theorem 2, entry will drive the equilibrium price to marginal cost (even given limited consumer information). Since $p = c + 1/M(n)$, showing that $\lim_{n \to \infty} M(n) = \infty$ is sufficient to show that $\lim_{n \to \infty} p = c$. The following lemmas establish that, if a is finite, then $\lim_{n \to \infty} M(n) = \infty$.

Theorem 2′: the $\lim_{n \to \infty} M(n) = \infty$.

Proof of Theorem 2′: Since $f(\theta) > 0$ for $\theta \in (a, b)$ and $f(\theta)$ is continuous, there exists an interval $(a, a + \delta)$ subject to $\theta \in (a, a + \delta)$, $f(\theta) \geq \xi > 0$. As a result,

$$M(n) = \int_a^{a+\delta} n(n-1)\{1 - F(\theta)\}^{n-2}\{f(\theta)\}^2 \, d\theta + Z$$

$$\geq \xi \int_a^{a+\delta} n(n-1)\{1 - F(\theta)\}^{n-2} f(\theta) \, d\theta + Z,$$

where

$$Z = \int_{a+\delta}^{b} n(n-1)\{1 - F(\theta)\}^{n-2}\{f(\theta)\}^2 \, d\theta.$$

Therefore,

$$\lim_{n \to \infty} M(n) \geq \lim_{n \to \infty} n\xi - \lim_{n \to \infty} \{1 - F(a + \delta)\}^{n-1} + \lim_{n \to \infty} Z = \infty.$$

We know, however, that

1. $\lim_{n \to \infty} n\xi = \infty$.
2. $\lim_{n \to \infty} n\xi\{1 - F(a + \delta)\}^{n-1} = 0$, since $1 > \{1 - F(a + \delta)\} > 0$.
3. $\lim_{n \to \infty} Z \geq 0$ since $n(n-1)\{1 - F(\theta)\}^{n-2}\{f(\theta)\}^2 \, d\theta \geq 0$ for all $\theta \in (a + \delta, b)$.

Thus, $\lim_{n \to \infty} M(n) = \infty$.

REFERENCES

AKERLOF, G. (1970). "The market for lemons: qualitative uncertainty and the market mechanism," *Quarterly Journal of Economics*, vol. 84, pp. 488–500.

ARROW, K. (1958). "Toward a theory of price adjustment," in P. Baran *et al.*, *The Allocation of Economic Resources*, Stanford University Press, Stanford.

BUTTERS, G. (1977). "Equilibrium distributions of sales and advertising prices," *Review of Economic Studies*, vol. 44, pp. 465–491.

CRASWELL, R. (1979). "Trademarks, consumer information and barriers to competition," Federal Trade Commission, Washington, D.C.

DEVINE, D. G. and MARION, B. W. (1979). "The Influence of Consumer Price Information on Retail Pricing and Consumer Behavior," *American Journal of Agricultural Economics*, vol. 61, pp. 228–237.

DIAMOND, P. (1971). "A model of price adjustment," *Journal of Economic Theory*, vol. 3, pp. 156–168.

DIAMOND, P. and ROTHSCHILD, M. (1978). *Uncertainty in Economics: Readings and Exercises,* Academic Press, New York, pp. 488 and 489.

DIXIT, A. and STIGLITZ, J. (1977). "Monopolistic competition and optimum product diversity," *American Economic Review,* vol. 67, pp. 297–308.

FEDERAL TRADE COMMISSION (1978). *Trade Regulation Rule on Advertising of Opthalmic Goods and Services,* 16 CFR 456, Washington, D.C.

FEDERAL TRADE COMMISSION (1979). *Consumer Information Remedies,* Washington, D.C.

FOOD AND DRUG ADMINISTRATION (1977). "Proposed monograph for OTC internal analgesic, antipyretic and antirheumatic products," *Federal Register,* vol. 42, p. 35382.

GABOR, A. and GRANGER, C. (1961). "On the price consciousness of consumers," *Applied Statistics,* vol. 10, pp. 170–180.

GROSSMAN, S., KIHLSTROM, R., and MIRMAN, L. (1977). "A Bayesian approach to the production of information and learning by doing," *Review of Economic Studies,* vol. 44, pp. 533–548.

GUASCH, L. and WEISS, A. (1980). "Wages as a sorting mechanism in competitive markets with asymmetric information," *Review of Economic Studies,* vol. 47, forthcoming.

HART, O. (1979). "Monopolistic competition in a large economy with differentiated commodities," *Review of Economic Studies,* vol. 46, pp. 1–30.

HOTELLING, H. (1929). "Stability in competition," *Ecomomic Journal,* vol. 39, pp. 41–57.

LANCASTER, K. (1979). *Variety, Equity and Efficiency,* Columbia University Press, New York.

LELAND, H. (1979). "Quacks, lemons and licensing: a theory of minimum quality standards," *Journal of Political Economy,* vol. 87, pp. 1328–1346.

MCCONNELL, J. (1968). "The development of brand loyalty: an experimental study," *Journal of Marketing Research,* vol. 5, pp. 13–19.

MONROE, K. (1976). "The influence of price differences and brand familiarity on brand preferences," *Journal of Consumer Research,* vol. 3, pp. 42–49.

MORRIS, R. and BRONSON, C. (1969). "The chaos of competition indicated by *Consumer Reports,*" *Journal of Marketing,* vol. 33, pp. 26–34.

NELSON, P. (1974). "The economic value of advertising," in Y. Brozen *et al. Advertising and Society,* New York University Press, New York, pp. 43–66.

PERLOFF, J. and SALOP, S. (1985). "Equilibrium with product differentiation," *Review of Economic Studies,* vol. LII, pp. 107–120.

PHELPS, E. (1972). "A statistical theory of racism and sexism," *American Economic Review,* vol. 62, pp. 659–661.

PHELPS, E. and WINTER, S. (1970). "Optimal price policy under atomistic competition," in E. S. Phelps *et al., Microeconomic Foundations of Inflation and Employment Policy,* W. W. Norton and Co., Inc., New York, pp. 309–337.

PITOFSKY, R. (1977). "Beyond Nader: consumer protection and the regulation of advertising," *Harvard Law Review,* vol. 90, pp. 661–701.

PLOTT, C. and WILDE, L. (1979). "Seller induced demand," California Institute of Technology, Pasadena, unpublished manuscript.

SALOP, S. (1980). "The monopoly matchmaker and the theory of brokerage," Federal Trade Commission, Washington, D.C., unpublished manuscript.

SALOP, S. and STIGLITZ, J. (1977). "Bargains and ripoffs: a model of monopolistically competitive price dispersion," *Review of Economic Studies,* vol. 44, pp. 493–510.

SATTINGER, M. (1984). "Value of an additional firm in monopolistic competition," *Review of Economic Studies,* vol. 51, pp. 321–332.

SCHWARTZ, A. and WILDE, L. (1979). "Intervening in markets on the basis of imperfect information: a legal and economic analysis," *University of Pennsylvania Law Review,* vol. 127, pp. 630–682.

SCHMALENSEE, R. (1979). "On the use of economic models in antitrust: the Rea–Lemon case," *University of Pennsylvania Law Review,* vol. 127, pp. 994–1050.

SCITOVSKY, T. (1950). "Ignorance as a source of oligopoly power," *American Economic Review,* vol. 40, pp. 48–53.

SEADE, J. (1980). "On the effects of entry," *Econometrica*, vol. 48, pp. 479–489.

SHAPIRO, C. (1980). "Dynamic models of imperfect information and quality," Massachusetts Institute of Technology, Cambridge, unpublished manuscript.

SMALLWOOD, D. and CONLISK, J. (1979). "Product quality in markets where consumers are imperfectly informed," *Quarterly Journal of Economics*, vol. 93, pp. 1–23.

SPENCE, A. M. (1973). "Job market signalling," *Quarterly Journal of Economics*, vol. 87, pp. 355–374.

SPENCE, A. M. (1974). "Competitive and optimal responses to signals," *Journal of Economic Theory*, vol. 7, pp. 296–306.

SPENCE, A. M. (1976). "Product selection, fixed costs and monopolistic competition," *Review of Economic Studies*, vol. 43, pp. 217–235.

STIGLITZ, J. (1975). "The theory of screening, education and the distribution of income," *American Economic Review*, vol. 65, pp. 283–300.

STIGLITZ, J. (1979). "Equilibrium in product markets with imperfect information," *American Economic Review, Papers and Proceedings*, vol. 69, pp. 339–345.

STIGLER, G. (1961). "The economics of information, *Journal of Political Economy*, vol. 69, pp. 213–225.

TUCKER, W. (1964). "The development of brand loyalty," *Journal of Marketing Research*, vol. 1, pp. 32–35.

UHL, J. N. and BROWN, H. L. (1972). "Consumer perception of experimental retail food price changes," *Journal of Consumer Affairs*, vol. 5, pp. 174–185.

VARIAN, H. (1980). "A model of sales," *American Economic Review*, vol. 70, pp. 651–659.

WILDE, L. and SCHWARTZ, A. (1979). "Equilibrium comparison shopping," *Review of Economic Studies*, vol. 46, pp. 543–553.

A MODEL OF INNOVATION WITH APPLICATION TO NEW FINANCIAL PRODUCTS

By RONALD W. ANDERSON *and* CHRISTOPHER J. HARRIS

1. Introduction

IN THIS paper we analyse a continuous-time model of innovation in an oligopolistic industry. Our model is distinguished from others by its emphasis of the possibility that firms which follow with imitative products may be disadvantaged to the extent their entry is delayed. This is a wide-spread phenomenon, typical of industries such as computers and military hardware where leaders are able to establish industry standards. In this sense our analysis is quite general. The features of our model also apply to innovations in financial markets. Indeed our study was originally motivated by the need to provide a foundation for the discussion of financial regulation. Consequently, competition among securities exchanges or primary dealers will receive particular attention in our discussion.

Many financial products are distinguished from durable products in general by the ease with which they may be traded on secondary markets. This liquidity is a highly desirable feature for the holder of the financial instrument. It derives from the homogeneity of many financial instruments. It is also promoted by the existence of a centralized marketplace for the product. For if buyers and sellers both go to the same place to trade, search time is reduced or, alternatively, the discount or premium demanded by a market maker is reduced.[1] This has important implications for competition in markets in these instruments. First, there is a tendency for secondary transactions to concentrate in a small number of locations.[2] Second, once liquidity is established at a marketplace, it would be relatively difficult for a rival to lure the trading activity away.[3] The net effect of this is that positive profits to market makers may persist even in equilibrium. Furthermore there is an advantage in establishing the market first. Overall, liquidity effects may result in a tendency for trading of a given financial instrument to concentrate in a small number of exchanges or dealers.

There is a further tendency for trading in related financial products to concentrate at the same group of dealers or exchanges. For example, in England futures trading for financial instruments is concentrated at a single exchange.[4] In the U.S., one exchange accounts for a high proportion of the

---

[1] The link between centralized markets and liquidity has been emphasised by Telser (1981) and Townsend (1984).

[2] The high degree of concentration of American futures exchanges is documented in Carlton (1984). In recent years the New York Stock Exchange has accounted for trading volume that is more than twice that of all other U.S. stock exchanges combined (see Sharpe (1981)).

[3] For example, this is reflected in the high failure rate of new futures contracts which directly imitate existing contracts (see Silber (1981)).

[4] The London International Financial Futures Exchange.

activity in exchange traded stock options.[5] There are a variety of economies of scope which contribute to this. In particular, the investment in communcations equipment necessary for price reporting and the apparatus of market clearing can be spread over several distinct financial instruments. As a consequence, the tendency towards concentration due to liquidity effects is strengthened so that market making for a group of financial instruments is apt to be oligopolistic.

A further characteristic of financial markets is that non-price competition among financial institutions may be as important or more important than price competition. For example, in futures markets the cost of transaction services consists of commissions and the expected execution loss reflected in the bid/ask spread. The latter is determined through the competitive interaction of a large number of individual market makers.[6] In the United States since antitrust actions in the early 1970's, commissions have been negotiated between customers and brokers. Consequently, futures exchanges are not directly involved in pricing market making services.[7] For such situations exchanges or their counterparts in other industries compete with one another through a variety of means including the quality of the trading and price reporting facilities provided, the quality of supervision of trade practices, and through providing some kind of performance guarantees. However, the most important form of non-price competition is often in designing and initiating trading in new financial instruments. For given the difficulty of diverting activity from an already established marketplace, the main opportunity to expand is through establishing new products. It is precisely this form of competition that we wish to analyze in the model considered here.

Finally, one characteristic common to most financial markets is that they are regulated to some extent. The rationale for the regulation may differ from market to market as does the form the regulation takes. However, the effect of regulation for the introduction of new financial instruments is similar for most markets. Any major innovation is likely to come under some form of public scrutiny. The consequence is that the innovator must count on sometimes considerable legal costs and quite possibly some regulatory delay before the proposed innovation is allowed to take place.

In sum, the distinctive features we wish to capture in a model are: (i) there are a small number of rivals, (ii) first-movers have advantages in establishing and maintaining market share, (iii) competition takes place through product development, and (iv) regulation can add to development

---

[5] The Chicago Board Options Exchange had 77 percent of stock option volume in the U.S. in 1976 (Sharpe (1981)).

[6] These are floor traders commonly called scalpers. The process of determining the bid/ask spread is modelled by Telser and Higinbotham (1977).

[7] Exchanges may indirectly affect the pricing of transactions services notably by determining the size of the pool of market makers. Anderson (1985) shows that the equilibrium exchange size generally results in non-zero profits to market makers even in the face of entry.

costs and time. Beyond this, the selection of our model is dictated by the questions we wish to address. In part, these are familiar concerns of analyses of oligopolistic R&D games. Does oligopolistic competition lead to under or over investment in new product development? Under what conditions will rivals introduce new products simultaneously and when will they do so sequentially? However, we are particularly concerned with the effect of regulatory cost and regulatory delay on the flow of new product development.

The organization of the paper is as follows. Section 2 describes the model and establishes the existence and uniqueness of a subgame perfect equilibrium. Section 3 is devoted to comparative static properties of the model and their interpretation. Section 4 discusses extensions to the model of Section 2, and its relation to other work.

2. The model

In this section, we consider the innovation decisions of two firms. For the sake of concreteness and with a view to our intended application to financial institutions, we shall refer to these as exchanges. The potential innovation is to introduce a new product. The nature of the product and the development time and cost are known and equal for the two exchanges. Until the product is introduced by either one of the exchanges the demand for the product is unknown. The decision of the exchange is whether to innovate in advance of knowing demand, to innovate after the other exchange so that demand is known, or to not innovate at all.

Our model is a simple two player dynamic game in continuous time. For convenience of notation we assume that the exchanges are identical. At any time an exchange may decide to introduce the product by incurring a fixed cost C to cover development costs including product design, marketing, legal work, and regulatory procedures. Once the decision to innovate is made the exchange must wait a period of length N before offering the product. This reflects time for development including possible regulatory lag.

Both C and N are fixed numbers independent of time or of the actions of either of the exchanges. This reflects our emphasis on new product development as opposed to more basic research. In the case of the former, the innovation requires certain product-specific development steps that are unlikely to be lessened by delaying the project. In contrast basic research may benefit from related discoveries elsewhere so that the innovation may become less costly with time. Our assumptions rule out the possibility of a trade-off of development cost and development time, of imitative products being developed more cheaply and quickly than pioneering ones, and that regulatory treatment may be unpredictable and may depend upon the actions of other exchanges. While any or all of these may be relevant to a particular industry of interest, allowing for them would complicate the analysis without commensurate increase in our understanding of the competitive interaction of financial institutions.

Once the product is introduced it will generate net revenues at the constant rate R for the industry as a whole indefinitely into the future. If a single exchange offers the product, it captures all the net revenues. If two exchanges offer the product they will split the market with the market share of a leader, who innovates earlier, higher than that of a follower. Let $S(M)$ be the market share of an exchange that has offered the product a period of length M after the other exchange ($M < 0$ for a leader). Thus $S(-M) = 1 - S(M)$. Furthermore, we assume that $S(0) = 0.5$, that $S' < 0$, and that $S(\infty) = 0$. (Note that $1 > S > 0$ for all M.) Demand for the product is uncertain before it is on the market. We assume that R takes on two possible values R^H and R^L with probabilities p and $(1-p)$ respectively, where $1 > p > 0$ and $R^H > R^L \geqslant 0$. (That $R^L \geqslant 0$ reflects the assumption of costless possible exit.) Finally, the exchanges discount profits and costs at the rate r.

In our formulation the exchanges compete only through their decision to develop a new product, and the random variable R and the function $S(\,.\,)$ are given. Implicit in this specification is some process determining the costs of transactions involving the new financial product. For example, if commissions are fixed by regulation or by a binding commitment among exchanges and if products are homogeneous, total commission income would be independent of the number of exchanges offering the product. Alternatively, Saloner (1984) has argued that the same is true if commission rates are determined by exchange members who engage in Bertrand type competition and who are jointly liable for all of exchange fixed costs.

Total industry revenues would not generally be independent of the number of firms in the industry if the unit profits were determined in a quantity setting game. In such a framework, adding an exchange offering an identical product would be likely to decrease total revenues. If products are differentiated, total revenues could rise, fall, or remain unchanged depending upon the degree to which the products are close substitutes. In our model we assume that the demand for both exchanges is known as soon as the good of one exchange is available. This will be plausible only for the case in which the goods are fairly substitutable. For the range of applications we have in mind, we think it is unlikely that total industry revenues would increase by much if a second exchange offered its product.

The assumption that the follower's share is decreasing in the length of the lag between the leader's and follower's innovation reflects the advantage which liquidity effect bestow on the exchange that innovates first.

In this model the two exchanges are entirely symmerical prior to play. The only way that the exchanges are ever distinguished is that some combinations of strategies may result in one being the leader and the other following. In this way an important feature of the model is to identify those asymmetries which arise from one exchange undertaking to lead. The leader produces an externality, for the introduction of the product reveals the level of demand. The follower benefits from this externality. Thus our model has the feature that first-movers have both an advantage (market share) and a disadvantage (lack of information) relative to followers.

That incumbent firms often generate externalities that benefit potential followers has been emphasised by von Weizsacker (1980). In such cases the welfare implications of barring entry must be judged on a case by case basis. here we are interested in assessing whether in financial markets liquidity effects, which may be viewed as creating a barrier to entry, necessarily lead to a misallocation of resources. Prior to doing so we first study the general features of equilibrium in our model.

Solution concept

Our solution concept is the natural analogue, in the present context, of the notion of (subgame) perfect equilibrium in pure strategies used in the analysis of games in discrete time. In order to state clearly what we mean by this, we must first outline the nature of the exchanges' strategies and explain how the outcome of the game is determined from these strategies.

An exchange's strategy specifies, for every conceivable contingency, the decision that it will make in that contingency. For concreteness let us refer to the exchanges as exchange A and exchange B. There are, broadly, three types of contingency that A may face. First, neither exchange may have innovated by time t. Secondly, only B may have innovated by t. Thirdly, both may have innovated by t. In the first case, A's strategy simply specifies whether or not he will innovate at t. In the third, no further action by A is possible. The second case is more complicated. For A must take account not only of the fact that B has innovated, but also of the time $t_1 < t$ at which he did so. If, furthermore, $t \geq t_1 + N$ then A must in addition take account of whether the revealed level of demand is high or low. (For example, if $t < t_1 + N$ and t is close to $t_1 + N$, then the reduction in A's potential market share may already be so great that he will only be able to cover the cost of innovating if the level of demand is high. In this case A will prefer to wait until this level is revealed at $t_1 + N$.)

Overall, exchanges observe what transpires in the interval of time $[0,t)$ and choose their actions at t accordingly.

We allow for effectively instantaneous reactions. Specifically, if a strategy calls for an irreversible action when a certain event is observed then, if the event occurs at t, the action will have been taken by t_1 for all $t_1 > t$. The action, which is a reaction to the event, occurs at t in the sense that t is the greatest lower bound of the times by which the action will have occurred. Thus the reaction is essentially instantaneous.[8]

---

[8] The nature of the difficulty is best illustrated by means of an example.

Suppose that A's strategy is to innovate if B has innovated, but not otherwise, and that B's strategy is to innovate at time t_1. (This example is slightly contrived, but it captures the essence

Finally, then, the exchanges strategies are in (perfect) equilibrium if there is no contingency in which either exchange can improve its expected payoff by a unilateral change in its strategy. The operational significance of this definition will be clear from the analysis that follows.

Analysis of the model

We begin by noting that if an exchange copies a successful innovation, then it will do so immediately. For with discounting waiting is intrinsically costly. Moreover, it results in a loss of revenue because potential market share falls with increasing delay. Similarly, it may be verified that if an exchange chooses to follow an innovation before observing demands then it will follow immediately. The analysis of the model can therefore be conducted entirely in terms of four expected payoffs: (i) the payoff from innovating at 0 and not being imitated under any circumstances (π_1); (ii) the payoff from innovating at 0 when the other exchange also innovates at 0 (π_2); (iii) the payoff from innovating at 0 when the other exchange imitates at N if the innovation is successful (π_4); and (iv) the payoff from imitating at N a successful innovation by the other exchange (π_3).

Consider first the case of an exchange which innovates at once, and whose rival never innovates. It incurs a cost C straight away, and receives flow profits of R^H from N onwards with probability p and flow profits of R^L from N onwards with probability $1-p$. Its expected discounted lifetime profits are therefore

$$\pi_1 = -C + e^{-rN}\bar{R}/r$$

where $\bar{R} = pR^H + (1-p)R^L$. Next, if both exchanges innovate at time 0, they each receive a payoff

$$\pi_2 = -C + e^{-rN}S(0)\bar{R}/r$$

since they each receive a fraction $S(0)$ of the final profit flow. Thirdly, in the case where exchange A innovates at 0 and exchange B innovates at N if the level of demand turns out to be high, B receives a payoff

$$\pi_3 = p(-e^{-rN}C + e^{-2rN}S(N)R^H/r).$$

footnote 8 continued.

of the difficulty in the simplest possible fashion.) Certainly B innovates at time t_1. A does not innovate at any $t_2 > t_1$. If he did then there would exist t, $t_1 < t < t_2$, such that B has innovated by t, but A did not innovate at t. Nor does A innovate at any $t_2 \leqslant t_1$. This is obvious if $t_2 < t_1$. For the case $t_2 = t_1$, note that B does not innovate in the interval $[0, t_1)$ observed by A at t_1, so that an innovation by A at t_1 would also violate his strategy. But A must innovate some time, for the same reason that he cannot innovate later than t_1.

Formally, we appear to have arrived at an impasse. Intuitively, however, it is clear that the outcome should involve simultaneous innovation at t_1. A cannot possibly innovate before t_1. Furthermore, he *will have* innovated by any $t_2 > t_1$. The impasse is nothing more than a minor 'closure problem', caused by describing the outcome too literally in terms of the times at which the players innovate. This intuition can be made rigorous, but we feel that it would be over-pedantic to do so here. We shall simply say that B innovates at t_1, and that A reacts immediately by innovating himself.

For he acts at all only with probability p, in which case he incurs a cost C at time N and then receives a fraction $S(N)$ of demand from $2N$ onwards. Finally, in the same case A receives

$$\pi_4 = -C + e^{-rN}(1 - e^{-rN})\bar{R}/r$$
$$+ e^{-2rN}(p(1 - S(N))R^H + (1 - p)R^L)/r,$$

since he receives all demand from N until $2N$, and shares demand from $2N$ onwards only if its level is high.

It is always the case that $\pi_1 > \pi_2$ and $\pi_1 > \pi_4$, as is obvious since in the case of π_2 and π_4 the leader must share demand with the follower when its level is high. Also, $\pi_4 > \pi_2$. For in the case of π_4 the leader monopolises the market for a period of length N, and possesses more than half of it thereafter. This is, however, all that one can say in general about the interrelationships among the π_i. In particular, each of the five possibilities envisaged by the following proposition obtains for a suitable choice of C, N, p, S, R^H and R^L.

Proposition 1: Equilibrium always exists. Furthermore, in equilibrium,
  (i) If $\pi_1 < 0$ then neither exchange ever innovates. Suppose then that $\pi_1 > 0$:
 (ii) if, in addition, max $\{\pi_2, \pi_3\} < 0$ then only one exchange ever innovates, and it does so immediately;
(iii) if $\pi_2 > $ max $\{\pi_3, 0\}$ then both exchanges innovate at once;
 (iv) if $\pi_3 > $ max $\{\pi_2, 0\}$ and $\pi_4 > 0$ then one exchange innovates immediately and the other innovates at time N if the level of demand is high;
  (v) if $\pi_3 > $ max $\{\pi_2, 0\}$ but $\pi_4 < 0$ then neither exchange ever innovates.

Notice that, for any π_2 and π_3, either max $\{\pi_2, \pi_3\} \leq 0$ or $\pi_2 \geq$ max $\{\pi_3, 0\}$ or $\pi_3 \geq$ max $\{\pi_2, 0\}$. Thus, aside from borderline cases, the five possibilities listed in Proposition 1 are mutually exclusive and exhaustive. As we have already noted, they are also not vacuous. Table 1 gives parameter choices for which the various types of equilibria occur.

Notice too that the equilibria of cases (ii) and (iv) are asymmetric, both in respect of the actions taken by the exchanges and the payoffs they obtain. There is nothing pathological abut this—such asymmetric equilibria are commonplace in sequential games. The question of which firm will in fact lead does of course arise. But this is just the familiar problem of how players will coordinate their expectations on a particular equilibrium from among multiple equilibria. As such it arises mainly from the excessive abstraction of the model. Thus, in a practical example of case (ii), one exchange would have a slight edge over the other. That exchange would be the leader.

The findings of Proposition 1 are intuitive. If $\pi_1 < 0$ then even monopoly is not profitable. hence one would not expect any innovation. This is case (i). Next, if monopoly is profitable ($\pi_1 > 0$), but it is not profitable to

TABLE 1
Examples of Equilibria

Type of Equilibrium	C	R^H	R^L
(i)	5	1	0
(ii)	2	0.4	0.3
(iii)	1	1	0.1
(iv)	1	0.3	0.1
(v)	1	0.3	0

In all cases we take $N = 1$, $p = 0.5$, $r = 0.1$ and $S(N) = 0.4$.

engage in a symmetric duopoly ($\pi_2 < 0$) or to copy a successful innovation ($\pi_3 < 0$), then monopoly will be the outcome. This is case (ii). It might arise if costs are high relative to average demand, and if a high level of demand is insufficient to compensate the market share lost due to entering with a delay of N. Thirdly, if symmetric dupoly is profitable ($\pi_2 > 0$), and more so than copying a successful innovation ($\pi_2 > \pi_3$), then simultaneous innovation will occur. This is case (iii). It might happen if average demand is high relative to costs, but the loss of market share $S(0) - S(N)$ due to a delay of N is also very large.

If, on the other hand, copying a successful innovation is profitable ($\pi_3 < 0$), and more so than engaging in a symmetric duopoly ($\pi_3 > \pi_2$), then we know that if one exchange does innovate then the other will follow suit, with a delay of N, if that innovation is successful. This might happen if average demand is low relative to costs, but R^H is considerably greater than R^L. There are then two possibilities. If the knowledge that the profits of a successful innovation will be creamed off by competition is sufficient to render the risk of innovation unworthwhile ($\pi_4 < 0$), then neither exchange will innovate. This is case (v). It is rather different from case (i). No innovation takes place for strategic reasons. Note that this could prevail even if $\pi_1 > 0$, in which case the availability of the innovation would be socially desirable.

Finally, competition with a successful innovation may not be sufficient to render the initial risk unworthwhile ($\pi_4 > 0$), perhaps because the development lag enables the innovator to establish a sufficiently large market share. Then one firm will innovate, and the other will copy the innovation if it is successful. This is case (iv). Notice that it may well be that copying is more profitable than undertaking the initial innovation ($\pi_3 > \pi_4$). It is not necessarily the case that there is an advantage to being first. If $\pi_3 > \pi_4 > 0$ then both exchanges would prefer to follow. But one exchange must go first otherwise there will be no profits at all.

Proof of Proposition 1

The verbal discussion above has described the principal considerations already. We therefore need only outline the proof of the proposition.

Suppose $\pi_1 < 0$, and suppose for a contradiction that innovation does take place. Then some exchange innovates first (possibly equal first), say at t. The payoff to this exchange is at most

$$\max \{e^{-rt}\pi_4, e^{-rt}\pi_2, e^{-rt}\pi_1\} = e^{-rt}\pi_1 < 0.$$

It would therefore do better not to innovate.

Suppose next that $\pi_1 > 0$ but $\max \{\pi_2, \pi_3\} < 0$. If neither exchange innovates then one exchange, say A, can improve its payoff by innovating, say at t. For it cannot pay B to copy at once (since $e^{-rt}\pi_2 < 0$) or to copy only successful innovations (since $e^{-rt}\pi_3 < 0$), so that A's payoff from innovating at t is $e^{-rt}\pi_1 > 0$. Thus one exchange, say A, must innovate at some t. Furthermore, if $t > 0$ then A can improve its payoff by innovating at 0. For B's optimal reaction is still to do nothing, and A's payoff becomes $\pi_1 > e^{-rt}\pi_1$. Thus in the present case one exchange innovates at once and the other never innovates.

Similar arguments establish parts (iii)–(v) of the proposition. We therefore have that, in the cases listed, equilibrium, if it exists, must have the respective forms described. It is easy to see that an equilibrium of the appropriate form does indeed exist in each case. To see that equilibrium also exists in the borderline cases, we need only note that the equilibrium constraints for any particular form of equilibrium are continuous in the parameters. Thus if, for example, we have a case on the borderline between case (iv) and case (v) (i.e. $\pi_3 > \max \{\pi_2, 0\}$ and $\pi_4 = 0$), then equilibria of both type (iv) and type (v) exist. Notice that, in contrast with the non-borderline cases, for which the outcome is unique, outcomes are never unique for a borderline case. This completes the proof of the proposition.

3. Policy analysis

It was emphasized in the introduction that competition among financial institutions is often shaped by a variety of governmental interventions. We now use our model to examine the implications of several types of policies for the pace of financial innovation. We are particularly concerned with the claim that governmental interference unnecessarily complicates the process of introducing new financial products and stifles worthwhile innovations as a result.[9]

We shall repeatedly compare the equilibrium under some policy with the exchange joint profit maximum in the absence of the policy. The reason for

[9]This criticism of government policy has been raised repeatedly with respect to American futures markets where the Commodity Futures Trading Commission has the legal responsibility of scrutinizing all new contracts or changes in existing contracts. See Anderson (1984).

this is that, when the products of the two exchanges are identical and when demand is the same whether one or two exchanges offer the product, joint exchange profits will be an acceptable proxy for total social surplus. We are principally concerned with cases when the products of competing exchanges are effectively the same. It should be clear that this formulation creates a presumption that the socially best outcome is to have at most one exchange offer the product. For if the second exchange enters it incurs the development cost without yielding any increase in the total market. Formally, in our model the outcome of a single exchange innovating results in joint exchange profits of π_1, a leader/follower outcome yields combined profits of $\pi_3 + \pi_4 = \pi_1 - pe^{-rN}C$, and simultaneous innovation yields $2\pi_2 = \pi_1 - C$. Note that $\pi_1 > \pi_2 - pe^{-rN}C > \pi_1 - C$, so that the three outcomes involving innovation are unambiguously ordered with respect to joint profits. It should be clear also that joint profits may not be an accurate guide to social welfare if the product offered by the second exchange differs significantly from that of the first. This should be borne in mind when considering the relevance of our comments below to any specific application.

The statement that having a second exchange offer a product does not increase benefits for the users of the product has immediate and important consequences for public policy. Specifically, conventional antitrust policies aimed at promoting entry are unlikely to increase welfare and may actually decrease it. To see this consider a policy which would have the effect of increasing a follower's market share above what would otherwise prevail. (We do not address here how such a result could be achieved but will comment on this below.) Thus instead of anticipating a share $S(N)$ if it follows, an exchange has a prospect of some $S^* > S(N)$. If the other parameters of the problem are unchanged, this increases follower's profits to $\pi_3^* > \pi_3$ and decreases leader's profits to $\pi_4^* < \pi_4$.

The consequences of such a policy depend upon the equilibrium that would prevail in its absence. If, in the absence of the policy, only one exchange would innovate, sufficiently great increases in the follower's share could bring about two possible changes. Either the second exchange could be prompted to follow, and the first exchange still innovates ($\pi_3^* > 0$ and $\pi_4^* > 0$); or the first exchange is discouraged from innovating ($\pi_4^* < 0$). In either case exchange joint profits are decreased by the policy. If the before policy equilibrium is of the leader/follower type, the policy would have no effect on joint profits ($\pi_3 + \pi_4 = \pi_3^* + \pi_4^*$) unless it discouraged the leader ($\pi_4^* < 0$) in which case combined profits fall to zero. If the before policy equilibrium involves no innovation the policy has no effect. Finally, if the before policy equilibrium involves simultaneous innovation, increasing the follower's share would either have no effect or would induce one exchange to be a follower. Only in this last case would joint profits be increased by the policy. Even then, the policy would be inadequate to bring about the joint profit maximizing outcome of only a single exchange innovating.

From this discussion we see that policies aimed at increasing the attractiveness of being an imitator can have perverse effects. As has been pointed out above, a follower naturally benefits from an informational externality. Here, if anything, the free market gives too strong an incentive to enter with an imitative product.

Patent protection is the public policy most directly aimed at correcting misallocation due to externalities of this type. It is obvious in the present context that costless, unending patent protection necessarily does bring about the joint profit maximizing outcome. With such a patent if $\pi_1 > 0$, a single exchange innovates, and the total profits are distributed according to the ownership of the patent rights. However, there is good reason to believe that for financial markets real patents would not operate in this manner. The basic problem is that it is often very difficult to distinguish imitative financial products from genuinely new products solely on the basis of their objective description. To see this consider the following hypothetical but quite plausible situation.

Suppose one exchange is offering a futures contract that calls for the delivery of tin to either port A or port B at the option of the seller. Suppose a second exchange wishes to offer a tin futures contract which would differ from the existing one only by allowing delivery in either port A or port C. If sellers find either location B or C preferable to A, the two contracts will be genuinely different. If, however, sellers prefer to deliver to A rather than to either B or C, then the two contracts would be effectively identical.[10]

Ultimately, of course, the market can distinguish genuinely new financial products from imitations. The problem is that it will be unable to do so if ease of entry for imitators discourages the innovator. This apparent impasse can be circumvented if there is some policy which has the effect of discouraging imitators but does not require a public authority to distinguish imitative from original products. In our model public authorities plausibly could affect two additional parameters—the development costs and the development lag. For given actions by the two exchanges increasing either parameter will decrease joint exchange profits. Nevertheless, because of the nature of competition, an increase in either may have the effect of raising equilibrium joint profits.

Von Weizsacker (1980) has already pointed out that cost increases may be welfare improving, and the same is true in our model for much the same reason. An increase in C decreases π_1, π_2, π_3 and π_4. If, in the absence of the cost increase, the equilibrium is either of the matching or the leader/follower type, the increase in cost may lead to only one exchange innovating. It can be confirmed that the net effect may be to increase joint profits. Of course, if prospects for the innovation are not particularly good, the equilibrium even with low development costs may involve only a single exchange. In this case increasing development costs necessarily is harmful.

---

[10] Seemingly slight differences of contract designs may be the difference between acceptance or rejection by the market. See Silber (1981).

It is worth noting that in practice the principal effect of patent laws may be to raise development costs. If an original innovator seeks protection under patent laws it is necessary to incur (possibly considerable) legal expenses to file patents on all relevant aspects of the product.[11] This protection may be imperfect in the sense that, at a cost, an imitator may be able to design the product so as to avoid infringing existing patents. However, if the costs of patenting even a purely imitative product are sufficently great, then imitation may be rendered unprofitable. Overall, patenting laws may have a role to play, albeit only inasmuch as they provide a means of raising costs.

Again, in spite of the superficial presumption to the contrary, increasing the development lag by means of an additional regulatory delay can be desirable. We now examine two examples of this in some detail. Similar examples of the desirable effects of raising costs can be given. We concentrate on regulatory delay because in practice it would seem to be more attractive. For small increases in development time could lead to a substantial fall in the follower's market share, making a regulatory delay a potent tool. Substantial cost increases may be necessary to discourage a follower, however, and these involve a waste of resources.

An increase in N decreases both π_1 and π_2, since all revenues are delayed. Also, π_3 decreases with N so long as $\pi_3 > 0$, and once negative it remains so. For the follower obtains a smaller share of the market at a later date. The effect of an increase in N on a leader's payoff π_4 is ambiguous in general. On the one hand, all revenues are received later, tending to decrease π_4. On the other, the leader monopolises the market for longer and holds a larger share of it once competition begins. If $S'(N)$ is strongly negative the latter effect might be expected to dominate, making π_4 increase with N.

The effect of changes in N on the relative magnitudes of the π_i is more complicated, allowing a variety of changes in the form of equilibrium. Much of this richness of response remains even when S cannot be varied freely. Indeed, we shall take S to be identically 0.5 in both our illustrations. Thus all effects will be due entirely to the relative magnitudes of revenues and costs, and to their timing. The parameters of the illustrations are given in Table 2.

In the first case, it turns out that equilibrium is of type (v) for $0 < N < 1.82$. That is, innovation does not take place because of the fear of imitation. For $1.82 < N < 4.70$, however, equilibrium is of type (ii). Thus, by introducing a regulatory delay, it is possible to allow an innovation that would, for strategic reasons, never have taken place otherwise.[12]

---

[11] See Temin (1979) for a discussion of how costly and imperfect patenting has been in the pharmaceutical industry.

[12] With $S \equiv 0.5$, π_4 becomes a quadratic in e^{-rN}. This quadratic is strictly negative for all N if its discriminant, $(\bar{R}/pR^H)^2 - 2rC/pR^H$, is negative. This is the case for the parameter choices shown. An immediate corollary of $\pi_4 < 0$ everywhere is that $\pi_2 < 0$ everywhere too. Next, $\pi_3 > 0$ so long as $e^{-rN} > 2rC/R^H$ (and $\pi_3 \leqslant 0$ thereafter). Finally, $\pi_1 > 0$ so long as $e^{-rN} > rC/\bar{R}$. Thus we have that equilibrium is of type (v) for $N < 10 \log 6/5$ (≈ 1.82), of type (ii) for $10 \log 6/5 < N < 10 \log 8/5$ (≈ 4.70), and of type (i) if $N > 10 \log 8/5$.

TABLE 2
Parameter values for the illustrations

Illustration	R^H	R^L	p	C
1	6	1	0.6	25
2	6	5	0.8	23

(i) We take $r = 0.1$ and $S \equiv 0.5$; (ii) N is not given explicitly since the purpose of the illustrations is to consider variations in N.

Our second illustration is a little more involved. In this case there exist $N_3 > N_2 > N_1 > 0$ such that equilibrium is of type (iii) on $[0, N_1)$, of type (iv) on (N_1, N_2), of type (ii) on (N_2, N_3), and of type (i) on (N_3, ∞). Since π_2 decreases with N, the welfare attainable from equilibria on $[0, N_1)$, namely $2\pi_2$, is bounded by $2\pi_2(0) = 12$. Similarly, π_3 and π_4 decrease with N, so the welfare $\pi_3 + \pi_4$ attainable on (N_1, N_2) is bounded by $\pi_3(N_1) + \pi_4(N_1) = 10.97$. Finally, $\pi_1(N_2) = 21.47$, so that a substantial welfare gain is obtained if the regulatory lag is chosen so that N is larger than, but close to, N_2.[13]

The two illustrations demonstrate how a policy of increasing the development lag can serve to discourage imitative innovations and bring about an increase in equilibrium joint profits. In the illustrations the follower's share was not affected by change in N. As was emphasized above, liquidity effects are likely to mean that in many financial markets, $S' < 0$. As a result, increases in N will be even more potent in discouraging imitative products. Consequently, a small increase in N may suffice, and the departure from the (infeasible) joint profit maximizing outcome of one exchange innovating with a minimal development lag may be slight.

4. Extensions and relation to other work

The model can easily be extended to take account of asymmetries between the exchanges in respect of development costs and development

---

[13] Note first that $\pi_2 - \pi_3$ is a negative quadratic in e^{-rN}. Hence $\pi_2 > \pi_3$ on a bounded interval (if at all). Also, $\pi_3 > \pi_2$ when $\pi_2 \leqslant 0$. Hence, if $\pi_2(0) > \pi_3(0)$ then there will exist $N_1 > 0$ and $N_2 > N_1$ such that $\pi_2 > \pi_3 > 0$ on $[0, N_1)$, $\pi_3 > \max\{\pi_2, 0\}$ on (N_1, N_2), and $\max\{\pi_2, \pi_3\} < 0$ on (N_2, ∞). But $\pi_2(0) > \pi_3(0)$ if $c < R^L/2r$, which is the case in the present example. Thus we have a type (iii) equilibrium on $[0, N_1)$. It remains to determine the form of equilibrium on (N_1, N_2) and (N_2, ∞). It turns out that equilibrium is of type (iv) on (N_1, N_2) and that there exists $N_3 > N_2$ such that equilibrium is of type (ii) on (N_2, N_3) and of type (i) on (N_3, ∞).

In order to see that equilibrium is of type (iv) on (N_1, N_2), remember that π_4 is a negative quadratic in e^{-rN}. Indeed, the turning point of this quadratic occurs at a point larger than 1. Thus, since $e^{-rN} \leqslant 1$ for all $N \geqslant 1$, π_4 is decreasing in N. Thus equilibrium will be of type (iv) on (N_1, N_2) rather than of type (v), which is the only other possibility here, if $\pi_4(N_2) > 0$. But N_2 is the point at which π_3 vanishes, so $e^{-rN_2} = 2rc/R^H$. Also, $\pi_4(N_2) = \pi_1(N_2) - pe^{-2rN_2}R^H/2r = -c + e^{-rN_2}\bar{R}/r - e^{-2rN_2}pR^H/2r = 7.36 > 0$, as required.

Finally, we already know that equilibrium must be of either type (ii) or type (i) on (N_2, ∞), since $\pi_3 < 0$ there. Also, π_1 is decreasing in N, so that equilibrium is either of type (i) everywhere on (N_2, ∞), or it is of type (ii) on some positive interval (N_2, N_3) and then of type (i). To show that there is such a positive interval we need only show that $\pi_1(N_2) > 0$. But $\pi_1(N_2) > \pi_4(N_2) = 7.36$.

lags, to allow for the possibility that it is cheaper to develop an imitative product, and so on. Doing so raises no new issues of principle, although the finding that equilibrium is essentially unique will no longer hold.

It has already been noted that the assumption that the total net revenue flow is a constant, R, no matter whether one or two exchanges are active might be violated if the exchanges' products were differentiated. It may also be violated with homogeneous quantity setting game played by exchange members. However, by modifying the specification of the market share function the model can be adapted to cover these possibilities. Indeed, the positive analysis above is unchanged.

Suppose that $S(0) = \lambda/2$, for some $\lambda > 0$, and that $S(M) = \lambda - S(-M)$. Previously we had $\lambda = 1$. To the extent that joint duopoly profits fall below monopoly profits, we would expect to find $\lambda < 1$. Any expansion of the market due to the presence of differentiated contracts would tend to increase λ. Overall, at the very most, we would not expect to find λ much greater than 1. However, provided $\lambda < 2$, Proposition 1 holds without alteration. For the classification given there requires only that $\pi_1 > \max\{\pi_2, \pi_4\}$.

The policy analysis, on the other hand, will change if λ exceeds 1 by a large margin. For then there is a social gain from having two exchanges in the market rather than one. This gain might outweigh the social cost arising because of duplication of effort. We explained in Section 2 why we think it is unlikely that this case will arise.

Turning to the related literature, we have already observed that the basic principles which arise in our model are identified by von Weizsacker (1980). He emphasizes that barriers to entry need to be evaluated on a case by case basis. We have simply taken this recommendation to heart and have analyzed the issues as they apply to financial market innovations.

More recently, a model similar to ours has been analyzed by Fudenberg and Tirole (1985). In one respect their model is more general; it allows for the possibility that the cost of innovation may fall with time. On the other hand, players' market shares depend only on the order in which they innovate, and not on the delay between innovations. More importantly, they do not take into account the uncertainty associated with a new product. Consequently, they cannot model the informational externality produced by the leader in the financial innovation.

A second aspect of Fudenberg and Tirole (1985) is worthy of comment. A major preoccupation of their paper is to develop a solution concept for continuous time models that allows representation of the limits of discrete-time mixed-strategy equilibria (Fudenberg and Tirole (1985; Section 4A)). This is undoubtedly a worthwhile undertaking.

However, such a solution concept may not be ideal for the analysis of continuous time models as such. After all, the structure of the integers, used to represent discrete time, is very different from that of the real numbers, used to represent continuous time. And certainly one would not want to make it a *requirement* of a solution concept for continuous time models, that it allow representation of the limits of discrete-time equilibria.

Anyway, having developed such a solution concept, Fudenberg and Tirole (1985; Section 4B) analyse their model in terms of it. It seems fair to say that, compared with the informal analysis of pure strategy equilibrium that they sketch (Fundenberg and Tirole (1985; Section 3)), their formal analysis yields little economic insight. We analyse pure strategy equilibria because they seem to mirror the economics of the problem more closely.

Finally, Benoit (1985) analyses a model that is closely related to ours. Formally, the main difference between the models is that his uses discrete time, which makes the analysis somewhat more cumbersome than in continuous time. More substantively, our focus on financial markets, the consequent concern with liquidity as a determinant of market share, and the analysis of changing development lag are all absent from that paper. Benoit does consider the comparative static analysis of costs (which we have merely touched on) and probability of high demand (which we have omitted entirely) at length, but his main concern is to show that the leader's equilibrium payoff may not be monotonic in these variables.

5. Conclusion

We have analysed a continuous-time model of innovation in an oligopoly. The model was seen to be particularly relevant to competition among exchanges, securities dealers, and other financial institutions which provide the marketplace for secondary trading in financial instruments. Our analysis shows that because leaders in introducing new products generate an informational externality, competition may discourage worthwhile innovations or may result in an excess of imitative products. Conventional patent protection may not solve this problem either, because weak patent protection may arbitrarily inhibit genuinely new products. In contrast, it is argued that a slight regulatory lag applied to all new products has two advantages. First, it may encourage innovation which might otherwise be deterred. Second, it allows the market, and not the regulators, to determine which new products are genuinely new and which are imitative.

C.U.N.Y. Graduate Centre, New York, USA.
Nuffield College, Oxford, UK.

REFERENCES

ANDERSON, R. W. (1984), "The Regulation of Futures Contract Innovations in the United States", *Journal of Futures Markets*, 4, 297–332.

ANDERSON, R. W. (1985), "Competition Among Futures Exchanges in the United States", mimeo.

BENOIT, J.-P. (1985), "Innovation and Imitation in a Duopoly", *Review of Economic Studies*, 52, 99–106.

CARLTON, D. W. (1984), "Futures Markets: Their Purpose, Their History, Their Growth, Their Successes and Failures", *Journal of Futures Markets,* 4, 237–272.

FUDENBERG, D. and TIROLE, J. (1985), "Preemption and Rent Equalisation in the Adoption of New Technology", *Review of Economic Studies,* 52, 383–402.

SALONER, G. (1984), "Self-Regulating Commodity Futures Exchanges" in R. Anderson (ed.), The Industrial Organisation of Futures Markets, Lexington Books.

SHARPE, W. F. (1981), Investments, (2nd. ed.) Prentice-Hall.

SILBER, W. L. (1981), "Innovation, Competition, and New Contract Design in Futures Markets", *Journal of Futures Markets,* 1, 123–155.

TELSER, L. G. (1981), "Why Are There Organized Futures Markets?", *Journal of Law and Economics,* 24, 1–22.

TELSER, L. G., and HIGINBOTHAM, H. N. (1977), "Organized Futures Markets: Costs and Benefits", *Journal of Political Economy,* 85, 969–1000.

TEMIN, P., (1979), "Technology, Regulation, and Market Structure in the Modern Pharmaceutical Industry", *Bell Journal of Economics,* 10, 429–446.

TOWNSEND, R., (1984), "Theories of Contract Design and Market Organization: Conceptual Bases for Understanding Futures Markets", in R. Anderson (ed.) The Industrial Organization of Futures Markets, Lexington Books.

WEIZSACKER, C. C. von (1980), "A Welfare Analysis of Barriers to Entry", *Bell Journal of Economics,* II, 399–420.

SEQUENTIAL RESEARCH AND THE ADOPTION OF INNOVATIONS

By SUDIPTO BHATTACHARYA, KALYAN CHATTERJEE and LARRY SAMUELSON

I. Introduction

IN THE last decade, the literature on equilibrium models of research and development (R & D) has addressed the problem of strategic interactions in the adoption of innovations with known distributions of payoffs. This line of inquiry is exemplified by the work of Fudenberg and Tirole (1985) and Reinganum (1981b, 1981c), which extends work by Jensen (1980); and Reinganum (1982a, 1983), which extends work by Weitzman (1979).

More recently, attention has turned to the problem of learning about innovations with unknown distributions of payoffs. Examples include Bhattacharya (1978), Jensen (1981, 1983), and Roberts and Weitzman (1981) (see also Marschak (1968) and Whittle (1983)). This paper continues this line of research. We examine cases in which the payoff distribution of a potential innovation is unknown. We assume that costly experiments can be conducted by firms, which yield stochastic information regarding the innovation's profitability. The firm's problem is to select an optimal decision rule, specifying for each partition in its information structure whether the firm should adopt the innovation, reject it, or continue to experiment. We consider the normative theory and positive implications of such optimal choices by firms.

Our investigations extend the R & D literature in three directions. The first contribution of our analysis is to the theory of the diffusion of innoivations. Beginning with the work of Griliches (1957) and Mansfield (1968), the empirical regularities of diffusion have been extensively studied. However, theoretical links between a decision-theoretic model of individual firms' behavior and the diffusion of innovation are rare. The primary exceptions are Jensen (1982, 1983), in which firms are assumed to observe the same sample realizations of a random variable which is informative as to the (mean) profitability of an innovation. This leads to a diffusion curve of adoption times across firms which is dependent upon divergences in firms' prior beliefs.

In contrast, we exploit the approach of Bhattacharya (1978) to examine a model in which firms have identical priors but privately observed samples. We find that naturally arising random differences in observed samples are sufficient to yield a diffusion curve matching the commonly observed

The first author would like to thank Professor Herman Chernoff for discussions some years back, and the Berkeley Program in Finance for research support. Chatterjee and Samuelson thank the National Science Foundation (SES-8419931) for financial support. The authors are grateful to Belgacem Raggad for computational assistance. The authors retain responsibility for errors or ambiguities.

empirical regularities in diffusion. Our methodology also yields comparative statics for these diffusion curves with respect to important parameters such as the true mean profitability and sampling variance.

Our next contribution concerns strategic interaction across firms. Strategic interdependencies among firms may arise for two reasons. First, the profitability of the innovation for a particular firm may depend upon how many other firms adopt the innovation, and when they adopt it. The most obvious example is the case in which the first adopter secures exclusive patent protection without possibility of imitation, relegating others' profits to zero. Reinganum (1981–1983) examines these types of strategic relationships under the assumption that firms know the distribution of payoffs.

In our framework involving an unknown payoff distribution, there is an additional dimension to inter-firm interaction. The R & D decisions of other firms may reveal information to an expeimenting firm. This information will be pooled with the experimenter's own observations in forming posterior beliefs, and is then relevant to the optimal accept/reject decision. We construct a model in which the effects of these two types of strategic interaction on firms' optimal research strategies can be examined. The complexity of the problem prohibits an explicit solution at the level of specificity of the independent sampling case. However, the qualitative implications of the basic forces in the problem are revealed.

Our third contribution is a methodological one. We first observe that an optimal research strategy should be modeled as the solution to a well-specified sequential decision problem. The established literature on sequential sampling, pioneered by Wald (1947) and Chernoff (1972), provides techniques to address the realistic complexity implicit in sequential R & D decisions. We apply these techniques to construct a model of optimal R & D that is grounded in an explicit process of information revelation via sampling. This model constitutes the paper's third contribution.

An alternative analysis is provided by Roberts and Weitzman (1982). Two potential difficulties arise with adopting the Roberts and Weitzman model of experimentation for our purposes. Their model exogenously specifies the evolution over time of the standard deviation of the Normal posterior distribution describing the innovation's profitability, while we derive it from a repeated sampling process.[1] Secondly, their results do not extend in a straightforward way to the interactive learning models which we introduce in this paper.

Jensen (1982) considers a model of R & D which is based on a well-specified sequential decision problem. The uncertainty in Jensen's model concerns a state variable which can take one of two values. The analysis thus fits into the framework of Wald (1947). Again, however, the

---

[1] Various forms for the standard deviation of the posterior distribution appear in Roberts and Weitzman, but all retain the characteristic of banishing uncertainty at some finite, known time, unlike in our model. They do suggest that residual uncertainty could be accommodated if it is uncorrelated with the random variable being estimated.

approach appears to encounter difficulties when examining interactive learning.

In Section II, we develop the theory of optimal research and development on the part of a single firm. Section III demonstrates how this naturally leads to a diffusion of innovation curve based on common prior information but different (statistically independent) sample realizations. These diffusion curves are shown to have properties consistent with empirical findings in this area. Section IV develops the analysis of strategic interactions between firms. Section V offers concluding remarks.

II. Noninteractive research

In this section, we develop a model of a single firm's decision to adopt an innovation. The profitability of the innovation is subject to some uncertainty. The firm has the option at each date of making an irreversible decision to either adopt or reject the innovation, or to delay that decision to conduct research on its profitability. The benefit of research is that information regarding the innovation is revealed, reducing the risk that the firm adopts an unprofitable innovation or fails to adopt a profitable one. The costs of research include the direct cost of both conducting the research and of delaying the decision (e.g., maintaining research capabilities). The problem is to select a decision rule which optimally balances these two forces.

(II.1) *The model*

The performance of an innovation to be considered for adoption is described by a normally distributed random variable, X, with mean μ and variance σ^2. For example, X may be a (dollar) value of prototype output minus costs of input requirements. The profits of the firm from adoption are given by kX, where k represents a scale variable as well as a multiplier capturing the fact htat the performance of the innovation may be realized for many periods. Since X is subject to some uncertainty, the firm is concerned with expected profits, or $k\mu$.

The mean profit parameter of the innovation, μ, is not known with certainty, though we assume that the variance σ^2 is known. In time period t ($t = 1, 2, \ldots$), the firm has the option of making a decision to adopt or reject the innovation, or of postponing the decision by conducting an additional experiment. An experiment provides a realization of the random variable X, allocating an inference to be drawn concerning μ. Experimentation costs c (dollars) per experiment. The firm chooses an experimentation strategy which maximizes expected profits minus experimentation costs.

The experimenter has prior beliefs about the distribution of μ, expressed by a normal distribution with mean μ_0 and variance σ_0^2.[2] Suppose that t experiments have been conducted, yielding independent realizations of the variable X of $X_1,\ldots, X_t$. For convenience, let $\sum_{i=1}^{t} X_i \equiv X(t)$. Then the firm's prior beliefs are updated via Bayes' rule to yield a Normal posterior distribution with mean μ_t and variance σ_t^2 given by

$$\mu_t = \frac{\mu_0 \sigma_0^{-2} + \sigma^{-2} \sum_{i=1}^{t} X_i}{\sigma_0^{-2} + t\sigma^{-2}} = \frac{\mu_0 \sigma_0^{-2} + \sigma^{-2} X(t)}{\sigma_0^{-2} + t\sigma^{-2}} \tag{1}$$

$$\sigma_t^2 = \frac{1}{\sigma_0^{-2} + t\sigma^{-2}}. \tag{2}$$

As is customary, we refer to σ_0^{-2} and σ_t^{-2} as the prior and posterior precisions.

(II.2) *The optimal strategy*

To solve this problem, we borrow techniques from the sequential sampling literature. Chernoff (1972) has observed that as the length of the time periods between experiments approaches zero, we can approximate μ_t by a Gaussian diffusion process. The optimal stopping sets for this problem, and hence the optimal experimentation strategy for the firm, can be determined by solving a free-boundary problem involving the heat equation that emerges from the Gaussian diffusion process. The resulting solution is quite complex. However, if c is small relative to k, so that a large number of experiments will be conducted, a convenient and asymptotically accurate approximation is available (Chernoff (1972, 17.6.7); Whittle (1983, section 41.9)).[3] As t gets large (and hence σ_t^2 becomes small), the optimal stopping rule becomes:

Accept if $\quad \mu_0 \dfrac{\sigma^2}{\sigma_0^2} + X(t) \geq \dfrac{k}{4c(\sigma_0^{-2} + t\sigma^{-2})}$ $\qquad$ (3)

Reject if $\quad \mu_0 \dfrac{\sigma^2}{\sigma_0^2} + X(t) \leq \dfrac{-k}{4c(\sigma_0^{-2} + t\sigma^{-2})}$ $\qquad$ (4)

Continue to
Experiment $\qquad$ otherwise.

[2] Perhaps the most natural way to think of this process is that nature first draws a "true" value of μ from the distribution $N(\mu_0, \sigma_0^2)$.

[3] An approximation is required because an explicit solution to the free-boundary problem has not appeared in the sequential sampling literature. Chernoff (1972) has shown that the solution can be approximated arbitrarily closely by an algebraic function in t of sufficiently high degree. For sufficiently large t, all but one of the terms in the algebraic function become arbitrarily close to zero, yielding the stopping sets given in (3)–(4).

The economic intuition underlying (3)–(4) is easily revealed. At any time t, the innovation should be adopted if the accumulated experimental results have increased the (prior) estimate of mean profitability above a cutoff level, and should be rejected if the accumulated experimental results have decreased the estimate of profitability below a cutoff level. The cutoff levels are chosen so as to achieve an optimal balance between the risk of an incorrect decision and the cost of continued experimentation.

We can offer four observations to attest to the plausability of the cutoff levels involved in this stopping rule. First, the absolute value of each cutoff level decreases over time. This reflects the fact that the precision of the firm's information increases over time, reducing the risk of an incorrect adoption or rejection and prompting the firm to adopt or reject on the basis of a smaller absolute value of experimental performance. Second, the cutoff levels for adopting or rejecting the innovation are mirror images of one another. This follows from the symmetry of the problem, since the opportunity loss or penalty in terms of forgone profits is the same whether an unprofitable innovation is incorrectly adopted or a profitable one incorrectly rejected. Third, an increase in k/c, ceteris paribus, has the effect of increasing the experimental performance required before a decision will be made. This is expected, since increasing k/c increases the penalty attached to an incorrect decision relative to the costs of experimentation. Finally, suppose that either the precision of the prior (σ_0^{-2}) goes to zero or the prior mean is zero, so that all information is derived from sample observations. The level of performance required before a decision will be made is then increasing in σ^2, the uncertainty connected with the innovation. Hence, as the information conveyed by experimentation gets less precise, the firm requires greater experimental performance before making a decision.

This provides us with a convenient model of a firm's research and development activities. The model addresses the process of learning about an innovation which is available at any time, but whose profitability is unknown. This contrasts with the complementary approach taken in R & D models with known payoff distributions (e.g., Reinganum (1981a, 1982b)). In these models, the profitability of an innovation is known but the innovation is not available immediately, with research and development (stochastically) advancing the date at which the innovation is available.

III. *The diffusion of innovations*

We would now like to examine the diffusion rate for an innovation subject to the experimentation process described in the previous section. As noted by Jensen, studies of innovation diffusion have generally been confined to the documentation of empirical regularities in industry-wide adoption behavior, and are generally not based upon a decision-theoretic model of individual firms' optimization. Our goal is to construct an empirically plausible theory of aggregate diffusion behavior from our model of the firm.

(III.1) *Interpretations of diffusion rates*

The diffusion rate can be given two interpretations, based on the following two questions. Given a single firm, how long is the firm likely to experiment before it reaches a decision? Alternatively, given a large number of identical firms conducting independent experiments, how does the proportion of firms that has ceased experimenting and reached a decision change over time? When discussing the case of a large number of firms, we must assume that the profitability to a single firm of adopting the innovation does not depend upon the number or proportion of other firms who have adopted the innovation. This will be true of "process" innovations, such as numerically-controlled machine tools, which affect the costs of production in a wide variety of industries. We must further assume that the innovation under consideration is a "landmark" one, for which the true (mean) profitability drawn by nature, μ, is likely to be approximately the same across all firms. However, firms do not know μ ex ante. Hence, they experiment independently, and ignore the adoption behavior of other firms' when making their decisions because of observability difficulties. We shall relax this independence assumption in Section IV.

(III.2) *Stylized facts of diffusion*

We would like our model to accommodate the generally recognized stylized facts of diffusion. These include the observation that the cumulative proportion of firms adopting an innovation (1) is an increasing function of time; (2) follows a curve which is initially convex and subsequently concave; and (3) is such that the inflection point of thius curve occurs at a value of time for which the proportion of firms who have adopted the innovation is less than 1/2 (cf. Jensen (1982) and Nabseth and Ray (1974)). In addition, the speed of diffusion depends upon the characteristics of the innovation. For example, diffusion proceeds more quickly for an innovation with a higher mean profitability (higher realized μ). We shall examine the diffusion curve predicted by our analysis to see if it exhibits these characteristics, and examine its sensitivity to the model's parameters.

(III.3) *Shape of predicted diffusion curve*

We shall restrict attention to cases in which firms have unbiased prior expectations, or $\mu_0 = 0$. We shall also restrict attention to innovations which happen to be profitable, so that $\mu > 0$, and will accordingly be interested in the decision to adopt the innovation. The natural symmetry of the problem ensures that analogous results could be obtained for cases of $\mu < 0$ and decisions to reject the innovation.

Let $G(t)$ be a function identifying the cumulative proportion of firms who will have adopted the innovation by time t given that the firms started at time zero with prior mean $\mu_0 = 0$, and given that our model of sequential research is applicable, so that firms follow the behavior specified in (3)–(4). The function $G(t)$ can be described technically as a first passage "distribution" identifying for any t the probability that the (Wiener) process $X(t)$ will hit the upper boundary given in (3) before time t (without having first hit the lower boundary).[4] Standard statistical techniques can be invoked to derive a differential equation which this first passage time distribution must satisfy (cf. Cox and Miller (1965, chapter 5)). Because this derivation is conceptually straightforward but tedious, it is relegated to the Appendix. This differential equation can then in principle be solved to obtain the distribution $G(t)$. Unfortunately, the equation in question is a second order partial differential equation with time-dependent coefficients, and an analytical solution to the problem is not known. We accordingly solve the differential equation numerically. This is accomplished by choosing various representative values for the model's parameters, and for each set of values calculating the value of $G(t)$ for a large number of values of t.[5] The Appendix again contains details.

The question now arises of how to present the calculated values of $G(t)$ in a form which is both readily interpreted and will allow us to test whether the diffusion behavior exhibits the characteristics identified in the empirical diffusion literature. We begin by plotting the calculated values of $G(t)$ for selected values of the model's parameters. The results are shown in Fig. 1 (with $\sigma^2 = 1$ and $\sigma_0^2 = 0.01$ (cf. note 5)).

To examine these issues further, we fit a curve to the calculated values of $G(t)$. Since $G(t)$ is a cumulative distribution, an appropriate and suitably flexible choice concerning the functional form of $G(t)$ is that it is a

---

[4] Some firms will reject the innovation, so that the cumulative proportion of adopting firms will not approach unity $(\lim_{t \to \infty} G(t) < 1)$. The characterization of $G(t)$ as a distribution is accordingly not quite accurate, though it is standard terminology (e.g., Cox and Miller (1965)). Our calculations (reported in Table 1) reveal that the proportion of firms adopting always passes 0.95 as t gets large (given our choices of parameter values). This occurs because our choice of an unbiased prior expectation of $\mu_0 = 0$ causes the process to start at the midpoint of the adoption and rejection boundaries, and our choices of μ and σ^2 yield processes with very strong positive drifts relative to their variances, so that the probability of absorption at the lower barrier is virtually zero.

[5] To obtain the numerical results, we will have to fix the values of the system's parameters, or μ, k, c, σ_0^2, and σ^2. We will investigate the implications of various values of μ, k, c, and σ^2, but will be less concerned with σ_0^2, and will assume $\sigma_0^2 = 0.01$ throughout. The motivation behind choosing this value is that we would like to examine a process for which a relatively large number of experiments will be conducted. Hence, we have in mind a case in which individual experiments are relatively inexpensive (compared to payoffs), but in which a large number of experiments are required to reveal substantial information. This equivalent to assuming that the prior precision $(1/\sigma_0^2)$ is large relative to the precision of any individual experiment $(1/\sigma^2)$. We initially take the latter to be unity $(\sigma^2 = 1)$, and hence our choice of σ_0^2. This is consistent with the assumption of relatively short time periods under which our diffusion process approach is applicable.

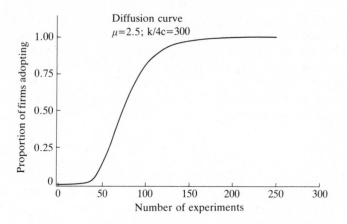

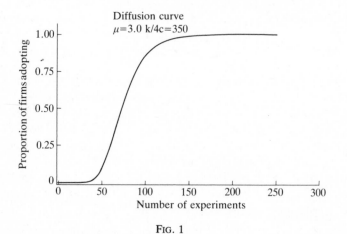

Fig. 1

generalized logit function, or (if $f(t)$ is linear in t, this is a simple logistic model):

$$G(t) = \frac{e^{f(t)}}{e^{f(t)} + 1}.$$ (5)

We can rearrange (5), take logs, and then expand $f(t)$ in a Taylor series to yield

$$\ln\left[\frac{G(t)}{1 - G(t)}\right] = f(t) = \beta_0 + \beta_1 t + \beta_2 t^2 + \varepsilon_t,$$ (6)

where ε_t is a remainder.

For various values of μ, k, c, and σ^2 (cf. note 5), we can use our calculated values of $G(t)$ to estimate the parameters β_0, β_1, and β_2 in (6). Since it is somewhat inconvenient to keep track off our exogenous parameters, we temporarily set $\sigma^2 = 1$. We also notice that only the ratio $k/4c$ and not the absolute magnitudes of k and c enters into the firm's decision problem (cf. (3)–(4)). Hence, we can estimate (6) for various values of μ and $k/4c$. The Appendix contains more details concerning this estimation.

The estimates are shown in Table 1. Each cell, corresponding to a value of $k/4c$ and μ, contains information in the following format:[6]

$$
\begin{array}{|c|}
\hline
b_0 \\
b_1 \\
b_3 \\
\underline{t}/\bar{t} \\
\hline
\end{array}
$$

where

b_i—estimate of β_0; for $i = 0, 1, 2$.

$\underline{t}$—initial passage time (min $\{t : G(t) \geqslant 0.05\}$)

$\bar{t}$—last passage time (max $\{t : G(t) \leqslant 0.95\}$).

The initial and last passage times identity points at which 5 and 95 percent

TABLE 1

μ	200	250	$k/4c$ 300	350	400
1.5	-4.73 7.01×10^{-2} -1.64×10^{-4} $34/225$	-5.38 7.03×10^{-2} -1.51×10^{-4} $44/238$	-6.01 7.11×10^{-2} -1.44×10^{-4} $53/250$	-6.54 7.15×10^{-2} -1.37×10^{-4} $62/261$	-7.08 7.25×10^{-2} -1.33×10^{-4} $70/271$
2.0	-5.46 10.43×10^{-2} -3.27×10^{-4} $31/146$	-6.27 10.36×10^{-2} -2.92×10^{-4} $39/159$	-6.97 10.30×10^{-2} -2.67×10^{-4} $47/170$	-7.58 10.22×10^{-2} -2.46×10^{-4} $55/180$	-8.21 10.28×10^{-2} -2.34×10^{-4} $62/189$
2.5		-6.88 13.54×10^{-2} -4.59×10^{-4} $35/122$	-7.63 13.25×10^{-2} -4.05×10^{-4} $42/133$	-8.30 13.06×10^{-2} -3.67×10^{-4} $49/142$	-8.90 12.87×10^{-2} -3.36×10^{-4} $56/150$
3.0		-7.33 16.56×10^{-2} -6.43×10^{-4} $32/100$	-8.15 16.19×10^{-2} -5.63×10^{-4} $38/110$	-8.76 15.61×10^{-2} -4.90×10^{-4} $45/118$	-9.41 15.32×10^{-2} -4.43×10^{-4} $51/126$
3.5			-8.54 19.00×10^{-2} -7.32×10^{-4} $35/194$	-9.26 18.45×10^{-2} -6.45×10^{-4} $41/101$	-9.79 17.64×10^{-2} -5.53×10^{-4} $47/109$

[6] The somewhat triangular shape of Table 1 arises from a reluctance to examine cases in which relatively few experiments are conducted prior to adoption, since the approximation underlying (3)–(4) might then be suspect.

of the firms have adopted. This provides an indication of the number of periods or experiments which pass before the first few firms adopt, and before virtually all firms have adopted (cf. note 4).

We find that $G(t)$ very nearly matches our generalized logistic behavior. The R^2 values for the regressions reported in Table 1 fall between 0.98 and 1.00. More importantly, the estimates all have such small standard errors that each of the confidence level (probability of a type one error) when concluding that $\beta_0 < 0$, $\beta_1 > 0$, or $\beta_2 < 0$ is 0.0001.

We can now test whether our model yields diffusion behavior which matches the stylized facts. From (6), we have

$$\frac{\partial G}{\partial t} = (\beta_1 + 2\beta_2 t)(G(1 - G)) \tag{7}$$

$$\frac{\partial^2 G}{\partial t^2} = 2\beta_2 G(1 - G) + (\beta_1 + 2\beta_2 t)(1 - 2G)\frac{\partial G}{\partial t}$$

$$= G(1 - G)[2\beta_2 + (\beta_1 + 2\beta_2 t)^2(1 - 2G)]. \tag{8}$$

From (7), the hypothesis that the proportion of firms who have adopted the innovation is an increasing function of time is equivalent to $\beta_1 + 2\beta_2 t \geqslant 0$.[7] It is clear that the diffusion curve must be initially convex and subsequently concave, since (7)–(8) ensure $\partial^2 G/\partial t^2 < 0$ for sufficiently large t (and hence G) as well as $\partial^2 G/\partial t^2 > 0$ for sufficiently small t. Finally, the stipulation that the diffusion curve encounter its inflection point before half of the firms have adapted is equivalent to $\beta_2 < 0$. The hypotheses that correspond to the stylized facts are then $\beta_1 + 2\beta_2 t \geqslant 0$ and $\beta_2 < 0$.

As we have mentioned, the estimations in each cell of Table 1 allow us to accept $\beta_2 < 0$ at a confidence level of 0.0001. Examination of the appropriate test statistic also yields strong support for $\beta_1 + 2\beta_2 t \geqslant 0$ (cf. note 7), so that our hypotheses are verified. We have thus established that the diffusion process matches the stylized facts (increasing, S-shaped cumulative distribution with right-skewed density) cited in section III-2.

(III.4) Comparative statics

We now examine the relationship of the model's parameters (μ, k, c, and σ^2 (cf. note 5)) to the speed of diffusion. Notice that two notions of the

---

[7] The appropriate test for the slope requires some care. We cannot take $\beta_1 + 2\beta_2 t > 0$ for all t as an alternative hypotheses (with $\beta_1 + 2\beta_2 t = 0$ or $\leqslant 0$ as the null), since the slope of a distribution function is expected to approach zero as t gets large, so that failing to reject the null in this case would be uninformative. Letting $\beta_1 + 2\beta_2 t \geqslant 0$ be the alternative and $\beta_1 + 2\beta_t < 0$ the null is inappropriate, since the null is here not sufficiently well specified to construct the necessary sampling distribution when the null holds. Letting $\beta_1 + 2\beta_2 t \geqslant 0$ be the null and $\beta_1 + 2\beta_2 t < 0$ the alternative leads to an acceptable test in which the null is invariably accepted, supporting our hypothesis. The test of alternative $\beta_1 + 2\beta_2 t > 0$ rejects the null for almost all values of t, as expected.

speed of diffusion arise. One is the length of time before the first few (or some fractile of) adoptions take place, and is represented in the initial passage times in Table 1. The second is the speed at which subsequent adoptions take place after firms have begun to adopt, and is represented by the slope of the diffusion curve. Empirical examinations of innovation diffusion inevitably confine attention to the latter. This may be misleading, since there is no guarantee that the two notions of the speed of diffusion move in the same direction in response to parameter variations. A parameter variation may increase the slope, causing an empirical examination to pronounce that innovation adoption has been accelerated, while postponing the initial or median passage time, casting doubt upon this assessment.

Consider first μ and k/c. (We recall that only the ratio of k/c and not the individual values enter the problem). An increase in mean profitability (μ) can be expected to reduce the initial passage time, since an innovation with a higher mean profitability will more quickly yield a level of experimental performance sufficiently favorable to surpass the adoption boundary. An increase in k/c increases the cost of a mistake relative to the cost of an experiment, and hence can be expected to induce the firm to conduct more experiments. This will delay initial passage. The initial passage times reported in Table 1 confirm these expectations.

Assessing the impact of variations in μ or k/c on the slope of the diffusion curve after a given initial passage time has been reached is more difficult. The expectation is that an increase in mean profitability will increase teh slope (so that increasing μ unambiguously accelerates innovation), while the effect of an increase in k/c is not immediately obvious. To address these issues, we reformulate (6) as (letting $k/c \equiv K$, for notational convenience):

$$\ln\left[\frac{G(t, \mu, K)}{1 - G(t, \mu, K)}\right] = f(t, \mu, K). \tag{9}$$

We would like to accumulate enough information about the roles of μ and k/c in (9) to reveal whether increases in μ or k/c increase or decrease the slope of the diffusion curve. We begin by expanding the right side of this equation in a Taylor series. It is evident from Table 1 that if the effects of μ and k/c are to be adequately represented, then a third order approximation is required. This follows from the observation that μ and (to a lesser extent) k/c affect the coefficients on t^2 in Table 1. Such a variation is not captured by a second order expression. We accordingly have

$$\Gamma \equiv \ln\left|\frac{G(t, \mu, K)}{1 - G(t, \mu, K)}\right| = \gamma + \gamma_\mu u + \gamma_K K + \gamma_t t$$
$$+ \gamma_{\mu\mu}\mu^2 + \gamma_{KK}K^2 + \gamma_{tt}t^2 + \gamma_{\mu K}\mu K + \gamma_{\mu t}\mu t + \gamma_{Kt}Kt$$
$$+ \gamma_{\mu\mu\mu}\mu^3 + \gamma_{KKK}K^3 + \gamma_{ttt}t^3 + \gamma_{\mu\mu K}\mu^2 K + \gamma_{\mu\mu t}\mu^2 t$$
$$+ \gamma_{KK\mu}K^2\mu + \gamma_{KKt}K^2 t + \gamma_{tt\mu}t^2\mu + \gamma_{ttK}t^2 K + \gamma_{\mu Kt}\mu Kt. \tag{10}$$

Notice that the possibility that the coefficients on t^2 vary in μ and k/c does not arise until third-order terms appear on the right hand side of (10).

We use the data underlying Table 1 to estimate this equation. Results are reported in Table 2. It is clear that the third order terms in the approximation are necessary (e.g., see $\gamma_{\mu\mu K}$). The results reported in Table 2 allow us to test for the effects of variations in μ and k/c on the slope of the diffusion curve. We find that an increase in either μ or k/c will increase the slope of the diffusion curve in the range of values considered in Table 2.[8]

We can conclude that an increase in mean profitability unambiguously hastens innovation, advancing initial passage time and increasing the slope of the first passage distribution given an initial passage time. An increase in k/c, however, has ambiguous effects. It delays initial passage, but increases the slope of the distribution given initial passage. This suggests that care must be taken in examining the effect on the speed of diffusion of variations in parameters which affect the cutoff performance required for adoption.

Equation (10) does not allow us to directly ascertain the effects of variations in σ^{-2} (the sampling precision) on the rate of diffusion. The potential ambiguity can be revealed by noting two basic relationships. First, from (3)–(4), an increase in the sampling precision reduces the performance required for adoption (given by $k/4c(\sigma_0^{-2} + t\sigma^{-2})$), much like a decrease in k/c. The initial reaction is then that an increase in sampling precision should mimic the effect of a decreasing k/c by hastening initial passage but reducing the slope of the distribution and hence slowing diffusion once first passage occurs. However, a second effect appears. An increase in σ^{-2} reduces the variance of $X(t)$, and hence reduces the probability that the experimental performance strays very far from its expected value. This should delay initial passage, as fewer exceptionally high values of experimental performance will appear which would exceed the adoption boundary. Its effect on the slope of diffusion once first passage occurs is unclear. The Appendix exploits a transformation of the problem's variables to resolve these conflicting effects. It shows that an increase in σ^{-2} accelerates initial passage and increases the slope of the diffusion curve. We can therefore conclude

---

[8] To examine the effects of μ and k/c on the slope of the diffusion curve (given an initial passage time), we test the hypotheses $\partial^2\Gamma/\partial t\partial\mu = 0$ and $\partial^2\Gamma/\partial t\partial k = 0$. We reject both hypotheses, with test statistics of 33.25 and 521.75 (see below). We then calculate $\partial^2\Gamma/\partial t\partial\mu$ and $\partial^2\Gamma/\partial t\partial K$ for representative values of μ, K, and t. This reveals that $\partial^2\Gamma/\partial t\partial\mu > 0$ and $\partial^2\Gamma/\partial t\partial K > 0$ for values within the relevant range. To construct the test statistics, we reestimate the model with the restriction $\partial^2\Gamma/\partial t\partial\mu = 0$ ($\gamma_{\mu t} = \gamma_{\mu\mu t} = \gamma_{t t\mu} = \gamma_{\mu Dt} = 0$) imposed and then with the restriction $\partial^2\Gamma/\partial t\partial D = 0$ ($\gamma_{Dt} = \gamma_{DDt} = \gamma_{t t D} = \gamma_{\mu Dt} = 0$). We compare the resulting sum-of-squares-errors with the test statistic given by

$$\frac{(\text{Restricted SSE} - \text{Unrestricted SSE})/q}{(\text{Unrestricted SSE})/n - k} \sim F_{q, n-k}$$

where q is the number of restrictions (four in each case), n is the number of observations (2446), and k is the number of variables including intercept (twenty).

TABLE 2

Coefficient	Estimate		Standard Error		Probability of Type I Error When Rejecting H_0: Coefficient = 0
Intercept	−3.74		1.13		0.0009
γ_μ	4.40		0.74		0.0001
γ_K	−1.74	$\times 10^{-2}$	0.20	$\times 10^{-2}$	0.0002
γ_t	3.75	$\times 10^{-2}$	0.71	$\times 10^{-2}$	0.0001
$\gamma_{\mu\mu}$	−1.07		0.27		0.0001
γ_{KK}	0.063	$\times 10^{-4}$	0.016	$\times 10^{-4}$	0.0001
γ_{tt}	−1.25	$\times 10^{-4}$	0.27	$\times 10^{-4}$	0.0001
γ_μ	−0.36	$\times 10^{-2}$	0.061	$\times 10^{-2}$	0.0001
$\gamma_{\mu t}$	3.64	$\times 10^{-2}$	0.44	$\times 10^{-2}$	0.0001
γ_{Kt}	−0.11	$\times 10^{-4}$	0.051	$\times 10^{-4}$	0.0338
$\gamma_{\mu\mu\mu}$	0.12		0.031		0.0001
γ_{KKK}	−0.0016	$\times 10^{-6}$	0.00048	$\times 10^{-6}$	0.0011
γ_{ttt}	0.66	$\times 10^{-6}$	0.047	$\times 10^{-6}$	0.0001
$\gamma_{\mu\mu K}$	0.055	$\times 10^{-2}$	0.010	$\times 10^{-2}$	0.0001
$\gamma_{\mu\mu t}$	−0.79	$\times 10^{-2}$	0.069	$\times 10^{-2}$	0.0001
$\gamma_{KK\mu}$	−0.0030	$\times 10^{-4}$	0.0030	$\times 10^{-4}$	0.3201
γ_{KKt}	−0.00064	$\times 10^{-6}$	0.0020	$\times 10^{-6}$	0.7491
$\gamma_{tt\mu}$	−1.67	$\times 10^{-4}$	0.091	$\times 10^{-4}$	0.0001
γ_{ttK}	−0.047	$\times 10^{-6}$	0.011	$\times 10^{-6}$	0.0001
$\gamma_{\mu Kt}$	0.26	$\times 10^{-4}$	0.018	$\times 10^{-4}$	0.0001

Notes: *Number of Observations* = 2446. $R^2 = 0.98$. *F-value* = 5523.

that an increase in the precision of the sampling distribution unambiguously hastens diffusion.

Our general conclusion is that our model of research and development yields innovation diffusion patterns which match the commonly cited stylized facts of such models. We can contrast our approach with that of Jensen (1981, 1982; see also Nabseth and Ray (1974, especially Chapter 6)). In our model, firms have common prior information, and the diffusion pattern is generated by naturally occurring differences in sample realizations. Jensen assumes that firms have identical sample realizations, but different priors. The common sample realizations then cause the posterior probability distribution to mirror the pattern of prior differences. The entire distribution drifts upward toward the acceptance barrier, and the differences in prior expectations cause firms to adopt at different times.

IV. Interactive experimentation

Models of research and development which emphasize learning, such as Jensen (1981, 1982), Roberts and Weitzman (1979), and our previous analysis, have generally assumed that firms make their decisions in isolation.[9] In contrast, a growing literature examines the impact of the firm's realization that the profitability of adoption depends upon whether and when other firms adopt the innovation (e.g., Reinganum (1981b, 1981c), Jensen (1980)), because of competition from other adoptees, patent protection or similar factors. However, this analysis has been conducted in the context of an innovation of known profitability. In this section, we examine these issues in the context of learning about an innovation of unknown profitability. For convenience, we restrict our analysis to the case in which payoffs are potentially linked because of the availability of perfect patent protection fro the first firm to adopt the innovation.

Examining these issues in a model of learning introduces a second form of interaction between firms which we also examine in this section. We now assume that the true (mean) profitability μ is inherently common (modulo first adopter advantage) to firms, and that the experimental realizations $\{X_t\}$ are conditionally independent samples across firms. Firm i cannot observe firm j's experiments. However, firm i can observe whether or not j has adopted the innovation, and (we assume) whether j has rejected. The former ability is obviously present in the case of potential patent protection. The latter ability will arise if rejecting and innovation requires a conspicuous adjustment in a firm's research activities, facilities, and personnel. Firm i can accordingly infer information from the observation that j is still experimenting, and will incorporate this information in optimal experimentation decisions.

(IV.1) *Extensive form*

Our analysis must begin with a specification of the game played by the potentially interdependent firms. We will consider cases with and without patent protection. The firms in the model are as in Section II, but there are now potentially n firms, ordered from 1 to n. In each period t, the first firm makes a decision to adopt, reject, or continue. The last choice commits the firm to an experimentation cost of c. If the first firm adopts, and perfect patent protection is available, the game ends. If the firm decides to reject or continue, or if patent protection is not available, the the decision passes to the second firm, which faces similar alternatives. This sequence proceeds until each firm has made a decision (in the specified order). If the game has not been ended by either an adoption protected by a patent or by all firms having either adopted or rejected, the sequence is repeated in period $t + 1$.

The alternating-decisions formulation of this game is adopted to preserve comparison between the discrete formulation and a corresponding continuous-time formulation. If we formulate the discrete version as a simultaneous move game, as initially appears most natural, there is a

---

[9] The nearest exception to this is the search models of Reinganum (1982a, 1983; see also Weitzman (1979)).

probability that two or more firms will adopt the innovation simultaneously. The resulting profits are presumably lower than those accruing from sole adoption; perhaps because the patent must either be shared or is randomly allocated to one firm. The probability of joint adoption thus enters the firm's optimality calculation. In the continuous time formulation, the probability of simultaneous adoption is zero, and does not enter the firm's calculations. The presence or absence of a simultaneous adoption probability then makes a qualitative difference in the types of calculations which enter the firms' decisions. In order to preserve comparability of the discrete and continuous-time formulations, we accordingly stagger the decision opportunities in the discrete model so as to eliminate the possibility of simultaneous adoption.[10]

(IV.2) *Equilibrium*

To formulate an equilibrium, we observe that the information available to firm i at time t is the sum of firm i's sample realizations, denoted $X_i(t)$, the number of firms who have adopted the innovation, and the number of firms who have rejected the innovation. A strategy is then a decision rule that specifies, for any period and any observation on how many firms have rejected and how many firms have adopted the innovation, an upper and lower cutoff level with the properties that the firm will accept (reject) the innovation if its experimental performance lies above (below) the upper (lower) cutoff. A sequential equilibrium (cf. Kreps and Wilson (1982)) results if for every period and every possible history of rejections and adoptions, each firm finds that adhering to its strategy is optimal as long as other firms adhere to theirs.

A proof of the existence of a sequential equilibrium can now be outlined. We first observe that if the game is truncated after a finite number of periods, say T, then the existence of an equilibrium can be easily established. This can be accomplished by approximating the experimental performance $X(t)$ by a binomial process which allows two possible outcomes in each period, one favorable and one unfavorable. This approximation, which can be made arbitrarily fine by suitably shortening the model's time periods and appropriately modifying the size of the outcomes in the binomial process, allows experimental performance $X(t)$ to be represented

---

[10] Fudenberg and Tirole (1985) also observe the potential inconsistencies in passing between discrete and continuous formulations of problems involving strategic interactions between firms. They respond by reformulating a continuous-time model to allow nonzero probabilities of simultaneous actions, thus allowing it to be essentially equivalent to a simultaneous-move discrete-time formulation. Our approach to this problem is motivated by the observation that in practice, simultaneous patenting of innovations is exceedingly rare. The most appropriate model then appears to be a conventional continuous time rather than simultaneous-move discrete-time formulation, with a primary virtue of the former being the fact that simultaneous actions do *not* occur with positive probability. The continuous-time model can then be employed without modification, while the discrete model requires some alteration if it is to be used. We modify the discrete model by introducing sequential moves in order to preserve comparability with the continuous model.

almost surely by a sequence of successes and failures. It also causes the firms to be faced with finite strategy sets, since a strategy now specifies the pattern of successes in each period which are sufficient for acceptance or rejection. This allows us to apply Nash's theorem to demonstrate the existence of an equilibrium.

We then apply the limiting argument of Fudenberg and Levine (1983) to show that because an equilibrium exists in a finite horizon model for any finite horizon T, then a sequential equilibrium exists in the infinite horizon model. The primary element in this argument is the requirement that the game be "continuous at infinity." This stipulates that the change in agents' ex ante payoffs from the game that can be effected by changing only actions which occur after period T approaches zero as T gets large. In many applications, discounting ensures that this requirement is satisfied. In our model, we can invoke the observation that as T gets large, the period 1 expectation that the game proceeds for at least T periods approaches zero. The effect on period 1 payoffs of variations in strategies after period T then also approaches zero. This establishes the continuity requirement and hence existence.

A complete analytic exposition of the equilibrium is not presented in this paper. Instead, we examine the characteristics of key interest. We have seen that two types of strategic interaction arise; the possibility of being preempted by a rival firm and the possibility of drawing inferences from a rival firm's decisions. We examine the effect of each of these on optimal adoption behavior.

(IV.3) *Preemption and strategic interaction*

We first examine the effects of possible preemption. We assume that the first firm to adopt an innovation receives perfect patent protection, and that other firms receive no profit from the innovation. The basic question in which we are interested is whether the threat of preemption causes a firm to expand or contract the boundaries of its continuation region (compared with the case in which rivals and possible preemption do not exist), hence either delaying or hastening probable adoption or rejection. We concentrate on the adoption decision. Intuition readily suggests that the risk of preemption which accompanies continued experimentation in the presence of potential rival innovators will prompt firms to more readily adopt.[11] This effect will manifest itself in a reduction of the optimal (acceptance) stopping barrier.

We can easily verify this intuition. The adoption boundary (expressed in terms of the posterior mean profitability) is characterized by the relationship that if the posterior mean lies on the adoption boundary, then the expected opportunity loss from adoption must equal the sum of expected opportunity loss and sampling costs from continuing. The period t expected opportunity

---

[11] Such questions are examined in models without learning by Reinganum (1981a, 1982b), Loury (1979), and Lee and Wilde (1980).

loss from adopting is obviously decreasing in the period t posterior mean, because a higher mean lowers the probability that an unprofitable innovation is mistakenly adopted. The expected opportunity loss from continuing is higher if preemption is possible than it is in the no-preemption case, since the risk of preemption introduces a new source of opportunity loss which does not exist in the no-preemption case. In order to preserve the boundary relationship, the adoption boundary with preemption must then lie below (or at least as low as) that without preemption, so as to reduce the expected payoff from adopting (with preemption) to equality with the (lower than no-preemption case) expected payoff from continuing. Equivalently, the threat of preemption reduces the profitability of continuing and accordingly induces the firm to undertake riskier adoption decision.

This reveals that in the presence of possible preemption, firms more readily readily adopt the innovation. This result relies neither on asymptotic arguments nor on the specific form of the stopping bouindaries, and is hence quite general. Reinganum (1981a, 1982b) also finds that the threat of preemption hastens innovation. Notice that preemption induces firms to spend *less* on R & D in our model, since on average fewer experiments are conducted before an adoption decision is made. Potential preemption thus increases the probability that an incorrect decision is made in our model.

(IV-4) *Interactive learning*

We now consider the implications of interactive learning. For convenience, we presume that preemption possibilities do not exist and that the value of adoption is independent of whether or when other firms adopt. We also assume that there are only two firms, labelled i and j.

Our interest again concerns whether interactive learning hastens or delays the decision to adopt or reject an innovation. For convenience, we again consider the decision to adopt the innovation. We can first observe that interactive learning generates a bandwagon effect which tends to hasten decisions to adopt. To see how this arises, suppose that firm j adopts the innovation in period t. This immediately reveals the results of firm j's experiments to firm i, since firm j must have just crossed its equilibrium adoption barrier. Before j's adoption occurred, firm i had available only the information that j's experimental performance ($X_j(t)$) lay between j's adoption and rejection boundaries. The information that $X_j(t)$ has just reached j's adoption boundary thus suddenly increases the expected value and the precision of information available to firm i from observing firm j. This will yield a reduction in the performance firm i requires from i's experiments in order to adopt, and hence a reduction in i's adoption boundary. Firm i then accepts more readily, yielding the bandwagon effect.

While the observation that firm j has adopted makes firm i more likely to adopt, the effect of the observation that firm j continues to experiment remains an open question. Conflicting forces arise in this case. For convenience, assume that firm i's experimental realization in period t lies on the adoption boundary that would prevail without interactive learning, so that firm i would be just indifferent between adopting and continuing on the basis of its own information. Then consider the effect on this indifference of observing that firm j has not yet adopted or rejected. This observation of firm j provides unfavorable information, since the failure to adopt reveals that firm j's experimental performance must lie below j's adoption boundary. Factoring this information into firm i's calculations reduces firm i's posterior estimate of the mean and hence reduces the expected profitability of adoption. Firm i will then require a higher performance from its own experiments before it accepts. Hence, the adoption boundary (measured in terms of i's performance) increases, and adoption is delayed.

There is, however, an opposing force. The observation of j's continued experimentation provides information to firm i, and hence increases the precision of i's current information. The ability to observe whether firm j continues to experiment in the future also increases the precision of the future information to be gained by firm i. The information gained from firm j thus behaves much like an increase in i's sampling precision. We have seen that an increase in precision reduces the adoption boundary and hence hastens innovation, because it allows the firm to have more confidence that adopting an innovation with a positive expected mean does not involve a mistake. This effect then works in the opposite direction to that identified in the previous paragraph.

We can illuminate further the role played by these two effects. Let μ_t and σ_t^2 be firm i's posterior mean and variance without inclusion of information from firm j, and let $\bar{\mu}_t$ and $\bar{\sigma}_t^2$ be the posterior estimates with such information. Suppose further that we can treat the effect on $\bar{\sigma}_t^2$ as if it has been an increase in i's sampling precision. Let σ^2 be i's sampling variance. Let $\bar{\sigma}^2$ be the effective or "as if" sampling variance which would prevail if the sampling precision is to capture the effect of the information provided by j's continuing to experiment. From (3)–(4), the criterion for adoption without and with interactive learning is given by

$$\mu_t\sigma^2(\sigma_0^{-2} + t\sigma^{-2})^2 \geq k/4c; \qquad \bar{\mu}_t\bar{\sigma}^2(\sigma_0^{-2} + t\bar{\sigma}^{-2}) \geq k/4c. \tag{11}$$

The question is then whether observing firm j's continued experimentation increases $\mu_t\sigma^2(\sigma_0^{-2} + t\bar{\sigma}^{-2})^2$ and hastens adoption or, alternatively, decreases $\mu_t\sigma^2(\sigma_0^{-2} + t\sigma^{-2})^2$ and delays adoption.

We can place some bounds on the relative magnitudes of μ_t, σ_t^2, σ^2, and $\bar{\mu}_t$, $\bar{\sigma}_t^2$, and $\bar{\sigma}^2$. First, notice that the information that firm i gleans from firm j would be of the highest quality if firm i actually observed the outcomes of firm j's experiments. In this case, each period would allow two experimental observations, and each period would be twice as informative. The sample precision would be doubled (σ^2 would be halved) and the posterior precision $\sigma_0^{-2} + t\sigma^{-2}$ would be approximately doubled (exactly doubled iff $\sigma_0^{-2} = 0$). In practice, the information gained from observing firm j is less informative, since j's precise sampling outcomes cannot be observed, and less drastic alterations in σ^2 and σ_t^2 will be accomplished. Notice next that if firm j employs a symmetric decision rule, as in (3)–(4), and if we continue to assume $\mu_0 = 0$, then the best estimate of $X_j(t)$ that does not invoke information from firm i is $X_j(t) = 0$. Factoring this information into firm i's calculation of $\bar{\mu}_t$ could then at most halve firm i's posterior estimate of μ_t, with this halving potential occurring only if $X_j(t) = 0$ were actually observed. In practice, less precise information on $X_j(t)$ is gained, and μ_t will be reduced by a factor less drastic than half. We can now observe that if each effect attained its maximum, the two adoption boundaries given in (11) would be approximately (exactly iff $\sigma_0^{-2} = 0$) equal. Interactive learning would then have no impact. The question remains open as to how far each effect falls short of its bound, and hence the actual impact of interactive learning on the adoption boundary.

To address this problem, we once again resort to simulation techniques. We first note that firm i's posterior distribution with interactive learning, conditional on observing sample $X_i(t)$ and conditional on firm j's continuing to experiment, is given by

$$g_i(\mu, t) = \frac{\eta_i(\mu \mid \mu_0, \sigma_0^2)[1 - Y_j(t \mid \mu)]\eta_i(X_i(t) \mid \mu, t\sigma^2)}{\int_\mu \eta_i(\mu \mid \mu_0, \sigma_0^2)[1 - Y_j(t \mid \mu)]\eta_i(X_i(t) \mid \mu, t\sigma^2)}, \tag{12}$$

where $\eta_i(\cdot \mid \mu, \sigma^2)$ is a normal density with mean μ and variance σ^2, and $Y_j(t \mid \mu)$ is the cumulative first passage (to either barrier) distribution characterizing firm j's behavior (for a given μ). Equation (12) is a direct application of Bayes' rule. The prior information on μ is given by $\eta_i(\mu \mid \mu_0, \sigma_0^2)$. The probability that firm j is still continuing for given μ is given by $[1 - Y_j(t \mid \mu)]$, and the (independent, for any given μ) probability of firm i observing sample realization $X_i(t)$ is given by $\eta(X_i(t) \mid \mu, t\sigma^2)$.

We now temporarily assume that firm j follows the decision rule given in (3)–(4) for the case without interactive learning. We can then employ our estimate of the first passage distribution given in Table 2 to numerically solve the posterior density (12) for various values of μ and t. This is a straightforward functional evaluation problem, and requires no special assumptions or programming. These calculated values can then be used to calculate $\bar{\mu}_t$ and $\bar{\sigma}_t^2$. If we treat the reduction in the posterior variance from σ_t^2 to $\bar{\sigma}_t^2$ as having been caused by a reduction in the sampling variance (increase in the sampling precision), we can calculate the "as if" value of $\bar{\sigma}^2$ which will have to prevail to capture the effect of drawing information from firm j. This allows us to calculate values of $\mu_t \sigma^2 (\sigma_0^{-2} + t\sigma^{-2})^2$ (without interactive learning) and $\bar{\mu}_t \bar{\sigma}^2 (\sigma_0^{-2} + t\bar{\sigma}^{-2})^2$ (with interactive learning). We perform these calculations for various points in time and various values of k/c. We assume that σ_0^{-2}, σ^{-2}, and μ_0 are as in section III, while no assumption on μ is required. We further assume that firm i's experimental performance lies on the adoption boundary that would prevail on the basis of i's information alone.

Table 3 presents the calculations. In each case, we find that interactive learning reduces $\mu_t \sigma^2 (\sigma_0^{-2} + t\sigma^{-2})^2$. This pushes firm i's posterior information below the acceptance boundary, and prompts firm i to continue experimenting.

We conclude that the mean-reducing effect of the unfavorable information that firm j continues to experiment outweighs the extra precision gained from observing j's continuation. The net effect of the observation that firm j has not yet adopted is thus unfavorable.

Consider now our temporary assumptions. First, the use of a rule of the form given in (11) depends upon the distribution given in (12) being approximately normal, so that the type of analysis pursued by Chernoff can be employed. In the absence of normality, statistical theory is silent as to the appropriate rule. Secondly, we have treated the effect of observing firm j as if it were an increase in i's sampling precision which is consistent across time periods. In fact, this increase will be more pronounced in later time periods. Finally, consider the assumption that firm j follows the decision rule which prevails in the absence of interactive learning. In reality, firm j will accomplish an adjustment in this rule. Given our preliminary indication

TABLE 3

$k/4c$	T	$\dfrac{\mu_t \sigma^2}{(\sigma_t^2)^2}$ *	$\dfrac{\bar{\mu}_t \bar{\sigma}^2}{(\bar{\sigma}_t^2)^2}$ †
300	100	3.0	2.3
300	125	3.0	2.3
400	100	4.0	3.3
400	125	4.0	3.2
400	150	4.0	3.2
400	175	4.0	3.2
500	100	5.0	4.3
500	125	5.0	4.3
500	150	5.0	4.3
500	175	5.0	4.4
500	200	5.0	4.3
600	100	6.0	5.6
600	125	6.0	5.6
600	150	6.0	5.7
600	175	6.0	5.6
600	200	6.0	5.7

* Calculated on assumption firm is on noninteractive-learning adoption boundary.
† Simulated.

that the mean effect dominates in interactive learning cases, firm j will expand its adoption boundary. This will increase the uncertainty associated with the observation that j is continuing to experiment, which may further increase i's posterior variance and hence adoption boundary. This reinforces our results.

These remarks identify the issues involved in formulating optimal decision rules in the presence of interactive learning. A complete treatment of the problem requires the development of a more complete statistical analysis, perhaps building on the work of Chernoff. Our identification of the relevant issues provides a first step in analyzing this problem.

V. Conclusion

We have examined the optimal sequential research strategy of a single firm, with the firm's beliefs generated by an explicit sampling procedure. We have demonstrated that this model of experimentation leads to a diffusion of innovation curve that matches commonly observed empirical behavior. This provides an explanation of diffusion which is not dependent upon variations in firms' priors. Finally, we have provided the first investigation of strategic interaction between firms in a model of learning via experimentation. Our results suggest that such interaction may be important in devising optimal experimentation strategies.

University of California, Berkeley
The Pennsylvania State University

APPENDIX

This appendix presents the details of the analysis underlying Section III. We begin with the observation that under our approximation of μ_t as a Gaussian diffusion proicess (cf. Section II.2), the magnitude $X(t) = \sum_{i=1}^{t} X_i$ is also a Gaussian diffusion process. In particular, it is a Wiener proces with incremental drift and variance given by

$$E[dX(t)] = \mu \, dt \qquad \text{Var}\,[dX(t)] = \sigma^2 \, dt.$$

Notice that $X(t)$ is a time-homogeneous diffusion process, with values of $E[dX(t)]$ and Var $[dX(t)]$ that are independent of t.

A probability density describing the likelihood of a firm adopting the innoivation (or proportion of firms adopting) at each time t is a first passage density for the Wiener process $X(t)$ to the acceptance boundary. First passage time problems are most tractable if the boundary in question is constant over time. Unfortunately, this is clearly not the case with the boundary described by (3)–(4).

We surmount this obstacle by accomplishing a transformation. We define

$$X'(H) = \mu_0 \sigma_0^{-2} + X(t^{-1}(H))\sigma^{-2} = \mu_0 \sigma_0^{-2} + X\left(\frac{H - \sigma_0^{-2} - t_0}{\sigma^{-2}} + t_0\right)\sigma^{-2}. \qquad (A1)$$

$$H(t) = \sigma_0^{-2} + (t - t_0)\sigma^{-2} + t_0 (=1/\sigma_t^2 \text{ if } t_0 = 0). \qquad (A2)$$

The initial time period is given by t_0, which will generally be taken to be zero. We now define a new variable

$$Z(H) = X'(H)(H - H_0 + \sigma_0^{-2}) + D, \qquad (A3)$$

where $H_0 = \sigma_0^{-2} + t_0$ and

$$D = \frac{k}{4c}\sigma^{-2}. \tag{A4}$$

We collect some information on $Z(H)$. First, notice that $Z(H)$ is again a diffusion process, with

$$
\begin{aligned}
E[dZ(H)] &= X'(H)\,dH + (H - H_0 + \sigma_0^{-2})E[dX(H)]\sigma^{-2} \\
&= X'(H)\,dH + (H - H_0 + \sigma_0^{-2})\frac{E\,dX(t)}{dt^{-1}(H)}\frac{d_t^{-1}(H)}{dH}dH\sigma^{-2} \\
&= X'(H)\,dH + (H - H_0 + \sigma_0^{-2})\mu\,dH\sigma^2\sigma^{-2} \\
&= \left[\frac{Z(H) - D}{(H - H_0 + \sigma_0^{-2})} + (H - H_0 + \sigma_0^{-2})\mu\right]dH.
\end{aligned} \tag{A5}
$$

$$
\begin{aligned}
\text{Var}\,[dZ(H)] &= [H - H_0 + \sigma_0^{-2}]^2(\sigma^{-2})^2\,\text{Var}\,[dX(H)] \\
&= (H - H_0 + \sigma_0^{-2})^2(\sigma^{-2})^2\frac{\text{Var}\,dX(t^{-1}(H))}{dt^{-1}(H)}\frac{dt^{-1}(H)}{dH} \\
&= (H - H_0 + \sigma_0^{-2})^2(\sigma^{-2})^2\sigma^2\sigma^2\,dH \\
&= (H - H_0 + \sigma_0^{-2})^2\,dH.
\end{aligned} \tag{A6}
$$

The useful aspect of this transformation is that it gives flat decision boundaries. In particular, we note that

$$Z(H) = \pm 2D \Leftrightarrow X'(H) = \pm\frac{D}{(H - H_0 + \sigma_0^{-2})}, \tag{A7}$$

which is in turn equivalent to the decision rule given in (3)–(4).

While we have achieved flat decision boundaries, we have sacrificed the time homogeneity of the diffusion process. This is clearly indicated by (A5) and (A6), which are not independent of H. Notice, however, that (A5) and (A6) include the time variable only in the form of $H - H_0$.

Let $g(H, Z_0, H_0)$ be a density function in H describing the likelihood that the first passage time for the diffusion proicess $Z(H)$ to the upper boundary of $2D$ is H, given that the process begins from Z_0 at time H_0 (cf. note 4). Let $G(H, Z_0, H_0)$ be the corresponding distribution, so that $G(H, Z_0, H_0) = \int_{H_0}^{H} g(\tau, Z_0, H_0)\,d\tau$. It is well known that the latter function satisfies the Kolmogorov backward equation (cf. Cox and Miller (1965, Chapter 5)). For a diffusion process which is not time homogeneous, the Kolmogorov backward equation is:

$$\tfrac{1}{2}[\text{Var}\,[dZ(H_0)]]\frac{\partial^2 G}{\partial Z_0^2} + [E[dZ(H_0)]]\frac{\partial G}{\partial Z_0} = -\frac{\partial G}{\partial H_0}. \tag{A8}$$

In order to solve this equation, boundary conditions involving the "forward" variables $Z(H)$ and H must be provided. Unfortunately, we have no boundary information on H. For example, such information could take the form of a date at which all firms were known to ahve adopted the innovation. This is the type of information that we are attempting to discover, and is accordingly not known. The standard technique in diffusion studies is to note that if the diffusion process is time-homogeneous, then $-\partial G/\partial H_0 = \partial G/\partial H$. This holds because the behavior of the diffusion process depends only upon the elapsed time between initial and terminal times, with the process' time homogeneity ensuring that the identity of the initial and terminal times is irrelevant. Hence, postponing the initial time is equivalent to advancing the terminal time. Unfortunately, our diffusion process is not time-homogeneous. However, we have noted that the characteristics of the process depend only upon $H - H_0$. Though the process varies over a time interval, its characteristics are again a function only of the length of the interval and not the identity of its endpoints. Hence, we have $-\partial G/\partial H_0 = \partial G/\partial H$ and (A8) is (using (A5)–(A6) and initially setting $\sigma_0 = 1$ in order to concentrate on the variables of interest):

$$\frac{1}{2}\frac{\partial^2 G}{\partial Z_0^2} + [Z_0 - D + \mu]\frac{\partial G}{\partial Z_0} = \frac{\partial G}{\partial H}. \tag{A9}$$

To help in solving (A9), we have available the boundary conditions

$$G(H, 0, H_0) = 0 \tag{A10}$$

$$G(H, 2D, H_0) = 1. \tag{A11}$$

To interpret these, notice that if $Z_0 = 0$ (as in (A10)), then $X'(H_0) = -D/(H' - H_0 + \sigma_0^{-2})$, which is to say that the process starts at the rejection boundary. It is then immediately rejected, and adoption of the innovation does not occur, giving a distribution function of adoption times everywhere equal to zero (as in (A10)). Similarly, $Z_0 = 2D$ implies $X'(H_0) = D/(H - H_0 + \sigma_0^{-2})$, which gives immediate adoption and hence a cumulative distribution everywhere equal to one. We also have the initial conditions

$$G(H_0, Z_0, H_0) = 0 \qquad 0 \leqslant Z_0 < 2D \tag{A12}$$

$$G(H_0, 2D, H_0) = 1. \tag{A13}$$

These indicate that at time H_0, the proportion of firms adopting is zero if the process is not at the adoption boundary (cf. (A14)), and unity if it is at the boundary (cf. (A13)).

Equation (A9) is a second order partial differential equation. Unfortunately, an analytical solution to this problem is not known. We accordingly resort to numerical methods in order to obtain the first passage time distributions. In particular, the fortran subroutine DPDES (Partial Differential Equation Solver) is employed to calculate the value of the function $G(H, Z_0, H_0)$ which satisfies (A9)–(A13) on a grid of points of the form (H, Z_0), each of which identifies an initial condition Z_0 and a time H at which the distribution is to be evaluated.[12] We temporarily fix $\sigma_0^{-2} = \sigma^{-2} = 1$, and then for various values of D and μ we employ this method to calculate values of $G(H, Z_0, H_0)$ for (generally 10,000–25,000) representative values of (H, Z_0).

We now consider whether these calculated values of $G(t)$ exhibit logistic behavior which matches commonly observed empirical regularities. We first note that we can confine our interest to initial conditions Z_0 which correspond to the unbiased prior expectation of $\mu_0 = 0$. Letting $\mu_0 = 0$ in (A3) gives $Z_0 = D$, and we accordingly examine $G(H, D, H_0)$. We also recall that we have set $\sigma_0^2 = 1$ and have temporarily set $\sigma^2 = 1$. Now recognizing that $H = t + 1$ when $\mu_0 = 0$ and $\sigma^2 = \sigma_0^2 = 1$, we can use our observations on $G(H, D, H_0)$ to construct values of $G(t) = G(H - 1, D, H_0)$. The latter calculations are then used to estimate (6), or $\ln(G(t)/(1 - G(t))) = \beta_0 + \beta_1 t + \beta_2 t^2 + \varepsilon_t$, for various values of μ (ranging from 1.5 to 3.5) and $D = k/4c\sigma^2$ (ranging from 2 to 4).

It is apparent that (6) cannot hold over the entire range of t, since $G(0) = 0$ (hence

---

[12] The partial differential equation is defined on a rectangular subset of R_+^2, with the horizontal axis measuring time and the vertical axis measuring initial conditions. The rectangle is bounded above by a horizontal barrier corresponding to an initial condition of $Z_0 = 2D$ and below by an initial condition of $Z_0 = 0$. On the left, it is bounded by a vertical barrier corresponding to a time of H_0. The boundary and initial conditions given by (A10)–(A13) identify the values of $G(H, Z_0, H_0)$ along these boundaries. The task is then to find values of $G(H, Z_0, H_0)$ at interior points which are consistent with (A9). The numerical solution technique uses the method of lines to expand the solution in a series of cubic Hermite basis functions. Solving for the coefficients of these functions yields values of $G(H, Z_0, H_0)$ and $\partial G/\partial Z_0$ on a grid of points within the rectangle of interest, where the solution is achieved under the requirement that (A9) be satisfied at two Gaussian quadrature points between each pair of grid points. We choose the grid finely enough that the accuracy of the result is on the order of at least 10^{-4}. For details, see Sewell (1982).

$\ln(G/(1-G)) \cong -\infty)$; and for t large enough $G(0) \cong 1$ (hence $\ln(G/(1-G)) \cong \infty$). We suspect, however, that (6) is applicable to a substantial range. We estimate (6) on the set $\{t : G(t) \in [0.05, 0.95]\}$. In addition, this time series estimation entails significant risk of autocorrelation. We accordingly apply a correction for first order autocorrelation to the ordinary least squares estimates of β_0, β_1, and β_2. We report the corrected estimates, though the correction has insignificant effects on parameter estimates.

To obtain the results shown in Table 1, it remains to transform our units of measurement. We let the new time unit be one one-hundredth of the old unit. In the process, we reduce the experimentation cost ("per unit of time") by a factor of one hundred (increasing D from 2–4 to 200–400) and increase the prior precision ("per unit of time") from 1 to 100, reducing the prior variance from 1 to 0.01 (cf. note 5). *This provides the case examined in the text, and the results reported in Table 1.*

Finally, consider the comparative static implications of σ^{-2}. As σ^{-2} increases, two effects appear in our transformed version of the problem. The height of the barrier D increases (cf. (A4)) and the increment of real time Δt associated with any interval of transformed time ΔH decreases (cf. (A2)). Both of these effects tend to incresse the slope of the diffusion curve measured in real time units, and in this sense increasing σ^{-2} hastens innovation. However, the effect of σ^{-2} on initial passage time is potentially ambiguous. Increasing barrier height delays initial passage in ΔH units, but increasing σ^{-2} causes smaller real time units Δt to be associated with ΔH units. These effects conflict. Letting $\underline{t}$ be the initial passage time in real units, we have $\underline{t} = (\underline{H} - G_0^{-2})/\sigma^{-2}$ (cf. (A2) and let $t_0 = 0$). Differentiating $\underline{t}$ with respect to σ^{-2} and evaluating at the values of $\sigma_0^{-2} = \sigma^{-2} = 1$ chosen for our transformed simulations, we have $(\partial D / \partial \sigma^{-2} = 1$ in this case)

$$\frac{\partial \underline{t}}{\partial \sigma^{-2}} = \frac{\partial \underline{H}}{\partial D} - (\underline{H} - 1). \tag{A14}$$

Converting the regression results in Table 1 from t units back into H units reveals that $\partial \underline{H} / \partial D$ is comfortably less than half of $\underline{H} - 1$, giving $\partial \underline{t} / \partial \sigma^{-2} < 0$. An increase in σ^{-2} thus hastens diffusion, as measured by the initial passage time and increases the slope of the diffusion curve given initial passage time.

REFERENCES

BHATTACHARYA, SUDIPTO (1976), "Informational Efficiency and Intertemporal Rates of Return," Sloan School, MIT.

—— (1978), "Diffusion of Innovations: A Sequential Experimentation Approach," in "Essays in Financial Theory," MIT Ph.D. Thesis.

CHERNOFF, HERMAN (1972), *Sequential Analysis and Optimal Design,* Society for Industrial and Applied Mathematics, Philadelphia.

COX, D. R. and MILLER, H. D. (1965), *The Theory of Stochastic Processes,* Chapman and Hall, Ltd., London.

FUDENBERG, DREW and LEVINE, DAVID, (1983), "Subgame-Perfect Equilibria of Finite- and Infinite-Horizon Games," *Journal of Economic Theory* 31, 251–268.

—— and TIROLE, JEAN (1985), "Preemption and Rent Equalization in the Adoption of New Technology," *Review of Economic Studies* 52, 383–402.

GRILICHES, Z. (1957), "Hybrid Corn: An Exploration in the Economics of Technological Change," *Econometrica* 25, 501–522.

JENSEN, RICHARD (1980), "A Duopoly Model of the Adoption of an Innovation of Uncertain Profitability," CMSEMS Discussion Paper 434, Northwestern University.

JENSEN, RICHARD (1982), "Adoption and Diffusion of an Innovation of Uncertain Profitability," *Journal of Economic Theory* 27, 182–193.

JENSEN, RICHARD (1983), "Innovation Adoption and Diffusion Where There Are Competing Innovations," *Journal of Economic Theory,* 29, 161–171.

KREPS, D. M., and WILSON, R. (1982), "Sequential Equilibria," *Econometrica* 50, 863–894.

LEE, TOM and WILDE, LOUIS L. (1980), "Market Structure and Innovation: A Reformulation," *Quarterly Journal of Economics* 94, 429–436.

LOURY, GLENN C. (1979), "Market Structure and Innovation," *Quarterly Journal of Economics* 93, 395–410.

MANSFIELD, E. (1968), *The Economics of Technological Change*, Norton, NY.

MARSCHAK, T. (1968), *Strategy for Research and Development*, Rand Corporation Memorandum.

NABSETH, L. and RAY, G. F. editors (1974), *The Diffusion of New Industrial Processes*, Cambridge University Press.

REINGANUM, J. (1981a), "Dynamic Games of Innovation," *Journal of Economic Theory* 25, 21–41.

—— (1981b), "On the Diffusion of New Technology: A Game Theoretic Approach," *Review of Economic Studies* 48, 395–406.

—— (1981c), "Market Structure and the Diffusion of New Technology," *Bell Journal of Economics* 12, 618–624.

—— (1982a), "Strategic Search Theory," *International Economic Review* 23, 1–15.

—— (1982b), "A Dynamic Game of R & D: Patent Protection and Competitive Behavior," *Econometrica* 50, 671–688.

—— (1983), "Nash Equilibrium Search for the Best Alternative," *Journal of Economic Theory* 30, 139–152.

ROBERTS, KEVIN and WEITZMAN, MARTIN, L. (1981), "Funding Criteria for Research, Development, and Exploration Projects," *Econometrica* 49, 1261–1288.

SEWELL, G. (1982), "IMSL Software for Differential Equations in One Space Variable." IMSL Technical Report Series 8202, IMSL, Houston, Texas.

WALD, A. (1947), *Sequential Analysis*, J. Wiley & Sons, NY.

WEITZMAN, M. L. (1979), "Optimal Search for the Best Alternative," *Econometrica* 47, 641–654.

WHITTLE, PETER, (1983), *Optimization Over Time*, John Wiley & Sons, NY.